A Dictionary
of
North East Dialect

at the Lit n Phil
1 Dec 2004
Bill Griffiths.

Bill Griffiths

Published by Northumbria University Press
Trinity Building, Newcastle upon Tyne NE1 8ST, UK

First Published 2004
Copyright © Bill Griffiths

British Library Cataloguing in Publication Data. A Catalogue Record for this book
is available from the British Library.

ISBN 1-904794-06-8

Designed and printed by External Relations, Northumbria University

Typeset in Baskerville

Cover illustration: "*Easington '94*" by kind permission of J. B. Curtis.

Northumbria University is the trading name of the
University of Northumbria at Newcastle. ER–119139

A Dictionary *of*
North East Dialect

northumbria
UNIVERSITY PRESS

Acknowledgements

With grateful acknowledgement for the use of extracts from:

BL MS Egerton 2868 (James Raine's dialect word list) at the British Library.

BL MS Lansdowne 1033 (vol. 99 of Bishop *Kennet's* Collection – Bishop Kennet's 'Etymological Collections of English Words and Provincial Expressions') at the British Library.

Rev. J.E. Hull's typescript *'Popular Introduction to the Tyneside Dialect'* at the Archives of the Natural History Society of Northumbria, Hancock Museum.

Michael Dodd's card index *'List of Geordie Words'* at the Beamish North of England Open Air Museum's Regional Resource Centre.

Bell-White MS 12 *'A Glossary for Newcastle, Durham and Northumberland'* by permission of the Special Collections and Archives Librarian, Robinson Library Special Collections, University of Newcastle.

The co-operation of the staff of the Local Studies Centre, Newcastle Central Library, is gratefully acknowledged; access to their excellent collection of dialect literature has been an essential help in preparing this book.

Contents

Preface

This dictionary project began in the mid-1990s and has grown ever since. Its intention was to provide a straightforward guide to the language used in current North East dialect speech as well as 'classic' texts of the nineteenth and twentieth centuries. So much extra material has been sent in, collected and researched, that it has outgrown its original format: the words now speak for themselves through quotations illustrating the way they are used. It would be nice to think of this as a dictionary that also makes interesting reading! As well as the dictionary section, it seemed helpful to provide some background on how North East dialect developed over the centuries – not in isolation, but interacting with a surprising number of factors including immigration, local industry and trade contacts abroad. Words, like ideas, soon pass frontiers. These issues are addressed in the introduction, which gives new insights into the story of North East dialect.

A general thanks is warmly extended to all who have sent in dialect material in response to our website, newsletters and publications. All the same, much remains to be collected and explained. It is hoped you will not be simply a passive reader of this book, but actively participate by sending in comments and further information on 'What words were/are used where, and when, and by whom' – see contact note (p.191). There has been little effort to record the dialect of the urban and industrial North East during the twentieth century, so there is a lot to catch up on! Plus making a record of what is new in the twenty-first century...

To this end, we have taken 'dialect' to mean words typically in use in the North East, that are not an accepted part of 'standard' English. Few words are unique to any county or region. A special use of even a common word will be worth noting; new coinings are not to be automatically dismissed as 'slang'. North East dialect is at heart a spoken language, a flexible experience, and open to change. This book is not intended to fix it, but to encourage a better appreciation of what is becoming recognised at last as an essential part of the region's 'intangible heritage'.

Bill Griffiths
Centre for Northern Studies
Northumbria University

Historical introduction

If we take language as the attribute of a nation and dialect that of a region, this is not to suggest that dialect is subordinate to 'national' language. In the case of English dialects, their roots go back to the fractionalising of society in the era of Viking and Norman invasions, so that many features of Northern English precede the efforts to set up a national English in the fifteenth and sixteenth centuries. The model is more one of parallel development and it would be more useful to think in terms of varieties of English, developing and interacting over a long period.

To what extent the 'dialects' of Old English ('OE' – the language of the Anglo-Saxons) can be taken as the direct source of Medieval dialects is debatable. Language is continuous, but the slight differences between Anglian (Mercian and Northumbrian) in the North, and West Saxon in the South give little warning of the divergence that was to take place. In vocabulary the Anglo-Saxon North already preferred 'bairn' to 'child' for example, and uncontracted forms of the verb to contracted ones, e.g. *cyme* than *cym* (comes), *weorest* than *wyrst* (become); but even these distinctions were likely to be minimised by the spread of Late West Saxon as a written norm in the late tenth century, at a time when Wessex had absorbed the other 'kingdoms' into a recognisable England.

The real jolts that led to language change came with the arrival of the Vikings in the ninth century and the Normans in the eleventh, though there are understandably no exact records of how the spoken language changed or when. The Vikings contributed many new words to Northern English, some of which also entered Southern speech early on. The Normans effected a more total takeover of the state: under their rule, Anglo-Saxons were replaced by Normans in key positions and the status of English demoted. Instead of English being the language of government and literature, charters, wills and other administrative and legal records would be kept in Latin, while the business of the ruling class would be conducted in Norman-French.

Deprived of any central supervisory machinery that might have secured its cohesion and consistency, spoken English diversified, curiously along the line from London to Cheshire that had served as the dividing line between West Saxon and Viking influence in King Alfred's day (880s). To the north of that line was the Danelaw, to the south the Saxon kingdoms with West Mercia and Kent. Either these traditional loyalties were very persistent or – a distinct possibility – the divergence between Northern and Southern English had begun earlier, its effects obscured by the traditional nature of the written language. This affects the question of when words from Old Norse ('ON', the Viking language) entered English: in the ninth and tenth centuries, when Viking power was considerable and the cultural current ran (as it were) from Viking to Anglian; or in mid eleventh to twelfth centuries, when Viking power was on the wane, and the once-dominant settlers assumed a lower profile in Anglo-Norman society.

The making of Middle English

In the Middle Ages, English in the South exhibited many sound changes but was more conservative in its grammar; the North proved more conservative of vowel sounds, but more innovative in its vocabulary and grammar. It is these changes that lay the real basis of Medieval and Modern dialects.

For example, the long OE vowel /a/ can change into /o/ in the South: the OE word *ac* becomes *oak* in the South, but stays as *ac* in the North, later breaking to give *yek; finnd* 'find' retains a short vowel in the North, but lengthens and breaks to a diphthong in the South; the Northern /u/ (sometimes written 'oo') retains its OE value, while in the South it later changes to the dark *uh* sound.

In the North it is to be expected that more words from ON would be absorbed than in the South. Many of these were never adopted into 'national' English, and either died out in the North (e.g. *maugh* 'brother-in-law' or *tawm* 'a fishing line') or survived to give a distinctive feel to Northern dialects (e.g. *marra* 'work-mate', *cree* 'animal pen'). Paradoxically, while many OE words had died out by the end of the Middle Ages, examples can be better preserved in Northern than Southern English, e.g. *thoo* for you, *neep* for turnip. (Perhaps this was because of the keenness in the South to introduce new words based on French and Latin.)

The extent of Viking influence in the North East is a point of debate. When, in an East Durham charter of 1155 we find side by side as names of witnesses: Eilwin de Saham, his son Raven de Slinglawe, John son of Herebert de Saham, Roger Dreng, Ranulf de Hassewelle, Ailmar de Daltune, and the aristocratic Reinald Escolland – mixing Viking, French and Anglo-Saxon name elements – we are at a loss to determine whether this apparent mix is the result of chance relocation, intermarriage or a cross-cultural fashion in Christian names. It is to be remembered that language is a cultural, not a genetic matter; and it is certain that words of ON origin have long been in use in areas not believed to have been settled directly by Vikings. An example is *beck* (from ON) which corresponds to OE *burn*(e) 'stream'. If dialect followed the lines of Viking settlement, *beck* should not be found in Co. Durham or Northumberland. It is true these areas show a relative lack of ON place-names and memorials, but it unlikely this early exemption continued long, and *beck* is now the standard term in Co. Durham for a local stream.

Tendencies to regional consistency were at work even in the Middle Ages – for there was mobility as well as stability inherent in the feudal system: in interchange between manorial estates, in the access to local and regional markets and fairs, in the realities of feudal warfare, and in the obligation of pilgrimage. It is likely that throughout the Middle Ages the Church provided a channel of communication and a degree of cohesiveness within and between the fledgling dialects. It was not after all the Normans' aim to extinguish English society, rather they acted as a super-class exploiting, but at the same time depending on the English population. They would hardly want their serfs to converse in Norman-French.

Major changes also occurred in grammar. Old English was an inflected language (like German or Latin) with different endings for masculine, feminine and neuter nouns, strong and weak adjectives, and the four cases (nominative for the subject of a sentence, accusative for the object, genitive for the possessive, and dative for indirect object or instrumental).

Plus different endings for singular and plural! Of these, only apostrophe-s for the genitive (*king's*, etc.) and –s for the plural (*kings*, etc.) have survived for the noun.

An inflected language means the role of a word in the sentence is clear whatever the word order; in Modern English we need to observe the order subject-verb-object to make the meaning clear: 'the king killed the lion' is very different from 'the lion killed the king'. The loss of inflexions (case endings) was the major change that gave Modern English its simple, streamlined grammar.

One theory is that when Viking had to speak to Anglian, the niceties of inflexion tended to be lost, and a compromise language, a sort of mix or 'pidjin' resulted, with a simpler structure. However, it should be noted that OE itself did not satisfactorily distinguish between subject and object cases, leading early on to a risk of ambiguity. Even in the Anglo-Saxon period there was a tendency to adopt 'sense order' to make the meaning clear. Moreover, case endings (suffixes) were unaccented tags at the end of a word; because they were little emphasised, over time they tended to level (become similar). This led to greater dependence on sense order and that in turn reduced the usefulness of suffixes – a circular process that could, in itself, account for their loss. Vulnerable and disestablished as English was, the spoken language had no way of monitoring or regulating change.

Some steps in the process, however, may have been deliberate. In the case of verbs, the endings for the present tense are also reduced to plus-s or non-s (*speaks* and *speak*). There is no precedent for this in OE or ON, and the conclusion is that the useful formula for nouns was applied to verbs, perhaps as a conscious improvement (simplification).

Many of these grammatical changes had their basis in the North. The South retained more of the OE verb inflections, and as late as 1611 these are found in the King James Bible (e.g. *saith, hath, casteth...*). Not that Southern English had not changed also, but whether independently or in awareness of the North is less clear.

There may be differences, for example, in the rate North and South adopted French words. These came in two waves – Norman-French (also called Anglo-Norman) of the late eleventh to early thirteenth centuries, and Parisian or Central French of the thirteenth and fourteenth centuries. Norman-French often had initial /w/ where Parisian French had /gu/, e.g. *William/Guillaume, warrant/guarantee*; also /k/ for /ch/ as in *cauldron* and later *chauldron*. A strong early influence from Anglo-Norman may be assumed in the North East, given the importance of the Norman 'Palatinate' of Durham; but this seems more evident in the commonness today of Norman-French personal names and French elements in place-names than in the dialect.

National English and the reaffirmation of dialect

With the break-up of the Angevin Empire in the early thirteenth century, the Anglo-Norman nobility faced the need to commit themselves to either England or France. In time, those noble families settled here came to think of themselves as English, and this opened the way for the reversal of the eclipse of the English language. The shock and destabilisation of the Black Death may equally have served to revise notions of identity and national structure. By the fourteenth century, impressive works of poetry were being composed in English dialects (*The Green Knight*, Langland's *Piers Plowman* and Chaucer's more French-aware *Canterbury Tales*), each in some way with the approval of noble patronage; and in 1362 Parliament and the Courts were first conducted in English.

In the fifteenth and sixteenth centuries, national unity became an urgent political consideration after the War of the Roses, and a form of English that seems largely a fusion between the vocabulary of the South and the syntax of the North is favoured as a new standard written English. (It is not necessary to invoke Midlanders moving to London to account for this; it could have been purely an executive decision. Indeed, it might be less accurate to speak of the Tudor revolution in government than the Tudor revolution in English.) The new 'national' English is employed in government documents; it is taught as the written norm in the new Grammar schools; it is promoted by printing and (in the seventeenth century) defined in dictionaries. It achieved a stability that has not been radically challenged since. It increasingly affected the speech of the educated class – and though it is true a written language usually follows the spoken language, it can equally be the case that written language can influence what is spoken.

Dialects might have been expected to weaken or even disappear under this competition from an 'official' English. In fact, during the seventeenth century, when arguments became violent over what England stood for and what path it should take, regional dialect returned to prominence. Perhaps there was no clear political purpose to this move – there were risings both in favour of James II and William and Mary in Yorkshire in 1688; rather Northern dialect was reasserted as a general symbol of ancient rights or regional identity against the presumption of the South.

In 1673 (in Moorman's words) "the York printer, Stephen Bulkby, had issued, as a humble broadside without author's name, a poem which bore the title *A Yorkshire Dialogue in Yorkshire Dialect; Between an Awd Wife, a Lass, and a Butcher.*" This was followed in 1683 by a booklet *A Yorkshire dialogue* by George Meriton (1634–1711), a lawyer and antiquary of Northallerton; and his sequel *The Praise of Yorkshire Ale* (1697).

These are non-political, even dully commonplace in their material. George Meriton was also author of a history of England, which, while it condemned the execution of Charles I, gave a detailed and impartial account of the Civil War. Whether the Yorkshire of this time be deemed separatist or radical (it included the home of General Fairfax; and Andrew Marvell was MP for Hull), we seem to be evidencing a county beginning to use its history and language as a means towards current identity rather than as an assertion of ready-made historical allegiances. One clue here is that Meriton included a *clavis* – a key or glossary – with his work, showing he was associating his efforts with a broader audience, and intended to be part of an intellectual as well as local scene.

In the same decades, it was the Royal Society (RS) that was providing the main initiative in the field of dialect research. Thomas Sprat (1635–1713), Bishop of Rochester in 1684, and historian of the Royal Society, set the ground rules by which dialect and common language in general was to be admired and imitated:

> "... They [the RS] have exacted from all their members, a close, naked, natural way of speaking; positive expressions; clear senses; a native easiness: bringing all things as near the mathematical plainness, as they can: and preferring the language of Artizans, Countrymen, and Merchants, before that, of Wits, or Scholars." *(History of the Royal Society, 1667)*

John Ray (1628–1705), better known as a pioneer of botany and plant classification, was also the first author of a major dialect study, the *Collection of English Words, Not Generally Used* (London, 1674), which lends dialect for the first time an acknowledged academic status. His may also be the claim to have undertaken the first dialect research, as he "toured around the country in the course of his language investigations" (Fox, 2000, p.81).

White Kennet (1660–1728) was Dean and afterwards Bishop of Peterborough; his manuscript *Etymological Dictionary* (preserved in the British Library as Lansdowne MS 1033) goes further than Ray, in that his national collection of dialect words was provided with notes on word origins in Old English or the Norse languages, and – important for our purposes – notes of which counties a word was used in. It is supposed he benefited from having the great scholar of languages, George Hickes, as a lodger in the 1690s; he may also have had access to the material Ray was collecting.

These were the sort of people who were giving dialect a new status and a dual future – as living language and academic discipline. They can be helpfully viewed as scientists – men who were concerned with collecting the evidence of language around them, much as they would be with natural history specimens. Presumably it was in this sense that dialect was seen as one of the legitimate focuses of the Royal Society.

None of these pioneers should be viewed as primarily political activists. But it is worth considering that some of the appeal of dialect at this time may have been as a symbolic counterpoise to an over-centralised and arbitrary (Stuart) government. If so, it pointed the way forward to the role of dialect in the next century and more.

In the North East

In the 1720s a Newcastle schoolmaster, Edward Chicken, produced a poem, *The Collier's Wedding*, in which the narrative is in flawless 'national' English rhyming couplets, but the speech of the collier hero is given in dialect, and the wedding customs of the collier class, settling in Benwell near Newcastle, are described with some merriment. The force of the satire depends on a city audience that spoke and thought Metropolitan English and practised Metropolitan manners. It must have seemed to more urbane Novocastrians like a step back in time.

The language that served as the currency of North Eastern culture was the traditional speech of rural areas, brought into urban centres by migrating workers and their families. They responded to the new opportunities in what we could broadly call 'industrial' work – ship-building, coal mining, chemical manufacture and transport. The key to all this was the potential for deeper mining, made possible by the atmospheric engine in the eighteenth century and the steam engine in the nineteenth century that effectively pumped out water from the mine workings. But where did the new workers come from? The wedding customs described by Edward Chicken seem to derive from rural Northumberland, or so Brockett assures us in his dictionary (s.v. 'bride-ale'). Heslop (1892–96, p.xvi) held a similar opinion:

> "... To these dalesmen [i.e. from Tynedale and Riddesdale] we owe the strong clanship of the colonies of pitmen and keelmen scattered along Tyneside and throughout the colliery districts."

However, Thomas Wilson, writing of Gateshead speaks of similar customs his side of the river:

> "But feast and fun, and fuddled heeds,
> The stockin'-thrawin', and the beddin',
> Here nyen o' maw description needs—
> Thou'll find them i' the Collier's Weddin'."

> *(Pitman's Pay,* pt.3)

How the agricultural was transformed into the industrial can be seen in particular words. 'Goaf' from ON *golf,* meaning the bay of a barn with its wooden supports, and attested in that sense in East Anglia at least, becomes the part of a coal mine where the coal has been removed and only the structure of props held up the roof. Similarly, *inbye* and *outbye* are found in the North East relating both to directions around a farm and in the workings of a pit. *Cavil* – to choose work station by lot – was probably the same process used to allot shares of the olden common field.

It is wrong, in this sense, to see urban dialect as less authentic or 'ancient' than rural speech: it is rural speech transformed – with both innovative and retentive tendencies. It was and remains 'living' dialect.

If the North East was a little slower than Yorkshire and Lancashire in publishing its dialect, this changed in the 1790s, when a flood of broadsheets presented songs to a ready market in the growing industrial settlements of Tyneside and Co. Durham. Publishers tended to be also collectors of songs, like John Bell: he himself compiled a manuscript dictionary of Tyneside words (Newcastle University Library, MS, Bell-White 12). John Trotter Brockett, another Tynesider, published his extensive *North Country Words* in 1817, with new editions in 1829 and 1846. A transformation was underway – economic, social and cultural, with dialect as a marker of its progress.

Dialect and immigration

Mining fuelled the growth of North East industry and brought Newcastle to prominence as the major centre of coal finance and export. But it is well to remember that mining was also typical of the Upper Pennines, and that what we now regard as quintessential open countryside was once a fever of lead and copper mining. Copper mining was encouraged in Cumberland by Queen Elizabeth's minister Cecil in 1566, lead mining was put on a commercial basis in the Pennines by the seventeenth century; Wakelin (1977, p.24) refers to German assistance in the reign of Henry VIII. How much this Pennine industry exhibited continuity with the coal mining to the east is uncertain: a lead mine was called a 'groove' rather than a 'pit', and a list of mining terms from Derbyshire by Thomas Houghton in 1681 has little in common with later North East coal mine usage. In Parliamentary Papers (1861, XXI, Pt.2, p.323) there is this note on the west of Co. Durham:

> "… The general character of the lead miners presents a striking contrast to that of the colliers. They consist of families which have lived for ages on the spot – a steady, provident, orderly, industrious people, engaged from year to year by the lead-owners, and generally, besides their work underground, cultivating a small farm, which in many cases is their own freehold… They have been subjected to very little intermixture for ages past, as appears by their language, which differs considerably from that of the neighbouring country, approximating more to the dialect of the lowlands of Scotland." (Lowland Scots being the most conservative of dialects based on English.)

A more active influence on Tyneside dialect may have come from maritime connections with the Dutch. While some words could have been transmitted by Flemish settlers under Norman rule (see Wakelin, 1977, p.23; Llewellyn, 1936) – the loan-words *plack* and *dacker* are likely examples – the expected route might rather be through maritime contact between Tynesiders and the Dutch in the seventeenth to nineteenth centuries. The Dutch were a major sea-faring nation then, and although the Eastland Company, founded 1568, handled English cloth exports to the Baltic, "the trade between England and the Netherlands (in the seventeenth century) was largely in the hands of the Dutch, while much of England's trade with other countries was carried on in Dutch vessels" (Llewellyn, 1936, p.43). Most notably, exports of coal from the Tyne to Europe were handled via Amsterdam from the second half of the eighteenth century on. The Dutch and English shared herring fishing grounds, whaling grounds, trade routes, and in the eighteenth and early nineteenth centuries a strong mutual interest in smuggling (a word that itself comes from Dutch).

It may well be this link to Dutch that first sets North East industrial speech a little apart from its rural source, with words like 'pea-jacket', 'hoy', 'geck', 'gliff', 'haar', 'mizzle', 'plote', 'pluff', 'stot', 'yuke' and so on. Admittedly, it is often difficult to be certain of exact word origins: if you go back far enough, English, Dutch, Danish and other Germanic languages share a degree of common ancestry; but if the word is not noted down till 1700 or 1800 in English, we have good reason to look for a more modern source outside our borders or at least outside our main culture.

A further influence on Tyneside dialect surely came from Scottish immigrants in the early nineteenth century. There was a strong Scottish contingent in the keelmen who loaded the coal onto the ships in the Tyne. By 1700 there was an estimated 1,600 such keelmen servicing a fleet of come 400 keelboats (Haswell, p.35). As a class, they tended to settle on the Quayside area, and their occupancy of Sandgate is reflected in the well-known dialect song *The Keel Row*. According to W. Stanley Mitcalfe (1937, p.2), "… In the seventeenth and eighteenth centuries a considerable number of the keelmen were of Scottish origin, and many of these men were accustomed to return to Scotland in the winter. Lists of keelmen at the town hall dated 1729 show a surprising number of keelmen originating from near Edinburgh, and in some lists as many as fifty percent."

This raises some very interesting speculations, not only about the sources of nineteenth century Tyneside dialect, but about the origin of the word 'Geordie' itself. The word *divvent*, for example, may well be Scottish in origin – it is found as standard in the dialogue in George MacDonald's novel *Castle Warlock* (1882). MacDonald, born 1824, was brought up in Aberdeenshire, but left Scotland in 1848, living afterwards in the south of England and abroad. *Divvent* is entirely absent from the long poems on mining by Thomas Wilson (written in Gateshead (1826–30) but referring back to the early century); in Brockett only *div* is mentioned briefly as "very common among the vulgar" for 'do'; he also lists *dinna* and *disna* (without location). *Divvent* could well be a Scotticism brought direct by Scottish workers to Tyneside. Another Scottish mannerism may be the frequent word-ending -ie/y (*smaaly, Santy, forky-tail*, etc.). There are many examples of this in Scottish dialect, but few in the North East until the nineteenth century.

Scots influence also worked in a more intellectual sphere. A North-Easterner well enough placed to attend university would likely choose Edinburgh rather than Oxford or Cambridge. Political sensibilities also tended to be linked. In reaction to the 'unreformed' Corporation (City Council) in Newcastle, and the dominance of an unreformed Parliament in London, the tone of popular politics veered to the radical, embracing republicanism and democracy, and more aligned to feeling in Scotland than London. Booklets of songs published on Tyneside in the 1800s and 1810s contain both reformist and anti-French texts, plus a fair proportion of Scottish songs and imitations of Burns' work.

> "For nearly a hundred years the main cultural current in Britain had flowed from south to north. Now [late eighteenth century] it reversed itself. Out of Scotland came thinkers, politicians, inventors and writers who would restore Britain's self-confidence, and equip it with the tools to confront modernity on its own terms. They remade its politics. They galvanised its intellectual and educational institutions; they gave it a new self-image and a new sense of its place in history. They also redid its infrastructure and refitted its empire. The 'Scottish invasion' of the first three decades of the nineteenth century prepared the way for the great triumphs of the Victorian age." (Herman, 2003, p.256)

Irish immigration became a major factor after the tragic famine of the mid 1840s. Their impact on North East dialect should have been considerable, but is less easy to trace. Of words, perhaps *skilly* has an Irish origin. Their influence on pronunciation may have been more significant, but again it not easy to assess. In a poem *The Bombardment of Berry Edge*, written in Newcastle (1856) there is a parody of the Irish accent which shows little evident link with North East dialect. The text includes as Irish /sh/ for /s/ e.g. *shlip* for slip, *shtop* for stop, *shcamp* for scamp, *mishter* for mister; confusion of /th/ and /t/ e.g. *betther* for better, *tundering* for thundering; a rejection of the fronted form of long /e/: *lave* for leave, *spake* for speak, *complately* for completely, *plaise* for please, etc. and plus *jine* for join.

It may be that Tyneside dialect had settled and confirmed itself by the mid nineteenth century and resisted further change; or it may be that Irish immigrants served as unskilled labour, with little status and cultural impact, whereas, "The Scots who came South were very often skilled men seeking better pay and wider opportunities" (Clarke, 1977, p.113). In another interpretation, Shields (1974) suggests that Irish settlement in the mid Tyne area led to an audible dilution of dialect.

The many publications on dialect in Tyneside in the nineteenth century give the impression of a stable dialect, its non-standard form emphasised by phonetic spellings. But this cannot disguise the fact that, compared, say, with the Northern English of the fifteenth century, it had moved a good deal closer to 'standard' English. Its grammatical framework had much in common with the South (either because of interaction or because many features of 'standard' grammar originated in the North anyway). It certainly cannot be said to be a separate language. Yet the North East had in its own way developed a pronunciation and a lexis that was increasingly distinctive from Lancashire, Cumbria and Yorkshire.

The wonder is that dialect had not been completely overwhelmed by centuries of State English. The sheer number of dialect speakers is one reason for this, and their increasing concentration in urban centres during the course of the nineteenth century. This new urban population had little access to education and no reason to identify themselves with the speech of the Metropolis. Rather, the need for local identity and the growing strength of regionalism during the nineteenth century helped affirm the role of dialect. But there is another factor, in that the 'ruling class' may have preferred the lower orders to retain a different 'language' – not unlike the feudal dichotomy. In pursuit of a settled society, nineteenth century England was close to creating a caste system, in which one's status, work and type of language was decided by one's parentage. Dialect then, was a useful social marker, a matter to be regretted or to be proud of, according to one's viewpoint.

The Great North Coalfield

Extending from Ashington in the north to Trimdon in the south, the Great North Coalfield would be expected to be synonymous with North East dialect. Consistency in communication would surely be an essential precaution for the safety and efficiency of a coal mine, though in fact Greenwell's list of technical mining terms (1848) has relatively few obvious dialect words. The factor of mobility of workers within the coalfield would seem to support the argument for consistency. Thus, looking at a random street (German Row) at Seaham Colliery in the 1871 census, we find it holds some 60 adults born inside County Durham but some 68 born outside the County. Of the 60 from within Durham, only five were actually born in Seaham; of those from outside the County, 18 came from Northumberland, 22 from the Tyne area, and 28 from elsewhere, e.g. Ireland, Wales, Cornwall and Cumberland.

Through the birth-places of successive children in one family, we can see a marked tendency for the mine-workers to move around from pit to pit, sometimes making almost a yearly change of abode.

A sense of identity as miners and dialect speakers is evident in the following report of Durham miners taking part in a rally in Newcastle to extend suffrage in 1873:

"... A great many of the lads, especially from the Durham district, had evidently never been in Newcastle previously, and the air of wonder with which they gazed at the crowds, at the buildings, and especially at the fine folks who occupied the windows, was very amusing. If the quality criticised and quizzed them, the lads returned the compliment, and it was entertaining enough to catch snatches of criticism on the manners and customs of the upper ten thousand of Newcastle, reduced to the purest 'pitmatical', shouted across the streets, as the men and lads belonging to collieries swept by where I stood in the crowd." *(Newcastle Weekly Chronicle,* 19 April 1873, Supplement)

This is the first mention of 'pitmatical' as a name for North East dialect – deriving from 'pitmatics' (the craft or science of mining, itself modelled on words like 'mathematics'). 'Geordie' was first applied to the talk of Tyneside by Scott Dobson in his 1969 book *Larn yersel Geordie.*

The capital of the coalfield is indisputably Newcastle; its international links and high proportion of immigrant workers made it also the centre of innovation in dialect. Some but not all features of Tyneside English were adopted generally (like 'stot' and 'hoy'); yet there is also a considerable degree of local variation throughout the coalfield, with terms like *butterloggy* (butterfly) or *spell* (splinter) in the south that can be viably seen as pre-industrial forms, and likewise *fadge* (round loaf) or *bagie* (turnip) in the north. Such innovations as transpired on Tyneside (and perhaps Wearside) are understood but not used throughout the region; they seem to have spread patchily and survived even more patchily.

Of course there are no precise borders which you step over and find the dialect transformed. Rather there are focuses of loyalty, perhaps based on which central town people look to for recreation, shopping and social activities. In former days, these would have been the main market towns, ecclesiastical centres, and focuses of organised entertainment; today it is likely to be governed by public transport routes or the supermarket you take your car to. (I recall ladies in Trimdon in the 1990s bemoaning the downgrading of their bus services to Durham in favour of services to Peterlee; people in Wheatley Hill spoke of Hartlepool as their main shopping centre, etc.)

The survival of local loyalties in dialect reminds us that an agricultural world exists side-by-side with the industrial (and sometimes overlaps in personnel); it reflects the scattered nature of the industrial settlements away from Tyneside and Wearside; a further factor may be the growing interest in dialect exhibited by all classes as the nineteenth century progressed (with the emphasis on the 'pure' rural form); and indeed, the lack of linguistic cohesion within the mining community. Jack Lawson's autobiography *A Man's Life*, published in 1932, gives the following picture of Boldon Colliery ca.1900:

"... Its population consisted of people from every part of the British Isles, some of the first generation and some of the second, all boasting they were Durham men, though their parents spoke the dialect or had the accent of the distant place of their birth... there was a combination of Lancashire, Cumberland, Yorkshire, Staffordshire, Cornish, Irish, Scottish, Welsh, Northumbrian, and Durham accents, dialects, and languages. It was a polyglot population, and the Durham dialect, so marked among the children, did not hold unrivalled sway among their elders." (ch.5)

(This last comment is revealing, for it indicates that children influenced each other more to a consistency of speech than parents influenced them; their acute hearing and accurate miming, along with their own pressures to reach a youthful standard could be a major unrecognised factor in the perpetuation of local dialect.)

Social variations

There are variations in lexis other than geographical ones. The vertical strata of society make a difference, and Palgrave in Hetton-le-Hole in the 1890s noted that people would tend to try to speak more refinedly to him (as the minister). Those, like Thomas Wilson, who escaped the mining world for a desk job, would have to learn Standard Written English at least.

Other pressures applied. As early as 1845 it was noted:

> "... Increased opportunities of intercommunication with other provincials or the metropolis (dependent upon increased facilities of locomotion, the improvement of roads and the spread of mechanical devices) sweeps away much of these original [dialect] distinctions, but it never destroys them all." (Kemble, 1845, p.121)

Schooling seems to have been a more formidable discouragement to dialect, intentionally or unintentionally. National primary schooling, introduced in the early 1870s, did not overtly outlaw dialect (in the way it stopped Welsh being spoken in Wales). But many saw it as a discouragement:

> "... The decline [in dialect] would set in with education easier of attainment and would be hastened from 1870 onwards by compulsory education. Many of us remember being told to speak properly and drop the 'Weardale twang'. No dialect words were in the school books, nor were any ever written and this alone was sufficient to bring about its decline. Some schoolmasters did their best to ridicule it out of existence, describing it as coarse, vulgar and gawkish." (Lee, 1950, p.222)

But schooling also had less predictable effects:

> "... As we were put into higher classes we were taught to read by the phonetic method, that is to split the word in syllables and pronounce each to form the word." (Wade, 1966, p.75)

It is to this mode of teaching that we might trace examples of 'spelling pronunciation' that are still apparent and have helped to modify certain pronunciations. Thus, long /o/ in the North East broke to /iu/ (*biuts*, *skiul*, etc.). But either in imitation of the south or from teaching practices, a new long vowel has emerged in this context (almost 'coooker') unlike the shorter southern equivalent. *Fakade* for 'façade' is another example. (This possibility of spelling influencing pronunciation was first noticed in the 1920s by Harold Orton.)

The potential of dialect does not appear to have been exploited by nineteenth century Chartists or Trade Unionists, who used printed notices in 'Standard' English, either for the convenience of their printers or as an indication of the national level of their aspirations. Despite the affirmation of the triple role of dialect in regional identity, class identity and counter-identity, and the strong record of composition and publication in dialect (especially on Tyneside) that give the impression that the nineteenth century was the heyday of dialect appreciation – culminating in the great six-volume *English Dialect Dictionary* of 1898–1905 – there was a warning sign in the publication of *The Queen's English* by Henry Alford, Dean of Canterbury Cathedral in 1864. Insistence on 'correct' English needed no more defence than did patriotism...

The twentieth century

In the twentieth century, North-Easterners have been bombarded by other forms of English – American English in the cinema, Army Slang English in two world wars (with Commonwealth as well as US input), BBC 'proper' English on radio and TV, School English in the form of correct diction classes (in some grammar schools!), and Specialist Jargons in endless official forms and professional reports. This in itself need not have disadvantaged dialect: North-Easterners are adaptable and capable of understanding and even speaking a second language.

However, something of the creativity and egalitarian humour of the earlier nineteenth century use of language was in abeyance. Windows, the Newcastle music shop, printed editions of favourite songs; this tradition was properly kept alive in schools and local choirs; but where was the inventiveness? If the 1900s were arguably the heyday of the North Eastern economy, this optimism died down by the 1920s, with all the agony of low pay and unemployment; a confident mobility of population gave way to fixed conditions and few prospects of improvement.

Lawson (1932) claimed, "There are no strange dialects now, because there are no strangers from other parts, for, as is well known, the county cannot even employ all its own. There is only one dialect now, and only Durham people. The melting-pot process is complete" (ch.6).

The 'stability' and the rather scattered and small-scale nature of Co. Durham pit villages perhaps brought about some of the local variations in words now evident. However, local differentiation should not be over-stressed. (We should be sceptical of Shaw's *Pygmalion*, where Professor Higgins seems able to identify London accents not only by area, but even by street. That is good fun, but denies the whole point of language, which is communication.)

During the twentieth century there was arguably less enthusiasm for dialect among womenfolk than men. Lady Londonderry in election campaigning in the 1930s addressed her attentions to the womenfolk of Seaham ward as the most rewarding way of boosting votes for the Conservative cause (Lynne, 1997). Similarly, we learn:

> "... Happily, the younger miners, while possessing a liberal reserve of 'pitmatic'
> for street-end and other familiar uses, are able to converse in a near approach to
> conventional English. The younger womenfolk are better still. They take more
> pride in appearance and correct speaking..." (*Northern Daily News*, 31 May, 1919)

A correspondent who grew up on Tyneside in the 1940s writes:

> "... My idea would be that women tend to be more socially aspirational than men, hence strive after a less broad way of speaking. It was always my mother (and never dare call her Mam) who corrected me when I used such expressions as – 'Give us a one' – but of course in the 1940s these things mattered much more than either before or since. (A curious postscript to this is that recent information on dialect has come in to us from women correspondents.)" (AK)

A preliminary survey of North East dialect in 2001 showed considerable knowledge of and support for dialect among the over-60s; a good knowledge of dialect among those in their 30s to 50s; but relatively little dialect awareness among younger adults. Assuming this tentative result to be valid, what has happened to dialect in the last 50 years?

The 1950s, with its radio programmes *What Cheor Geordie* and *North Countryman*, seemed to augur well for dialect. The 1970s 'revival' of Geordie on Tyneside in the brilliant comic writing of Scott Dobson likewise. But Dobson's picture of the average beer-drinking, leek-growing pitman has all but passed from the picture. The loss of so much heavy industry in the region from the 1960s on – culminating in the pit closures of the 1990s – highlighted the reality that dialect was not so relevant to other employment contexts.

The introduction of compulsory secondary schooling after World War 2 is properly seen as a great advance, but without the guarantee of a job in the pits or shipyards, pressures for education have become paramount; the English 'O' Level exam has proved a powerful vehicle of change simply because it is an unavoidable passport to white-collar status.

Mobility of population has returned to the North East, but this time in the form of emigration. Economic regeneration is badly needed, but how to achieve it is another matter. The standard political solution has been a reliance on Modernism and (it seems to me) a distrust of the past. The risk that dialect itself might be viewed as a 'conservative' force is not particularly encouraging.

Internationally, the stream of ideas has run from a politically and culturally dominant America to Europe in recent decades, paralleled by a purely independent youth culture. Identities are under challenge. ("We might as well," a North East MP remarked to me, "put all the pieces in a bag and shake them up.") Would a Regional Assembly for the North East help?

The twenty-first century

The dialect situation has deteriorated, but...

The 2001 survey – alluded to previously – showed the continuity of a core of dialect vocabulary that remains useful and popular. New elements (like the Romany of Charver Taak) are reaffirming the fun and character of North East speech; the traditional pronunciation
and musical cadence of the dialect remains largely in place. Strategies of survival become evident: dialect words are doubled up to make their meaning clear (*guissie pigs, hacky-dirty, mell-hammer, clag-candy*, etc). Semi-redundant words find new uses – *keks, sneck, dut*. Words with an interesting sound take on an emphatic role (*stot, clag, ploat*). New compounds and word-formations are around.

There is certainly change, but it would churlish to regard this simply in terms of loss. Discoveries in genetics seem to have boosted an interest in family history that gives us a new way to view continuity and approach the past. Curiosity at least has been aroused, new identities are being forged, and as part of this process of renewal, dialect (past, present and future) is arguably attracting more attention than ever.

The Dictionary

Sample entry

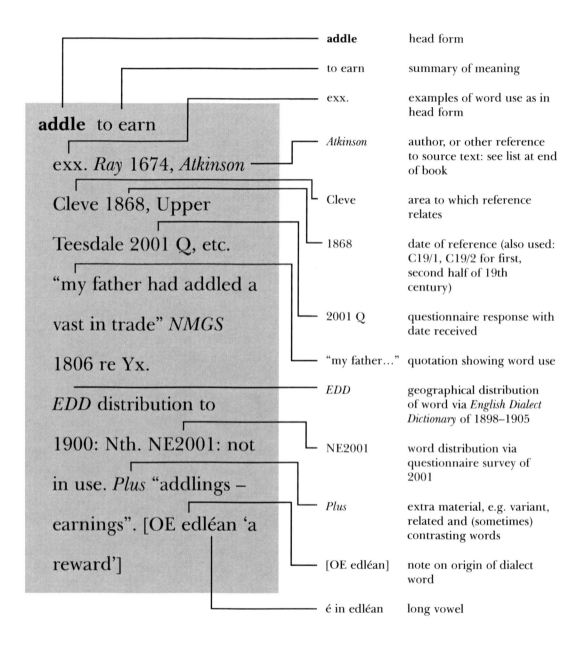

addle	head form
to earn	summary of meaning
exx.	examples of word use as in head form
Atkinson	author, or other reference to source text: see list at end of book
Cleve	area to which reference relates
1868	date of reference (also used: C19/1, C19/2 for first, second half of 19th century)
2001 Q	questionnaire response with date received
"my father…"	quotation showing word use
EDD	geographical distribution of word via *English Dialect Dictionary* of 1898–1905
NE2001	word distribution via questionnaire survey of 2001
Plus	extra material, e.g. variant, related and (sometimes) contrasting words
[OE edléan]	note on origin of dialect word
é in edléan	long vowel

The entry text:

addle to earn

exx. *Ray* 1674, *Atkinson* Cleve 1868, Upper Teesdale 2001 Q, etc. "my father had addled a vast in trade" *NMGS* 1806 re Yx. *EDD* distribution to 1900: Nth. NE2001: not in use. *Plus* "addlings – earnings". [OE edléan 'a reward']

aa, aw I (first person sg. pronoun)

exx. *Bewick* Tyne 1790s, Coxhoe 1916, etc. "Aa divvin' knaa" *Graham* Geordie 1979. [OE ic (pronounced 'ich') becomes long 'i' in Middle English; breaks to 'ia', then reduced to long 'a'. Though conventionally spelt 'aw' on Tyneside, the sound in fact is that of a long 'a' (aa, ah)]

aa to own

exx. *Brockett* Newc & Nth 1829, *Dinsdale* mid-Tees 1849, Tanfield Lea C20/2. "whee's aa this?" *Hull MS* wNewc 1880s [OE ah '(he) owns']

aabut ...but, almost

"aabut overtyen us" *Pitman's Pay* G'head, 1826. "Thoo will, will thi? Abbut thoo'll not!" *Hull MS* wNewc 1880s. *EDD* distribution to 1900: Nth [all... but or aye... but]

aad, aud, aald old

"alde walles" *Cuthbert* D'm C15/mid; "coal wis nowt but aad trees an' things" *Haldane* Newc 1879; "aad milk – skimmed milk" *Hull MS* wNewc 1880s; "aad bodee – old person" *Dodd* Tanfield Lea C20/2. [OE (Ang) ald rather than WS eald]

aad-farant old-fashioned, strange

"as audfarandly as a man of threescore" *Raine* Yx 1702; "an audfarand bairn – a child of promising abilities, also grave, sober, etc." *Bell MS* Newc 1815. *EDD* distribution to 1900: Sco, Nth. [ON fara]

aal, aw, a' all

"my putting's a' done" 'Collier's Rant' Newc, C18/2; "aal ees watter, aal ees puff – all his capacity" *Hull MS* wNewc 1880s; "aal the world and pairt of Gyetside" *Geeson* N'd/D'm '1969'. [OE (Ang) all rather than WS eall]

aall togither altogether

"aall togither like the folks o' Shields" Graham *Geordie* 1979

aan, awn, ain own (adj)

"his awen pople" *Cuthbert* D'm C15/mid; "he's ma ain for ever mair" *Bobby Shaftoe* C18/mid; "wor aan bonny river" *Allan's Tyneside Songs* p.531 1879; "let him ax for 't his aansel" *Geeson* N'd/D'm 1969. [OE agan, g changing to w]

aareet alright

"thats irrit" CT New Herrington 1930s; "aareet?" (a greeting) NE 2004

aback, abacka behind, on the other side of

"a wreck abacker the pier" *Green* Wearside 1879; "hoyed aback o' the fire" (to the back of) *Dobson* Tyne 1970. *EDD* distribution to 1900: Nth, Sco. [OE on bæce]

abackabeyont, etc. far, far away

"aback-a-behint where the grey mare foaled the fiddler" *Brockett* Newc & Nth 1829; "he lives abacka beyont" *Graham* Geordie 1979; "bakabiyont – far away" *Dodd* Tanfield Lea C20/2; "Abackabeyont – Gateshead" *Leslie* Newc 1992. *EDD* distribution to 1900: Nth

aboon above

"she's aboon ith' chamber" *Kennet* 1690s Yx; "wor steeple stands abuin St Nicholas'" *Oiling* G'head 1826; "thoo... was niver abi'an three mile fra' the' oon door sti'ans" *Egglestone* Weardale 1870s; "abyun – above" Tanfield Lea 1960. *EDD* distribution to 1900: Sco, Nth, eMids [OE abúfan]

ace see **excellent**

addle to earn

exx. *Ray* 1674, *Atkinson* Cleve 1868, Upper Teesdale 2001 Q, etc. "my father had addled a vast in trade" *NMGS* 1806 re Yx. *EDD* distribution to 1900: Nth. NE2001: not in use. *Plus* "addlings – earnings". [OE edléan 'a reward']

afear'd afraid

"thor's nowt to be afeared on" *Graham* Geordie 1979. *EDD* distribution to 1900: general. NE 2001: low use. *Plus* "as fear'd as a moose" *Allan's Tyneside Songs* p.27 1805. See also **flay**

afore before (adv, conj)

"afwore" *Bewick* Tyne 1790s; "byeth hint and afore" *Allan's Tyneside Songs* p.245 1827; "While ye toast yor shins afore the lowe" (fire) *MC May* Tyne 1891; "we'll git up afore the sparrow farts" Ashington C20/mid. *EDD* distribution to 1900: general. NE 2001: low use

afterdamp gas containing Carbon Monoxide

"after-damp – the residual gases after an explosion in a coal pit" *Brockett* Newc & Nth 1829; "after-damp – carbonic acid" *Nicholson* 1880. *EDD* distribution 1900: N'd, D'm, wYx

again against

"All that is agayn ye pes, or ye right" *Raine* York 1415; "mind ye're riddy agyen ee gets back" (for when) *Hull* MS wNewc 1880s; "I used to work agin him" (alongside) *JR* Seaham C20/1; "Ah'm agyen this sortathing" *Dobson* Tyne 1972

ahad 1. a grip; 2. on fire

1. "Aa gets ahaad on't" *Hay* Ushaw Moor C20/1;
2. "yer stacks is ahaad!" *Hull* MS wNewc 1880s; "the chimlas ahad" *Dobson* Tyne 1969

ahint behind (prep, adv)

"ahint the coonter he sat i' the shop" *Allan's Tyneside Songs* p.316 1827; "he's close ahint" *Atkinson* Cleve 1868; "come in ahint" (drover's cry to dog) *Geeson* N'd/D'm 1969; "she's away ahint one them trees" *Irwin* Tyne 1970. *EDD* distribution to 1900: ahind – Sco, N.I., Nth; ahint – Sco, N'd [OE æthindan].
See also **behint**

airt quarter of the compass, direction

"the wind is in a cold airt" *Kennet* 1690s Yx; "fra a' airts 'n' pairts" *Egglestone* Weardale 1870s. *EDD* distribution to 1900: Sco, N'd, Yx, Lx. NE 2001: not in use [Gaelic aird]

aix axe

"Lukey's aix and saw" *Pitman's Pay* 2, G'head 1828

ajee, agee aslant, crooked

"a bonnet agee" *Bell* MS Newc 1815; "with his short blue jacket; and his hat agee" *Allan's Tyneside Songs* p.336 C19/1; "agee [ajee] – awry, crooked" *Dinsdale* mid-Tees 1849; "ajee-wagee" cenD'm 2001 Q. *EDD* distribution to 1900: Nth, Sco, Ire. *Plus* "jee – crooked, awry" *Brockett* Newc & Nth 1829. See also **jee-wye**

aller see **eller**

amain out of control

"two waggons coming after me amain" *Errington* Felling/Heworth re 1790s; "amain – vehicle running out of control"

amain cont.

Dodd Tanfield Lea C20/2. *EDD* distribution to 1900: N'd, D'm, C'd, Yx [*OED* gives as C16 formation]

amang among

"amang thur hills" *Egglestone* Weardale 1870s. *Plus:* "inamang" *Hull* MS wNewc 1880s

amell amidst, among

"amell, ameld – among" *Ray* 1674; "amel – between" *Bailey* D'm 1810; "amell 7 and 8 o'clock" *Atkinson* Cleveland 1868. *EDD* distribution to 1900: N'd, C'd, Yx. NE 2001: not in use [ON ámilli]

annanters see **enanters**

ane see **yan**

anenst, nenst beside, towards

"for pavyng anenst the kyrk lone, ii d." *Raine* York 1530; "I sat close anenst him" *Atkinson* Cleve 1868; "The cash was paid nenst his year's rent" *Brockett* Newc & Nth 1829. *EDD* distribution to 1900: general. NE 2001: not in use [OE on efn 'face to face'].
See also **forenenst**

arf, arfish, erf timorous

"Ise arf" (I am afraid) *Grose* 1787; "its an awfish hike" (frightful) *Bell* MS Newc 1815; "erf or ergh – afraid" *Bell* MS Newc 1830s; "ah felt arfish in the dark" *Atkinson* Cleve 1868. *EDD* distribution to 1900: Sco and East Coast. NE 2001: not in use [OE (Ang) arg, ON argr]

argie to argue

"argy – the popular pronunciation of argue" *Brockett* Newc & Nth 1829; "divvent argie" *Graham* Geordie 1979. *EDD* distribution to 1900: general. NE 2001: in use. *Plus* "argufy – to argue" *Atkinson* Cleve 1868; "argify" *GP* S'm 1998

arles, earles a retaining fee, deposit

"arles – earnest or advance of wages" *Ray* 1674; "Given the smith in arles for the bell, 1 s." *Raine* Bedlington 1674; "arles... the money that was commonly given in Northumberland and Durham to confirm a hiring or binding" *Evening Chronicle* 18 Oct 1938. *EDD* distribution to 1900: Sco, Ire, Nth. NE 2001: not in use [OFr arres, erris 'earnest, pledge']. *Plus* "the fitters... arled the keelmen

arles, earles cont.

for their services during the coming year" *Mitcalfe* re Tyne ca. 1800

arran-web spider-web

exx. Nth 1829, mid-Tees 1849. *EDD* distribution to 1900: D'm, Yx. NE 2001: not in use [OF arraigne 'spider']. *Plus* "yrayn" (a spider) *Durham* C15/2; "atter-cop – a spider (also D'm, N'd, S.Scots)" *Atkinson* Cleve 1868; "spinner-mesh – a spider's web" *Atkinson* Cleve 1868

arsy-varsy head over heels

ex. *Grose* 1787. *EDD* distribution to 1900: NE, Mids

ashet dish

"serving dish or pie dish" *Geeson* N'd/D'm 1969. *EDD* distribution to 1900: Sco, N'd [Fr assiette]

ask, asker newt

"ask, asker, esk – a water newt" *Brockett* Newc & Nth 1829; "ask – a newt or small lizard, distinguished as a drie ask and a water ask" *Bell* MS Newc 1830s; "lizard or newt... a newt is only a wet ask when found in water... when found elsewhere it is classed with the dry asks and like them is reputed to be poisonous" *Hull* MS wNewc 1880s. *EDD* distribution to 1900: ask – Nth, Sco, Ire; asker – Yx, Mids [OE aexe]

ass ashes

ex. *Brockett* Newc & Nth 1829. *Plus* "ass-midden – a heap of ashes collected for manure" *Brockett* Newc & Nth 1829; "ass-midden – the heap of ashes... of the household" *Atkinson* Cleve 1868

astite as soon as, as willingly

"Aw'd astite de nought as de that" *Bell* MS Newc 1815. *EDD* distribution to 1900: Nth, Sco, NE 2001: not in use [ON títt 'often']. See also **stite**

'at see **that**

atop, atoppa on the top (of)

"a-top o' the dike" *Hull* MS wNewc 1880s. *EDD* distribution to 1900: general

atwee in two

"Eneugh to rive atwee the heart" *Pitman's Pay* 2, G'head 1820s. *EDD* distribution to 1900: atwee –NE; atwo – general

atween between

"atween the twee leets" (at twilight) *Embelton* Tyne 1897. *EDD* distribution to 1900: general. *Plus* "inatween" (after verbs of motion) *Hull* MS wNewc 1880s; "atwix" *Graham* Geordie 1979

aud see **aad**

aup see **yep**

aw see **aa**

awn see **aan**

ax, ast ask

"axing pennies ti buy backy" *Oliver* Newc 1824 p.9; "ast fer sumthing ta eat" *Egglestone* Weardale 1870s; "we mun ax Geordie" *Haldane* Newc 1879; "Ye may weel ax" *Parker* Tyne Valley 1896 p.88; "he was assin' where they'd getten hed?" (hid) *Dunn* B'p Auck 1950; "the aad chep axed him whe dun it" *Irwin* Tyne 1970. *EDD* distribution to 1900: general. [OE axian, acsian, variant of ascian]. *Plus* "he jus' come roond unaxed" *Leslie* Newc 1992

axletooth molar

"assil tooth or axle tooth – a grinder" *Brockett* Newc & Nth 1829. *EDD* distribution to 1900: Nth, Sco. [ON jaxl 'molar']

aye 1. ever, always. 2. yes

1. "haldand ay his first will" *Cuthbert* D'm C15/mid; "yer aye fashin yen wi somethin or other" *Bewick* Tyne 1790s; "the gimmers aye are short of milk" *Northumbrian Words III* C20/mid re Kielder. *EDD* distribution to 1900: Sco, N'd, W'd [OE a (long 'a') 'ever, always'] 2. yes: "aeyh, eyeh" *Bewick* Tyne 1790s etc.; "aye, sartly..." *Embelton* Tyne 1897. "Oh-aye – reet oh" *Dobson* Tyne 1970–71. *EDD* distribution to 1900: general; NE 2001: in common use. [derived from aye 'ever'] *Plus* "yis" *Allan's Tyneside Songs* p.480 1869; "u'm, h'm or umhim – an indifferent, careless manner of assenting to what is said... very common in Newcastle" *Brockett* Newc & Nth 1829; "aha" (mild assent) B'd Castle 2001 Q

ayont beyond

"far ayont the hill" *Geeson* N'd/D'm 1969; "ten miles ayont Hell" *Graham* Geordie 1979. *EDD* distribution to 1900: Sco, Ire, Nth. See also **beyont**

babby baby

ex. *Dobson* Tyne 1974. *Plus* "babba" *JB* Shildon C20/mid; "babby-hoose is a playtime 'house' outlined on the ground with the most ornamental material available, usually pebbles or boodies" *Hull MS* wNewc 1880s

baccy tobacco

"we'll tak a bit baccy" *Bell* Newc 1812 p.89; "Ah's off me bakky!" *Embleton* Tyne 1897; "bacca" *Coxhoe* 1916. *EDD* distribution to 1900: general

backcast 1. to change retrospectively, 2. a reversal

1. "We canno' backcast it – we cannot now order it differently" 1892 *Palgrave* Hetton 1896. *EDD* distribution to 1900: Sco, parts of Nth

2. "back-cast – a relapse of health, etc." *Atkinson* Cleve 1868; "Thoo's getten a back-cast" – you've got a relapse" *Palgrave* Hetton 1896

back-by back there

"If ye lamp shoud gan oot hinny divvent leave it way back-by" *Taylor* Dawdon C20/2

back end latter part, autumn

"back-end – the autmnal part of the year, the latter end of any given time" *Brockett* Newc & Nth 1829; "end of a week, a month, a year" *Atkinson* Cleve 1868; "part of the year after harvest" *Hull* MS wNewc 1880s. *EDD* distribution to 1900: Sco, Nth, Mids. NE 2001: in low use

back ower backwards, back again

"they cam back ower hyem" *Allan's Tyneside Songs* p.451 1862; "back ower" (backwards) *Haldane* Newc 1879; "so a cam back ower" S'm 2004 per BG. *EDD* distribution to 1900: N'd, D'm, Yx

back shift the second shift

"back-shift – the second shift of hewers in each day. It commences about four hours after the pit begins to draw coals" *Nicholson* 1880; "In the back shift one worked from 9 a.m until 5 p.m." *Hitchin* re Seaham 1910s p.62; "in bakk – afternoon shift" *Dodd* MS Tanfield Lea C20/2. *EDD* distribution to 1900: N'd, D'm, Yx. See also **fore shift**

bad unwell, ill

"bad, badly – poorly, indisposed, ill or sick" *Atkinson* Cleve 1868; "bad wi' the beor" *Dobson* Tyne 1970; "Ee, I was dead bad last night" *PG* H'pool C20/2. *EDD* distribution to 1900: general

baff week/end non-pay week/end

"the baff week is o'er" *Bell* Newc 1812 p.38; "baff-week – the week in which the pitmen receive no pay; a card not a trump is a baff one" *Brockett* Newc & Nth 1846; "baff Saturday – the day... when the men's work is made up, the wages being paid on the succeeding Friday." *Nicholson* 1880; "it's the baff week, thoo sees, an ah hae ne brass!" *Embleton* Tyne 1897; "The alternate weekend to 'pay' weekend in the days of fortnightly payments" *Northumbrian III* 1990 re Backworth. *EDD* distribution to 1900: N'd, D'm. [*Brockett* 1846 and *Geeson* N'd/ D'm 1969 equate 'baff' with 'blank'. *EDD* suggests variant of bauch, which from ON bágr 'hard up']

bagie see **turnip**

baggy stickleback, etc.

"baggies – small fish that youngsters catch and put in a jam jar" *RV* Winlaton, 1950s. *EDD* distribution to 1900: sSco, N'd

bain ready, etc.

"sho made hir bayne", "to ete... we were bayne" *Cuthbert* C15/mid; "bain – willing, forward" *Ray* 1674; "bain – ready, near" *Bailey* Co.Dm 1810; "bainer way – nearer route" *Dinsdale* mid-Tees 1849. *EDD* distribution to 1900: Nth, Mids, Sco, Ire. [ON beinn 'direct, ready']

bairn child

"sho was with barne" *Cuthbert* C15/mid; "barn, bearn – a child... bearn-teams – boods of children" *Ray* 1674; "Bobby Shaftoe's getten a bairn" Co.D'm C18/mid; "a heap o' hungry bairns" *Pitman's Pay* G'head 1820s; "en a little bairnie's pot" *Armstrong* Tanfield C19/2; "seeben lad bairns" *Egglestone* Weardale 1870s; "it's a clivvor bairn that knas its own fathor" Ashington C20/mid; "hee's aawnly a bairn" *VIZ* 42. *EDD* distribution to 1900: Sco, Ire, Nth, eMids. NE 2001: in common use. [ON barn, OE (Anglian) bearn as against West Saxon cild].

bairn cont.

Plus "**bairn time** – the time of life during which females bear children" *Bell* MS Newc 1815; "**bairn-team** – a large family, a brood of children" *Brockett* Newc & Nth 1829; "**bairnsplay** – a task easily done; also any kind of frivolity" *Hull* MS wNewc 1880s. *Alternatively:* "thine own wayns" *Noah's Ark* Newc C15/16; "sprog" *MG* Teesdale C20/2; "pit-rats" *Bell* Newc 1812 p.51; "kid" *Allan's Tyneside Songs* p.458 1862

bait, bate portable meal

"bate – a lunch taken on the road" *Bell* MS Newc 1815; "bait – food taken by a pitman to his work" *Nicholson* 1880; "when at wor bate, we'd had some confidential crack" (in pit) *Barrass* Stanley 1892; "my 'bait' of bread and jam" *Hitchin* re Seaham 1910s p.62; "bait – mid-shift food" *McBurnie* Glebe Colliery, C20/mid; "bait – the local word for food taken at work is bait... from the 1920s the most general food was bread and butter and sugar" *Northumbrian III* C20/2 re Durham collieries; "bait or bate – food tied in a handkerchief" *Geeson* N'd/D'm 1969; "bayut – lunch" *Dobson* Tyne 1970. *EDD* distribution to 1900: general. NE 2001: in common use [ON beita]. See also **scran**

bait-poke lunch box or bag

"bait-poke – a bag in which a pit-lad carries his provisions: 'Aw put the bait-poke on at eight'" *Pitman's Pay* G'head 1820s; "a sandwich outa me bait box" *Hay* Ushaw Moor C20/1; "baite-poke – a white bag... slung on the arm" *Wade South Moor* C20/mid. *EDD* distribution to 1900: N'd, D'm [?ONF poque, Ice. poki, Gaelic poca, OE pohha]. See also **tommy box**

ban to curse (someone)

"'Why dost thou bann Robin Hoode?'" C16 ballad; "banning – cursing" *Bell* MS Newc 1830s. *EDD* distribution to 1900: general. [OE bannan]

bane, byen bone

"for to breke and bryst his banes" *Cuthbert* C15/mid; "Thou hast full weary baynes" *Noah's Ark* Newc C15/16; "buain" *Armstrong* Tanfield C19/2 [OE bán]. See also **shackle(-bane)**

bang to beat, exceed

"bang – rush; surpass, excel" *Pitman's Pay* G'head 1820s; "we can bang them at canny Newcastle" *Allan's Tyneside Songs* p.243 1842. *EDD* distribution to 1900: Sco. [?ON banga 'to hammer']. *Plus* "to bang up – to get with chlld" *Bell* MS Newc 1830s

bangle bracelet

ex. NShields C20/mid Q

bank hill, hillside

"bank – hill. The word 'hill' is practically unknown in the dialect" *Palgrave* Hetton 1896; "bank – hill, slope on road" *JB* Shildon C20/mid; "a steep road or incline" *Graham* Geordie 1979; "hilly bank" *GJ* Spennymoor C20/2. *EDD* distribution to 1900: general. NE 2001: in use [Probably ON, since OIce. bakki 'ridge']. *Plus* "**banky** – hilly" *Dobson* Tyne 1973

bank aboveground at pit

"we made all possable speed out, to go to bank" *Errington* p.60 Felling/Heworth re 1800s; "bank – the top of mouth of a coal pit – 'are ye gawn to ride 't Bank?'" *Bell* MS Newc 1815; "iv a heap like coals at bank" *Haldane* Newc 1879; "The lads at bank [i.e. in heaven] 'ill greet us" *Barrass* Stanley 1890s; "At bank or doon the pit" *Barrass* Stanley 1890s; "the 'pit'-surface, top of 'shaft'. To 'work at bank' is to do the colliery work above ground" *Palgrave* Hetton 1896; "'the' rapped the cage ter bank" *Hay* Ushaw Moor C20/1; 'on surface near shaft' *JP* Dawdon C20/2. *EDD* distribution to 1900: N'd, D'm

banksman supervisor at top of pit shaft

"James Carre, then bankeman of the said cole pitts" *Raine MS*: Houghton-le-Spring, 1604; "banksman – a higher order of pitmen who take care of the pit heaps or mouth of the coal pit" *Bell* MS Newc 1815; "banksman – a man employed in taking the coals from the mouth of the shaft... to the skreen" *Brockett* Newc & Nth 1846; "banksman – shoves last few men into cage and makes sure the gate comes down and signals to the engine room 3 raps for 'men riding' and 2 raps for release the keps" *GP* S'm C20/mid; 'the man in control at the top of the shaft of a pit' *Graham* Geordie 1979. *EDD* distribution to 1900: N'd, D'm

bantling infant

"Here, then, is the end of your Lordship's bantling [Shaftesbury's baby, i.e. his Bill on child employment], dressed in your swaddling-clothes, it was stripped and despoiled before you took it back to your nursery..." *3M* Seaham 1842; "bantling – (anything) small or young. East Castle was called 'The Bantling'" *JG* Annfield Plain 1930s. *EDD* distribution to 1900: Sco, Mids. [*OED* suggests possible from Gm bänkling 'bastard']

banty 1. breed of chicken, 2. troops

1. "but wheest! the banty's craw aw hear" *Allan's Tyneside Songs* p.374 1849; "bantee – bantam [hen]" *Dodd MS* Tanfield Lea C20/2. [bantam, name and breed from the Far East]
2. "Bantams/Bantys – name for Durham troops in 1914-18 War" *CT* New Herrington 1930s

barguest apparition boding ill

"bar-guest – a ghost, all in white with large saucer eyes, commonly appearing near gates or stiles, there called bars (Yorks)" *Grose* 1787; "bar-guest – a local spirit or demon... accustomed to howl dreadfully at midnight before any dire calamity" *Brockett* Newc & Nth 1829; "barguest – an apparition in the form of some animal, most frequently a large shaggy dog, but always characterised by large saucer eyes and a terrible shriek or roar" *Atkinson* Cleve 1868. *EDD* distribution to 1900: Nth, eMids [Gm Barg-geist, mountain-demon, gnome; cf. OE gast 'spirit']

barley to 'bag', to reserve

"An' ay wad Johnny barley" [i.e. claim as husband] *Allan's Tyneside Songs* p.46 1812; "barley me that – I bespeak that" *Bell MS* Newc 1815; "To claim, to speak for first: 'Barley me the big 'un'" *Palgrave* Hetton 1896; "Aa barleyed forst kick" *Graham* Geordie 1979. *EDD* distribution to 1900: Nth [English 'parley']

barm yeast

ex. *Atkinson* Cleve 1868. *EDD* distribution to 1900: general. [OE barm] *Plus* "barm-cake" EP eD'm 1945; "barm-cake – idiot" H'pool, Teesside, Wingate 2001 Q; "barm-pot – idiot" *PG* H'pool C20/2, MB Coxhoe re C20/1, Ho'ton 2002 Q. NE 2001: only in phrases; otherwise 'yest' is used. See also **yest**

bastle border dwelling

"The English bastle was essentially a defensible farmhouse consisting of two floors, where the family lived above and the animals sheltered below" Reed *Border ballads* p.29

bat 1. a blow, 2. to hit

1. "we'll gie him his batts, and let him gae" Reed *Border Ballads* C16; "the bairns then hits her door such bats" *Allan's Tyneside Songs* p.335 C19/1; "nivor struck a bat – used in *Easington* and Horden to descrive a lazy sod" *JS* Easington C20/mid; "gets a bat in the mooth" *Irwin* Tyne 1970. *EDD* distribution to 1900: Nth, Mids
2. "they fit en they bat it" *Armstrong* Tanfield C19/2; "I'll bat thy gob in a minute" *IA* S'm 1950s, '60s. *EDD* distribution to 1900: general. NE 2001: in use [Fr battre] *Plus* "batterfanged – beaten and scratched" *Atkinson* Cleve 1868. *EDD* distribution to 1900: Yx, Lincs

bate see **bait**

bat end pit electrcian's term

'end of an electric cable, nearest the panel' re Houghton Pit 2001 Q

batts flat land

"batts – islands in rivers, or flat grounds adjoining them" *Bailey* Co.Durham 1810; "batts – low flat grounds adjoining rivers, and sometimes islands in rivers" *Brockett* Newc & Nth 1829. *EDD* distribution to 1900: N'd, nYx

bauk, balk beam of wood, e.g. in a building

"balks, bawks – poles laid over a stable or other building for the roof [i.e. a beam]" *Ray* 1674; "hen-bawks – the hen-roost, the bawks or cross poles or sticks in a hen-house" *Kennet* 1690s as Nth; "bauk – ...a pole or beam, such as are used under the roofs of small buildings; land left unplowed, to divide the property of different persons in common or open fields" *Grose* 1787 re N'd; "balk – a strong piece of timber for supporting the roof in a coal pit" *Brockett* Newc & Nth 1846; "propped up with barks" (planks) *JR* Seaham C20/1. *EDD* distribution to 1900: general. [ON bjalki 'beam']

bays see **hopscotch**

(to) be 1. I am, etc., 2. you are (sg.), 3. he is, etc., 4. we are, 5. you are (pl.), 6. they are

1. "Aze suer aws reet" *Bewick* Tyne 1790s; "sair fail'd is I" *Allan's Tyneside Songs* p.10 1834; "Aa is a feul" *Haldane* Newc 1879; "eff he thinks aw'se a fule, he's a lang way wrang" *Wearside Tales* 1879; "I'se sure!" (ironically) *EP* Southwick 1940s; "A's – I am" *Dunn* B'p Auck 1950; "aaz – I'se" *Dodd* MS Tanfield Lea C20/2; "awm stuck" *Allan's Tyneside Songs* p.408 1862; "Aa'm / Aa's" *Tyneside grammar* 1880s; "A'm" *Barrass* Stanley 1890s; "ahm – I am" *Dobson* Tyne 1972.

2. "thou is", "thou's" *Chicken* Benwell 1720s; "Wi, how is thou?" *Marshall* Newc 1823 p.10; "thoo is" *Armstrong* Tanfield C19/2; "thouse varney ten minits late" West Stanley C20/1

3. [as in standard southern]. *Plus* "ben't, baint (pronounced beeant) – be not" *Atkinson* Cleve 1868

4. "wese" *Meriton* nYx 1683; "as lang as wour yebble" *Marshall* G'head 1806; "wah" (we are) *RF* Gateshead C20/mid

5. "yor, yer" *EDD* N'd C19

6. [as in standard southern] *Plus* "thai bene" *Cuthbert* C15/mid

[there are two OE verbs, forms from beon (not favoured in the North East) and forms like is, earun (more Anglian) that underlie the above dialect forms]. See also **shall, was, will**

beal to roar (of animal or human)

"to cry out, weep, lament" *Bell* MS Newc 1830s; "to roar, as of a child" *Dinsdale* mid-Tees 1849; "to bellow, to low as a cow; to raise the voice" *Atkinson* Cleve 1868; "beel – bellow like a bull" *Gibson* C'd 1880. *EDD* distribution to 1900: Nth. [OE bellan 'to roar', ON belja 'to bellow']

beb, bev 1. a sub, a gift or loan of money, 2. assisting

1. "So I'm all right for a beb then?" per *Wood* Stockton/M'bro 2002

2. "bevving" (helping out at pitch n toss) *LG* S'm C20/mid. *EDD* distribution to 1900: beb – N'd

beck stream, local watercourse

"a brook or rivulet" *Bailey* Co.Durham 1810; "small rivulet" *Dinsdale* mid-Tees 1849; "the general name for a stream of running water" *Atkinson* Cleve 1868; "Beck. Used indifferently with 'burn.' A stream." *Palgrave* Hetton 1896;

beck cont.

"rowled in beck – fell in the stream" *Dunn* B'p Auck 1950; "gan play down th' beck" *TC* S'm 1940s; exx. Trimdon, Lanchester, Wheatley Hill 2004 Q. *EDD* distribution to 1900: Nth (not N'd), eMids. NE 2001: in use for local stream. "While the Norse beck crowds the banks of Teesdale, it does not exist in Weardale" *Egglestone* Weardale 1886; "the name occurs 63 times in Durham but not in Northumberland" *Graham* Geordie 1979 [ON bekkr]. See also **burn**

beclarted dirtied

"beclarted – bemired, smeared over with dirt" *Atkinson* Cleve 1868. *EDD* distribution to 1900: Sco, Nth. [first noted C13th, source uncertain]. See also **clarts, clarty**

bedstock, stocks frame of bed, the bed itself

"Ower the bedstock" *Marshall* Newc 1823 p.17; "At this Aw lowpt clean ower the stock, An' fand that Aw wiz waken..." *Barrass* Stanley 1890s (waking from a nightmare); "bedstock – the side beam of a bed" *Hull* MS wNewc 1880s; "she gov us a dunch an' then shuved us ower the bedstock" *Cuddy Cairt* Newc 1917; "A'm tired out, A'm off to the bedstocks/ stocks", "It's time you were in the stocks" *BJ* re Cockfield, ca.1900, Ho'ton, B'p Auck 1940s. *EDD* distribution to 1900: Nth, Sco. ['stock' as piece of wood]

bee-hive 1. bee-bike, 2. bee skep

1. "bee-bike – a bee's nest, or hive, in a wild state" *Brockett* Newc & Nth 1829; "byke – the nest of a bee or wasp" *Luckley* Alnwick 1870s; "a wasp's byke or a bummler's byke" *Nth Words* Bensham 1938; "When the scythe cuts and the sock rives / No more fairies and bee-bikes" Denham Tracts C19. *EDD* distribution to 1900: N'd, D'm, nYx [Brockett analyses as bee-wick; or from big 'to build'?]

2. "bee skep – a bee hive" *Bell* MS Newc 1815, *Atkinson* Cleve 1868; "skep – a hive for bees, also measure for corn, etc... made of ropes of straw fastened together with the tough bark of hazels, etc." *Bell* MS Newc 1830s; "skep – beehive" wD'm 2001 Q

beeld shelter, protection

"some traist of thair belde" (protection) *Cuthbert* C15/mid; "& do think you a great beald to me" *Raine* MS York 1588; "beeld – a high fence or skrean to defend cattle from the

beeld cont.

cold" *Kennet* 1690s as Nth; "beild – sheltered as 'it has good beild'" *Bell* MS Newc 1830s; "beild – shelter" *Gibson* C'd 1880. *EDD* distribution to 1900: Nth, Sco. [?OE bieldo 'boldness, confidence']. *Plus* "beeldy – warm, affording shelter from cold: 'beeldy flannel'" *Brockett* Newc & Nth 1829

beestlings rich milk

"beeslings, beestlings – the first milk which a cow gives after her calving" *Kennet* 1690s as Yorks; "beestlings" *Bell* MS Newc 1815; "beestlings or beastings" *Brockett* Newc & Nth 1829; "beastlings, beeslings (pronounced bizlins)" *Atkinson* Cleve 1868. *EDD* distribution to 1900: general. [OE biesting]

behint behind

"behint yon auld fail dyke" Reed *Border Ballads* C16; exx. *Bewick* Tyne 1790s, *Atkinson* Cleve 1868, Tanfield Lea 1960. *EDD* distribution to 1900: Nth, Mids. "but ahint is commoner" *Graham* Geordie 1979. See also **ahint**

belang to be born in or live in

"Hey lad, dista b'lang plyess?" *NDN* 31 May 1919; "whare de yea belang?" *Armstrong* Tanfield C19/2; "a man ed belang'd Middlesborro" *Egglestone* Weardale 1870s; "'War dis thoo belang?' 'Aa belang canny Shields'" *Palgrave* Hetton 1896; "Aa belongs Pittington" Coxhoe 1916; "Where the hell thee's belang? – where do you come from / live?" *Dunn* B'p Auck 1950; "belang Seaham" S'm 1990 per BG. NE 2001: low use

bell in phrase 'bears the bell' – is victorious

"thou greitly bears the bell" Reed *Border ballads* C16; "The Bayly berith the bell away" *Durham* C16/2

belk see **bowk**

bent type of grass

ex. *Brockett* Newc & Nth 1829; "the whins and bents and strang sea air" *Allan's Tyneside Songs* p.468 1862; "bent – a kind of short, wiry, dark-coloured grass... of the moors and moor-banks" *Atkinson* Cleve 1868; "a coarse grass growing on sandhills near the shore" *Geeson* N'd/ D'm 1969. *EDD* distribution to 1900: general

bere barley

"bear – four-rowed barley" *Brockett* Newc & Nth 1829; "bear, bere – a variety of barley, otherwise called bigg" *Atkinson* Cleve 1868; ex. Aberdeens, 1993. *EDD* distribution to 1900: general. [OE bere] See also **bigg**

berries

"Berries. Generic name for all fruit of the berry kind" *Palgrave* Hetton 1896

bet beaten [perfect participle]

"seldom be't" *Allan's Tyneside Songs* p.209, 1842; "bet – exhausted" *Dodd* MS Tanfield Lea C20/2

beuk book

"beuk" *Armstrong* Tanfield C19/2; "byuk" Coxhoe 1916; "yen o' the beuks thet tellt ye hoo it's aall dyun" *Robson* Newc C20/1; "boouk" S'm 2003 via BG. See also library

beuts, byuts boots

"guid pair of buits" *Bell* MS Newc 1830s; "beuts en shoos" *Armstrong* Tanfield C19/2; "fill thi beuts" (eat as much as you can) *CT* New Herrington 1930s; "Aav nae biuts" *Dunn* B'p Auck 1950; "byuts" Coxhoe 1916, Dinnington 1950s, Tanfield Lea 1960 (Q); "...brings new byeuts te wor bairns" *Dobson* Tyne 1972. See also **skeets**

bewer girl, young woman

"bewer – a disrespectful word – more Tyneside" *GP* S'm C20/mid; 'girl' *TP* S'd 1960s; "esp. a girl who tarted herself up for a night out" *SM* H'pool 2003; "woman, a lass – not exactly uncomplimentary but it's on the level of 'totty': 'Looka that bewer at the bar'" *Wood* re H'pool, Teesside 2003; "she was a bewer" (implying loose morals) *GD* S'm 2004 via BG. [*OED* gives as 'north dialect and tramps' slang']

beyont beyond

ex. *Atkinson* Cleve 1868. *EDD* distribution to 1900: general. See also **ayont**

bid to invite

"Are you bodden or invited to the wedding, burial, etc." *Bell* MS Newc 1815; "he's bad to the funeral" *Luckley* Alnwick 1870s; "When a miner dies, a 'bidder' goes round to all his fellow-workmen to bid them attend his funeral" *Palgrave* Hetton 1896. *EDD* distribution to 1900: Sco, Nth. [OE biddan]

biddy a louse

ex. *Dinsdale* midTees 1849. [Gael. videach 'very small']

bide wait, remain

"to stay, stop or continue" *Bell* MS Newc 1815; "to wait; to dwell; to bear, endure" *Atkinson* Cleve 1868; "Newcassel's fame 'ill bide / lang as its coaly tide" *Allan's Tyneside Songs* p.535 1882; "aw'll bide at yem" *Armstrong* Tanfield C19/2; "Don't let them bide out night" *Palgrave* Hetton 1896; "Bide where tha is" *Hitchin* re Seaham 1920s p.107; "if you are not coming bide at yem and sulk" *JS* Easington 20/mid. *EDD* distribution to 1900: general. NE 2001: only in phrases like 'bide your torn', 'bide your time'. [OE bídan]

big build

"hys newe house that he byggys" *Raine* MS York, 1376; "he bigged thare housyng" *Cuthbert* C15/mid; "big – to build: 'they bigged a bower'" *Bell* MS Newc 1815. *EDD* distribution to 1900: Nth, Sco, but obsol. *Plus* "biggen, bigging – a building... now generally used for a hut covered with mud or turf" *Brockett* Newc & Nth 1829

bigg, big barley

"otes, bygg, both ry and whete" *Durham* C16/2; "the Big-Market" (Newcastle) Owen Macdonald, 1752; "bigg – a coarse kind of barley; properly that variety which has six rows of grain on each ear" *Brockett* Newc & Nth 1829; "bigg – a variety of barley, known as 'four-rowed'" *Atkinson* Cleve 1868; 'now obsolete' *Hull* MS wNewc 1880s. *EDD* distribution to 1900: Sco, Nth, e Mids. [ON byggja]. See also **bere**

billy marra or campanion

"billie, billy – a companion or comrade, a brother" *Brockett* Newc & Nth 1846; "a companion" *Graham* Geordie 1979. *EDD* distribution to 1900: Nth, Sco. [? bully]

bind, binnd to bind; to contract to work in pit

"When wour bund" (*Marshall* G'head 1806); "thou's fast boon... thou's bun te Tyne Main" *Allan's Tyneside Songs* p.218 1827; "Gat fettl'd up a set of geer – and bun' to hew." *Pitman's Pay* G'head 1820s. *EDD* distribution to 1900: N'd, D'm

bindin' annual signing on for pit work

"the pranks that were play'd at the last binding" *Bell* Newc 1812 p.39; "binding or bindin – the contract or hiring for the year; the colliery bond" *Brockett* Newc & Nth 1846; "not varry lang 'fore wor bindin' cam roon" *Allan's Tyneside Songs* p.485 1862; "bindings – the time at which the yearly bond used to be signed, which was on the Saturday previous to March 22nd" *Nicholson* 1880; "The aud men tawk'd ... of what the binndins used te be" *Barrass* Stanley 1890s. *EDD* distribution to 1900: N'd, D'm

bing a container

"bing – a chest in a stable to keep the horses corn in" *Bell* MS Newc 1815; "stone recesses, called bing steads" (in mine) *Alston* 1833; as a measure of lead: "—— [number omitted] pokes make a horse [load] & two horses make a bing" *Raine* MS Alston 1675. *EDD* distribution to 1900: Sco, Nth, eMids. [?ON bingr 'heap', compare Dan. bing 'bin']

bink bench

"binks & forme" *Raine* MS Mollescroft 1613; "bink – a seat of stones, wood, or sods, made mostly against the front of a house" *Bailey* Co.Durham 1810; 'a ledge or platform-like hill, also a stone bench...' western Northumbria via *Hull* MS wNewc 1880s; "bink – stone bench for milk cans etc." *Blenkinsopp* Teesdale 1931; "bink – stone bench (as in farm dairy)" JB Shildon C20/mid. *EDD* distribution to 1900: with sense 'shelf' – Nth, Sco. [Nth version of bench]

binn external horizontal strip of wood on a coble

"acts like a rubbing strake" *Hill* Flamborough 1970s; "listin's, not binns" *FT* Cullercoats 2003

birk birch tree

"seaven score birk trees and allers" *Raine* MS Medomsley 1615. *EDD* distribution to 1900: Sco, Nth, eMids. [ON bjǫrk]

bishop to scorch

"to bishop – to let milk or sauce burn... in boiling." *Bell* MS Newc 1815; "bishoped – burnt (e.g. milk)" *Blenkinsopp* Teesdale 1931. *EDD* distribution to 1900: general

bit

bit [adj.] little, small or [noun] small amount or piece of

"the trap-door bit laddy" *Marshall* G'head 1806; "a bit backy" *Bell* Newc 1812 p.89; "bit – as in 'a bit pie'" *Dinsdale* mid-Tees 1849; "maw bit bairn", "she gave a bit smile" *Armstrong* Tanfield C19/2; "this bit paper", "any little bit thing" Coxhoe 1916

biv by

"biv it" *Allan's Tyneside Songs* p.48 1812; "on the road biv hissel" *Haldane* Newc 1879; "biv her side" *Chater* Newc 1880. *EDD* distribution to 1900: N'd, Yx. [intrusive intervocalic 'v' – or by analogy with forms like 'div', 'hev']

bizon see **bysen**

blaa, blaw 1. to blow, 2. a breather

1. "blaa – [to] blow (as with wind, gale, etc.)" *JB* Shildon C20/mid
2. "getting the men to work after their blaa was finished" *JS* Easington C20/mid; "'Let's hev a blaa' means 'Let us take wind' – that is, have a rest – or 'Let us have a smoke'." Tanfield Lea 1960

blackberries – 1. **bumblekites**, 2. **brambles**, 3. **black-kites**, 4. (other)

1."bumble-kites – bramble-berries" *Kennet* 1690s as Yx, *Bailey* Co.Durham 1810, *Bell* MS Newc 1815 as Durham, *Atkinson* Cleve 1868. *EDD* distribution to 1900: Nth. ["from its bering supposed to cause flatulency when eaten in too great a quantity" *Brockett* 1849]
2. "brambles (pronounced bramm'ls, brumm'ls) – blackberries, the fruit of the bramble" *Atkinson* Cleve 1868; "blackberry bushes and their fruit" *Palgrave* Hetton 1896, D'ton 1940s (Q); 'the fruit, not the plant' *JB* Shildon C20/mid. *Plus* "as freendlee is a brammel bush" Ashington C20/mid
3. "black-kites – brambles" *Gibson* C'd 1880. *EDD* distribution to 1900: N'd, C'd
4. "black bow-wowers – bramble berries (N'd)" *Bell* MS Newc 1815; "black-bowowers – blackberries – plus bumbly kites" *Luckley* Alnwick 1870s; "wicks or wickens – blackberries" *JS* E'ton 1950s; "hoggins, wicks, wickens – words used to describe blackberries in abundance" *JS* Easington C20/mid; "blackbarries" *Dobson* Tyne 1972

blackclock, clock cockroach, beetle

"a clock – a beetle or dor, a hot-chafer" *Kennet* 1690s as Nth; "clock – beetle" *Dinsdale* mid-Tees 1849; "Blackclock – cockroach (always used)" *Palgrave* Hetton 1896; "blaklok – black beetle" *Dodd* MS Tanfield Lea C20/2; "a cockroach was always called a blackclock" *ER* M'bro C20/2. *EDD* distribution to 1900: Yx. NE 2001: blackclock – low use [origin unknown]

blackie 1. a blackbird, 2. a black man

"blackie – blackbird" *JB* Shildon C20/mid, *Graham* Geordie 1979. *EDD* distribution to 1900: general. *Plus* "ouzel – the blackbird" *Atkinson* Cleve 1868
2. "We'd seed a Blackey... [boxing]" *Allan's Tyneside Songs* p.140 1816; "there's bonny wark oot here [Australia] wi' the Convicts, the Blackies, Robbers, en Bushrangers" *Allan's Tyneside Songs* p.403 C19/mid; "Twee Blackeys [statuettes?] sall mense the door-check" *Mitford* Newc 1888; ex. *TC* S'm 1980s. *EDD* distribution to 1900: N'd

blake 1. yellowish, 2. to make or become pale

1. "blake – yellow or of a golden colour; spoken of butter, cheese, etc." *Brockett* Newc & Nth 1829; 'yellow; bleak' *Dinsdale* mid-Tees 1849; "blake – of a fair, soft, yellow colour or tone: 'as blake's butter'" *Atkinson* Cleve 1868; 'butter-yellow' *Blenkinsopp* Teesdale 1931. *EDD* distribution to 1900: Nth. [OE blác 'pale' ON bleikr]
2. "thire enmys... sall blake" *Cuthbert* C15/mid. *EDD* distribution to 1900: Yx. See also **drunk**

blakes cow dung

"cow-blakes – cow-dung [for fuel]" *Ray* 1674. *EDD* distribution to 1900: Yx. See also **cassens**

blare 1. to cry (weep or shout), 2. to poke out the tongue, 3. an outcry, a shout

1. "she blaired out for a greet while" (cried our, wept) *Bewick* Tyne 1790s; "blare – to cry aloud, as the cow blares, etc." *Bell* MS Newc 1815, 1830s; "sae blind wi' blairin" *Allan's Tyneside Songs* p.180, 1824; "'Crikes!' Jemmy blair'd" *Allan's Tyneside Songs* p.187 1824; "the bairns begins an' shoots an' blairs" *Allan's Tyneside Songs* p.335 C19/1; "blair, blare – to bellow as a cow; to cry loudly or noisily [like] a child; to protrude the tongue" *Atkinson* Cleve

12

blare cont.

1868; "blaring – crying peevishly: 'You'r blaring like a calf'" *Luckley* Alnwick 1870s; "A'll gi' th' something to blare for, if aa start wi' th'" *Palgrave* Hetton 1896; "she blared her eyes out" *IA* S'm 1950s, 60s; 'to weep, cry loudly' Dinnington 1950s Q; "the bairns were blairin'" *Graham* Geordie 1979. *EDD* distribution to 1900: general. NE 2001: in use. [Du. blaren, Fr pleurer]
2. "blare – to poke out the tongue" *Dinsdale* mid-Tees 1849. *Atkinson* Cleve 1868
3. "aw set up a blare" *Allan's Tyneside Songs* p.49 1812. *Plus* "blary – noisy, of an infant" *Palgrave* Hetton 1896

blash to splash (trans., intrans.)

"blash – to splash" *Bell* MS Newc 1815; "blash – to plash [sic]" *Bailey* Co.Durham 1810; "t' watter blashes oot i' t' can" *Atkinson* Cleve 1868. *EDD* distribution to 1900: Sco, Nth, eMids [imitative]

blashy wet

"streets... brave and blashy" *Allan's Tyneside Songs* 1812 p.46; "blashy – thin, poor: 'blashey tea'" *Pitman's Pay* G'head 1820s, sim. *Brockett* Newc & Nth 1829, *Atkinson* Cleve 1868. *EDD* distribution to 1900: Sco, Nth, Mids

blast explosion (in pit)

"blast – an explosion of fire-damp" *Nicholson* 1880. *EDD* distribution to 1900: N'd, D'm

blate shy, modest

"bleit, blate – bashful" *Ray* 1674; "faith you're no blate" *Bell* MS Newc 1815, 'shamefaced' 1830s; "deeth o' late hez no been blate" *Oliver* Newc p.8 1824; "he's not forward, in fact he is blate" *Allan's Tyneside Songs* p.571 C19/2 re Choppington. *EDD* distribution to 1900: Nth, Sco, Ire. [possibly from OE blát 'pale'] *Plus* "blaytness – shyness" (*Pitman's Pay* G'head 1820s)

blather to gabble, talk nonsense, etc.

"blather – to stammer, also blather for bladder" *Bell* MS Newc 1830s; "Blather – gabble: 'she blathers away when there's no one here'" (of a baby's attempts to talk. 1891), 'hard (hold) thy blatherin' tongue'" *Palgrave* Hetton 1896. *EDD* distribution to 1900: general. NE 2001: in use. [ON blaðra]. *Plus* "blatha-skyt – person who talks rubbish" *Dodd*

blather cont.

MS Tanfield Lea C20/2; "blather skite – one who talks aimlessly" *Graham* Geordie 1979. See also **blether**

blaze to shoot

"blazed it ower the bar" (re football) Dinnington 1950s Q

blea livid colour

"few will keep a tuppe that is blea-faced" *Raine* MS EYorks 1641; "blee – bluish" *Bell* MS Newc 1815; "blea – bluish or lead-colour" *Brockett* Tyne & Nth 1846; "blae (pronounced bleea) – of a livid or pale bluish colour: 'he leuks bleea's a whetstone'" *Atkinson* Cleve 1868. *EDD* distribution to 1900: Nth, Sco, Ire. [ON blá 'blue, livid']

bleaberry bilberry

"blea-berry, blay-berry – the bilberry or black whortle berry" *Brockett* Newc & Nth 1829, *Atkinson* Cleve 1868; "Bleeberry – bilberry" *Palgrave* Hetton 1896, *JB* Shildon C20/mid; "bleeberry sauce" *Dobson* Tyne 1970–71. *EDD* distribution to 1900: Nth, Sco, Ire. [ON blá 'blue, livid'] See also **windberry**

bleb blister, droplet

"bleb – a drop" *Bailey* Co.Durham 1810; 'the watery bubble of a blister' *Bell* MS Newc 1815; "a drop of water or any other fluid; a blister: 'blebs iv his hands'" *Atkinson* Cleve 1868; "a bleb on her lip" *IA* S'm 1950s,60s; 'sore skin by burn, scald or friction' *Dodd* MS Tanfield Lea C20/2; "bleb was often restricted to a blood blister, e.g. when you 'brayed your finga end' with the hammer" *JS* Easington C20/mid; "bleb – extrusion in a bike inner-tube" *Wood* M/bro 2002; 'a carbuncle on a car-tire wheel' Gateshead per BL 2003. *EDD* distribution to 1900: Sco, Nth, Mids. NE 2001: in use. [imitative] See also **blush**

bleck dark dirt

"any blecked or coloured wooll" (?spotted) *Raine* MS Birstwith 1585/86 via Knaresborough; "bleck – grease... in machinery" *Atkinson* Cleve 1868; 'pitch' [tar] *Hull* MS wNewc 1880s; 'dirty grease, found on coal waggon-ways where rollers are used' *Palgrave* Hetton 1896. *EDD* distribution to 1900: N'd, Yx, Ches. NE 2001: not in use. [ON blek 'ink']

bleech a gale

"bleech – high wind with snow or rain" *Dodd* MS Tanfield Lea C20/2. *EDD* distribution to 1900: bleach – N'd

bleezer, blazer screen to help in lighting a fire

"bleezer – a sheet of iron for closing the open space above a grate to increase the draught" *Hull* MS wNewc 1880s; "blazer – a piece of sheet iron, put between the grate and the mouth of the chimney, in order to make the fire draw" *Palgrave* Hetton 1896; "bleezer" Spennymoor C20/mid, *JP* S'm C20/2, *Dodd* MS Tanfield Lea C20/2, Trimdon 2002 Q. *EDD* distribution to 1900: N'd, Yx. NE 2001: low use. *Plus* "chaakin on th bleezer" of a couple not talking to each other. eD'm 1990s

blether 1. to talk idly, 2. silly talk

1. "may blether an' crack" *Allan's Tyneside Songs* p.406 1862; "blether – to cry loudly like a fractious child" *Atkinson* Cleve 1868.
2. "'mang the noise an' the blether" *Allan's Tyneside Songs* p.489 1862; "blether" Gateshead, S'd 2001 Q. See also **blather**

blinnd blind

"blind as a bat" *Egglestone* Weardale 1870s, *Other Eye* Newc., ca.1890, GP S'm C20/2; "short vowel... a blind lonnin is one that ends abruptly without exit; a blind burn is one which disappears underground for part of its course" *Hull* MS wNewc 1880s; "What's the matter wi thoo ref are ye blinnd or what?" *JS* Easington C20/mid

blithe happy

"he was blithe of the myracle" *Cuthbert* C15/mid; "Whe's like my Johnny, / Sae leish, sae blithe, sae bonny?" *Allan's Tyneside Songs* p.45 1812; "Wor lasses then were blythe and bonny" *Pitman's Pay* G'head 1820s]. *EDD* distribution to 1900: general. [OE blíð]

blob 1. bubble [noun and vb], 2. condom

"blob – a bubble: 'soap-blobs', 'nose-blobs'; verb, to bubble" *Atkinson* Cleve 1868; "Blob – to bubble: 'it blobs up'" *Palgrave* Hetton 1896. *EDD* distribution to 1900: general. [imitative] 2. 'condom' exx. *IA* S'm 1950s, 60s; *TP* S'd 1960s, Stanley 1960s per BG

blogged blocked

ex. *JB* Shildon C20/mid

blonk, blank to thwart, to disappoint

"aw fand ma-sel blonk'd" *Allan's Tyneside Songs* p.47 1812; "blonk'd – disappointed" *Dinsdale* mid-Tees 1849; "to be blonked is to be baffled or disappointed" *Hull* MS wNewc 1880s. *EDD* distribution to 1900: N'd, D'm, nYx. [OFr blankir]

blue 1. bluestone or shale (pit term),
2. a uniform

1. ex. *Northumbrian III* 1990 re Backworth
2. "Then hurrah! hurrah! for the jackets of blue! / For the brave British tar in their jackets of blue." *Scrapbook* Tyne C19/1; "O this bonny moor hen she's got feathers enew / She's many fine colours but none of them blue" 'The Bonny Moor Hen' ca.1818; "Aw've even worn the blue" *Barrass* Stanley 1897

bluey lobster

ex. *GP* Seaham C20/2

blush blister (noun and vb)

"blush – a blister or puffing up of the skin... in Teesdale and elsewhere the word is blish" *Hull* MS wNewc 1880s; "his hand's all blushed" *Palgrave* Hetton 1896; "blush – blister" *Dodd* MS Tanfield Lea C20/2. *EDD* distribution to 1900: Sco, N'd, C'd, Yx. *Plus* "blish" *Dinsdale* mid Tees 1849. See also **bleb**

board portion of coal face

"bord – the space allotted generally to one man to work in, in a colliery" *Pitman's Pay* G'head 1820s; "Pillars and boards" (initial galleries driven inbye through the coal to the boundary.) *Hitchin* re Seaham 1920s p.105. *EDD* distribution to 1900: N'd, D'm, Yx

bobbersome frisky

"bobberous, bobbersome – hearty, elated, in high spirits" *Brockett* Newc & Nth 1829. *EDD* distribution to 1900: Nth. [?variant of bothersome; but compare Irish bob 'a trick']

boff see **pump**

bogey 1. industrial vehicle, 2. go-cart

1. "bogie – the tram or truck, used by the Newcastle Quayside cartmen" *Brockett* Newc & Nth 1846; "bogey – a low, two-wheeled sleigh-cart for carrying hay to the stack without the trouble of pitching" *Palgrave* Hetton 1896; "bogey (or tram) – used for transporting lengths of long materials into

bogey cont.

mine working places" *McBurnie* Glebe Colliery, C20/mid. *EDD* distribution to 1900: Nth, Sco, Ire. [origin unknown]
2. "bogie – a child's home-made carriage, generally made with four pram wheels and a sugar-crate" *Irwin* Tyne 1970

bogie stove on a coble

'cuddy stove' *Hill* Flamborough 1970s. *Note: not used, FT* Cullercoats 2003.

boggle, etc., 1. supernatural being, 2. of a horse rearing up

1. "bogel or bogel-bo – a ghost or bugbear" *Bell* MS Newc 1815; "boggle or bógle, boggle-bo – a spectre or ghost, a nursey bug-bear." *Brockett* 1829 re N'd and D'm; "boggle about the stacks – a favourite pastime among young people in the country villages" *Brockett* Newc & Nth 1829; "bo'man, bo-boggle – a kidnapper or hobgoblin" *Bell* MS Newc 1815, 'Bo, bo her[e] is a boggle come to get you' *Bell* MS Newc 1830s; "supernatural (sea) monster" RLS, Scots, 1891; "The manner in which he wishes to alarm his readers... put me in mind of the Bo-men and Bogles resorted to by nurses and old women, to intimidate children." *Newc Courant* 6 Jul 1822 p.2; "We hadn't gane far, till attacked we were, / By a bogle, frev out on a lane, man; / He a skeleton seem'd... Aw fancied him Death, in disguise, man" *Street Piracy* Newc 1822. *EDD* distribution to 1900: general. NE 2001: not in use. [origin – disputed; note "bogill" (buffalo or wild ox) C16 Scots] *Plus* "boman – bogeyman" *Dinsdale* mid-Tees 1849; "Bo-lo – a nursery ghost or hobgoblin: 'Gan to bed therecklies or aw'll bring the bo-lo!'" *Luckley* Alnwick 1870s; "boggart – a hobgoblin, a sprite" *Atkinson* Cleve 1868; "bogie – a sort of cross between a ghost and a paedophile" Thornley C20/mid Q. See also **scarecrow**
2. "boggle – to start or shy or swerve [e.g.] of a horse" *Atkinson* Cleve 1868; "His horse teuk the boggle, an' off flew he." *Crawhall* Newc 1888. *Plus* "'to take boggart', said of a horse that starts at any object in the hedge or road" *Grose* 1787

boilie bread and milk

"afore the young prince wi' spice boily was fed" *Allan's Tyneside Songs* p.352 C19/mid; "boily – properly, food prepared specially for

boilie cont.

an infant's use; milk with soft bread crumbled fine boiled in it" *Atkinson* Cleve 1868; 'chunks of bread in a basin, with a few raisins mixed in for flavour and scalded with boiling water; milk was added [if available]' *BJ* re Newbottle C20/1; "boiley – crustless bread with warm milk and sugar (invalid dish)" *JB* Shildon C20/mid; "boilee – milk and bread and sugar" South Moor (Stanley) 2003 per BG. *EDD* distribution to 1900: Nth

bonny handsome, pretty, fine

"My bonny keel-laddie" *Ritson* N'd 1793; "the bonny pit laddie" *Allan's Tyneside Songs* p.3 1812; "the bonny lads of Byker Hill" *Bell* Newc 1812 p.36; "The bonny lass of Benwell" *Allan's Tyneside Songs* p.29 1812; "a reet bonny half-crown" *Street Piracy* Newc 1822; "mi, mi, what bonny buttons!" *Allan's Tyneside Songs* p.180 1824; "Wor bonny river" *Oiling* G'head 1826; "bonny – beautiful, pretty, handsome, cheerful" *Brockett* Newc & Nth 1829; 'fair to look at, handsome, fine, beautiful; applied to either persons or things: "a bonny bairn", "the bonny beast" (greyhound), *MC* Tyne May 1881; "nuw here's a bonny mess!" (ironically) wNewc 1880s; "a bonny lot of difference" Coxhoe 1916; "bonny marked un" (a black eye) *Northumbrian III* 1990 re Backworth; "bonny lad" (of anyone younger, in friendly mode) S'd 2001 Q. *EDD* distribution to 1900: general. NE 2001: in use esp. in phrases. [Fr bon 'good']

boody, boudy piece of (broken) chinaware, earthenware

"boudy – broken earthenware; baby boudy's – broken earthen ware used by the chldren as play things" *Bell* MS Newc 1815; "babby-boodies – broken pieces of earthen ware or glass" *Brockett* Newc & Nth 1829; "boody – pieces of pots" *Dinsdale* mid-Tees 1849; "sparrars' byens... monkey's skeletons... an' lots o' boody styens" (fossils) Newc C19/2; "The boody pots went roond an' roond" (earthenware beer mugs) *Barrass* Stanley 1890s; "cheeny boodies – china or earthenware or glass fragments that children play with at baby houses, etc." *Embleton* Tyne 1897; "boody pob – cheap cups and saucers" *Nth Words* N'd 1938; "used as 'money' by girls when they played 'shops' and 'houses'" *JS* E'ton 1950s; "yerboodies clarty – the plate is dusty" *Dobson* Tyne 1969; "boody –

boody, boudy cont.

potware or plasterware" *Geeson* N'd/ D'm 1969, *Irwin* Tyne 1970; "boody – earthenware" *LL* Tyneside 1974; "boody-egg – a pot egg put in with a hen (or pigeon) to encourage them to lay" *Wood* Tees 2002. *EDD* distribution to 1900: N'd, D'm. NE 2001: low use. *Plus* "booly – shard" S'm 2002 Q; "glenters – pieces of earthenware or any thing else which shines or glenters or lay glenting in the sun shine" *Bell* MS Newc 1815. See also **babby**

booler child's hoop, etc.

"a child's iron hoop usually made at the pit by a friendly blacksmith" *JS* E'ton 1950s; "made up children's toy from a hoop of steel, wood, or a bike tyre" *ER* M'bro C20/2; "booler and hook" *Ferryhill* 2001 Q; "boolers were hoops, usually the rim of a bicycle wheel nowadays. You spread a net over it, with some bait, and attached a line. You sank it in the water next the pier, and after a while hauled it up to see if a lobster had come aboard" *JP* S'm C20/2; "egg-boolin' technology" (egg-rolling) *Dobson* Tyne 1972 [from vb. 'to bowl'? compare Romany boler 'a wheel']. See also **girth**

boose see **buse**

boot equalising payment

"bute or boot – money given in bartering horses, &c. to equalize the value." *Bailey* Co.Durham 1810; sim. *Brockett* Newc & Nth 1829. *EDD* distribution to 1900: Sco, Nth, Mids. [OE bóte] See also **beut**

born, brunt to burn

"an aaful smell o' bornin'" *Robson* Newc C20/1; "Born doon the Civic Centre!" *Irwin* Tyne 1970; "thou wylt be brentte" *Raine* MS Barwick in Elmet 1540; "brunt – usually for burnt, 'a brunt bairn dreads the fire'" *Bell* MS Newc 1830s; "some native com one day / an' brunt maw hut like hay" *Allan's Tyneside Songs* p.404 C19/mid. *EDD* distribution to 1900: born – N'd

borst to burst

"brussen – [bust, burst]" *Atkinson* Cleve 1868; "borsts" Coxhoe 1916, Tanfield Lea, 1960; "borst oot laffin", "aw cud brust an crie" *Armstrong* Tanfield C19/2. *EDD* distribution to 1900: borst – N'd

bottles medicine

"Bottles – medicine (always so)" *Palgrave* Hetton 1896. *EDD* distribution to 1900: eD'm, Sco

boudy see **boody**

bowdykite pot-bellied, cheeky

"bowdy-kite – a pot-bellied impertinant fellow" *Bell* MS Newc 1815; "bowdikite, or bowley-kite – a corpulent person... [also] applied to a mischievous child, or an insignificant person" *Brockett* Newc & Nth 1829; "pot-bellied" *Embleton* Newc 1897. *EDD* distribution to 1900: N'd, D'm, Yx

bowk, boke to belch

"he did boke & belshe" *Raine* MS Berrythorpe C17; "to boke – to belch, to be ready to vomit" *Ray* 1674; "bowk – to belch or rift" *Bell* MS Newc 1815; "bolk (pronounced boak or booak) – to retch, strain to vomit, with the usual sound implied" *Atkinson* Cleve 1868; "Aa'hm bowkin full" (have eaten well) Ashington C20/mid; "a bit gassy forbye which meks ye bowk" *Dobson* Tyne 1970; "bowk – to retch, vomit" Weardale, Teesdale, Teesside 2001 Q. *EDD* distribution to 1900: general. [ME bolk (vb)] *Plus* "belk – a belch" *Atkinson* Cleve 1868. See also **rift**

box a Friendly Society, or saving scheme

"at wor box-dinner" *Allan's Tyneside Songs* p.177 Newc 1824; "box – a club or society instituted for benevolent or charitable purposes" *Brockett* Newc & Nth 1829; "divn't ye knaw he's iv our box?" *Wearside Tales* 1879 (where also description of means of operation). *EDD* distribution to 1900: general

brae brow, slope

"on bra ne banke" *Cuthbert* C15/mid; "brae – the brow of a hill" *Bell* MS Newc 1830s; "brae (pronounced breea) the overhanging edge or margin of a river-bank" *Atkinson* Cleve 1868. *EDD* distribution to 1900: Nth, Sco, Ire. [ON brá]. *Plus* "we get wor breed by the sweet o' wor broo" *Allan's Tyneside Songs* p.150 1827

braffen horse collar

"brauchin – a horse collar made of old stocking stuffed with straw" *Grose* 1787 re C'd; "braugham – a collar which goes round a horse's neck to draw by. (braffen)" *Bailey* Co.Durham 1810; "collars or 'braffins'"

braffen cont.

[on the ponies] *Hitchin* re Seaham 1910s p.68; "My farming friend tells me he used a braffen when he fitted it across the chest of the horse to help reduce the strain on its shoulders when pulling a heavy load. Also he used it as a brake when he fitted across the haunchs of the horse to lean on when on downhill work." *CT* New Herrington 1930s; "braffen – horse collar (jokingly, man's shirt collar)" *JB* Shildon C20/mid. *EDD* distribution to 1900: bargham – Nth, Sco. [?OE beorgan (to protect) plus hame (covering) (*OED*); *Hull* MS mentions Welsh brefant (throat), Scottish brecham]

brag goblin

'a sprite or goblin usually attached to some particular locality, e.g. the Pelton Brag' *Hull* MS wNewc 1880s; 'a mischievous goblin' *Brockie* D'm 1886. *EDD* distribution to 1900: NE

braidin' 1, to vomit, 2. to broadcast

1. ."brade – to vomit" *Blenkinsopp* Teesdale 1931; 'retching without vomiting' Embleton, Newc 1897. *EDD* distribution to 1900: Nth, wMids
2. "to breade – to spread" *Ray* 1674; "brade, braid – to publish abroad: 'he brades it out everywhere...'" *Atkinson* Cleve 1868. *EDD* distribution to 1900: general. [OE brædan 'to spread']

brakesman man in charge of winding engine at pit

"brakesman – the engineman who attends to the winding machine" *Nicholson* 1880; "he rapped 'Men On' to the brakesman / and away Aa went in the cage" West Stanley C20/1. *EDD* distribution to 1900: N'd, D'm

brambles – see **blackberries**

brandreth iron bar to suspend cooking vessels from

"ye brendreth in ye kitchen chimney" *Raine* MS Dishforth / Norton 1672. *EDD* distribution to 1900: Sco, Nth, e Mids. [ON brandreið 'a grate']. See also **racken-crook**

brass money

"I didn't want for brass" *Marshall* G'head 1806 re Yx; "the brass aw've getten at the race" *Allan's Tyneside Songs* p.141 1816; "for provisions was dear, and they'd sav'd little

brass cont.

brass" *Allan's Tyneside Songs* p.398 C19/mid; 'brass – money; copper money' *Atkinson* Cleve 1868; "ah hae ne brass" *Embleton* Tyne 1897; 'money' *Dodd* MS Tanfield Lea C20/2. *EDD* distribution to 1900: general. [from similarity of brass to gold (exploited by counterfeiters)? or from low-denomination copper coinage]. *Plus* "she had ne tin" *Allan's Tyneside Songs* p.520 1872. See also **lowie, wedge**

brat item of clothing, apron

"brat – used contemptuously for Ragged Clothes; for a child, a name given to a slip or pinafore used as an apron by children" *Bell* MS Newc 1815; "Their bits and brats are varra scant" (food and clothes) *Pitman's Pay* G'head 1820s. *EDD* distribution to 1900: Nth, Sco, Ire. [OE (Ang) bratt, probably from OIrish brat 'cloth']

brattice wooden screening

"ye bretyshyng abowt ye churche" (scaffolding) *Raine* MS York 1543; "brattish – a wooden partition (a brattice), used for purpose of ventilation in coal mines... also... any slight partition dividing rooms" *Brockett* Newc & Nth 1846; "brattice – a partition, generally of deal, placed in the shaft of a pit, or in a drift or other working of a colliery, for the purpose of ventilation. Its use is to divide the place in which it is fixed into two avenues, the current of air entering by the one and returning by the other" *Nicholson* 1880; "brattice – in the house, a wooden boarding fastened at right angles to the door-frame, on the side where the door opens, so as to screen the room from draughts. Also, wood or canvas used in mines to help the air to travel" *Palgrave* Hetton 1896; "'brattish' or 'brattich'... used in our house (and others) to denote a wooden board or boards which were placed just inside and to the side of our back door and served as a sort of draught excluder for anyone sitting near to the door" DE Shildon C20/2. *EDD* distribution to 1900: Nth, Sco. [OFr breteske]

brattle the noise of thunderclap

"he makes such a thundering brattle" *Bell* Newc 1812 p.42; "brattle – to sound like thunder; 'a brattle of thunder' a clap of thunder" *Bell* MS Newc 1815; "brattle – the noise of a peal of thunder: 'what a brattle o'

brattle cont.

thunner that was!'" *Luckley* Alnwick 1870s. *EDD* distribution to 1900: esp. Sco. [imitative] *Plus* "rowly rattle bags – thunder clouds" *Bell* MS Newc 1830s

bravely fine, well

"I'se bravely, Bob!" *Bells* re Carlisle 1802. *EDD* distribution to 1900: general. NE 2001: low use. *Plus* "I'll... gar ilka thing look braw" (fine) Newc C19/1 as Scots.

bray to beat, smash

"Aw've bray'd for hours at woody coal" *Pitman's Pay* G'head 1820s; "bray – beat or thrash with violence: 'Ah'll bray thee'" *Atkinson* Cleve 1868; "to hit or smack" *Viereck* re Gateshead, 1966; "as when you brayed your finga end with the hammer", "that shop had its winders brayed in on Saturday neet" *JS* Easington C20/mid; "ifah findthelad that brayedthe winder inall brayhim" *Dobson* Tyne 1970; "he brays on the door" *Irwin* Tyne 1970. *EDD* distribution to 1900: Nth, Ire. NE 2001: in use. [OFr breier 'to crush, pound, rub']

brazen/ed bold, cheeky

ex. *Atkinson* Cleve 1868; "brazen ched – a cheeky child" Spennymoor C20/mid; "brazen (short 'a') – cheeky (often with 'fond')" *JB* Shildon C20/mid. *EDD* distribution to 1900: Nth. See also **fond**

breckens bracken, ferns

"breckens, breckins – ferns" *Bell* MS Newc 1815; "brekans" *Egglestone* Weardale 1870s. *EDD* distribution to 1900: N'd, D'm, nYx. [?ON, compare Swed. bräken]

breed bread

"butter an breed" *Bewick* Tyne 1790s; "breed – bread" Tanfield Lea 1960

breeks britches, short trousers

"yellow breeks" *Marshall* G'head 1806; "Ma breeks o' bonny velveteen" *Pitman's Pay* G'head 1820s; "noo for Tim Bodkin aw'll send, / For to darn my silk breeks at the knee" *Crawhall* Newc 1888; "breeks, briches – trousers" *Dodd* MS Tanfield Lea C20/2; "a bran new coat, but aad breeks" *Graham* Geordie 1979. *EDD* distribution to 1900: Nth, Sco, Ire. [Nth form of breeches, from OE bréc]. *Plus* "Ned's Sunday britches" *Allan's*

breeks cont.

Tyneside Songs p.425 1862; "britches is the common name for any kind of 'troosers'" *Hull* MS wNewc 1880s; "breeks or britches esp. britches; keks more Newcastle" South Moor (Stanley) 2003 per BG. See also **keks, trousers**

brent steep

ex. *Bailey* Co.Durham 1810; "rather steep as a brent hill or bank" *Bell* MS Newc 1815; "brant, brent – steep: 'as brent 's a hoos'-sahd'" *Atkinson* Cleve 1868; "Brent – steep (of stairs, ladders, and such-like erections)" *Palgrave* Hetton 1896; "ower brent – too steep" *Hull* MS wNewc 1880s; "brent or brant stairs – steep stairs" Spennymoor C20/mid. *EDD* distribution to 1900: Sco, Nth, Mids. [ME brant]

brick to break 1. present tense, 2. past tense

1. "fit te brik their necks" *Bewick* Tyne 1790s; "wad brick my sleep" *Allan's Tyneside Songs* p.75 1806; "till'd day brick" *Moore* Weardale 1859; "brick" *Wearside Tales* 1879
2. "aw warnt he hesint brokken his fast to day" *Bewick* Tyne 1790s; "we brak wor sweep oar" *Allan's Tyneside Songs* p.307 1862; "Aa think me neck's brocken" *Haldane* Newc 1879; "ah brak a tyum teapot" *Embleton* Tyne 1897; "brokken in te – burgled" *Dunn* B'p Auck 1950. See also **brockens**

brickies' brickyard

ex. *CT* New Herrington 1930s

brickwist breakfast

"a hevvent had ne brickwist" *Embleton* Tyne 1897

brig bridge

"aw went alang the brig" Bell Newc 1812 p.9; exx. *NChorister* D'm, C18/2, *Pitman's Pay* G'head 1820s, *Dinsdale* mid-Tees 1849; "Newcassel Brig" *Allan's Tyneside Songs* p.298 1831; "brigg – a bridge; a quasi-natural pier projecting into the sea" *Atkinson* Cleve 1868 [e.g. Filey Brig]. *EDD* distribution to 1900: Sco, Nth, Mids. [Nth form of bridge from OE brycg]. *Plus* "brigstuns" (flagstones) *Smith* Weardale 1883

brissel, brusle to dry or scorch

"brusle – to dry: 'brustled pease' *Grose* 1787 re N'd; "brissel – to scorch or dry very hard with

brissel, brusle cont.

fire" *Bailey* Co.Durham 1810; "brissle – to
scorch or burn meat" *Bell* MS Newc 1815.
EDD distribution to 1900: Nth, Sco, Ire.
[? Fr brusler of C15]

brock badger

"Jack's brock, that all the Chowden dogs
can bang" *Pitman's Pay* G'head 1820s; "Aa's
sweatin' like a brock" *Palgrave* Hetton 1896.
[OE, Gael. broc]

brokkens broken workings

"broken – the reworking of a colliery in the
pillars, etc left in first working the 'whole'
coal" *Bell* MS Newc 1815; "broken pillar
working, the removal of the pillars left in the
first working for the support of the roof"
Nicholson 1880; "coming back-broken...
[reclaiming more coal until] only a forest of
props supported the roof over a wide area",
"the roof in such broken districts was often
unsound" *Hitchin* re Seaham 1920s p.105;
"brokens – extracting pillars previously left
by Bord and Pillar" *Northumbrian III* C20/2 re
Durham collieries; "cum back brokkins – the
method used to recover pillars of coal which
had been left" *Northumbrian III* 1990 re
Backworth; *Coming back brokkens* – title of
book by Mark Hudson (London: Cape
1957). See also **brick**

broon brown 1. adj., 2. Newcastle Brown Ale

1. "broon – brown" Tanfield Lea 1960
2. "a pint of broon" *Dobson* Tyne 1972

brose barley broth

Nth Words, 1938, re Newcastle, originally
Scottish: "Eat your brose, barley brose, / and
when ye're an aad, aad wifie / Ye'll still can
touch your toes." (trad.). *EDD* distribution
to 1900: Sco, N'd. [OFr broez]

broth stew

"...few broth ... originally perhaps a few broes,
the Scotch for broth, and taken in England
for the plural" *Brockett* Newc & Nth 1829;
"Will ye hev a few broth?" *Luckley* Alnwick
1870s extra; "'a little broth ' is always 'a few
broth.'" *Palgrave* Hetton 1896; "a few broth"
(a bowl of broth) Dinnington 1950s Q. *EDD*
distribution to 1900: general. [*OED* says from
OE broð, with Irish broth, Gaelic brot coming
from the English]

brownie 1. supernatural being, 2. brown linnet

1. "brownie – a domestic spirit" *Brockett* Newc
& Nth 1829; "Browney or Browneys – certain
Scottish and Northumberland goblins...
Browney or a Guest – a ghost" *Bell* MS Newc
1830s. *EDD* distribution to 1900: Nth, Sco
2. "Brownie (broo:ni) – brown linnet. Singing
competitions of these birds for a wager are
held in public-houses, where they are always
advertised as Brownie Matches" *Palgrave*
Hetton 1896. *EDD* distribution to 1900: eD'm

browt brought

"aul th' geer wis browt te bank" *Armstrong*
Tanfield C19/2; "browt" Coxhoe 1916

browt up brought up, reared

"where was thoo browt up?", "disgraced
the family by showing me browt'ns up" *JS*
Easington, 1950s; "dinna show the browtens
up – don't show your ignorance" *Dunn* B'p
Auck 1950

brunt see **born**

bubble to cry

"aw'll bubble tiv aw dee, begox!" *Allan's
Tyneside Songs* p.397 C19/mid; "he [the
pitman] nivvor bubbles for a shillin' lost" Tyne
MC May 1881; "it macks mi mar bubble" *CT*
New Herrington 1930s; "bubbling – weeping"
FS Shotton Colliery 1930s; "divvent bubble
hinny" Dinnington 1950s Q; "giv-ower
bubblin' – cease your grizzling" *Dobson* Tyne
1969. *EDD* distribution to 1900: N'd, Sco.
[imitative] *Plus* "bubbly-baby" (cry baby) *AT*
Co.D'm C20/mid

bubbly snotty

"the bairn has a bubbly nose" *Grose* 1787;
"bubbly – snotty" *Brockett* Newc & Nth 1829

bubbly jock a turkey

'a turkey cock' *Bell* MS Newc 1815, *Brockett*
Newc & Nth 1829. *EDD* distribution to 1900:
Sco, N'd, C'd. [descriptive, or rhyming slang]

buer a gnat

ex. *Ray* 1674; "buer, buver – a gnat" *Atkinson*
Cleve 1868. *EDD* distribution to 1900: N'd,
Yx... obsol. See also **bewer**

bull-stang see **dragonfly**

bullets sweets

"Nelson's bullets – a sweetmeat in the shape of small balls" *Dinsdale* mid-Tees 1849; "black bullets en mint losengers" *Egglestone*, Weardale 1870s; "black bullets – black or sometimes brown spherical boiled mint sweets made by Welch's of Tyneside" *JS* Easington C20/mid; "toffees, mints, anything, were Bullets" Thornley 1940s Q. *EDD* distribution to 1900: N'd. NE 2001: in use. [supposedly in imitation of the bullets that killed Nelson]

bullies keelmen, comrades

"You will have a relation of the Keel bullyes in the colliers at Newcastle" *Raine* MS 1696; "...the keel went bump 'gainst Jarrow, / An' three o' th' bullies lap oot" *Allan's Tyneside Songs* p.27 1805; "bully – a Newcastle word for brother or companion" *Bell* MS Newc 1815; "bully – the champion of a party, the eldest male person in a family. Now generally in use among the keelmen and pitmen to designate a brother, companion, or comrade" *Brockett* Newc & Nth 1829; "bullee – comrade, bully" *Dodd* MS Tanfield Lea C20/2. *EDD* distribution to 1900: N'd, Ire. [?Du. boel 'brother'; compare Billy]. See also **keelman**

bumblekites see **blackberries**

bummin' making a continuous noise

"bummin' – a whirring noise arising from quick motion" *Pitman's Pay* G'head 1820s; "an organ grand was bummin' lood" *Allan's Tyneside Songs* p.357 1849. *EDD* distribution to 1900: general. [imitative]

bummler bumble-bee

"bumler – a bumble or humble bee" *Bell* MS Newc 1815; "as bissy as bumblers" *Egglestone* Weardale 1870s; "We usually said 'bummler' which were clasified as 'white arsties', 'red arsties' or 'sandies'" *JS* E'ton 1950s; "bummlor – bee or bluebottle" Roker C20/mid; "buzzin aboot like a bumbler bee" Ashington C20/mid; "dandelions bloom and bummlers hum" *Dobson* Tyne 1972; "bummlor" Trimdon 2002 Q. *EDD* distribution to 1900: Nth + Norf. NE 2001: in use. [imitative]

bummler box small box

"bummler-box – a small box for holding bees and insects" *Luckley* Alnwick 1870s; "bumler-box, or bumbler-box – a small wooden toy used by boys to hold bees. Also the

bummler box cont.

Sunderland name for a van for passengers drawn by one horse" *Brockett* Newc & Nth 1829; "bumla box – very small house" *Dodd* MS Tanfield Lea C20/2, *Graham* Geordie 1979. *EDD* distribution to 1900: N'd

bumly rucked up (of clothes)

ex. *MB* Coxhoe C20/mid

bums bailiffs, debt enforcers

"bum-baillee, bum-bailiff – a corruption of the word bound bailiff or sheriffs officer" *Bell* MS Newc 1815; "Thor com doctors, an' bairns, an' bums" *Barrass* Stanley 1890s. *EDD* distribution to 1900: general

bunch to kick

"bunch – to strike with the foot, to kick" *Brockett* Newc & Nth 1829; 'a blow with the knee' *Hull* MS wNewc 1880s; "bunch – to bump deliberately" *Wood* Tees 2002. *EDD* distribution to 1900: general. [compare Du. bonken 'to thrash']. See also **punch**

buntin 1. wood, 2. to line or reinforce with wood, 3. the cone of the fir-tree

1. "buntin – a balk or piece of timber" *Bell* MS Newc 1815; "buntins, buntings – balks of foreign timber, secured in rafts on the shores of the river Tyne; afloat at high water: "let's go hikey on the buntins" *Brockett* Newc & Nth 1829; "buntons – shaft supports to carry guides" *Dodd* MS Tanfield Lea C20/2. *EDD* distribution to 1900: N'd, D'm
2. "Thor shafts Aw've buntin'd" *Barrass* Stanley 1890s
3. "to pepper buntins is to throw buntins (fir-cones) in play" *Heslop* 1890s

burd young woman

"A U, hinny burd" *Allan's Tyneside Songs* p.29 1812; 'maiden' thus Basil Bunting and Thomas A. Clark quoting 'a glossary of Old Scots'. *EDD* distribution to 1900 – burd (young lady, maiden): Sco. [?OE brýd 'bride']

burn stream, anything smaller than a river

"wee saw 2 ducks come out of the burn" *Errington* p.34 Felling/Heworth re 1780s; "burn – a rivulet" *Bailey* Co.Durham 1810; "burn – a brook, or rivulet... any runner of water that is less than a river" *Brockett* Newc & Nth 1829; "...a burn winds slowly along meadows, and originates from small springs; while a beck

burn cont.

is formed by water collected on the sides of mountains, and proceeds with a rapid stream." *Brockett* Newc & Nth 1846; "Wi' smiths and potters frae the burn" *Allan's Tyneside Songs* p.381 C19/mid ff re Sandgate; "burn – a brook, a stream of water... a word very little used in this region" *Atkinson* Cleve 1868; "T' perk... wuv a burn runnin' throo' t'middle ont" *Egglestone* Weardale 1870s; 'a main stream' eD'm 1945 Q; exx. N.Shields, Ch-le-St C20/mid, N'd 1995 (rural/children). *EDD* distribution to 1900: Nth, Sco, Ire (but wider in place-names). [OE burne]. See also **beck**

buroo Bureau (of National Assistance)

"Burroo – the Labour Exchange... the pronunciation was a short u as in 'but', oo as in Jew, emphasis on the second syllable." Ch-le-St 1950s (E); "on the buroo – unemployed" *Dobson* Tyne 1969; ex. *AK* Newc C20/mid. *Plus:* "'The Nash' (National Assistance)" S'm C20 BG

buse, boose stall for an animal

"boose – an ox or cow-stall" *Ray* 1674; "ox-boose – ox/cow stall for winter nights" *Ray* 1674; "a stall; as cow buse, hay buse" *Bailey* Co.Durham 1810; "buse – cowstand, pig cree, pig stye" *Bell* MS Newc 1815. *EDD* distribution to 1900: Nth, eMids, Ire. [OE bósig – cow-stall]

buss to kiss

"buss – kiss" *Dodd* MS Tanfield Lea C20/2. *EDD* distribution to 1900: general. [?Fr baisser]

buss, busk decorate, dress up, prepare

"thai buske with speres hir to sla" (make ready) *Cuthbert* C15/mid; "busk – to dress or make smart, as 'busk you my bonny bride', 'busk you my winsome marrow'" *Bell* MS Newc 1815; "Jemmy, let us buss, we'll off / An' see Newcassel races" *Allan's Tyneside Songs* p.138 1816; 'Bussin' the tyup' is covering the coals with lighted candles... an expression of their joy at the gaudy days or holidays which take place generally after this event." *Pitman's Pay* G'head 1820s. *EDD* distribution to 1900: Nth, Sco. [ON búask 'to ready' Fr busquer]. See also **tup**

bussie

1. bus station eD'm 1990s
2. busfare or ticket *PG* H'pool 1998

but

"Eh, bud..." Embleton, Newc 1897; "A divvent knaw warrit means burra hard th' docta tella" (but Aa) *CT* New Herrington 1930s; used emphatically: "you can, but!" *Geeson* N'd/D'm '1969'

but and ben front and back parts of a two-room house

"but and ben – by-out and by-in... the outer and inner apartment, where there are only two rooms" *Brockett* Newc & Nth 1829; "but and ben – front and back areas of a two-room house" *Blenkinsopp* Teesdale 1931. *EDD* distribution to 1900: esp. Sco. [OE bútan, binnan]

butcher the stickleback

'the stickleback, without a red belly" *Palgrave* Hetton 1896. *EDD* distribution to 1900: eD'm

butt the halibut

ex. *Atkinson* Cleve 1868. *EDD* distribution to 1900: East Coast. [compare Swed. butta 'turbot']

butter

"wants burra on baith sides – likes the best of everything" *CT* New Herrington 1930s

butterfly 1. **butterflee**, 2. **flutter-by**, 3. **lowy, butterlowie**, 4. **butterloggy**, 5. other

1. "a fine butterflee coat with gowld buttons" *Allan's Tyneside Songs* p.146 1816; "butterflees" *Embleton* Tyne 1897, "buttaflee" *Dodd* MS Tanfield Lea C20/2
2. "flutterby" NShields C20/mid Q, eD'm 1990s, Stanley, G'head, Blyth, Byker 2002 Q. NE 2001: in use. [a modern childish or humorous variant of 'butterfly']
3. "like a lowey" (implying speed) *Wearside Tales* 1879; "lowie" (to rhyme with Joey) Spitaltongues 2004 Q; "butterlowy" *FS* Shotton Colliery 1930s, S'd, Ho'ton, Wash'ton, Ch-le-St 2002 Q. [not in *EDD* or *OED*]
4. "butterloggy" *PG* H'pool C20/2, Wingate, M'bro. 2001, Wheatley Hill 2004 Q; "butterloggy seems quite specific, that is to central Teesside, i.e. Stockton/Mbro and Hartlepool area" *Wood* 2003. [Not in *EDD* or *OED*, but log would generally be accorded an ON origin]

butterfly cont.

5. "scotchie – butterfly" 2001 Q. See also
loggerheed

buzzer the pit hooter

"Buzzer – the steam whistle or 'fog-horn' that
warns miners of the times for returning to
and from work" *Palgrave* Hetton 1896;
'factory siren' ER M'bro C20/2; "buzza – pit
siren" *Dodd* MS Tanfield Lea C20/2, *GP* S'm
C20/mid; "The steam whistle used to notify
surface workers of starting, break, and
finishing times" *Northumbrian III* 1990 re
Backworth. *EDD* distribution to 1900:
Nth, Mids

by

used emphatically: "By, I enjoyed myself!"
Geeson N'd/D'm '1969'

bygg see **bigg**

byke see ***bee-hive***

byre cow shed

"byer – a cow house" *Bailey* Co.Durham 1810;
"ye... that keep cows on the Moor, though ye
couldn't keep them iv a byre" *Allan's Tyneside
Songs* p.238, 1829; "Ah've... muck't (mucked
out) t' byre" *Egglestone*, Weardale 1870s. *EDD*
distribution to 1900: Sco, Ire, Nth, Mids.
[OE b´yre]

bysen anything shocking or spectacular

"bison or bizen – any thing thing that is too
shameful to be seen" *Bell* MS Newc 1815; "the
reck'ning (bill)... was a bizon" *Marshall* Newc
1823; "byson – a shame, scandal: 'It's...quite
a byson'" *Pitman's Pay* G'head 1820s; "bizon –
a scandal" *Luckley* Alnwick 1870s; "bizen –
somthing enormous and frightful" Embleton,
Newc 1897. *EDD* distribution to 1900:
Nth. [OE b´ysen 'something remarkable',
ON b´ysen]

byu- see **beu-**

caa, caw to urge forward, drive animals or vehicles

"ka!" (a signal in driving cattle) *Ray* Nth 1674; "he ca'ed a nail intill her tail" *Reed Border Ballads* C16; "caa – to drive: 'to caa the cart'" *Brockett* Newc & Nth 1846; "ca, caw – to turn, to drive: 'Tom, come an' caw the grindstone', 'Ca' the mangle, hinny'" *Luckley* Alnwick 1870s; "I've often cawed the kirn (churn)" *Nth Words*, N'd, 1938. *EDD* distribution to 1900: Sco, N'd. See also **caal**

caad cold

"cald or caud for cold" *Bell* MS Newc 1830s; "hoo het an' hoo caad" *Haldane* Newc 1879; "caad fire – a fire laid but not lit" wNewc 1880s; "parishment o' cahd" (infection) *Embleton* Tyne 1897; "a cup o' caad cocoa" *Irwin* Tyne 1970; "deethacaad" East Boldon 1985. *EDD* distribution to 1900: cauld – Nth; caad – N'd; caud – Yx

caal 1. to call, 2. to call someone names

1. ex. "caal – call" Tanfield Lea 1960. *EDD* distribution to 1900: caa – Sco; caal – N'd
2. 'to assail with offensive epithets' *Hull* MS wNewc 1880s; "to call someone is to speak ill of them" *PG* H'pool C20/2. *EDD* distribution to 1900: general

caalor, caller man who alerts pitmen for shift work

"caller – a person who goes round at a certain hour in the night, to let the pitmen know it is time to go to work: 'when the caller call'd at yen'" *Pitman's Pay* G'head 1820s; "caalor – a man employed to arouse pitmen of the fore-shift. The hour at which they wish to be called is usually chalked on the door" *Hull* MS wNewc 1880s; "sleep thi kaala – sleep in" *Dodd* MS Tanfield Lea C20/2. *EDD* distribution to 1900: N'd, D'm

cabbish cabbage

ex. *Dinsdale* mid-Tees 1849; "sum men delites in gardening, an' cabbish grows se big" *Creswell* Newc 1883. *EDD* distribution to 1900: N'd, Yx. See also **caskets**

cack, cacka, cacky excrement

"cack" (excreta) plus "cacky, cackhouse" *Brockett* Newc & Nth 1829; "cack" *Dinsdale* mid-Tees 1849, *KH* Stockton C20/2, *JB* Shildon C20/mid; "cack-ah" *RM* Norton C20/mid; "cacka" Gosforth C20/2 Q; "cacker"

cack, cacka, cacky cont.

Tyneside 2001 Q; "cackie" *AT* Co.D'm C20/mid, "kakee – human faeces" *Dodd* MS Tanfield Lea C20/2; "th's tark'n a load o' cacky" *CT* New Herrington 1930s; "cacky – animal or human waste" *Graham* Geordie 1979; "kakky pants" *PH* S'd C20/1; "cacky – skitters, with diarrhoea" Newc 2001 Q. *EDD* distribution to 1900: cack – general. [?Du kakken vb, earlier Lat. cacare; also ON kökkr 'a lump']

cadger itinerant seller of pots, etc.

"the cadgers call everyday" *Raine* MS EYorks, 1641; 'a packman or itinerant huckster' *Brockett* Newc & Nth 1829; 'hawkers and pedlars in general' *Hull* MS wNewc 1880s; "cadger – salesman" Aberdeens, 1993. *EDD* distribution to 1900: general

caff chaff, straw

"Luik upon as blisses / Scrimp meals, caff beds, and dairns" *Allan's Tyneside Songs* p.46 1812; "Caff – chaff" *Palgrave* Hetton 1896. *EDD* distribution to 1900: Nth, Sco, Ire. *Plus* "caffy-hearted – feint-hearted" *Dunn* B'p Auck 1950. See also **chisel**

cage pit lift

"cage – a frame of iron which works between slides in a shaft, and in which the tubs of coal and workmen are lowered into the pit and brought to the surface" *Nicholson* 1880; 'the lift which goes up and down in the shaft of a mine' *Palgrave* Hetton 1896. *EDD* distribution to 1900: N'd, D'm

caidie flat cap

ex. *AK* re Newc C20/1. [not in *EDD* or *OED*]

caingy peevish

'peevish, ill-tempered, whining' *Brockett* Newc & Nth 1829; "angry, apt to find fault or quarell, as a caingy ald carle" *Bell* MS Newc 1830s; "as caingy and cankery as an ill-clep'd cur" *Atkinson* Cleve 1868. *EDD* distribution to 1900: Nth

call etc. see **caal**

caller fresh

"callar – fresh, cool: 'callar air'" *Grose* 1787; "his breath's like caller air" Newc C19/1 (Scots); "caller – cool, refreshing: 'Caller herrings'; 'Caller ripe grosers'" *Brockett* Newc & Nth 1829; 'cold, fresh; esp. of the weather'

caller cont.

Hull MS wNewc 1880s. *EDD* distribution to 1900: Sco, Nth. [?Sco. calver]. See also **caaler**

cam a mound, etc.

"cam – a hill, a ridge, an earth dyke or mound" *Brockett* Newc & Nth 1829; 'a ridge or long earthen mound; a hedge-bank' *Atkinson* Cleve 1868; 'rising-ground' *Palgrave* Hetton 1896. *EDD* distribution to 1900: Sco, Nth. [ON kambr]

camsteery awkward

"ye're sic kamstarie fowk" *Bell* Newc 1812 p.38; "camsteeries – will not be guided, uncannie" *Bell* MS Newc 1815; "kamstary – mad. Perhaps the same as Sc[ots] camsterie, camstairie" *Brockett* Newc & Nth 1829. *EDD* distribution to 1900: Sco, Nth. [cam in sense of crooked, awry?]

can 1. positive forms, 2. negative forms

1. "kin" (can, vb) *Armstrong* Tanfield C19/2
2. "cannot ye gang yourself?" *Bewick* Tyne 1790s; "cannit" *Armstrong* Tanfield C19/2; "cudint" *Armstrong* Tanfield C19/2; "they canna wait a tide" *Haldane* Newc 1879; "ye canna deny that" *Egglestone*, Weardale 1870s, Coxhoe 1916, *JB* Shildon C20/mid, *Dobson* Tyne 1970–71, *VIZ* 72 (1995); "cannit" *Embleton* Tyne 1897, "we cannit foller" *Dobson* Tyne 1972; "They'll not can get any food" (not be able to); "I'll not can get" (I expect I shan't be able to come) *Palgrave* Hetton 1896; "you'll not can do that" *FS* Wingate 1940s; "he hadn't could do it" *FS* Wingate 1940s

canch, caunch obstructive stone in pit

"canch or caunch – a part of the roof or thill to be removed for the purpose of making height" *Nicholson* 1880; "Thor's law planks an' raggy kanches" *Barrass* Stanley 1890s; "canch – the stone below the thill or floor of a narrow coal seam that has to be removed as coal-getting proceeds" *Wade South Moor* C20/mid; "caunch – section of roof taken down, or section of floor taken up, to make [adequate] height to travel along" *McBurnie* Glebe Colliery, C20/mid; "canch – kerb" nwD'm C20/mid Q. *EDD* distribution to 1900: only in sense of a rise like a step – N'd, D'm, Yx, Mids [compare Mids. cank-stone]

candle coal a type of coal

"cannel or sometimes 'candle' coal – in the

candle coal cont.

collieries a thin piece of unmarketable [coal] at the top of the seam" *Bell* MS Newc 1815; "cannel coal – a fine, compact desription of coal, with a conchoidal fracture; burns with a bright flame like a candle, whence its name" *Nicholson* 1880

candies sweets

exx. Billingham 1940s, Ho'ton, Ch-le-St, 2002 Q

candyman 1. a vendor, 2. bailiff, esp. agent of eviction

1. "he was a candy man... he seld...candy for the bairns te lick, a tin trumpet then had Johnny" *Allan's Tyneside Songs* p.459 1862; "a rag-man who gives a kind of toffee in exchange for rags, etc." *EDD* 1900 re N.I.
2. "polisses and candymen met... te torn th' pitmen oot" *Armstrong* Tanfield C19/2; "kandeemen – evict miners in strike" *Dodd* MS Tanfield Lea C20/2; 'A bum bailiff. The man who serves notice of ejectment' *Graham* Geordie 1979. *EDD* distribution to 1900: N'd, D'm. *Note:* clearly there is a missing link: from candyman as scrapman or sweet-seller to eviction-processors – perhaps as casual workers? First used in strike of 1844 (*OED*). *Plus* "candy crew – blackleg miners... It originated when a local candy-seller turned blackleg hirer in the early days of north-east miners strikes. Afterwards blacklegs were called candy-men" www.muthergrumble.co.uk/issue03 re 1885

canny 1. adj. fine, admirable, fair, of a size to be reckoned with, etc., 2. adv. well, etc.

1. "my canny lad oh!" *Collier's Rant* Newc, C18/2; "canny – nice, neat, housewifely, handsome (Newcastle, N'b & Nth)" *Grose* 1787; "Canny Gateshead" *Marshall* G'head 1806; "The bonny pit laddie, the canny pit laddie" *Allan's Tyneside Songs* p.3 1812; "canny – the most comprehensive of all Newcastle words, as alluding to both men and things, i.e. a canny man, a canny dog, a canny house" *Bell* MS Newc 1815; 'a genuine Newcastle word, applied to any thing superior of the best kind' *Brockett* Newc & Nth 1825; "Things of all sorts, no sorts, lollipops / may be bought in Canny Shields!" *Shields Song Book* 1826; "canny – good, kind, mild, affectionate: 'Ma canny bairns luik pale and wan'" *Pitman's Pay*

canny cont.

G'head 1820s; "there's a canny little lad gawn up the riggin look'e" *JS* South Shields C19/mid; "Cannynewcassel" Surtees *Handley Cross* 1854; "a canny chap wi' horses", "a canny convenient house" *Atkinson* Cleve 1868; "canny – kind, gentle, etc... apparently derived from the Scotch" *Luckley* Alnwick 1870s; "sic a canny body for a wife as Fanny" *Haldane* Newc 1879; "be canny wi' the cream, i.e. use it with moderation" *Hull* MS wNewc 1880s; "Canny. A North-country catchword. 'A canny few' is a fair number, a 'canny man' is one with some sense in his head, a 'canny little body' would be a dapper little person, with some notion of briskness and neatness. 'It'll tak' a canny bit', i.e. take some time. Also, careful, gentle. A child is told to be 'canny' with a jug, a baby, or other perishable article entrusted to him. A juvenile letter to some one at Shields was inscribed on the envelope, 'Please, Mr. Postman, be canny with this letter'. 'Ma canny hinny', a term of endearment" *Palgrave* Hetton 1896; "a canny singa on wee carn't half joggle ho' voice" *CT* New Herrington 1930s; 'sweet, cute, nice' D'ton C20/2; "he did varry canny in that", *Dobson* Tyne 1970; "it's a canny way, mind" (fair distance) *LG* S'm C20/2"; 'nice, cute, having a pleasing personality', "dead canny" *Wood* Tees 2002. *EDD* distribution to 1900: Sco, Ire, Nth, eMids; first noted Sco 1596. NE 2001:in common use. [ME cunnand 'knowing, skilfull'... Though a root c(a)n – 'to be able, to know how to' is common to OE and ON, the formation can(n)+y is of uncertain date. It is first recorded in Scots in 1596 [*EDD*]; in Jamieson *Scots Dictionary* of 1808 there are 18 shades of meaning including gentle, fortunate, good, gentle, careful, etc., which could well be the sourcce of NE usage] *Plus* "uncanny – giddy, careless, imprudent" *Brockett* Newc & Nth 1829
2. "Aw can read the spellin'-byuk varry canny" *JA* Newc 1875, sim. Coxhoe 1916; "aw spent en oor an' a half very canny" (agreeably) *Armstrong* Tanfield C19/2; "gan canny [carefully] wi' the Broon [Ale]" *Irwin* Tyne 1970–71. *Plus* "on the ca canny – to with-hold full effort'" *Northumbrian III* 1990 re Backworth

canty cheerful, brisk, etc.

"Me cannie keel laddie / Se handsum, se

canty cont.

canty, and free" *Allan's Tyneside Songs* p.115 1812; "Half cock'd and canty hyem we gat" *Pitman's Pay* G'head 1820s; 'cheerful, hearty' *Bell* MS Newc 1830s; "with hearty chiels I've canty been" *Allan's Tyneside Songs* p.208 1842; "canty an' crouse" *Allan's Tyneside Songs* p.464 1860; "she's a canty au'd deeam for her years" *Atkinson* Cleve 1868; 'talkative, sociable' *Hull* MS wNewc 1880s; "contented wi little bit, canty wi mair" Ashington C20/mid; "kantee – pleasant, lively" *Dodd* MS Tanfield Lea C20/2. *EDD* distribution to 1900: So, Ire, Nth. [Du kant 'neat, clever']

cap to excel

"that caps aal – that beats everything" *Hull* MS wNewc 1880s. *EDD* distribution to 1900: general

carle 1. man, the male, 2. of male cat

"carle – a clown, an old man..." *Grose* 1787; "She's ta'en the carle and left her Johnny" *Marshall* G'head 1806; "carl, karl – a country fellow, a gruff old man, a churl" *Brockett* Newc & Nth 1829; "carle – an old man... the feminine is carling for an old woman" *Bell* MS Newc 1830s. *EDD* distribution to 1900: Nth (not D'm?), S.W. [ON karl, OE ceorl 'man'] 2. "a carl-cat – a he-cat" *Ray* 1674. sim. *Grose* 1787, *Brockett* Newc & Nth 1829; "...also applied to a cat as a carle cat, the feminine is carling for an old woman and also a cat" *Bell* MS Newc 1830s. See also **quean-cat**

Carling Sunday fifth Sunday in Lent

"Carling-day or Carling-Sunday – the second Sunday preceding Easter, when parched peas are served up at most tables in Northumberland" *Grose* 1787; "The proper Sunday for the ceremony was remembered by the Easter sequence 'Carlin, Palm, and Paste Egg Day'." *GA* re Thornley 1940s; "The Sunday when public houses used to give to all and sundry, bowls of carlings – bowls of cooked brown peas" *Crocker* re Woodland nr Middleton, C20th/mid. [either 'Care Sunday' or ON kerling, Sco carline 'an old woman']

carlings special cooked peas served during on Carling Sunday

"choice grey pease of the preceding autumn steeped in spring water for twelve or fifteen hours then drained of surplus water and

carlings cont.

toasted" *Gentleman's Magazine* for 1788 via *Graham* Geordie 1979; "carlings – pease birsled or boiled" Jamieson *Scots Dictionary* 1808; "carlings – grey peas fryed in butter or dripping used in Nothumberland and Durham... *Bell* MS Newc 1815; "carlings – grey peas steeped some hours in water, and then fried in butter, [and seasoned with pepper and salt 1846]. *Brockett* Newc & Nth 1829; "carlins – grey peas steeped in water for a time, then 'bristled' and mixed with butter and sugar; they are eaten on the Sunday before Palm Sunday" *Luckley* Alnwick 1870s; "Carling Sunday. Fifth Sunday in Lent, on which day the traditional dish is one of 'carlins' cooked in melted butter. A carling (kaa:lin) is a kind of pea, of a dark grey or brown colour. They are used by lads on 'Carlin' Sunday' for throwing at one another, and are boiled by publicans for their customers on that night" *Palgrave* Hetton 1896; "Carlins were cooked and eaten on their own – lots of public houses and working men's clubs gave them out for free" *JG* Annfield Plain 1930s; "Carlins – those unexciting grey peas we ate with vinegar once a year to commemorate something forgotten (some said a grounded ship whose looted cargo saved the starving poor of the Tyne)" *GA* re Thornley, 1940s; "those brown peas you get on Carling Sunday (or on the bar in old-fashioned pub)" *PG* H'pool C20/2; "Broon Ale and Carlins Evening" *Dobson* Tyne 1972; "only grey or maple peas" 2001 Q. *EDD* distribution to 1900: Sco, Nth. [named from Carling Sunday]. *Plus* "very hard orangish peas, pigeon food (and good for pea-shooters)" Sacriston 2004 E; "Carlings was also the name given to sheeps' dropping(s)." *Crocker* re Woodland nr Middleton, C20th/mid

carr 1. wet area, 2. rocky area

1. "in a moist yeare hard land... proveth better than carres or ing-grounds" *Raine MS* EYorks 1641; "a carre – a hollow place where water stands" *Ray* 1674; "carr – flat marshy ground" *Bailey* Co.Durham 1810. *EDD* distribution to 1900: Nth, eMids. [ON kiarr 'marshy land']
2. also in NE place-names. [ONorthumbrian carr 'rock'; compare Welsh carreg 'a stone']

carvinarse meteorite

ex. *Lore and language* re Maria Pit, Throckley C20/mid; "fossil easily dislodged" i.e. from pit roof, Wade *South Moor* C20/mid

cas because

"cas – because" *Haldane* Newc 1879; "what's that forbicahse?" (what's that for?) *Embleton* Newc 1897; "caas" Coxhoe 1916; "kaaz, kaz" *Dodd* MS Tanfield Lea C20/2

caskets (cabbage) stalks

"casket – a stalk or stem; as a cabbage-casket" *Brockett* Newc & Nth 1829, 'the stalk of a cabbage *Luckley* Alnwick 1870s; "cabbage caskets" *Allan's Tyneside Songs* p.376 C19/mid; *Embleton* Tyne 1897. *EDD* distribution to 1900: N'd, D'm. *Plus* "cabbish-skrunt – cabbage-stalk" *Gibson* C'd 1880

cassens dried cow dung used as fuel

"one mow of casens wt some other fewell" *Raine* MS Gt Driffield 1679; "casing, cassons – dried cow-dung used for fewel" *Grose* 1787 re N'd. See also (cow)-**blakes**

cast to throw

"kest, kusn" (p.pt) *Gill* re Lincs C17/1; "Now have I cassen away my care" Rothbury C18/2; "poor Robin was cast on the fire" *Bell* Newc 1812 p.43; "where me eyes wur cassin" *Marshall* Newc 1823; "casting the coals on board" *Mitcalfe* p.4 re1822; "Like ony chicken efter moot, / when its awd coat it fairly casses" *Pitman's Pay* G'head 1820s; "cassen clothes" *Brockett* Newc & Nth 1829; "weather's ower-kessen" *Blenkinsopp* Teesdale 1931; "he and his 'marra' had to 'cast' – that is, shovel – [the coal] from the keel into the hold of the vessel being loaded" *The Maister* p.35 re Tyneside, 1800–1840; "cassen, kessen – thrown down, as applied to an animal... that has falled... and is unable to rise again" *Atkinson* Cleve 1868; "to kest an evil eye" *Egglestone* Weardale 1870s; "yan was kessen" (one sheep was on its back) Alston 1992 per BG *Texts* p.96. *Distribution:* 'cast' (from ON) is reckoned as more general in the North than 'throw' (from OE); kest is nYx, Lx in *EDD*. [ON kasta] *Plus* "a lift was 'a cast along the road'" (*Nth Words*, Alnwick re 1880 approx). See also **backcast, upcast**

cat see **carle, quean**

cat-haws fruit of the hawthorn

ex. *Atkinson* Cleve 1868; 'hawthorn-berries, often shot by boys through a hollow hemlock-stalk' *Palgrave* Hetton 1896. *EDD* distribution to 1900: Nth. *Plus* "catace – hawthorn berry" *JO* re High Thornley/Rowland's Gill, 1930s–1940s in *Nth Words*

catched caught

exx. *JB* Shildon C20/mid, *Dodd* MS Tanfield Lea C20/2. *EDD* distribution to 1900: general.

cattijugs rosehip

"cat-a-jugs – wild rose hip" *Blenkinsopp* Teesdale 1931; "cattijugs – hips, the fruit of the cat-whin or dog-rose" *Atkinson* Cleve 1868. *EDD* distribution to 1900: cat-jugs D'm, Yx. See also **choups**

catty-keys catkins

"katty-keys – ash-tree seeds" *Dinsdale* mid-Tees 1849. *EDD* distribution to 1900: nYx.

caunch see **canch**

cavil, kyevil 1. to choose or allocate work(place) by lot, 2. the work station itself

1. "cavils or lotts being casten" *Raine* MS Durham 1594; "cavils –lots; a periodical allotment of working places to the hewers and putters of a colliery, usually quarterly; each person having assigned to him, by lot, that place in which he is to work during the ensuing three months" *Nicholson* 1880; "wor kyevelin days" (as young hewers) *Barrass* Stanley 1890s; "Piece-workers changed their working area every three months... The moves were based on a lottery, called 'cavils'" *Hitchin* re Seaham 1920s p.105; "cavil – method used to give workmen lots for work places. Names and work places drawn for by lot" *McBurnie* Glebe Colliery C20/mid; "kyeble not kyevil" South Moor (Stanley) 2003 per BG. *EDD* distribution to 1900: esp. N'd, D'm; in broader use – Sco, N'd, D'm, Lincs. [ON kafle 'bits'; compare Du kavel 'a lot'. Apparently developed from system of holding shares in a medieval common field, hence "cavilled – divided into ridges, spoken of a common field held in ridges" *Luckley* Alnwick 1870s extra, "Cavil... means also an allotment of ground in a common field" *Brockett* Newc & Nth 1829]. *Plus* "let's put th' cuts in fo' we's

cavil cont.

buck'n out – let's toss for who's fielding" (cricket) *CT* New Herrington 1930s
2. "Cavil is the place allotted to a hewer in a coal mine, by ballot. 'I've getten a canny cavil for this quarter, however.'" *Brockett* Newc & Nth 1829; "he's warked hard kyevils" *Tyne MC* May 1881; "But as sure's Aw rub me kyevel, it's the warst one o' the saw" *Barrass* Stanley 1890s. [ON kafli 'piece (of wood)']. *Plus* "quebble – actual work place on seam – payment made by production was often dependent on good or bad 'quebble'" *Northumbrian III* Winlaton/Marley Hill C20/mid

caw see **caa**

chaffinch 1. **sheelie**, 2. **spink**, 3. **chaffie**

1. "sheely or sheeley – the chaffinch" *Brockett* Newc & Nth 1829; "Sheelie (shae:li) chaffinch" *Palgrave* Hetton 1896. *EDD* distribution to 1900: N'd, D'm, Northants
2. "spink – chaffinch; a spark of fire" *Dinsdale* mid-Tees 1849; "bull-spink – the chaffinch" *Atkinson* Cleve 1868
3. "chaffie" NE 2001: in low use

chafts, chaffs jaws

"'tye yur chafts up' is to wrap your head up when ill of the tooth ache" *Bell* MS Newc 1815; "chafts, chaps or chops – the cheeks" *Bell* MS Newc 1815; "Chaffs – jawbones (plural only)" *Palgrave* Hetton 1896. *EDD* distribution to 1900: chaft – Sco, Nth. [?ON, compare Swed. käft]

chalder, chaldron a measure, a coal wagon

"chalder – the Newcastle pronunciation of the word chaldron a measure in the coal trade" *Bell* MS Newc 1815; "celdra – a chaldron or 36 bushels" *Finchale* 1836; "chalder – a chaldron. A Newcastle chaldron of coals weights fifty-three hundred weight. Eight of these chaldrons make one keel." *Brockett* Newc & Nth 1846; "chaldron – measure of coal, 36 bushels or 25.5 cwts' *Wearside Tales* 1879; "chaldron as coal wagon itself" *TC* Dawdon C20/2. *EDD* distribution to 1900: Sco and East Coast. [OF chaudière, chaldere, chauldron]

chalk a plastercast

ex. S'd Q 2001. See also **pot**

champion see *excellent*

chancetimes occasionally

> ex. *Palgrave* Hetton 1896 as in very common use. *EDD* distribution to 1900: esp. eD'm, C'd, but also in Sth

chare lane in town

> "in the chair at ye entrance into the yeate or stile of ye church yeard" *Raine* MS Hart 1596; "chare – a narrow street or passage in Newcastle" *Bell* MS Newc 1815; "in 1800 there were 21 chares on the Quayside" *Graham* Geordie 1979; "chare – street, steep street, e.g. Durham Chare in Bishop Auckland" *JB* Shildon C20/mid; found in Newcastle, Bishop Auckland, Morpeth, Hexham, Chester-le-St – *Geeson* N'd/ D'm 1969. *EDD* distribution to 1900: N'd, D'm, wMids. [OE cierr 'turning' – compare "chare – to stop or turn: chare the cow" *Grose* 1787]

charver club-goer or other alert young citizen of Newcastle

> "charver – rough person" Newc. 2001 Q. *Plus* "Charverland – Bowburn" www.urbandictionary.com 2004; "Charver Taak" per magazine *Newcastle Stuff* 2002 on. [Romany 'chavo' a lad]

checkweighman, checkie officer esp. in pit

> "Checkweighman – name for both the owner's and the people's representative, each appointed to check the other's dishonesty, in weighing coal-laden tubs, as they come from the pit" *Palgrave* Hetton 1896; "Collingwood... Nelson's chief checky at Trafalgar", "cheefcheky – managing director" *Dobson* Tyne 1970

checky of checked pattern

> "a blue checky shirt" eD'm 1990 per BG

cheeny chinaware, Chinese

> "fine Chenee oranges, four for a penny" (Chinese) *Allan's Tyneside Songs* p.299 1842; "Cheeny folks wi' silver hair" *Allan's Tyneside Songs* 1849 p.357; "the cheeney" (chinaware) *Wearside Tales* 1879; "a canny bit o' blue cheeny" *Embleton* Tyne 1897. *EDD* distribution to 1900: general

chenny pit lamp

> ex. Thornley Q 2001

chep chap

> "chep – a fellow spoken of as a companion"

chep cont.

> *Bell* MS Newc 1815; "a terrible chep for drinkin' beer"; "young cheps" *Armstrong* Tanfield C19/2; "another o' wor cheps" (workforce) *Haldane* Newc 1879; "cheps" BL re Blaydon C20/mid; "this chep Bert Oven" *Dobson* Tyne 1972. *EDD* distribution to 1900: ?N'd.

chew see **tew**

chewing gum 1. **chuddy**, 2. **gowie**, 3. **chewey**

> 1. "chuddy" *ER* M'bro C20/2, Teesside 2001, S'd, Ho'ton 2002 Q; "[in use in] Easington during the war; also used to name sticks of licorice root" *JS* Easington C20/mid
>
> 2. "gowie" S'd 2001 Q, S'm, B Auck, S.Hylton 2002 Q,
>
> 3. "chewey (gum)" Fencehouses 1930s, Chester-le-St C20/2 Q

chicken 1. **clocker**, 2. **chucky-hen**

> 1. "a hen sitting on her eggs is called a clocking hen" *Bell* MS Newc 1815; "Yon hen's clockin'" *Palgrave* Hetton 1896; "clucker – a broody hen" *HP* South Gosforth C20/mid; "clocker – broody hen or hen with chicks" *Dobson* Tyne 1973. *EDD* distribution to 1900: N'd, D'm, C'd. [OE e.g. "seo brodige henn sarlice cloccige..." (the broody hen insistently clucks) ca 1000 AD; an onomatopoeic word, that is imitating the sound a hen makes. Thus "clock – to cluck as a hen does" *Atkinson* Cleve 1868]
>
> 2. "chuckey – chicken" *Dinsdale* mid-Tees 1849, 'a chicken, a hen' *Atkinson* Cleve 1868; "only chucky-egg" *PG* H'pool C20/2; "chuckey-hen (not chucky on its own)" D'ton C20/2. *EDD* distribution to 1900: Sco, Nth. [imitative e.g. "chuck chuck chuck" (as call to a hen) Roker C20/mid]. *Plus:* "eftor he's hed a leuk at the chekkors an' the hens..." *Robson* Newc C20/1. See also **banty**

chiel person

> "wiv some varry canny chiels" *Marshall* Newc 1823; "Highland chields" *Oliver* Newc p.6 1824; "the (school) maistor was a canty chiel" *Allan's Tyneside Songs* p.353 1849; "chiel – young man" *Gibson* C'd 1880. *EDD* distribution to 1900: N'd, C'd, S.W. Noted as 'more a Border than a Geordie term' *Graham* Geordie 1979. [from child or possibly Romany chal 'chap, fellow']

chirm crooning sound

"chirm – cooing of a bird" *Dinsdale* mid-Tees 1849; 'chirping sound' *Blenkinsopp* Teesdale 1931; 'the crooning of birds at rest' *Hull* MS wNewc 1880s. *EDD* distribution to 1900: general. [OE cirm, pronounced chirm]

chisel bran

"to buye a peck of chesill" *Raine* MS Gateshead, 1622; "chisel – bran" *Bailey* Co.Durham 1810; "chisel – wheat bran, the characteristic component of the genuine Tyneside broon breed" *Hull* MS wNewc 1880s; "Chisel – a kind of bran with which boys feed rabbits" *Palgrave* Hetton 1896. *EDD* distribution to 1900: Nth. [OE ceosel (pronounced chossel) 'gravel, sand'] See also **caff**

chist chest

"chist – chest" *Dinsdale* mid-Tees 1849; "chist yor cards" (keep you cards up) *JP* S'm C20/2. See also **kist**

chocks wooden blocks to keep pit props wedged in place

"chocks – wooden pillars built up of oblong pieces of timber laid crosswise, two and two alternately" *Nicholson* 1880; ex. *JR* Seaham C20/1. *EDD* distribution to 1900: N'd, D'm, wYx

chod turd

ex. eD'm 1998 E. *Plus* "tod – turd" *Wood* Tees 2002

choke-damp Carbon Monoxide

"choke-damp – the products of the combustion of fire-damp or carburetted hydrogen; called also after-damp" *Nicholson* 1880

choller jowls

"choller – a double chin. Also the loose flesh under a turkey-cock's neck" *Brockett* Newc & Nth 1829; "chollers hanging ower his chin – cheeks" *Dunn* B'p Auck 1950. *EDD* distribution to 1900: Sco, Ire, N'd, C'd, S.W. [OE ceolur 'throat']

choppy pony feed

'chopped hay or straw for fodder' *Hull* MS wNewc 1880s; "corn-like food for the pony" *JM* Dawdon 1970s

choups hips

"choups – heps [sic], the fruit of briars" *Bailey* Co.Durham 1810; "choup, cat-choup – a hip; the fruit of the hedge briar or wild rose" *Brockett* Newc & Nth 1829. *EDD* distribution to 1900: Sco, Nth. [choup 'hip', compare Norw. kjupa] See also **cattijugs**

chow 1. to chew, 2. a quid of tobacco

1. "aw'll lairn te chow backy" *Allan's Tyneside Songs* p.397 C19/mid; "he smokes an' chows" *Allan's Tyneside Songs* p.426 1862. NE 2001: in use. [compare ON kjalki 'jawbone']
2. "rowlin his great backey chow" *Allan's Tyneside Songs* p.145 1816; 'usually tobacco chewed down pit' *JP* S'm C20/2

choz see *excellent*

chucks 1. seashells, 2. 'jacks', 'fivestones'

1. "chucks an' gravel" *Allan's Tyneside Songs* p.356 1849; "chucks... also [means] the shells themselves" *Luckley* Alnwick 1870s; "chuck – a shell, usually of snail or winkle" *Hull* MS wNewc 1880s
2. "chucks – a game among girls; played with five of these shells, and sometimes with pebbles, called chuckie-stanes" *Brockett* Newc & Nth 1829; "chucks – a game among girls played with shells; also the shells themselves" *Luckley* Alnwick 1870s; "chuckstones" *IA* S'm 1950s,60s; "chuckstanes or chuckie stanes" (dexterity game with shells or pebbles) *Geeson* N'd/ D'm 1969; "chucks – a game played by children with pebbles called chuckie stones" *Graham* Geordie 1979. NE 2001 – in use (chucks). *Plus:* "checks" (the game) M'bro. 2001 Q; "five-stones" eD'm 2001 Q

chucky a hearty fellow

ex. *Pitman's Pay* G'head 1820s. See also **chicken, tadger**

chuddy see **chewing gum**

chummin see **toom**

claa-hammer with 'tails'

"The maister appeared in a 'claa-hammer, swalley-tailed coat' in the evening" *Windows* 1917; "claa-hammer coat – tail coat" *Dobson* Tyne 1970, 1972. *EDD* distribution to 1900: as suit N.I. 1892, USA 1878. [from 'claw']. See also **claut**

claes clothes

"closse" *Anderson* Newcastle 1607; "claiths" *Bewick* Tyne 1790s; "my pit claes" *Marshall* G'head 1806; "he used te sell claes pins" *Allan's Tyneside Songs* p.459 1862; "on we thee clais" *Armstrong* Tanfield C19/2; "clays prop" *JP* S'm C20/2. *EDD* distribution to 1900: Sco, Nth. For singular see **clout**

clag 1. to stick or make something adhere, 2. to hit

1. "the crank of the engine broke, and we fell back 2 fathom... I said, 'Clag to, boys!' and all kept hold" *Errington* p.53 Felling/Heworth re 1790s; "clag – to adhere or stick together" *Bailey* Co.Durham 1810; "clagged tegither wi' summat" *Haldane* Newc 1879; "thoo'l see me clag on te th' skeets" *Armstrong* Tanfield C19/2; 'to stick' *JR* Seaham C20/1, Tanfield Lea, 1960, *LL* Tyneside 1974. *EDD* distribution to 1900: Sco, Ire, Nth, Mids. NE 2001: in common use. [?ON – compare Dan. klag 'sticky', OE clæg (pronounced and meaning clay)]. *Plus* "Aam claggin – sweating" Ashington C20/1 Q
2. "clag him one" (hit) *ER* M'bro C20/2; "clagged his lug" *Dobson* Tyne 1970; "arl clag the' one" eD'm 2001 Q; 'to hit' Newc, Thornley, M'bro 2001 Q. *Plus* "clagger – a right carry on" Ferryhill 2001 Q

claggum anything sticky, esp. toffee

"clagham, clagum – treacle bioled a considerable time so that when it is cold it becomes hard and brittle" *Bell* MS Newc 1815; "maw mooth a' covered wi' claggum an' clarts" *Allan's Tyneside Songs* p.396 C19/mid; "claggum – treacle lollipops, etc" *Atkinson* Cleve 1868; 'treacle toffee' *Dodd* MS Tanfield Lea C20/2, *Graham* Geordie 1979; 'paste for wallpaper' *MB* Coxhoe C20/mid; "claggums – brilliantine" D'ton 1930s Q. *EDD* distribution to 1900: Sco, Nth

claggy sticky

"claggy – sticky, glutinous, adhesive: 'desput claggy walking'" *Atkinson* Cleve 1868; "the ground was claggy at the shows (the fair)" *IA* S'm 1950s,60s; "claggy taffy" *Dobson* Tyne 1972

clam to glue and clamp together... hungry

"cleam – to glue together" *Ray* 1674; "aw'l claime yur eyes up" *Bell* MS Newc 1815; "clam

clam cont.

– to press, to hold an article tightly" *Brockett* Newc & Nth 1829; "clam – to pinch, compress, force together; to suffer from the pinching effects of hunger, to starve" *Atkinson* Cleve 1868; "clam'd – starved" *Ray* 1674; "clammin – very hungry" *Wood* Cleve 2002. [OE clæman, OE clamm (a fetter)]. See also **clemmed, crame**

clap to pat

"clapt and stroakt ma little [dog]" *Pitman's Pay* G'head 1820s; 'to touch gently, to fondle, to stroke' *Brockett* Newc & Nth 1829; "If you clapped them, they will be kind with you" (Boy's essay on Kindness to Animals) *Palgrave* Hetton 1896. *EDD* distribution to 1900: Sco, Nth. [ON klappa – cognates in Dan, Ice have a similar sense]

clart to muddy, to muck

"clart – to daub, smear, make dirty" *Atkinson* Cleve 1868; "all clarted up" *MB* Coxhoe C20/mid; "he's just clartin on" (messing about) *Graham* Geordie 1979; "clart on, clart about" S'm 2000 via BG. *EDD* distribution to 1900: Sco, Ire, Nth, eMids. [beclart C13; further origin unknown]

clarts 1. wet mud, 2. mess, messing about

"plishplash throw the clarts" (street mud) *Bewick* Tyne 1790s; "clarts – mud or wet street sweepings" *Bell* MS Newc 1815; "the vary clairts upon the street / is goold in Callerforney" *Allan's Tyneside Songs* p.361 1849; "always weel supplied wi' Newcastle amonishen – clarts" *Allan's Tyneside Songs* p.444 1862; "clarts – soft mud: 'She's fa'en i' the gutter and myed her frock a' clarts'" *Luckley* Alnwick 1870s; "rotten eggs en oranges, clarts en lumps e breed" (as bits of refuse) *Armstrong* Tanfield C19/2; "a gret clart o' snaw o' tha neb" *Atkinson* Cleve 1868; "as clear as clarts" *Haldane* Newc 1879; "the roads wes clarty" (after rain) *Cuddy Cairt* Newc 1917; "up to the neck in clarts – an expression used when men are working in wet, muddy conditions [in the pit]" *McBurnie* Glebe Colliery, C20/mid; "ower biut tops i' clerts" *Dunn* B'p Auck 1950; "A could eat a scabby monkey fried in clarts" *VIZ* 78 (1996)
2. "it's all clart" (not to be depended on)" *Atkinson* Cleve 1868; "he myed an aaful clart aall ower the harth" *Robson* Newc C20/1; "a

clarts cont.

lot of clart' – a delaying fuss or bother"
Viereck re Gateshead, 1966; "klaht on" *Dodd*
MS Tanfield Lea C20/2

clarty mucky

"clarty – muddy and wet" *Bell* MS Newc 1815;
"if it (the weather) be clarty" *Allan's Tyneside
Songs* p.245 1827; "gan an' wesh yor clarty
fyece" *Luckley* Alnwick 1870s; 'he likes gannen
doon the pit best, hard, rough, and clarty as
the life is' Coxhoe 1916; "clarty byeut-marks"
Dobson Tyne 1970–71; "clarty" Trimdon 2002
Q. *EDD* distribution to 1900: Sco, Nth. Mids.
NE 2001: in common use

clash 1. a talk, a chat, 2. to slam, bang, make a
noise, 3. of any energetic action

1. "I came to have a little clash" *Chicken*
Benwell 1720s; "clash, clashing – loose talk,
spending one's time in talking" *Bell* MS Newc
1830s; "clash – gossip" *Gibson* C'd 1880, *Dodd*
MS Tanfield Lea C20/2. *EDD* distribution to
1900: Sco, Nth. NE 2001: in use
2. "dinnet clash the door" *Allan's Tyneside
Songs* p.478 1863, "Dinno' clash the door so"
Palgrave Hetton 1896, "don't clash the door"
IA S'm 1950s, 60s; 'to throw violently, to
strike' *Luckley* Alnwick 1870s; "'Clash'd and
slap'd,' of milk which has been agitated
by hasty carriage" *Palgrave* Hetton 1896;
"divvent clash yerdesklids se" *Dobson* Tyne
1970. *EDD* distribution to 1900: Sco, Nth.
NE 2001: in use
3. "he clashed him doon" (dashed, hurled)
Armstrong Tanfield C19/2; "clashing around –
rushing about" D'ton C20/2; "Aall clash thy
bloody wick out – I'll knock hell out of you"
Dunn B'p Auck 1950; "Ah'm clashed" (under
the weather) Crook C20/2 Q. *EDD*
distribution to 1900: Sco, NE

clashy wet

"clashy – wet, e.g. weather, road" *Dinsdale*
mid-Tees 1849. *EDD* distribution to 1900: Nth

claut to claw

"claut – to claw" *Dinsdale* mid-Tees 1849;
"claut – to scratch with one's nails" *Atkinson*
Cleve 1868. *EDD* distribution to 1900: Sco,
NE. See also **claa**

clavver to clamber

"I... claver'd up to the window" *Bells* re
Carlisle, 1802; "claffer, clavver – to climb up;

clavver cont.

mostly applied to children" *Brockett* Newc &
Nth 1829; "clavver – to climb, as one does
a hill; or as a child does on to its father's or
mother's knees" *Atkinson* Cleve 1868. *EDD*
distribution to 1900: Nth

clavver clover

ex. *Dinsdale* mid-Tees 1849. *EDD* distribution
to 1900: ?general

clay substance like putty to anchor a candle

"clay – a substance used by pitmen as a
substitute for candlesticks" *Pitman's Pay*
G'head 1820s

cleed to clothe

"I wad cleed thee in the silk so fine" Reed
Border Ballads C16; "the nyek'd to cleed"
Oiling G'head 1826. *EDD* distribution to 1900:
Sco, Ire, C'd and East Coast. [ON klædda
(past tense)]

cleg horse-fly

"clæggs, cleggs – Flies... that sting beasts and
particularly horses" *Kennet* 1690s as Yorks;
"cleg – the gad-fly; very troublesome in hot
weather, particularly to horses" *Brockett* Newc
& Nth 1829; 'horsefly' *Dinsdale* mid-Tees 1849,
Atkinson Cleve 1868; "kleg – mosquito" *Dodd*
MS Tanfield Lea C20/2. *EDD* distribution to
1900: Sco, Ire, Nth, Mids. [ON kleggi]. Plus
"bree, breese – the gadfly" *Atkinson* Cleve
1868; "bumbore – the gadfly" *Atkinson* Cleve
1868

clemmed to feel the effects of hunger or thirst

"clemmed – hungry" *Atkinson* Cleve 1868;
"clemm'd – starved" *Gibson* C'd 1880, Roker
C20/mid; "Ahmclamin" (hungry) East Boldon
1985; "mask the tea thin am clammin" *Dobson*
Tyne 1970–71; "I'm clamming for a drink"
Graham Geordie 1979 [ON klæima, Du.
klemmen]. See also **clam, crame**

clemmie a stone

"hoy clemmies" BF Billingham C20/mid; 'a
stone to throw at someone' ER M'bro C20/2;
"clemmy – hard piece of clay suitable for
throwing" *Wood* M'bro 2002. *EDD* distribution
to 1900: Sco, Nth

cleugh ravine

"cleugh – a rocky valley" *Bell* MS Newc 1815;
'a narrow rocky glen or ravine' *Atkinson* Cleve

cleugh cont.

1868; 'a narrow ravine more like a cleft in the hill than a waterworn valley' *Egglestone* Weardale 1886 [OE cloh; also Dan. kloft, Norw. kliufa 'to split']

click 1. to catch, snatch, 2. a tear or rent (noun and vb)

1. "deeth was him... to cleke" *Cuthbert* C15/mid; "klick up – to catch up [Lincs]" *Ray* 1674; "to klick – to snatch, or catch up. as the glede (kite) klicks up the chicken" *Kennet* 1690s as Nth; "Aw've seen him... Click up his chalk" *Pitman's Pay* G'head 1820s; "click haud o' the rope, Cuddy" *Luckley* Alnwick 1870s; "klik – snatch, hole in cloth" *Dodd* MS Tanfield Lea C20/2; "he clicked it oot o' me hand" *Graham* Geordie 1979. *EDD* distribution to 1900: Sco, Nth [OE clyccan, AN kliket 'clapper, latch']
2. "a greet click iv her frock" *Graham* Geordie 1979; "'mind you don't click your jumper' i.e. catch it on someting (like barbed wire, say). The 'click' itself would be the loose loop of wool that the wire would pull out" *PG* H'pool C20/2. *Plus* "Click – a sudden twinge of pain [in the side], etc." *Palgrave* Hetton 1896

clinkin' see *excellent*

clippy mat rug made of cut-up spare material

"clippy mat – made from hessian base and fibre clippings trimmed to length with scissors" CT New Herrington 1930s; "curled up asleep on the clippy mat" *Cate*, B'p Auckland area 1987 p.82. [*EDD* 1900 gives clip 'an iron hook' as N'd etc; but source likelier clippings as offcuts – "Hessian sacks were cut up, stitched together and nailed to wooden frames. Rags were dyed to the required colours and cut into suitable sizes called 'clippings'." *Hitchin* re Dalton-le-Dale 1910s p.12]. See also **proggie mat**

clivvor, clever 1. amazing, skillful, 2. healthy

1. "Sir John's clivvor job / wi' the aaful Lambton Worm" 'Lambton Worm' 1867; "clivor – skillful" S'd 2001 Q. *EDD* distribution to 1900: general
2. "leukin clivver and reet as owt" *Other Eye* Newc ca.1890; "Aa'm not very clever today" *AK* Newc, 1940s, sim. *JS* Easington C20/mid; "How are ye the day, lad? – Man. aa's clivvor" *Graham* Geordie 1979; "Adivven't feelower

clivvor cont.

clivver" East Boldon, 1985; "I'm not feeling ower clivva today" Charver 2000–2002. *EDD* distribution to 1900: general

clocking-hen see **chicken**

clog 1. log, 2. wooden shoe

1. "clog – a log, block of wood" *Atkinson* Cleve 1868; "clog – a lump of wood: 'put a clog on the fire' W(elsh). cleg, clog, a lump" *Luckley* Alnwick 1870s, sim. *Smith* Weardale 1883; "block of wood as part of construction of a coble" – *Hill* Flamborough 1970s. *EDD* distribution to 1900: Sco, Nth, Mids. [origin unknown – not necessarily the same as 'log'] *Plus* "give it come clog – put some effort into it" *Wood* Tees 2002. See also **yule-clog**
2. "These industrious miners that walk in their clogs / They suit them to travel o'er mountains and bogs" 'Bonny Moor Hen' ca. 1818; "clog – a sort of shoe, the upper part of strong hide leather, and the sole of wood, plated with iron" *Brockett* Newc & Nth 1829; 'wooden shoes, also delays, hindrances' *Bell* MS Newc 1830s; "clogs – ancle-shoes of thick leather with wooden soles" *Atkinson* Cleve 1868. *Plus* "clogger – football player who has no finesse" *Wood* Tees 2002

clooty cloth

"claes o' clooty blue" (blue cloth) *Allan's Tyneside Songs* p.499 1881; "clooty mat – a mat made of pieces of assorted cloth" *Irwin* Tyne 1970; "a beard like a clooty mat" *Irwin* Tyne 1970; "clootie" (a cloth) Gateshead 2001 Q. *EDD* distribution to 1900: clootie mat – Sco, N'd. See also **clout, devil, hookie mat, proggie mat**

cloudberry

"cloud-berry – the ground mulberry or *rubus chamæmorus*" *Brockett* Newc & Nth 1829. [because it grows on hills "where the clouds are lower than the tops of the same all winter long" Gerard's *Herbal* C17] *Plus* "knoop – the cloud-berry" *Brockett* Newc & Nth 1846. *EDD* distribution to 1900: N'd. [perhaps from ON knappr 'knob']

clout a piece of cloth

"clout – a cloth of limited size; a patch; a rag" *Atkinson* Cleve 1868; 'clothes, rags or a good smack' Spennymoor C20/mid; "she's got a tongue that wud clip cloots" Ashington

clout cont.

C20/mid; "clout – article of clothing" *JB* Shildon C20/mid; "clout was the dish cloth and also a clout across the lug hole" *JS* Easington C20/mid. [?OE clut] *Plus* "dishkloot – dishcloth" *Dodd* MS Tanfield Lea C20/2; "puddin-clout" GP eD'm C20/mid. For plural, see **claes**; see also **clooty**

clove boat part

support for a toft (thoft). ex. Hill 1970s re Staithes

coal

"cwols uv fire" *Moore* Weardale 1859; "coal-heed" (idiot) G'head C20/2 Q; "Pity Me Costa Coal Cree Package Tours" *Dobson* Tyne 1972. See also **candle coal, roondy**

coble small square-sterned fishing boat with running-strakes for hauling onto beach.

"Item in factura cimbri novi, et reparacione antiqui, cum uno cobill'" *Finchale* 1406–7; "coble – a particular kind of boat, very sharp and wedge-shaped in the bow, and flat bottomed and square at the stern" *Brockett* Newc & Nth 1829; "coble – a kind of boat peculiar to the North East, in use among fishermen and pilots, with sharp bows, flat sloping stern, and without a keel" *Atkinson* Cleve 1868. *EDD* distribution to 1900: East Coast from Scotland to East Anglia – *Note* north of Sunderland (approx) the word is pronounced with a long 'o'. [ONorthumbrian cuopl; compare Welsh ceubol, Bretton caubal; but the modern form could be a reintroduction in Middle English]. For boat parts see **bogie, clove, corf, cuddy, dodger, draft, scutboard**

cockle to hawk, retch

'to bring up phlegm and spit it out' *CT* New Herrington, C20/mid; "the sight of blood makes me cockle (retch)" *IA* S'm 1950s,60s; 'to vomit or spit' Roker C20/mid; 'to retch, clear phlegm from throat' *JB* Shildon C20/mid, Upper Teesdale, S'd 2001 Q; 'to spit' *Dobson* Tyne 1973, Barnard Castle; *PP* S'm 2000, eD'm 2001 Q. *EDD* distribution to 1900: N'd. *Plus* "cockle – a quantity of spittle 'Tom spat a big cockle'" *Luckley* Alnwick 1870s

cod cushion

"codbar – pillowcase" *Finchale* (1411; "i codd broudyd wyth ymages" *Raine* MS York 1445;

cod cont.

"cod – a pillow" *Ray* 1674; "lay my cods a little higher" *Chicken* Benwell 1720s; "cod, codd – a pillow or cushion" *Brockett* Newc & Nth 1829. *EDD* distribution to 1900: Sco, Nth, eMids, obsolete 1900. [ON koddi]. *Plus* "fire-cods – bellows" *Atkinson* Cleve 1868; "princod – a pincushion" *Atkinson* Cleve 1868. *EDD* distribution to 1900: Sco, Nth, eMids, but obsol.

codger return end of conveyor belt in pit

ex. Ho'ton 2001 Q

cogley crooked, unsteady

"coggly – unsteady. moving from side to side, easily overturned" *Brockett* Newc & Nth 1829; "cockly – unsteady on its basis; easily moved or overthrown; wavering" *Atkinson* Cleve 1868; "a coggly tyebble" *Luckley* Alnwick 1870s; "Coggly – crooked, from side to side, as of an uneven swing's motion. Walking on high heels, or sitting in a hay-cart, would be so described" *Palgrave* Hetton 1896; "cogley described poor writing, unsteady riding of a two wheeler bike and learning to drive a booler (a hoop)" *JS* Easington C20/mid; "the plank wis se coggly at aa nearly tummeled off" *Graham* Geordie 1979. *EDD* distribution to 1900: Sco, Ire, Nth. [cf. Welsh gogi 'to shake' *Hull* MS wNewc 1880s]

coin to turn, go round

"coin – to turn from the straight" *Wade South Moor* C20/mid; "to coign a corner" *Viereck* re Gateshead, 1966; "coin – turn the corner" *JS* Easington C20/mid; "koin – to swing tub around, turn" *Dodd* MS Tanfield Lea C20/2; "coin left – turn left" *Dobson* Tyne 1970; "coin yer gord" (spin your hoop) *Dobson* Tyne 1969; "coin or quoin – to turn around" *Irwin* Tyne 1970; "coin oot o' the way" (turn aside) *Graham* Geordie 1979. [AN coign, coin 'angle']

colley 1. meat. 2. a lamplight

1. "colley – butcher's meat. A term chiefly among children" *Brockett* Newc & Nth 1829; "colley – meat (child's term)" *Dinsdale* mid-Tees 1849. *EDD* distribution to 1900: NE [?ON kolla 'cow', or "a corruption of collop" *Hull* MS wNewc 1880s]
2. "lamplighter" *Geeson* N'd/D'm 1969

come

"in cam little Jenny" *Bewick* Tyne 1790s; "they

come cont.

cam back ower hyem" *Allan's Tyneside Songs*
p.451 1862; "cum thee ways in – come in; it is
cumin on ti snaa" *Hull* MS wNewc 1880s; "just
cum'd oot" *Armstrong* Tanfield C19/2. *EDD*
distribution to 1900: cam – Sco, Nth

coo cow

"he milked a dozen coos" 'Lambton Worm'
1867; "yor like the coo's tail, elwis late"
Ashington C20/mid. [OE cu]. For plural see **ky**

copple to tip or topple

"to copple the creels" (turn a somersault)
Viereck re Gateshead, 1966; "koppel owa –
tip over" *Dodd* MS Tanfield Lea C20/2. *EDD*
distribution to 1900: East Anglia; not in *OED*.
Plus "cropple your creels" Shotton 2001 Q.
See also **cowp**, **creels**

corby see *crow*

corf basket or other container in pit

"I' yen corf we byeth gan belaw" *Marshall*
G'head 1806; "corf, the corves – the corf to
hold 20 peck or 87.249 imperial gallons" *Bell*
MS Newc 1815; "corf – a basket for bringing
coals out of the pit: 'lensda hand on wi' ma
corf'" *Pitman's Pay* G'head 1820s; "corf – a
large wicker-work basket, used for drawing
coals out of the pits; made of strong hazel
rods" *Brockett* Newc & Nth 1829; "corve, curve
– a small waggon, wheel-less but having iron
runners, in use in the coal-pits" *Atkinson* Cleve
1868; "hoo korves an' trams gov way te tubs"
Barrass Stanley 1890s. *EDD* distribution to
1900: Sco, Nth, Mids, Corn. [ON korfr, Du
korf]. *Plus* "Korvers and Machenicks on the
Tine and Wear" *Errington* Felling/Heworth
p.42/50 re 1790s

corf

'tender to a larger coble' *Hill* Flamborough
1970s. [?calf]

cotterels coins

"the loss o' the cotterels" *Marshall* Newc 1823;
"And when wark's flush, for time o' want, /
Lay by some cottrils" *Pitman's Pay* G'head
1820s; "She alwes selt hor butter an' eggs
at the best price, and whats better Bill,
she nivor forgat to fetch the cotterals
hyem" *Cuddy Cairt* Newc 1917; "kottoril –
money" *Dodd* MS Tanfield Lea C20/2. *EDD*
distribution to 1900: N'd, D'm, Yx. [cotterils

cotterels cont.

being washers]. *Plus* "ackers" G'head, Blyth
C20/2 Q, "shrapnel – loose change" NShields
C20/mid

coul to rake in

"coul – to scrape earth together" *Bailey*
Co.Durham 1810; "coul, cowl – to scrape
together dung, mud, dirt, etc." *Brockett* Newc
& Nth 1829. *EDD* distribution to 1900: Nth.
[AN coiller, cuillir 'to gather, collect'] *Plus*
"cowlings – bits raked together" *Blenkinsopp*
Teesdale 1931; "cowler – a sort of rake
without teeth for drawing mud together"
Hull MS wNewc 1880s; "cowl-ri'aks – rakes"
Egglestone Weardale 1870s

cowie pill

"cowie – drug, usually a pill" Charver
2000–2002. See also *left-handed*

cowp, coup 1. **to tip up, overturn**, 2. **coup cart**,
3. **cowp...creels**

1. "cowp'd the cars" *Bells* re Carlisle, 1802;
"cope or coup – to empty or turn out" *Bailey*
Co.Durham 1810; "he had got too much [to
drink] and cowped the cart at the Robers
Corner, the wife in the cart, near dark"
Errington Felling/Heworth p.84 re 1800s;
"coup – to empty by overturning, to overset,
to tumble over" *Brockett* Newc & Nth 1829;
"cowpt corves i' the barrow way" *Pitman's Pay*
G'head 1820s; "he riched ower for a bit o'
lump sugar, and cowped the cream jug"
Allan's Tyneside Songs p.395 C19/mid; "sea
sarpints tee may cowp the boat" *Allan's
Tyneside Songs* p.362 1849; "Bella cowp'd the
hyesty-pudding on her new goon" *Luckley*
Alnwick 1870s; "cowped is (us) aul iv a heep"
Armstrong Tanfield C19/2; "cowped ower"
(roll over) *JP* S'm C20/2; "cowp – overturn"
Tanfield Lea, 1960. *EDD* distribution to 1900:
Sco, Ire, Nth. [AN couper 'to strike'; but
compare Swed guppa 'to tilt up'] *Plus* "coupie
– sheep on back" *Northumbrian Words III*,
C20/mid re Kielder
2. "ii coupe waynes with clogge wheeles" *Raine*
MS Wensley 1575; "coup, coop... a lime coop
– a cart or wain made close with boards to
carry anything that would otherwise fall out"
Grose 1787; "coup-cart – a short team, closed
with boards" *Brockett* Newc & Nth 1825;
"couppes – 'carts for leading manure, so
called, not, as Mr Brockett states, from their

cowp cont.

being able to be couped or turned up in order to be emptied, but from having their sides and ends not open rail work, but cowped or tubbed with boards' – 'ii couppes pro fimo extrahendo'" *Finchale* 1836; "coop-cart – one made to coup, i.e. trip to discharge a load" wNewc 1880s; "Coup Cart (koop) – the common dung – or coal-cart" *Palgrave* Hetton 1896; "coop-cart" (collecting potatoes in field) *DB* Darlington C20/mid; "coop cart – two wheeled farmer's cart, with a tippable body" *JB* Shildon C20/mid; "cowp-cart – a cart with a tip-up back used, e.g. for collecting night-soil" *GP* C20/mid S'm. *EDD* distribution to 1900: Sco, Nth
3. "aw cowp'd me creels" (danced) *Marshall* Newc 1823; "creell – a pannier or kind of baskett also a child's play to stand upon the head and hands and turn over usually called cowping the creells" *Bell* MS Newc 1830s; "ye wid laft... to see me coup me creels" *Armstrong* Tanfield C19/2; "kowp their moral creels" *Barrass* Stanley 1890s; "dinnut crowp your creels an' crack yor cranny" Crook C20/1 Q; "Charlie Cowp-his-creels" – a toy with a wooden figure rotating along parallel bars, subject of story by Lisle Willis C20/mid; "cowp your creels" (do a forward roll) *IA* S'm 1950s, 60s; "cowpd yacreels" (turned somersaults) East Boldon 1985; "shu slipped o the clarts n cowped a creels" (fell over dramatically) Sacriston 2004 E. *EDD* distribution to 1900: Sco, N'd, C'd. [from image of creel as basket carried on head? – hence "tipple your creels" (somersault) *JB* Shildon C20/mid... or rhyming slang for 'heels'?]

cowp, coup to swop, sell, barter

"a good horse which he would cope for another" *Raine* MS York 1670; "to kowpe – to chop or exchange" *Kennet* 1690s as Nth; "cope, coup – to chop or exchange, used by the coasters of Norfolk and Suffolk, and also Yorkshire, probably from the low dutch word, copen, to buy, sell or deal" *Grose* 1787; "cope – to exchange, barter" *Bailey* Co.Durham 1810, "coup, cope" *Dinsdale* Mid-Tees 1849; "cowp" *Blenkinsopp* Teesdale 1931, *Palgrave* Hetton 1896; "coup, cowp, or cope – to barter or exchange" *Brockett* Newc & Nth 1829; "they couped horses" *Bell* MS Newc 1830s; "Jim coup'd his vine (pencil) for two roasted taties"

cowp, coup cont.

Luckley Alnwick 1870s; "will you coup seats with me?" *Atkinson* Cleve 1868; "cowp ya" (swop you) *JP* S'm C20/2, *Dobson* Tyne 1970–71; "kowp – overturn, swap" *Dodd* MS Tanfield Lea C20/2. *EDD* distribution to 1900: Sco, Nth. NE 2001: in use. [ON kaupa 'to barter, buy, etc', OE ceapian]. *Plus* "horse-couping" Rothbury, C18/2; "horse-couper – horse dealer" *Hull* MS wNewc 1880s

craa, craw see **crow**

crack 1. to boast, talk, 2. chat, news (noun), 3. expert sportsman

1. "he dyd not well to brag and crack" (boast) *Raine* MS Newcastle, C16/mid; "he had great cause to crack of wealth" Rothbury C18/2; "crakin oh the bayrn" *Bewick* Tyne 1790s; "may blether an' crack" *Allan's Tyneside Songs* p.406 1862; "the French may... crack aboot ther warrin'" *Allan's Tyneside Songs* p.470 1862; "thoo gat drunk en crak'd t'preest oot ta fight" (challenged) *Egglestone* Weardale 1870s. *EDD* distribution to 1900: Sco, Nth. [Fr craquer 'to talk boastfully']
2. "to... hear aw his cracks and his jwokes" (?boasts) *Bells* (Nth C'd) 1815; "What's your crack?" (news) *Brockett* Newc & Nth 1829; "a crack ower his glass o' beer" *Haldane* Newc 1879; "Wi' soft, sweet sugar-candy crack", "when at wor bate, ee'd had some confidential crack" *Barrass* Stanley 1890s; "a smoak an' a bit crack wiv a cock-eyed chep thit wes sellin' mushells i' the Bigg Markit" *Cuddy Cairt* Newc 1917; "his a bit o' good crack – interesting to talk to" *Dunn* B'p Auck 1950; "that's bad crack – bad news" *Dunn* B'p Auck 1950; "Time tu hev a crack" *Lakeland* re C'd C20. *EDD* distribution to 1900: Sco, Nth. NE 2001: in use
3. "he wun the crack men's loodest praise" (at bools) Tyne *MC* May 1881; "We cud lick the very myest o' cracks thit tackled us i' play" *Barrass* Stanley 1890s

cracket, cricket stool

"plac'd on a creckit near the fire" *Chicken* Benwell 1720s; "cricket – a small three legg'd stool" *Grose* 1787; "a three-footed cracket" *Egglestone* Weardale 1870s; "a cracket for the bairn" *Haldane* Newc 1879; "dash maw pit cracket!" *Barrass* Stanley 1890s; "Cracket – a low stool, found in most cottages. When coal is low, miners sit on a cracket to their work,

cracket cont.

one end of which is higher than the other" *Palgrave* Hetton 1896; "cracket – three-legged small (milking?) stool" *JB* Shildon C20/mid; "cracket' is a stool; we chldren all had our own" *HP* South Gosforth C20/mid; "cracket-lowping" *Dobson* Tyne 1972. *EDD* distribution to 1900: Sco, Nth. NE 2001: in use. [?Du kruk-stool]

crag prominent rock

"great earthfast craggs & great stones" *Raine* MS Rothbury 1607. [Irish/Gaelic creag]

crake rattle

"the miners union meetings were announced by the crake man going round the streets on a Sunday morning with a big wooden rattle – a crake" *JS* Easington C20/mid. *EDD* distribution to 1900: D'm. [similar stem to 'crack']

crame to mend, e.g. with wire or staples

"to mend by uniting; as joining broken china or wooden bowls" *Brockett* Newc & Nth, 1846; "crame – to clamp and glue" *Blenkinsopp* Teesdale 1931 [Du krammen]

cranch to crunch

"cranch – to crush a hard substance between the teeth" *Brockett* Newc & Nth 1829; 'to crush any substance [noisily]; to break with a crackling sound' *Atkinson* Cleve 1868. *EDD* distribution to 1900: Sco, Ire, Nth, Mids. *Plus* "cranch – hard brittle substance" *Dinsdale* mid-Tees 1849

crane mining lifting gear

"crane – formerly used to hoist the corves of coals from the tram to the rolley; the coals being put by the barrowmen from the working-places to the crane, and drawn thence by horses to the shaft. upon the introduction of tubs the crane was abolished" *Nicholson* 1880. *EDD* distribution to 1900: N'd, D'm

cranky 1. ill, 2. unsafe, 3. item of pitman's clothing

1. "cranky – sprightly, exulting, jocose... also used in the opposite sense of ailing, sickly" *Brockett* Newc & Nth 1829; "cranky – ill able to move from... injury... ailment... or age" *Atkinson* Cleve 1868; "kranky – weak, poorly, sickly: 'Ah'se very kranky'" *Embleton* Tyne 1897. *EDD* distribution to 1900: cheerful –

cranky cont.

Ire, Newc, Sth; ailing – Nth, Mids. [Gm krank 'ill'] *Plus* "are you still feeling a bit crook?" *GP* S'm 1950s, *SP* S'm 2003
2. 'tottering, unsafe' *Robson* Tyne 1849 [Du kreng 'lop-sided' (of a ship)]
3. "crankey – a sort of checked flannell worn by pitmen – hence they get the name of Bob Crankeys" *Bell* MS Newc 1815; "cranky – once the characteristic neckcloth of the pitman" *Hull* MS wNewc 1880s

cree shed or pen (for animals)

"ah shoved the pig inte the cree" *Embleton* Tyne 1897; "Cray (krae:) – a hutch, as 'pig's cray,' 'pigeon-cray,' etc. The only word in use" *Palgrave* Hetton 1896; "cree – shed, usually for pigeons" Spennymoor C20/mid; "homemade garden shed or hut" *Viereck* re Gateshead 1966, Ferryhill 2001 Q; "an old age pensioner's coal cree" *Dobson* Tyne 1972; "chicken cree" *Graham* Geordie 1979. *EDD* distribution to 1900: Sco, Nth. NE 2001: in use. [ON krá, Irish cró 'a fold'].
See also **ducket**

creel wickerwork basket

"creil or creel – a kind of semi-circular basket of wicker work, in which provender is carried to sheep in remote pastures" *Brockett* Newc & Nth 1829; "creell – a pannier or kind of baskett... " *Bell* MS Newc 1830s; "wi' a creel on mee back... aw'll supply ye wi' flat fish, fine skyet, or fresh ling" *Allan's Tyneside Songs* p.406 1862; 'trap... for crabs and lobsters... invariably called a pot in cobles' *Hill* Flamborough 1970s; "creel – basket for 1 stone weight of fish" B'd Castle 2001 Q. *EDD* distribution to 1900: Sco, Ire, Nth. NE 2001: in low use. [OIrish criel 'chest' or OFr greille 'wicker-work']. See also **cowp... creels**

creep movement in strata

"creep – a heaving or bursting upwards of the floor of a coal mine" *Brockett* Newc & Nth 1829; "creep – a state of the mine produced by an insufficiency of coal left to support the roof, and which often forces the top and bottom of the mine together, and renders the pit unfit for further use" *Pitman's Pay* G'head 1820s. *EDD* distribution to 1900: N'd, D'm

crew gang of men

"a body of men, e.g. Craaley's crew" (iron workers) *Hull* MS wNewc 1880s, and see song 'Swalwell Hopping'. See also **candymen**

crib bed

"crib – a child's bed" *Brockett* Newc & Nth 1829; "crib – where a Charver sleeps: 'Am gan hyem to me crib'" Charver 2000–2002. *EDD* distribution to 1900: general

crible to curry favour, suck up to

"Crible – to curry favour" *Palgrave* Hetton 1896; "kreibal/kryble – to 'creep': "dinnut ye gan oot thor an kryble ti that lot!" South Moor (Stanley) 2003 per BG. *EDD* distribution to 1900: N'd, D'm

crine to shrink

"crine – to shrink, pine" *Bailey* Co.Durham 1810; "let yor hearts nivvor crine" *Allan's Tyneside Songs* p.538 1886. *EDD* distribution to 1900: Sco, Ire, N'd, C'd. [Gaelic crionan 'to lessen']

croggie a ride on a bike's crossbars

'sharing a bike' D'ton C20/2; "a croggie – a ride on a bike's crossbar: 'hey, give us a croggie home'" *RM* Norton C20/mid

crouse, croose cheerful, active

"crowse – brisk lively, jolley: 'as crowse as a new washen louse'" *Ray* 1674 sim, *Kennet* 1690s as Nth; "A cock's ay crouse on his awn midden" *Brockett* Newc & Nth 1846; "canty an' crouse" *Allan's Tyneside Songs* p.464 1860; "crouse – bumptious" *Gibson* C'd 1880; "as cruse as onny" *Northumbrian Words III* C20/mid re Kielder. *EDD* distribution to 1900: Sco, Ire, Nth. [Middle Eng (Nth) crous, compare Fris. krús 'free-growing, jolly']

crow 1. **craa, craw**, 2. **corby**, 3. **dowp**, 4. other

1. "craa" Rothbury C18/2; "black an' tidy as a craw" *Chater* Newc 1881; "craa – crow; 'Ralphy Crow' ('Ralph' pronounced 'raaf')" *JB* Shildon C20/mid; "midden-crow – the carrion crow" *Brockett* Newc & Nth 1829.
2. "corby – the raven. The carrion crow is also called a corby, or corby-crow" *Brockett* Newc & Nth 1829; "corby – a carrion crow" *Bell* MS Newc 1830s. *EDD* distribution to 1900: Sco, Ire, Nth. [Fr corbet]
3. "dowp – a carrion crow" *Bailey* Co.Durham 1810; "doup, dowp – the carrion crow"

crow cont.

Atkinson Cleve 1868. *EDD* distribution to 1900: Nth
4. "black-neb – the carrion crow" *Brockett* Newc & Nth 1829; "midden-crow – the carrion crow" *Brockett* Newc & Nth 1829

crowdy a mash made by pouring boiling water on oats

"crowdie an milk" *Bewick* Tyne 1790s; "grudge for haver-meal (oatmeal) to pay / to make them crowdies once a day" *Bell* Newc p.51 1812; "crowdie – oatmeal and water mixed together and used with milk, butter or the fat from off the pot when beef is boiled, the last is called fat crowdie" *Bell* MS Newc 1815; "crowdy – oatmeal and hot water mixed together: 'The crowdy is wor daily dish'" *Pitman's Pay* G'head 1820s; "crowdy and treacle" *Shields Song Book* (1826); "crowdy – oatmeal porridge, made thick enough to turn out of the basin, like a pudding, when cooled" *Atkinson* Cleve 1868; "crowdy – oatmeal and boiling water stirred together till thick, and then 'supped' with milk, treacle, dripping, or beer sweetened with sugar" *Luckley* Alnwick 1870s; "oatmeal well stirred with boiling water was a 'crowdie'. I am reported to have told my granny, that's what we feed our hens on' the first time I saw it mixed!" *Nth Words* Alnwick re 1880 approx; "crowdy – a sodden mess given to pigs, poultry, etc. the staple is meal stirred up with hot water and mingled with hosuehold scaps" wNewc 1880s; "Crowdy (kraaw:di) – a kind of porridge. (Teaspoonful of oatmeal, in plate of hot water, and half a glassful of milk added, when cold.)" *Palgrave* Hetton 1896; "efter Aa'd getten me claes on and etten me croody..." *Cuddy Cairt* Newc 1917; "oatmeal, peper and salt, a dollop of good dripping, with hot water poured onto it" *Nth Words* N'd, 1938; "save yor wind to cool yor crowdie" (shut up) Ashington C20/mid. *EDD* distribution to 1900: Sco, Ire, Nth. [compare Ice. groutr 'porridge']
See also **brose, skilly**

cuddy 1. short for Cuthbert, 2. donkey, 3. ?horse, 4. small cabin on a coble

1. "Cuddy – an abbreviation of Cuthbert" *Brockett* Newc & Nth 1829; "Cuddy's swine" (pig) *Pitman's Pay* G'head 1820s; "cuddy-duck – eider-duck" Newc 2001 Q
2. "cuddy – an ass, likewise a name given to a

cuddy cont.

weak minded person" *Bell* MS Newc 1815;
"wor Cuddy... 'll bray" *Allan's Tyneside Songs*
p.177 1824 Newc; "the cuddies... gov a terrific
he ha! he ha! he ha!" *Allan's Tyneside Songs*
p.438 C19/mid; "awkward as a cuddy" (clumsy
and obstinate) *Hull* MS wNewc 1880s; "Cuddy
– donkey (always used)" *Palgrave* Hetton 1896;
"Matthew, Mark, Luke and John / Haad the
cuddy while ah get on" *Irwin* Tyne 1970–71;
"the indigenous wild whippet, the horned
cuddy and the winged moggie" *Dobson* Tyne
1970–71. *EDD* distribution to 1900: Nth, Sco,
Ire. NE 2001: in use. *Plus* "neddy – donkey"
D'ton C20/mid
3. "On a cuddy thou's ride to the Toon"
Crawhall Newc 1888; "an ass or small horse"
Irwin Tyne 1970; "cuddy – horse" Wheatley
Hill 2004 Q
4. 'small cabin on a fishing coble' S'm C20/2
per BG; 'cuddy-decked over shelter in the
forepart of a coble... tilt: canvas shelter ofer
the bows of northern cobles' *Hill* Flamborough
1970s. [likely from Du. kaiute, with similar
meaning. (thus *OED*)] *Plus* "dodger, hud, or
sheet, not cuddy... cuddy might be used for a
small locker or the like" *FT* Cullercoats 2003.
See also **dodger, huddock**. For **cuddy-handed**
see **left-handed**

cull 1. a fool, 2. foolish

1. "cull – a Newcastle word for silly or foolish"
Bell MS Newc 1815; 'silly person' Tanfield Lea
1960; 'a stupid fellow' *Graham* Geordie 1979.
EDD distribution to 1900: Sco, N'd, C'd
2. "cull cheps for his worm cake frae far an'
near ride" *Ross* Tyne C19/1 p.11; "all the cull
cuckolds in Sunderland town" *Allan's Tyneside
Songs* p.5 1834. [*OED* suggests as slang term]

cullish foolish

"to refuse them is cullish" *Bell* Newc p.105
1812. *Plus* "consarn... that my Lord should
sae cullishly come by his deeth" *Marshall*
G'head 1806

cundy conduit, covered drain

exx. *Bell* MS Newc 1815, *Brockett* Newc &
Nth 1829, *Luckley* Alnwick 1870s; "doon the
cundy" (where Geordie's penker went) C20/1;
"kundee – small tunnel, drain" *Dodd* MS
Tanfield Lea C20/2; "a sewer" *Graham* Geordie
1979; "a small drivage to ventilate inaccessible
places" (in pit) *Northumbrian III* 1990 re

cundy cont.

Backworth; "cundy – pipe or gully for
draining water" B'p Auck 2001 Q. *EDD*
distribution to 1900: Sco, Nth, Corn.
[AN cunduit 'conduit, pipe']

curran-berry currant

"curran-berries – any kind of currant"
Dinsdale mid-Tees 1849; "curran or corran
barries – garden currants black and red" *Hull*
MS wNewc 1880s. *EDD* distribution to 1900:
corran – N'd; curran – D'm, Yx, Lx, nLincs

currick cairn

" a carrock of stones" *Raine* MS Ronaldskirk
1550; "corrock, currack, or kirock – a large
heap of stones formerly used as a boundary
mark, burial place, or guide for travellers"
Brockett Newc & Nth 1829; "it ed mak a better
guide post ner t' curricks" (re Cleopatra's
Needle) *Egglestone* Weardale 1870s; "currack –
dry stone pillar (landmark on moors)" *JB*
Shildon C20/mid. *EDD* distribution to 1900:
N'd, C'd, D'm

cushat dove, wood pigeon

"to shoot cowshets" *Raine* MS Askham 1672;
"cushat – a wild pigeon" *Kennet* 1690s as Nth;
'the ring dove or wood pigeon'; "cushat was
used for a wood pigeon... also 'woodies'"
JS Easington C20/mid; "cushat – a dove,
ring-dove or wood-pigeon" *Irwin* Tyne 1970;
"cushat – pigeon" South Moor (Stanley) 2003
per BG. *EDD* distribution to 1900: Sco, Nth,
Mids. [OE cusceote]. See also **skemmie**

cushy 1. cow, 2. a call to cows

1. "cushy-cow – a cow" *Brockett* Newc & Nth
1829; "cushie – cow (child's term)" *Dinsdale*
mid-Tees 1849; "cushy – cow, also 'cushy-cow'"
JB Shildon C20/mid; "cushy" D'ton C20/mid,
C20/2; "cushy-cow" *PG* H'pool C20/2, *JS*
Easington C20/mid, B'p Auck 2001 Q. *EDD*
distribution to 1900: Nth
2. "cush-cush – used in calling a cow" *Hull*
MS wNewc 1880s; "Cush – a call to cows at
milking-time" *Palgrave* Hetton 1896. *EDD*
distribution to 1900: Nth, Mids. [ON kus! kus!
'milkmaid's call']

cush, cushty see *excellent*

(short) cut 1. cut, 2. **bolt**, 3. **ginnel**, 4. **snicket**

1. "cut – short cut from road to road, e.g.
between houses" *TC* S'm C20/2; "short cut,

cut cont.

passage" Trimdon 2002 Q; "cut – path between houses from one road to another" cenD'm, eD'm, M'bro 2001 Q. [Celtic cut 'short' – *Hull* MS wNewc 1880s]

2. "bolts – narrow passages... between houses" *Atkinson* Cleve 1868

3. "ginnel – path between houses" Thornley 1940s Q

4. "snicket – back road, short cut" *JS* Ch-le-St

cutty 1. short, 2. a short tobacco pipe

1. "cutty sark" (short petticoat) Burns' poem 1791; "cutty – little, short, a short knife, cutty gun, a short tobacco pipe" *Bell* MS Newc 1830s. *EDD* distribution to 1900: Sco, Ire, Nth, S.W. [Celtic cut 'short']

2. "Aw sat i'the nuik, and my cutty aw smuik" *Street Piracy* Newc 1822; "me feet on the hob an' me cutty full o' twist" *Robson* Newc C20/1; "kuttee – short pipe" *Dodd* MS Tanfield Lea C20/2; "cutty-gun... a short pipe" *Graham* Geordie 1979. *EDD* distribution to 1900: Sco, Ire, N'd

dacker uncertain, unsettled

ex. *Brockett* Newc & Nth 1846. [MDu daeckeren]

dad 1. to beat, 2. a lump, 3. a blow

1. "dad – to shake by striking one thing against another... dad is likewise used when a person is struck...; to 'dad a hat' is to shake the wet off it" *Bell* MS Newc 1815; "I'll dad thy gob" *IA* S'm 1950s,60s; "the clippy mat and the door mat were dadded off the wall... to get the dust out" *JS* Easington C20/mid; "dad your pit claes off the wall" (get dust out of) *TC* S'm C20/2, also cenD'm C20/2 Q; "I'll dad thee lug" *Wade* South Moor 1966. *EDD* distribution to 1900: Sco, N'd, C'd. [*OED* as imitative]
2. "dad... also a lump, a large piece, a thick slice, as of bread or cheese" *Brockett* Newc & Nth 1829; "dads o' duff" (lumps of coal-dust) *Allan's Tyneside Songs* p.379 1849; "Dawd – slice: 'Cut him a dawd o' breed'" *Palgrave* Hetton 1896. *EDD* distribution to 1900: Ire, Nth
3. "dad – a blow, a thump, etc." *Brockett* Newc & Nth 1829; "he gat sic a dud as he'll not forget." *EDD* distribution to 1900: Sco, N'd. 'In N'd the word is now obsolete' *Graham* Geordie 1979

dad, daddy, deddy see **father**

daffle to confuse or be confused

"daffle – to puzzle" *Bell* MS Newc 1815; 'to betray loss of memory and mental faculty' *Brockett* Newc & Nth 1829. *EDD* distribution to 1900: Nth. [ME daff, 'fool' c.1325; ON dauf 'deaf, dull';... or same root as 'daft'?]

daffy to smarten up

"'E thowt he'd daffy th' dog up wirra notha culla" *CT* New Herrington 1930s

daft fond, foolish

"daft – fond, doting" *Kennet* 1690s as Yx; "daft – foolish, stupid, insane" *Bailey* Co.Durham 1810; "daft – foolish" *Bell* MS Newc 1815, "mad, disorderly" *Bell* MS Newc 1830s; "daft on or about (s.thing, s.one)" D'ton 1940s (Q); "daft over a lass" *IA* S'm 1950s,60s. *EDD* distribution to 1900: general. *Plus* "daftlike – embarrassed, having the appearance of folly, approaching to insanity" *Brockett* Newc & Nth 1829. [OE gedæfte 'meek' etc.]

daftie a simpleton

"oh you daftie" (used in an affectionate way if someone is careless) *KH* Stockton C20/2; "daftee – fool" *Dodd* MS Tanfield Lea C20/2; "dafty – a fool: 'ye'll hit somebody, ye dafty'" *Graham* Geordie 1979. *EDD* distribution to 1900: Sco, N'd, Yx

dag, daggy 1. drizzly, 2. to drizzle

1. "dag, daggy, dagging – small rain: "It's a dag", "It's daggy weather", "It's dagging on" *Bell* MS Newc 1815; "daggy – drizzly" *Blenkinsopp* Teesdale 1931; "dag – a drizzling rain" *Brockett* Newc & Nth 1846; "daggy – damp, wet: 'A daggy day'" *Brockett* Newc & Nth 1846. *EDD* distribution to 1900: Sco, N'd, C'd, D'm, EA
2. "15 Apr [1672] mizling, drizling, dagling, small rain" *Raine* MS Askham, "dagg – to drizzle: 'a fine daggling rain'" *Atkinson* Cleve 1868; "it's daggin on" *Heslop* N'd 1890s. *EDD* distribution to 1900: N'd, Yx, Lx, EA. [ON dögg 'dew']

dairns type of fish

ex. *Bell* Newc 1812 p.6; 'small unremarkable fish' (*EDD*)

dale valley

"dale – the distinctive name of the valleys... of Cleveland" *Atkinson* Cleve 1868. [OE dæl, ON dalr] See also **dene**

dame 1. mother, 2. a woman

1. "in credill laide, his dame before" *Cuthbert* C15/mid; "give my service (regards) to your dame" *Chicken* Benwell 1720s; "deame, d'yame or dame – the matron or mistress of the house" *Brockett* Newc & Nth 1829
2. "hold thee still le dame" *Noah's Ark* Newc C15/16; "the snuffy au'd dyem" *Ross* Tyne p.23 C19/1; "dame (pronounced deeam) – one's wife, the mistress of his house; also applied to an aged woman" *Atkinson* Cleve 1868 [OFr dame]

dare

"there was not ane durst come him near" Rothbury C18/2; "folks dorsent say owt tiv him" *Allan's Tyneside Songs* p.423 1862; "They dore just as seun lowp frae the land above the meun" (present tense) *Barrass* Stanley 1890s; "dursent" (dare not) Coxhoe 1916; "dairsent for dare not" *JR* Crook C20/mid; "darsent" *KH* Stockton C20/2; "dawsint – dare not"

dare cont.

Dodd MS Tanfield Lea C20/2; "aa dorna; he dorsent" *Todd* Tyne 1977 [OE durran, a pret-pres. vb]

dark to eavesdrop

"darking – listening obscurely or unseen" *Bailey* Co.Durham 1810; "dark – to listen insidiously, to eavesdrop: 'what are you darking at?'" *Atkinson* Cleve 1868. *EDD* distribution to 1900: Nth

darkening

"darkening – twilight" *Dinsdale* mid-Tees 1849. *EDD* distribution to 1900: Sco, Nth

darrak a day's work

"darg" *Pitman's Pay* G'head 1820s; "He has not had a darroc this three months" *Brockett* 1846 re Durham; "darrak – day's work" *Gibson* C'd 1880. *EDD* distribution to 1900: darg – Sco, Ire, Nth [day plus work] See also **daytal**

dats a rubbish dump

ex. *BL* Blaydon 1950s

davy davy lamp, safety lamp

"said, me Deavy for a new-aw'd had a cowpey (swop)" *Allan's Tyneside Songs* p.148 1827

daw, dow

"daw – to thrive, to recover from an illness" *Brockett* Newc & Nth 1829; "he neither dees nor dows" *Grose* 1787. *EDD* distribution to 1900: Sco, Nth. See also **dow**

the day today

"the day – a N'd and Scottish idiom for 'to-day'" *Brockett* Newc & Nth 1846; "How are ye the day, lad?" *Graham* Geordie 1979

daytal work on a day to day basis

"daytal – by the day: [of] a labourer... or the work done by him: 'on'y a daytal-man'" *Atkinson* Cleve 1868; "daytaleman – a day labourer, chiefly in husbandry... a man whose labour is... reckoned by the day, not by the week or year. Daytalemen, about coal pits, are those who are not employed in working the coal." *Brockett* Newc & Nth 1829; "dattle – miners paid at the 'County Average'" *BL* Winlaton 1950s. *EDD* distribution to 1900: Ire, Nth, eMids. [day plus tale in sense of tally]. See also **darrak**

daza see *excellent*

dazed feeling cold

"I's dazed – I'm very cold" *Ray* 1674; "daized – numb from cold" *Grose* 1787, *Brockett* Newc & Nth 1846. *EDD* distribution to 1900: Sco, Nth. [assumed ON root, since Ice. dasa-sk, to become numb (with cold)]. See also **nithered**

deave to deafen

"wi' lang sangs a'm deave'd" *Allan's Tyneside Songs* p.93 1812; "the timber merchints will ne mair with 'ten a penny' deave us" *Allan's Tyneside Songs* p.237 1829; "deave – to deafen, to stupify with noise, to din" *Brockett* Newc & Nth 1829; "a din fit to deave yan" *Atkinson* Cleve 1868. *EDD* distribution to 1900: general. [OE deafian]

dee, de to do: 1. positive forms, 2. negative forms

1. "while he was deand his office" (doing) *Cuthbert* C15/mid; "What shall I outher dea or say?" (Rothbury, C18/2); "eneough to de"; plus "to dih" *Bewick* Tyne 1790s; "How, smash! Skipper, what mun a' dee?" *Allan's Tyneside Songs* p.27 1805; "aw may drink, aw may fight, or dee owt" *Ross* Tyne p.5 C19/1; "marmaids dein' queer feats" *Allan's Tyneside Songs* p.409 C19/mid; "ta di'ah" *Egglestone* Weardale 1870s; "did te did? wilt te did?" (do it) *Smith* Weardale 1883; "Diz thi fatha still jump on an' off [the trams] like hi diz o' th' buses" *CT* New Herrington 1930s; "mind what ya deein..." Dinnington 1950s Q; "get did away – hurry up" *Northumbrian III* C20/2 re Hazelrigg Colliery; "thordeeincanny" *Dobson* Tyne 1969; "they had four or six gates so that in times of danger the garrison could dee off like" *Dobson* Tyne 1970–71; "worra wuz ganna dee?" *VIZ* 48, 1990s; "what Ah dud heer", "what duddy see?" *Egglestone* Weardale 1870s; "to get it o deughn" (done) *Bewick* Tyne 1790s; "Whiet dyun ower" tired out *Marshall* G'head 1806; "dyeun" (done) Coxhoe 1916; "diun out on't – swindled" *Dunn* B'p Auck 1950

2. "dinna / dinnot – do not" *Blenkinsopp* Teesdale 1931; "dinna sit there leyke steuke" (a stook of hay) plus "aw dinnit leyke te..." *Bewick* Tyne 1790s; "dinna whinge an' whipe" *Allan's Tyneside Songs* p.75 1806; "the loss o' the cotterels aw dinna regard" *Allan's Tyneside Songs* p.50 1812; "dinna be blind" *Allan's Tyneside Songs* p.244 1842; "dinna – do not" *Luckley* Alnwick 1870s extra; "dinna put it on

dee, de cont.

see strang" *Haldane* Newc 1879; "Aa didna bother him aboot it" (did not) Coxhoe 1916; "disna – does not" *Brockett* Newc & Nth 1846; "disn't thou think sham..." *Wearside Tales* 1879, etc. "dinnot – do not" *Dinsdale* mid-Tees 1849; "dinnet say thou winnet, hinney!" *Allan's Tyneside Songs* p.385 1849; "Aw shoor aw dinnot knaw what the lads are gettin' to now" *JS* South Shields C19/mid; "dinnet muaik thawsel se fast" *Armstrong* Tanfield C19/2; "Aw nivor did, nor div Aw noo" *Barrass* Stanley 1890s; "we dinnet want te myak ne brag of worsells" Coxhoe 1916; "dinnot / din't tell me what to dee" *IA* S'm 1950s, 60s; "dinit – do not" *Dodd* MS Tanfield Lea C20/2; "dissent matter where th' tram gans" *CT* New Herrington 1930s, etc. "Hold! doan't go yet" (*Marshall* G'head 1806); "deant" M'bro *MWN* 28 Jan 1860; "daint" (don't) Cleadon Park, South Shields C20/2 Q; "durd do that – don't do that" *MG* Teesdale C20/2; "dee-ant" (don't) *Wood* re Cleveland C20/2. *EDD* distribution to 1900: Nth re pronunciation; esp. divvent – Tyne, dimmut – D'm, C'd, deeant – Yx]. NE 2001: in use [OE (Ang) doen] See also **div**

dee to die

"And ever an ill death may they die" (rhymes with 'be') *RR* Weardale 1569; "I'll love thee till the day I dee" *Chicken* Benwell 1720s; "...that had deed" (died) *Bewick* Tyne 1790s; "if ever these worthies should happen to dee" *Allan's Tyneside Songs* p.239 1829; "he sais he'll dee in Scotland" *Armstrong* Tanfield C19/2; "when he fun oot he was gannin to dee" *Embleton* Tyne 1897. *EDD* distribution to 1900: Nth re pronunciation. [ON deyja]

deed dead

"as deed as a stane" *Marshall* G'head 1806; "I'd roast him deed" *Bell* Newc p.38 1812; "as deed as bacon" *Allan's Tyneside Songs* p.193 1842; "deed folk" (the dead) Embleton, Newc 1897; "fell doon in the street, deed" Coxhoe 1916; "deed-house – mortuary" *Graham* Geordie 1979; "guess whee's deed!" S'm C20/mid. *Plus* "aside the church wher ah the quiet folks ly" *D'm Chron* 28 Apr 1865

deef deaf

"yammering and shouting as kin (as if) yen was deef" *Bewick* Tyne 1790s; "deef – deaf" *Dodd* MS Tanfield Lea C20/2. *EDD* distribution to 1900: N'd, D'm, C'd, Dev, Corn.

deek look at!, see!

ex. *LL* Tyneside 1974. [Romany deek, dick 'look']

deeth death

"deeth" (death) *Bewick* Tyne 1790s; "Deeth cried, 'Jacky, come!'" *Allan's Tyneside Songs* p.235 1829; "the rope o' cawd deith seun'll stop Matty's breeth / on a life crushin' hang-gallas tree" *Allan's Tyneside Songs* p.366 1849; "Deeth follows on mee track" *Allan's Tyneside Songs* p.429 1862; "the darkest deeth" *Barrass* Stanley 1890s; "deethacaad" (East Boldon, 1985). [OE déað]

dele to share out

"to take and dele" *Cuthbert* C15/mid; possibly also in place-names, e.g. Dalton-le-Dale – shared land? *EDD* distribution to 1900: Sco, Nth. [OE daélan]

delve to dig

exx. *Atkinson* Cleve 1868, *Palgrave* Hetton 1896. *EDD* distribution to 1900: general. [OE delfan]

denched queasy

ex. *Blenkinsopp* Teesdale 1931. *EDD* distribution to 1900: densh 'dainty/squeamish' Nth

dene valley

"dene – a dell or deep valley" *Bailey* Co.Durham 1810; "Dene (dae:n) – the picturesque wooded hollows, each traversed by a stream, which line the sea-coast of Durham" *Palgrave* Hetton 1896; "dean, deane, or dene – a dell or deep valley, between two steep hills, with running water at the bottom" *Brockett* Newc & Nth 1829; "the narrow wooded valleys which we called the Denes" *Hitchin* re Seaham p.35 1910s; "all the steep side wooded valleys in the Magnesian Limestone are called denes from Ryhope Dene to Crimdon Dene in the south" *JS* Easington 2003. [OE denu 'valley']

deppity deputy, mine official esp. one in charge of tools, woodworking, and tracks

"deputies – a set of men employed in setting timber for the safety of the workmen; also in putting in brattice and brattice stoppings. They also draw the props from places where they are not required for further use" *Nicholson* 1880; "the deputy overman... wrote reports, rendered first aid, fired the explosive charges, and maintained discipline by example or sheer cussing" *Hitchin* re Seaham p.69 1910s; "deppity – the man in charge of a section of a mine" *Graham* Geordie 1979; "deputy – pit foreman" *JM* Dawdon 1970s; "The deputy was in charge of a working district, and the overman in charge of a number of districts" *Northumbrian III* C20/2 re Shilbottle Colliery. *EDD* distribution to 1900: N'd, D'm

deppity's kist tool chest

"the deputies' kist is used to keep their tools, plate and brattice nails, &c., in" *Nicholson* 1880; "The deputy... assembled his workmen at the kist, to check attendance and delegate work areas. In this chest he kept tools and first-aid equipment." *Northumbrian III* C20/2 re Shilbottle Colliery; "depitee's kist – holds tools and papers" *Dodd* MS Tanfield Lea C20/2; "also for first aid" *GP* Dawdon C20/2; "Box or large wood chest which has lid and locks. Used for keeping any special tools in, also report and time books for all accounts of work in a district of the mine. Always placed at a meeting station where the deputy places workmen to their daily jobs" *McBurnie* Glebe Colliery, C20/mid

des bed 1. folding bed, 2. bench

1. "the top o' the desk-bed where the wife kept all her fancy things" *Wearside Tales* 1879; "des' bed" *Barrass* Stanley 1890s; "dess bed – a large cupboard bed" Spennymoor C20/mid; "desk bed" *Irwin* Tyne 1970. *EDD* distribution to 1900: Sco, Ire, N'd. [AN deis, desse 'high table, dais']
2. "satt doune upon the dese" (dais) *Cuthbert* C15/mid; "deas, deis, deys, or dess – a seat or bench, a throne. In N'd it is now only applied to a seat made of stone and covered with green turf, at cottage doors." *Brockett* Newc & Nth 1846; "dess – a layer or course in any pile...; the entire pile, e.g. a haystack, or 'a dess of stones' *Atkinson* Cleve 1868; "deas – an old-fashioned wooden settle or sofa, which could be turned into a table, bed, or seat"

the **devil** 1. **De'il**, 2. **Scrat**, 3. **Cloutie**, 4. **Old Nick**, 5. **the Bad Man**, 6. **Old Horney**

1. "Mächil is hanged, / And brened iz hiz buks.... The dïl haz 'im fanged / In his krvked klvks." re Michael Scot, in Alexander Gil 1621; "De'il rive their sark gangs hame to night" *Chicken* Benwell 1720s; "he sits in his keel as black as the deil" *Allan's Tyneside Songs* p.4 1812; "When you ha' to do with the Deil, mind his horns" *Bell* MS Newc 1830s; "he's a limb of the deevil" *Allan's Tyneside Songs* p.309 1862; "the blue divels" *Allan's Tyneside Songs* p.408 1862; "Deel tyek ye!" *Graham* Geordie 1979. [OE deofol]
2. "Scrat, Aud Scrat – the Devil, the Evil One" *Atkinson* Cleve 1868". ON skratte (goblin) for 'Old Scratch' (re his claws)
3. "Clootie – an old name for the Devil, derived from the clute, the half of the hoof of any cloven-footed animal" *Pitman's Pay* G'head 1820s; "Clootie's gang" *Allan's Tyneside Songs* p.269 1843 (T. Wilson). *EDD* distribution to 1900: Clootie – Sco. N'd, NW. [?compare claut 'to claw']
4. "Auld Nick, Old Bendy, Aud Hooky, Old Scratch" *Geeson* N'd/D'm '1969'. [*Geeson* N'd/D'm '1969' offers OE nicor (water monster), Gm Nickel (goblin), and Nicholas as sources]
5. "the nasty Bad Man" *Allan's Tyneside Songs* p.312 1827; "the Bad Man" *Hull* MS wNewc 1880s
6. "awd Horney" *Allan's Tyneside Songs* p.303 1848

devil technical mining term

"what wi' deevils, bulls, an' cows" *Barrass* Stanley 1890s; "devil – a device for detaching the rope from a set of tubs whilst in motion" Wade *South Moor* C20/mid

dhan float for line of lobster pots, etc.

"A long line could contain some six pieces joined together; there would be a dhan-end or buoy at each end, and next to that a 'watcher' made of corks where the long line dipped." *JH* Sm re 1930s; ex. *FT* Cullercoats 2003

dickers to dare s.one

"Aa'll dickers ye te dee it" att. *GP* S'm C20/mid. *EDD* distribution to 1900: eD'm

dickies head lice

ex. *CT* New Herrington, C20/mid

diddums pre-talk to suit an infant

"diddums-wassums", "diddums-doddums-wassums" *MB* Coxhoe C20/mid

dight to prepare, dress

"she dighted her father's bloody wounds" Reed *Border Ballads* C16; "the dightynge of the house" *Raine* MS Newcastle 1593; "Item paid to iiij laboreres for dightinge the hill agaynst the playes" *Anderson* Newc C16; "dight – to dress, to clean" *Bailey* Co.Durham 1810. *EDD* distribution to 1900: general. [OE dihtan 'to compose, appoint'] *Plus* "keel dighter – a woman who scrape[s] or clean[s] out the floor of the keels, and get what small coals may have been left after the delivery of the keel" *Bell* MS Newc 1815

dike see **dyke**

dill to soothe

"the paralisy first dilde..." (benumbed?) *Cuthbert* C15/mid; "dill – to soothe pain, to still or calm, to dull" *Brockett* Newc & Nth 1829; 'to allay pain' *Dinsdale* mid-Tees 1849; 'to soothe' *Atkinson* Cleve 1868. *EDD* distribution to 1900: Sco, Nth, part Mids [ON dilla 'to lull']

ding to push or strike

"he manast [menaced] him to dyng" (beat) *Cuthbert* C15/mid; "none shall ding down ackornes of the trees" *Raine* MS Ilkley, 1552; "Ise ding him, I shall beat him" *Grose* 1787 as Nth; "ding-down – to throw down, used in Durham and Northumberland" *Bell* MS Newc 1815; "ding – also to dr[ive] in, as to ding in nails, etc." *Bell* MS Newc 1830s; "at last a great thrust dang him ower" *Allan's Tyneside Songs* p.147 1816; "The ducks dang o'er my Daddy" *Bell-Harker* Newc C19/1; "They dung doon the peep show" *Luckley* Alnwick 1870s extra; "when the blast dings frae the North" *Northumbrian III* C20/mid re Kielder; "ding you on the heed" Birtley 2003 per BG. *EDD* distribution to 1900: general. [?ON – compare Ice. dengja 'to hammer'; but also Romany ding 'to throw']

dinnot see **dee** (do)

dint to dent

"the tin was dinted" *IA* S'm 1950s,60s

dippy spoiled (of birds' eggs) i.e. too aged to blow out

ex. *JS* Easington re 1950s, GP S'm C20/mid. *Plus* "gollied – a bird's egg which could not be blown" *Wood* M/bro C20/2

dirdum see **durdum**

dirl to drill or twirl

"dirl – to vibrate: 'dirls my lug like wor smith's hammer'" *Pitman's Pay* G'head 1820s; "dirl – to move round quickly" *Brockett* Newc & Nth 1829. *EDD* distribution to 1900: Sco, Nth. [from drill?] See also **thirl**

dither to tremble

"her body quaking & dithering" *Raine* MS Bolling 1649/50; "to didder – to quiver with cold" *Ray* 1674. *Plus* "dithery docks – moorland grass with trembling seed head' D'ton 1940s Q, 'a particular species of grass with quaking seeds'. *PG* H'pool C20/2 See also **dother**

div, divvent 1. do, 2. do not

1. "div – often used for 'do" I div – I do; I div na, I do not" *Jamieson Scots Dictionary* 1808; "div – for do. Very common among the vulgar" *Brockett* Newc & Nth 1829; "div – to do: 'what div I knaw?'" *Luckley* Alnwick 1870s extra; "Aye, div Aa" *Haldane* Newc 1879; "div aa knaa him?" *Graham* Geordie 1979

2. "divent laugh at poor folks" *Bell* Newc p.89 1812 re 1811; "div'nt ye mak' sic a rout" beside "if ye din't knaw" *Allan's Tyneside Songs* p.47,48 1812; "divent – 'divent dive that' i.e. do not do that" *Bell* MS Newc 1815; "divvent say nowt" *Allan's Tyneside Songs* p.511 C19/mid; "divn't ye knaw..." *Wearside Tales* 1879; "divint get excited" Shield Row C20/1 Q; "Aa still divvent knaa" *Hay* Ushaw Moor C20/1; "A divvent knaw warrit means" *CT* New Herrington 1930s; "divvent bubble (cry) hinny" Dinnington 1950s Q; "divvent – do not, don't" *Dodd* MS Tanfield Lea C20/2; "divvent ride the ponies" *JM* Dawdon 1970s; "A divvent feel ower clivver" East Boldon 1985; "divvent fash yersel" S'd. 2001 Q; "divvent" South Moor (Stanley) 2003 per BG; exx. G'head, Blyth, NShields, Lanchester 2001 Q. *EDD* distribution to 1900: Tyne [Forms like 'div' are common in George MacDonald's novel *Castle Warlock*, apparently representing the sort of dialect he encountered as a youth in Aberdeen and area in 1830s. An

div cont.

earlier ex. is Scott's poem 'O Mortality' stanza 37 ("Div I ken...?") - the *Scottish National Dictionary* comments 'The /v/ is due to analogy with /hiv/, emphatic form of /hae/, have.' This intrusive /v/ is an occasional feature of North East English, but divvent may well be a Scottish import to Tyneside. "I find the dialect of Newcastle different from South Shields for instance they say divvint whereas we say dean't" *GA* S.Shields 1950s] See also **de** (do)

dobbie ghost or spirit

"dobby or dobbie – a spirit or demon" *Brockett* Newc & Nth 1829; "dobby – ghost or spirit" *Dinsdale* mid-Tees 1849; 'prankster or boggle' *Brockie* D'm 1886. *EDD* distribution to 1900: Nth. [form of name, 'Robin']

docken the dock plant

"a supposed witch struck a man on the neck with a docken stalke" *Raine* MS Rothwell 1654/55; "docken – the plant called the dock" *Bell* MS Newc 1815; "his (the dog's) lugs like twe dockins hung ower his jaws" *Allan's Tyneside Songs* p.141 1816; "amang these green dockins" *Allan's Tyneside Songs* p.334 C19/1. *EDD* distribution to 1900: general. NE 2001: in low use. [OE doccan (pl.)]

Dode George

"Dody – a corruption or diminutive of George" *Brockett* Newc & Nth 1829; "wor Dode'll bring maw picks te bank" *Chater* Newc p.6 1885; "aud Doad" *Barrass* Stanley 1890s; "Dohd – George" *Dodd* MS Tanfield Lea C20/2

dodger forward canvas 'cabin' on a coble

"There was not a lot of water in the coble when we transferred to the lifeboat as it had been deflected by our 'dodger.'" Seaham 1962. See also **cuddy, huddock**

doggins affectionate term for (any) dog

ex. S'm via BG 2001

doll to hit

"They've a chance to doll you" (bus conductor warning re drunks) *AM* South Shields C20/2

doll a clay stopper

"[Meanwhile] I had been rolling clay into cylindrical shapes about the diameter of the hole. These clay dolls were rammed tightly into the hole so as to throw the force of the

doll cont.

explosion inwards." *Hitchin* re Seaham p.101 1920s

dolly-muck small coal

"dolly-muck – small coal or coal-dust, used for banking up a fire" Wheatley Hill 2004. *Plus* "Dolly-wash – coal-dust in beck" Wheatley Hill 2004 Q

dook, jook to duck

"jouk – to stoop down to avoid a blow: 'jouken down'" *Pitman's Pay* G'head 1820s; "douk – to bow down; to dive or plunge under water" *Atkinson* Cleve 1868; "dookin – drenched" *Dodd* MS Tanfield Lea C20/2; "dook yor heed" *Graham* Geordie 1979. *EDD* distribution to 1900: dook – Sco, Nth, Mids; jouk – Sco, Ire, Nth, USA. [possible OE *ducan; compare Swed dyka] *Plus* "have ye had a dook yet?" (a bathe) *Graham* Geordie 1979

doon dejected

ex. *Dodd* MS Tanfield Lea C20/2

doon-bye down there, over there

"doon-by – down somewhere" *Dodd* MS Tanfield Lea C20/2; "Aa's gaan doon-bye" *Graham* Geordie 1979

doot, doubt think, suspect

"dowtyne to dye intestate" *Raine* MS Hull 1487; "wor life sure is ne joke, whativvor we may doot" *Haldane* Newc 1879; 'the equivalent to 'think'" *Palgrave* Hetton 1896; "Aa doot aa cannot" *NDN* 31 May 1919; "Aa doubt you're not going to rear that one, Maggie" (of a sickly child) *MR* S'm 1920s; "clear dividing line between me and my mother – we live in the same house and she'd use it naturally, but I wouldn't dream of it – it confuses me!" *PG* H'pool C20/2. *EDD* distribution to 1900: general. [AN duter, doubter 'to fear, suspect, surmise, think that']. *Plus* "ye mevvies misdoot me" *Graham* Geordie 1979

dother, dodder, etc. shaky

"dather – to quake or shake with cold: 'my teeth dather in my heed'" *Kennet* 1690s as Yx; "dother – to shake" *Bell* MS Newc 1815; "dodder, or dother – to shake, to totter, to tremble" *Brockett* Newc & Nth 1829; "dother – shiver or tremble: 'I'm dothering' on a very cold day" *RV* Winlaton C20/2.

dother cont.

EDD distribution to 1900: dother – gen.; dodder – Sco, Nth, S.W.; dather – C'd, Yx
See also **dither**

dothery shakey

"excuse bad writ'n' fer mi hand's dodthery" *Egglestone* Weardale 1870s; "Dothery (daudh:uri) – shaky, failing; of old age" *Palgrave* Hetton 1896; "as shivvery as a dothery duck" (grass) Coxhoe 1916; "dothoree – shakey" *Dodd* MS Tanfield Lea C20/2. See also **dither**

dottle a remnant, a lump

"a dottle, a bit left ower from glass-making, like a paperweight, used as a marker in hitchy-dabber" *TC* S'm C20/2; "dottle – the remain of a pipe of tobacco put upon the top of a fresh pipe for the purpose of lighting it" *Brockett* Newc & Nth 1846; "dottle – hot ash (from a cigarette)" *Dobson* Tyne 1969; "divvent drop yer dottle on me best proggy mat" *Irwin* Tyne 1970; "the tobacco left at the bottom of a pipe after smoking" *Graham* Geordie 1979, var. dozzle. *OED* as Scots word. [?from rare OE dot 'clump']

douce polite, etc.

"they ne'er saw nyen sae douce yet" *Marshall* Newc p.16 1823; "douce – respectable" *Gibson* C'd 1880. *EDD* distribution to 1900: Sco, Ire, Nth. [AN duz 'sweet, gentle', Fr douce]

dover ower nod off to sleep

"dover – to slumber, to be in a state between sleeping and waking" *Brockett* Newc & Nth 1846; "he'd dovered ower to sleep" *Embleton* Tyne 1897, sim. *GP* S'm C20/2. *EDD* distribution to 1900: Sco, N'd. [OE dofun 'dotage', ON dofna]

dowly dismal, melancholy

"dowly – melancholy" *Kennet* 1690s as Nth; "dowly thowts are mair wor friends than foes" *Allan's Tyneside Songs* p.192 1824; "dowly – lonely, dismal, melancholy, sorrowful, doleful: 'A dowly place', 'A dowly lot'" *Brockett* Newc & Nth 1829; "my bairn's a canny bairn, and never looks dowley" *Allan's Tyneside Songs* p.118 re Co.D'm, 1830s; "dowly – of persons: heavy with sorrow or anxiety; of things: lonely, melancholy; of weather: dull, gloomy: 'he's as dowly as deeath'" *Atkinson* Cleve 1868; "On a pay Friday neet, one reel dowly

dowly cont.

Decembor, / Reel dowly, for wages wor awefully law..." *Barrass* Stanley 1890s; "Chorch is se dowly" (dull) *Palgrave* Hetton 1896; "We said it (the Blast Beach) was 'dowelly' – lonely and threatening" *Hitchin* re Seaham p.30 1910s; "to be dowly – to be lonely" Spennymoor C20/mid; "dowly – out of sorts, depressed" *Wood* re Cleveland C20/2; "dowlee – dark or dismal" *Dodd* MS Tanfield Lea C20/2. *EDD* distribution to 1900: Sco, Nth. [?OE dol... compare dull; ON daufligr; Irish doiligh].

downcast shaft (in a pit)

"downcast shaft – the shaft by which the air enters a coal pit, by which the men descend to their work, and by which the coals are drawn up" *Brockett* Newc & Nth, 1846. See also **upcast**

dowp bottom, posterior

"hardly flig'd ower the doup" (of a near-fledged bird) *Allan's Tyneside Songs* p.49 1812; "his drawers on his doup luik'd se canny" *Allan's Tyneside Songs* p.334 C19/1; "doup, dowp – [buttock]: 'As fine as F**ty-Poke's wife, who dressed her doup with primroses' – Newc." *Brockett* Newc & Nth 1829; "thy canny dowp is fat and round" (to a baby) *Allan's Tyneside Songs* p.341 1842; "doup – the buttocks or posteriors: 'look thee! there'a a gret fat doup!'" *Atkinson* Cleve 1868; "clout y' dowp" (smack your bottom) *TP* G'head C20/2. *EDD* distribution to 1900: Sco, Nth. [ON dawp ?of rounded shape]. *Plus* "the varry dowpie [baby] on my lap / can tell his A B C" *Allan's Tyneside Songs* p.380 1849. See also **crow**

dozzen'd numbed

"dozened – spiritless, impotent, withered, benumbed – in a daze" *Brockett* Newc & Nth 1829; "dozzen'd, dozen'd, dozand – wrinkled or withered (of people, fruits, etc)" *Atkinson* Cleve 1868; "dozzint – dozy, stupid" *Dodd* MS Tanfield Lea C20/2. *EDD* distribution to 1900: Sco, Nth. [?ON dúsa 'to doze']

draft side-runner on keel of coble

"draft (draught)" *Hill* Flamborough 1970s; 'pronouned drawt, Seahouses' per BG 2003. *Plus* "Scorbles than drafts" Amble per BG 2003

drag, dreg improvised brake

"...te grape for the dregs when Aw com' tiv a hitch" *Barrass* Stanley 1890s; "I could stop a moving tub by spoking its wheels with a 'dreg'" *Hitchin* re Seaham p.70 1910s; sim. *GP* S'm 1950s, *Dodd* MS Tanfield Lea C20/2, "drag – metal or wooden rod used to slow a tub down by thrusting it between the spokes" *JM* Dawdon 1970s. *EDD* distribution to 1900: N'd, D'm, Yx. [OE dragan 'to draw', perhaps influenced by ON as in Swed dragg 'grapnel']

dragonfly 1. **fleeing ether**, 2. **fleeing ask**, 3. **tenging-ether**, etc., 4. **bull-stang**, etc.

1. "fleeing-eather – the large dragon fly" *Brockett* Newc & Nth 1829; "fleeing-aither, fleeing-eather or ether – the dragon-fly" *Atkinson* Cleve 1868
2. "fleeing-ask, fleeing-esk – the dragon-fly" *Atkinson* Cleve 1868
3. "tenging-ether – large dragonfly" *Dinsdale* mid-Tees 1849; "tanging-nadder – the large dragon-fly" *Brockett* Newc & Nth 1829; "stangin'-ether" *Brockie* D'm 1886
4. "bull-stang – the dragon-fly" *Atkinson* Cleve 1868; "bull-stang – a dragonfly (C'd)" *Grose* 1787; "bull-ether" wNewc 1880s

drawk, drark, drouk to soak, drench

"drawk – to saturate with water" *Bailey* Co.Durham 1810; "drouck – to drench" *Atkinson* Cleve 1868; "A've gotten drawked throu" (soaked) *Palgrave* Hetton 1896; "getten hisel weel drooked wi' rain" *Cuddy Cairt* Newc 1917; "drarked" *CT* New Herrington 1930s, *JS* Easington C20/mid; "drawked" S'd, Upper Teesdale 2001 Q. *EDD* distribution to 1900: Sco, Ire, N'd, D'm, C'd. [ON drekkja 'to drench']

dree long and dreary

"dree – long, tedious" *Ray* 1674; "dree-rood – a long and weary road" *Bailey* Co.Durham 1810; "dree - lonely, wearisome" *Dinsdale* mid-Tees 1849; "dree – long and dreary" *Gibson* C'd 1880. [ON drjúgr 'long-lasting', OE dréogan (vb)]

dreich gloomy etc.

"it's a dreich night" (very dull, gloomy, wet) Morpeth C20/2 Q; "dreak – cold; guy dreak – very cold" Dawdon 2001 Q. [same as **dree**]

drift connecting passage in a mine

"Drift is a passage... cut out under the Earth betwixt Shaft and Shaft, or Turn and Turn, or a passage or way wrought under the Earth to the end of a Meer (29 yards) of Ground or part of a Meer" Derbyshire, 1681; "Oh! marrow, oh! marrow, where has thou been? / Driving the drift from the low seam" 'Collier's Rant' C18/2; "drift – horizontal entrance to mine" *JB* Shildon C20/mid; 'tunnel through stone to link faces' *Douglas* D'm 1973. *EDD* distribution to 1900: NE, Derbys, Corn. [OE drifan 'to drive']

drive to excavate, etc.

"drive – to excavate; to carry forward, as driving a drift, &c." *Nicholson* 1880; "drave" (pret.) Dinsdale midTees 1849; "drov" (pret) *GP* S'm 1950s. [OE drífan 'to drive']

driver (in pit context)

"driver – a boy who has charge of a horse in the pit" *Pitman's Pay* G'head 1820s

drook see **drawk**

droonded drowned

ex. *Wearside Tales* 1879; "he droonded he' sell" *Graham* Geordie 1979; "drooned-oot" (of a colliery that has been flooded) *Graham* Geordie 1979

drouth/y thirst(y)

"Their drouth was sae surprizen" *Oiling* G'head 1826; "I'm really drouthy" Morpeth C20/2 Q; "droothee – thirsty" *Dodd* MS Tanfield Lea C20/2. *EDD* distribution to 1900: general. [OE drugað is root of both drought and drouth]

drumly, drubby muddy

"drumly – muddy" *Bell* MS Newc 1815; "drumly, drummely – muddy, thick; as applied to the mind, confused" *Brockett* Newc & Nth 1829; "druvy – muddy" *Robson* Tyne 1849; "drubby: "yon dark and drubby river" *Pitman's Pay* G'head 1820s; "drumly – muddy, turbid: 'aw cuddint drink't, it was sae drumly'" *Luckley* Alnwick 1870s extra. *EDD* distribution to 1900: drumly/drubly – Sco, Nth. [?OE droflic 'turbid, disturbed'] *drunk* 1. **drucken**, 2. **palatic**, 3. **mortal**, 4. (other)

1. "iv some drucken spree" *Oliver* Newc p.7 1824; "drucken – drunk" *Dinsdale* mid-Tees 1849, Tanfield Lea 1960, Stanley 2002 Q. [ON drukken]

2. "politic" (stress on second syllable) *AK* Newc 1950s; "palatic" nwD'm C20/mid Q; "pallatik – very drunk" *Dodd* MS Tanfield Lea C20/2, sim. *Dobson* Tyne 1969, S'd 2001, Blyth 2002 Q. [for paralytic]

3. "poor Fanny gat mortal wiv tyestin' [brandy]" *Allan's Tyneside Songs* p.367 1849; "An incident which amused my father in the 1940s occurred when a drunken woman subsided into his lap on the bus with remark 'Ee dear, Aa's mortal.'" *AK* Newc 1940s; "Bob went one neet an' gat mortil drunk" *Armstrong* Tanfield C19/2; "mortal" G'head C20/2 Q. *Plus* "mawtallee-us – very drunk" *Dodd* MS Tanfield Lea C20/2; "mortalious" *Graham* Geordie 1979 re 1898, Ch-le-St 2004 Q

4. "the said Anne was foxed, meanyng... that she was dronk" *Raine* MS York 1616; "you pist fool" *Bell* Newc p.45 1812; "in a state of indescribability" *Bell* Newc p.64 1812; "muzzy – half stupid with drink" *Pitman's Pay* G'head 1820s; "ower wet" *Allan's Tyneside Songs* p.252 1829; "nazzy – drunk, intoxicated" *Atkinson* Cleve 1868; "drunk as a mungkee..." *Dodd* MS Tanfield Lea C20/2; "blinnd drungk " *Dodd* MS Tanfield Lea C20/2; "blaked" Hartlepool 2003 via *Wood;* "blaked meaning inebriated 'ahm ganna get blaked the neyt'" *TH* Wheatley Hill/Peterlee 2002; "mullered – drunk" plus "mortal – very drunk" *Charver* 2000–2002; "flanged – drunk" S'd 2001 Q.

druvy see **drumly**

dub a pool

"whare gat she the wee fishie?... in a dub before the door" Reed *Border Ballads* C16; "the devill & he danced in a dub together" *Raine* MS Lumley 1624; "dub – a pool" *Bailey* Co.Durham 1810; "dub – a small pool of water; a piece of deep and smooth water in a rapid river" *Brockett* Newc & Nth 1829. *EDD* distribution to 1900: Nth. [ON djúp]

ducket pigeon loft

"see the skemmies tiv his duckit flee" *MC* Tyne May 1881; "pigeon-ducket" (carillon of Newc Civic Centre) *Dobson* Tyne 1970; "duccot, pigeon-duccot" (dovecot) *Graham*

ducket cont.

Geordie 1979; "duckat – pigeon loft, but cree is a shed, e.g. hen cree" South Moor (Stanley) 2003 per BG. [dove-cot]. See also **cree**

duds clothes

"duds – clothes of a dirty or inferior kind" *Brockett* Newc & Nth 1829; "fresh herring... hanging out to dry, among the newly-washed 'duds' which bellied out in the wind" *The Maister* re Shields p.34 1800–1840; "dudds for old tattered cloaths" *Bell* MS Newc 1830s; "new duds" *Allan's Tyneside Songs* p.485 1862; "duds – pit clothes" *Dodd* MS Tanfield Lea C20/2; 'working clothes' *Graham* Geordie 1979, South Moor (Stanley) 2003 per BG; "duds – 'boxer shorts'" *GD* S'm 2002. *EDD* distribution to 1900: general. [ME dudde 'a garment'; ON duði; 'dudes' for clothes appear in a late 16th century vocabulary of thieves' slang, along with several Romany words, originating from Kent – see *Fox* p.96...] *Plus* "fling off their black duddies" *Allan's Tyneside Songs* p.70 1805; "Ere he puts off his duddin for bed, man" *Street Piracy* Newc 1822

duff fine coal

"Duff (doof) – fine coal, or coal dust (the only name in use)" *Palgrave* Hetton 1896; "duft – small coal" *Dodd* MS Tanfield Lea C20/2. *EDD* distribution to 1900: Sco, Nth. *Plus* "Duffy – trashy, cheap and nasty (e.g. of sugar)" *Palgrave* Hetton 1896

dummickin

'running the gauntlet, in a circle' *GP* S'm 1940s

dunch, dunsh to bump, jog, collide

"dunsh or dunch – to push or jog with the elbow" *Brockett* Newc & Nth 1829; "Divvent dunsh's th' cans fulla scadden het watta" *CT* New Herrington 1930s; "dunched" (crashed) *JP* S'm C20/2; "dunch – to run into with force, as, the tubs dunched" *Wade* South Moor 1966; "dunsh 'im – tackle your opponent" *Dobson* Tyne 1969; "dunch – crash into" *LL* Tyneside 1974; "somebody dunched his airm" (knocked against) *Graham* Geordie 1979; "givowerdunshin" East Boldon 1985. *EDD* distribution to 1900: Sco, Ire, Nth, wMids, EA. NE 2001: in use [modern cognates in Icelandic, Swedish, Danish, suggest an ON root. The OE equivalent is dencgan 'to strike']

durdum, dirdum uproarious activity

"dirdum – noise, confusion" *Pitman's Pay* G'head 1820s; "such a durdum on his nose the little monkeys led" *Stobbs* Woodhorn, C19/mid; "dordum, durdum, dirdim – uproar and confusion: 'the street's iv a durdum'" *Atkinson* Cleve 1868. *EDD* distribution to 1900: Sco, Nth. [?Gaelic diardan 'bad temper']

dut hat

"bowler hat" *JO* re High Thornley/Rowlands Gill, *Nth Words* 1930s–1940s, *HP* South Gosforth C20/mid, N.Shields C20/mid Q, *Dodd* MS Tanfield Lea C20/2, *Graham* Geordie 1979; "duts off fer the Queen" *Dobson* Tyne 1969; "dutt – bowler cap or best cap, but not flat cap" South Moor (Stanley) 2003 per BG; "dut – woolly cap" *PG* H'pool 1998; 'small woolly hat' Tyne 2001 Q; "with my white tracksuit on and my dut" (seaham.com website 2002)

dwalm faintness

"dwalm – a sudden feeling of faintness, a suddent fit of illness." *Viereck* re Gateshead 1966; 'a swoon' *Brockett* Newc & Nth 1846. *EDD* distribution to 1900: Sco, Ire, Nth, S.W. [OE dwolma 'confusion', Du dwelm 'giddi-ness'] *Plus* "Bet turned dwamy, like to fall" *Allan's Tyneside Songs* p.386 1849; "Dwarmy (dwaa:mi) – faint, languid" *Palgrave* Hetton 1896; "dwalmish – likely to swoon" *Atkinson* Cleve 1868

dwine, dwiny diminish, fade away

"dwine – to pine, to be in a decline or consumption, to waste away" *Brockett* Newc & Nth 1846; "dwine – to pine away" *Atkinson* Cleve 1868. *EDD* distribution to 1900: gener-al. [OE dwínan, ON dvína] *Plus* "men are se dwiney nooadays" *Allan's Tyneside Songs* p.243 1829; "dwiny-twiny – tiny" Embleton, Newc 1897

dyke 1. wall, hedge, etc., 2. ditch, 3. break in strata

1. "behint yon auld fail dyke" *Reed Border Ballads* C16; "a dike – a dry hedge" *Kennet* 1690s as C'd "dike – an earthen fence" *Bell* MS Newc 1830s; "When I was young and lusty / I could loup a dyke" *Allan's Tyneside Songs* p.10 1834; "dike – a hedge, fence" *Dinsdale* mid-Tees 1849; 'a bank or long

dyke cont.

earthen mound; a rude stone wall on a dike-bank-top' *Atkinson* Cleve 1868; "a gert hee dyke" (wall) *Egglestone* Weardale 1870s; "Dyke – a hedge. This word is never used to mean a ditch" *Palgrave* Hetton 1896; "thick as snaa on a dike's back" GP S'm 1950s; "dry-dike – a stone wall built without lime" *Graham* Geordie 1979; 'hedge' Teesdale 2001 Q, Wheatley Hill 2004 Q; 'wall' Upper Weardale, Upper Teesdale 2001 Q. *EDD* distribution to 1900: as hedge/fence – D'm, C'd; as wall – Sco, N'd,Yx. [OE dic could be source of both ditch and dyke, meanings linked by the common element of digging. Compare also OFris dík and Middle Dudijc 'dam'] *Plus* "dyke stowers – hedge stakes" *Bell* MS Newc 1815; "diker – a hedger or ditcher" *Brockett* Newc & Nth 1846; "dike-loupers – transgressors" *Brockett* Newc & Nth 1846; "dike-lowper" (trespasser) *GP* S'm 1950s; "gan ti th' dyke" (take a pee), "diker – an unofficial break" *GP* S'm 1950s 2. "For he that bears his head so high, He oft-times falls into the dyke" *RR* Weardale 1569; "a dike – Any little pond or watering place" *Kennet* 1690s as Yorks; "three i' the dyke and two i' the lonnin" 'Pelton Lonnin' C19/1; "dike – a ditch or channel for carrying off water; a pool" *Atkinson* Cleve 1868; 'both hedge and ditch' *Graham* Geordie 1979; "dyke – hedge-side ditch" Wheatley Hill 2002 Q 3. re pit: "the fire returned back to the dyke and went out" *Errington* p.39 Felling/Heworth re 1790s

earwig 1. **forkytail**, 2. **twitchbell**, 3. other

1. exx. *Graham* Geordie 1979, N'd 1995 (rural/children), G'head C20/2 Q. *EDD* distribution to 1900: Sco, Nth. *Plus* "forkin-robbin – an earwig" *Brockett* Newc & Nth 1829, *Atkinson* Cleve 1868
2. "twitch-bell – the earwig" *Brockett* Newc & Nth 1829, *Atkinson* Cleve 1868, *Palgrave* Hetton 1896, S'd C20/mid Q; "twitchy-bell" eD'm 2001 Q, Stanley, S.Hylton, Wheatley Hill 2002 Q. NE 2001: in use. [?wriggly belly; compare also twitch 'couch-grass', and OE *twicele 'forked']
3. "cat-with-two-tails" Ray, Nth, 1737; "eariewig" *Wood* Tees 2002

eathor see **dragonfly**

ee, een

1. eye (sg): "Lo, lo, fast I sweat / It trickles all o'ur myn ee" *Noah's Ark* Newc C15/16; "the white of Johnny's ee" Bell Newc p.6 1812; "the pride o' maw e'e" *Allan's Tyneside Songs* p.465 1860; "eye (pronounced ee, plural een or eyen) – eye" *Atkinson* Cleve 1868. *Plus* "the ogle of the unfortunate monkey" *Allan's Tyneside Songs* p.420 1862
2. eyes (pl): "baith her eyne" Rothbury C18/2; "Deil stop out thy een!" *Collier's Rant* Newc C18/2; "Sae bonny blue her een" Bell MS Newc 1830s; "when yan gans away inted world yan gits yan's een op'n'd" *Egglestone* Weardale 1870s; "Een (ae:n) – eyes: 'Aa'll put thee een oot!' – only used in this single expression, and that by old people" *Palgrave* Hetton 1896; "een – eyes" Tanfield Lea 1960. *EDD* distribution to 1900: Sco, Nth. [OE eagan, ME eyen] *Plus* "wi mee eyes shut" *Allan's Tyneside Songs* p.408 1862, "ies" (plural) *Barrass* nDm 1893

eer see **year**

eftor after

"eftir" *Anderson* Newcastle 1460; "eftor" *Armstrong* Tanfield C19/2; "efter – after" *Atkinson* Cleve 1868; "eftor" Coxhoe 1916, Tanfield Lea 1960. [OE æftor]

eggtaggle a waste of time

ex. GP S'm 1990s. *EDD* distribution to 1900: Sco.

elby elbow

exx. N.Shields C20/mid Q, Wheatley Hill 2004 Q

eld-father, eld-mother grandparents

"thou haiest a witch to thy eldmother" *Raine* MS Blaydon 1586; "eld-father – grandfather" *Kennet* 1690s as D'm. *EDD* distribution to 1900: Sco... obsolete. [OE eald- 'ancestral']

eldin fuel

"& other eldinge & feuell" *Raine* MS ?York 1647/48; "eldin, elding – fuel; such as turf, peat, or wood" *Brockett* Newc & Nth 1829; "fire-eldin – fuel generally" *Atkinson* Cleve 1868. *EDD* distribution to 1900: Sco, Nth. [ON elding]

eliven 11

"eliven" *Dinsdale* mid-Tees 1849; "elivon" *Armstrong* Tanfield C19/2

eller, aller the alder tree or elder bush

"aller bushes" *Raine* MS Rothbury 1607; "eller – the alder tree" *Brockett* Newc & Nth 1829. *EDD* distribution to 1900: general. [OE alor 'alder', ellærn 'elder']

elsin awl

"elsin – an awl" *Bailey* Co.Durham 1810; "elshin – a crooked awl used by shoemakers" *Luckley* Alnwick 1870s extra. *EDD* distribution to 1900: Sco, Ire, Nth. [MDu elssene]

endlang lengthways, along

"all the coaste grounds endelange the Border" *Raine* MS 1548; "endlang – lengthways" *Brockett* Newc & Nth 1846; "endlang – along or forwards in the direction... of the length of an object or person; from head to tail" *Atkinson* Cleve 1868. *EDD* distribution to 1900: Sco, Nth, Mids. [OE andlang]

endways with narrow side foremost

"gan endways" *Brockett* Newc & Nth 1846. *EDD* distribution to 1900: Sco, Nth

eneugh enough

"weel eneugh" *Bewick* Tyne 1790s; "eneugh" *Armstrong* Tanfield C19/2. [OE genog] *Plus* "enow – for the present" *Atkinson* Cleve 1868

ennanters in case...

"ennanters – in case of" *Bailey* Co.Durham 1810, 'lest, in case' *Brockett* Newc & Nth 1829; "ananters – in the event of" *Dinsdale* mid-Tees 1849. *Plus* "anauntrins – if so be, if perchance" *Ray* 1674.

enter-common open to use

"Enter-common – a place open to everybody. For instance, Hetton Hall grounds, being presumably private, during the strike were 'enter-common,' roamed over at will, used by anybody" *Palgrave* Hetton 1896

esh ash tree

"esh – the ash tree" *Brockett* Newc & Nth 1829. [OE æsc]

ether adder

"athers and ethers for adders, the great dragonflie is usually called a flying adder" *Bell* MS Newc 1830s; "deef ez en ether" (deaf as an adder) *Egglestone* Weardale 1870s. *EDD* distribution to 1900: Sco, Ches, Leics. [OE nædre, ON naðra]. See also **dragonfly**

etten eaten

"he's etten th' lot" *Dunn* B'p Auck 1950

ettle to intend, aim to

"eckle, ettle – to aim, intend, design" *Ray* 1674; "ettle – to intend, to attempt, to contrive" *Brockett* Newc & Nth 1829; "a machine Aa ettled to meyk mesel" (tried) *Haldane* Newc 1879; "A ettled to gan to Hetton" *Palgrave* Hetton 1896; "hettled equals arranged, e.g. hev ye anything hettled for the week?" Crook C20th/2 Q; "ettle – my dad still says ettle in 2004" *JR* Sacriston. *EDD* distribution to 1900: Sco, Ire, Nth. NE 2001: low use or obsol. [ON ætla]

excellent 1. ace, 2. champion, 3. choz, 4. clinkin', 5. cush/ty, 6. daza, 7. mint, 8. other

1. "been having an ace time" 'Mackem Abroad' online 2004. [World War 1 slang]
2. "How are you... I'm champion" Tyneside 1930s Q; "champion cake/pie/beef" Tyneside 1930s Q, "I feel champion" *Viereck* re Gateshead, 1966; "champee-on – doing well" *Dodd* MS Tanfield Lea C20/2; 'first class' *Graham* Geordie 1979; ex. *RM* Norton C20/mid
3. "choz was used to express brilliant/good. But I knew it as chos" *CT* New Herrington 1930s; "choz, choss, choller" *JS* re Ryhope 1950s; "choz – brilliant, good" S'd 2001 Q. [?choice]
4. "clinking – first rate" wNewc 1880s "some clivor thraws at boolin', or some other clinkin' fun" *Barrass* Stanley 1892

excellent cont.

5. "cushtie-chock" (excellent) *PG* re D'm City C20/2; "custy – good" *JR* Sacriston C20/2; "a cush batchla pad" *VIZ* 72 (1995); "That's cushtie, that is." (Comment re decorated stall, Durham Miners Gala, 2001); "cush or cushty – cool" *Charver* 2000-2002, "cushty – neat" B'p Auckland 2001 Q. [Romany kushti 'good, fine, nice, all right'; there is also Anglo-Indian cushy from Hindustani khush ('pleasant'); not forgetting TV's 'Only Fools and Horses']
6. "daza – great or excellent" Tyneside C20/mid E; 'very good' Newc. 2001 Q; "darzer – slang for a good one: 'It's a darzer' (it's a smasher.)" *RV* Winlaton 2003. *Plus* "douse – thriving; dousy, same meaning" *Bell* MS Newc 1815; "dowser – a lively lad, a champion anything, e.g. pigeon, girlfriend: 'That's a dowser!'" *GP* S'm 1950s. [?Fr douce]
7. ex. eD'm 1990 per BG; "mint – good/great: 'That's mint, man'" *Charver* 2000–2002. [from mint as source of money]
8. "git-good – excellent" Wheatley Hill 2004 Q; "geet gud" NShields C20/mid Q; "rarker – said of s.thing exceptionally good" *LG* S'm C20/2; "some people in parts of Sunderland use cushty and others use topper as in 'it's topper that...' re something that they think is very good." *GA* 2003; "hellish – stylish, daring: "we said 'hellish' at school, always with the accent on 'ish,'" *PG* H'pool C20/2; "waxa – used for expressing how good something is" *Charver* 2000–2002

exclamations (some)

"Ee!" *Bell* MS Newc 1815; "Ye boolie allies!" *Windows* Newc 1917; "My certies!" *Allan's Tyneside Songs* p.237 1829; "'Crikes!' *Allan's Tyneside Songs* p.187 1824; "crikey mick" *ER* M'bro C20/2; "dee-a naaz – nobody knows" *Dodd* MS Tanfield Lea C20/2; "kae! – an interjectional expression of disbelief, contempt, or abhorrence; very common in Newcastle" *Brockett* Newc & Nth 1829; "Loak!" *Allan's Tyneside Songs* p.53 1823; "pitee aboot yi" (no sympathy) *Dodd* MS Tanfield Lea C20/2; "Well, arl gan t' Shields" (an exclamation of disbelief) CT New Herrington C20/mid. See also **hoot/s, haad, howay, why-aye** and **oaths**

face the coal face

"face, feace – the coal wall" *Brockett* Newc & Nth 1846

fadge round, flattish wheaten risen loaf

"fadges – thick cakes, baked on girdle or iron plate on the fire [partly deleted and corrected to read:] thick cakes, baked in an oven being too thick to bake on the fire" *Bell* MS Newc 1830s; "fadge or tharf cake – bun made out of spare dough left over when a baker's tins are all filled" Embleton, Newc 1897; "stotty fadges" *JG* Annfield Plain 1930s; "'fadges – not stotties" *GJ* Spennymoor 1960s; "yer fadge is ower femmer – the bread is too crumbly" *Dobson* Tyne 1969; "certified fadge-fillers labourer" *Dobson* Tyne 1972; "a small flat loaf of bread generally made up from the dough left over from a baking" *Graham* Geordie 1979; "fadge a properly risen round loaf, stottie means flat one" (i.e. two risings, not just one) South Moor (Stanley) 2003 per BG. *EDD* distribution to 1900: Sco, Ire, N'd, Lx. Note: fadge is perhaps older and more northerly in its distribution than stottie. [?OFr fais 'bundle' – compare "fad – a bundle of straw" *Brockett* Newc & Nth 1846; "fadge – a bundle; one that is short and thick in person" *Atkinson* Cleve 1868]. See also **stottie**

fairin' a present from a fair

exx. *Dinsdale* mid-Tees 1849, *Graham* Geordie 1979; 'a prize at a fair' *GP* S'm re C20/1. *EDD* distribution to 1900: general

to fair up improve (of weather)

"fair, fair-up – to become good weather again" *Atkinson* Cleve 1868, sim. *Palgrave* Hetton 1896. "It'll fair up" *GP* S'm C20/2

for fairs in earnest, seriously

"so haud the bairn for fairs / ye've often deund [done it] for fun" *Allan's Tyneside Songs* p.476 1863; "Thinkin thae wor gon for fairs" (for sure, for real) *Armstrong* Tanfield C19/2; "faw fairs – in earnest" *Dodd* MS Tanfield Lea C20/2; "This wan for fair – it coonts" *Leslie* Newc 1992. *EDD* distribution to 1900: N'd

farand manner, bearing

"fighting-farand – ready to fight" *Ray* Nth 1737; "ill-farand – ill-looking" Brockett Newc & Nth 1846. [ON fara 'to suit'; OE farende 'travelling', compare "farand-man – travelling merchant" *Brockett* Newc & Nth 1846].

farand cont.

See also **aad-farant**

farantly decently

"farantly – handsome e.g. fair and farantly" *Ray* 1674; respectable; neat, orderly' *Atkinson* Cleve 1868

farntickles freckles, etc.

"fairn-tickled – sunburnt in the face" *Bell* MS Newc 1815; "freckled, like the seed or small spots on the under side of the fern leaves" *Bell* MS Newc 1815; "fanticles, farentickles, farnticles, ec. – freckles on the skin" *Atkinson* Cleve 1868. *EDD* distribution to 1900: Sco, Ire, Nth

fash 1. to trouble, bother, 2. bother (noun)

1. "me he'll never fash nor flyte" 'Bobby Shaftoe' C18; "donnet fash me – don't teize me" *Grose* 1787; "yer aye fashin yen with somethin or other" *Bewick* Tyne 1790s; "And if thou say the tap's the bung, / Aw wadent fash ma thoom about it." *Pitman's Pay* G'head 1820s; "I cannot be fash'd (bothered)" *Brockett* Newc & Nth 1829; "he waddn't fash te carry'd hyem" 'Lambton Worm' 1867; "fash – to occasion trouble or inconvenience, to worry or annoy; to take trouble, or put oneself ot inconvenience: 'deeant thee fash theesel' about it'" *Atkinson* Cleve 1868; "He disn't fash the hoose mooch" (said of one seldom in) *Palgrave* Hetton 1896; "Aw canna be fashed wi' ye" *Nth Words* Bensham, 1938; "fash – worry" *Dodd* MS Tanfield Lea C20/2; "she cudn't be fashed ter stand aroond fettling all day" MS North Shields C20/2. *EDD* distribution to 1900: Sco, Ire, Nth, Mids. [OFr fascher; *Scottish National Dictionary* p.xiv gives as from French 15–16C]

2. "ye're nought but fash" *Chicken* Benwell 1720s; "we'd ha' some fash to git it (Cleopatra's Needle) alang t'fell" *Egglestone* Weardale 1870s. *Plus* "fashious – troublesome: 'to be a constable is both fashious and charge'" *Bell* MS Newc 1830s; "Aa've had a fashous job on't" (troublesome) *Graham* Geordie 1979

fast fixed, immovable

"let me past... dinnet muaik thawsel se fast" *Armstrong* Tanfield C19/2. *Plus* "Bedfast. Bed-ridden (always used)" *Palgrave* Hetton 1896; "earthfast – fastened or firmly fixed in the ground: 'great earthfast craggs & great

fast cont.

stones'" *Raine* MS re Rothbury, 1607. [OE fæst 'firm']

father 1. forms in –th-, 2. forms in –d-, 3. **dad, da**

1. "fayther" *Bewick* Tyne 1790s; "faither – father: "faither" *Pitman's Pay* G'head 1820s; "wor faithers" Wilson T *Allan's Tyneside Songs* p.266 1843; "fethur" *JA* Newc C19/mid, *Allan's Tyneside Songs* p.480 1869; "wor fethers afore mevvies wes'nt see wise" *Haldane* Newc 1879; "feather", "feathor" *Barrass* Stanley 1890s; "fethor and mother" *Allan's Tyneside Songs* p.335 C19/1; "me fethor's an engine driver" *Dobson* Tyne 1970-71; "fethor – father" Tanfield Lea, 1960
2. "fader, fadder" *Kennet* 1690s as Nth, sim. *Bells* re Carlisle, 1802, *Dinsdale* mid-Tees 1849, *Blenkinsopp* Teesdale 1931; "fedder, fayder, fayther" Tweddell, Cleve 1875. *EDD* distribution to 1900: forms in 'd' typical of N'd, D'm, C'd, nYx. [OE fæder]
3. "wour lads, like their deddy" *Allan's Tyneside Songs* p.46 1812; "deddy – father" *Pitman's Pay* G'head 1820s; "daddy" *Brockett* Newc & Nth 1829; "Da and Ma" *Palgrave* Hetton 1896; "Dar, for father" *JR* Crook C20/mid; "wor da" *Dobson* Tyne 1969; "me da sez..." *Cate* p.145 B'p Auck area 1987 [probably from infant babble; note also Romany 'dadrus'] *Plus* "paw, pau or paa – a term used in the North as father" *Bell* MS Newc 1815

faw, faa gipsy

"Francis Heron, King of ye Faws" *Raine* MS Jarrow 1756; "feaws – ragged beggars or gypsies (N'd)" *Grose* 1787; "Faws or Faas – gipseys or Faw Gangs, very numerous formerly in Northumberland and Durham" *Bell* MS Newc 1815; "faw – an itinerant ticker, a travelling besom-maker, mugger, etc." *Pitman's Pay* G'head 1820s; "And aw the faws... that went stravagin wi' them" *Oiling* G'head 1826; "Faw or Faw-gang" *Brockett* Newc & Nth 1829; "a fah – a gypsy" *Embleton* Tyne 1897; "ye clarty Faa" *Graham* Geordie 1979. [John Faw... recognised by the Scotch King in 1594 – Hoyland ca.1800 via *Raine* MS] *Plus* "fawlike – gipsy-like" *Blenkinsopp* Teesdale 1931

feal to hide (s.thing)

"she fealed them in the snowe" *Raine* MS Richmond 1631–32; "he that feales can find"

feal cont.

Ray Nth 1674; "feal – to hide, specially any thing surreptitiously obained: 'He that feals can find'" *Brockett* Newc & Nth 1829; "felt – to hide s.thing away" *Wood* Cleve 2002. *EDD* distribution to 1900: Ire, Nth. [ON fela]

feck 1. portion, 2. ability

1. "feck – the most or greatest part" *Kennet* 1690s as Yorks; "feck – a good quantity" *Gibson* C'd 1880; "the main feck" *Barrass* Stanley 1890s; "He did the main feck of the work" *Palgrave* Hetton 1896. *EDD* distribution to 1900: Sco, Ire, Nth. [OFr pek 'a measure']
2. "feck – might, activity, abundance" *Brockett* Newc & Nth 1829; "feck – activity, ability, might; number, quantity, mass" *Atkinson* Cleve 1868. *EDD* distribution to 1900: Sco, Nth. [?effect]. *Plus* "feckless – uncaring of personal appearance, careless" *JB* Shildon C20/mid

feg 1. fig, 2. anything valueless

1. "feg – the name invariably given by the vulgar to fig" *Brockett* Newc & Nth 1829; "then a' the things aw'd eatin last 'eer [year], / fegs, grosers, reed herrins, an' yell, did appear" *Allan's Tyneside Songs* p.410 C19/mid; "feg-tree" *Moore* Weardale 1859; "Canary-seed, raisins, and fegs" *WM* Newc C19/2. *EDD* distribution to 1900: N'd, D'm, W'd, S.W.
2. "feg – a dead grass-stem; anything without worth" *Atkinson* Cleve 1868. *EDD* distribution to 1900: general

fell hill, high land, moorland

"men dare not drive their goods (cattle) to t' fell" *RR* Weardale 1569; "fell – a moor or common" *Bailey* Co.Durham 1810; 'a rocky hill... frequently used for any moor or open waste' *Brockett* Newc & Nth 1829; 'a hill, bleak, barren and lengthened in outline; a long moorland summit' *Atkinson* Cleve 1868; "fells i' Wardle're littel else b'd ling, 'n' peat-pots, 'n' moss-broks" *Egglestone* Weardale 1870s; 'hill' *Graham* Geordie 1979. *EDD* distribution to 1900: Sco, Nth. [ON fiall 'mountain', OE fel]

felled worn out

"Sair fail'd is I / Sin' I kenn'd thee" *Allan's Tyneside Songs* p.10 C19/1; "Ah's sair felled" *FS* Wingate 1940s. *EDD* distribution to 1900: general

felter to tangle

"felter or feltre – to entangle, to clot together" *Brockett* Newc & Nth 1829; "feltered – rough, shaggy (of pony's coat)" *Blenkinsopp* Teesdale 1931. *EDD* distribution to 1900: general. [OFr feltrer]

femmer frail, not strong

"femmer, fremmer – weak, slender, feeble" *Brockett* Newc & Nth 1829; "femmer – slender, slightly made, weak" *Atkinson* Cleve 1868; "Femmer – frail; of persons and things. (Always used)" *Palgrave* Hetton 1896; "Femmer we used for anything weak – a rickety table leg, that might give way at any moment..." *Nth Words* Benwell 1938; "femmer – delicate, easily broken or damaged" *JB* Shildon C20/mid; "not used of people" *AK* Tyne C20/mid; "wouldn't be applied to persons, but to things – 'ricketty, frail, unable to bear weight or pressure'" *PG* H'pool C20/2; "it's aal femmer – it's too weak (to take weight)" *Dunn* B'p Auck 1950; "that chair's femmer, mind..." *TC* Dawdon C20/2; "she's nobbut femmer, poor body" *Graham* Geordie 1979; "femmer – easily broken or weak, can be used of cloth, etc" South Moor (Stanley) 2003 per BG. *EDD* distribution to 1900: Nth. NE 2001: in use. [ON fimr]

fend 1. defence, 2. a living, 3. to make shift

1. "the sorrowful fend that they can make" *RR* Weardale 1569
2. "we'll make a decent fend" *Pitman's Pay* G'head 1820s; "he oft had sair wark for ti myek a bit fend" *Allan's Tyneside Songs* p.489 1862. *EDD* distribution to 1900: general
3. "to fend – to shift for" *Ray* 1674; "fend – to endeavour, to make shift, to be industrious, to struggle with difficulties, to ward off" *Brockett* Newc & Nth 1829. [AN fendre 'to protect, defend']

fendy energetic, capable

"fendy – endeavouring" *Bell* MS Newc 1815; 'clever at providing for oneself' *Brockett* Newc & Nth 1829; 'industrious' *Dinsdale* mid-Tees 1849. *EDD* distribution to 1900: Sco, Nth. "a fendable fellow" *Kennet* Nth 1690s

fettle 1. to mend, fix, 2. condition

"fettle – to set or goe about any thiny, to dress or prepare" *Ray* 1674; "fettle – to make ready" *Bailey* Co.Durham 1810; "fettle – to put in order" *Bell* MS Newc 1815; "The house

fettle cont.

aw'll fettle up masell" *Pitman's Pay* G'head 1820s; "th' tee wis fettled" *Armstrong* Tanfield C19/2; "fettle – to adapt, arrange, fit up; to prepare, equip, get ready,supply; to put into a state of repair; to beat, overcome: 'ah'll fettle him', 'ah fun' him fettling's au'd sled'" *Atkinson* Cleve 1868; "he's elways fettlin' on wi summic or another" (busy) *Haldane* Newc 1879; "can the fettle this? – can you mend this?" *Dunn* B'p Auck 1950; "will you fettle this for me?" (repair) *McBurnie* Glebe Colliery, C20/mid; 'to bait a line or a pot' *Hill* Flamborough 1970s; "...will fettle yer bad leg" *Dobson* Tyne 1972; "the lock wants fettlin" *Graham* Tyne 1980; "fettlin department – in a foundry, handling the finishing process" *TC* S'm C20/2. *EDD* distribution to 1900: general. NE 2001: in use. [OE fetel, strap. ON fetla 'to bind up']
2. "fettle – order, good condition, proper repair" *Brockett* Newc & Nth 1829; "out o' fettle – out of repair; out of health" *Atkinson* Cleve 1868; 'state of health or repair' *CT* New Herrington 1930s; "fine fettle – fit" Wheatley Hill 2002 Q. See also **greetings**

fifie see **mule**

finnd to find

"find (pronounced finnd) – to find; preterite fand, fund; p.p. fund" *Atkinson* Cleve 1868; "finnd" *Egglestone* Weardale 1870s, *Dodd* MS Tanfield Lea C20/2; "thai him fande" *Cuthbert* C15/mid; "fand" (pret.) *Marshall* G'head 1806. *Egglestone* Weardale 1870s; "when he fund oot he was gannin to dee" *Embleton* Tyne 1897; "fund – p.p. found" *Dinsdale* mid-Tees 1849. *Allan's Tyneside Songs* p.533 1882. *EDD* distribution to 1900: pronunciation 'finnd' given as nYx]

fir-apple fir-cone

ex. Dinsdale mid Tees 1849. *EDD* distribution to 1900: D'm, C'd, W'd. See also **buntin**

fire-damp methane, explosive once admixed with air

"fire-damp – the inflammable air, or carburetted hydrogen gas of coal mines" *Brockett* Newc & Nth 1829; "after-damp. – carbonic acid; stythe. the products of the combustion of fire-damp" *Nicholson* 1880; "fire-damp – light carburetted hydrogen gas

fire-damp cont.

it is found in most coal mines; being most abundant in the vicinity of slips and dykes" *Nicholson* 1880

fired exploded

ex. [re a pit] *Nicholson* 1880

first see **forst**

fit fought

"thae fit freh five o'clock te six" *Armstrong* Tanfield C19/2

fizz to hiss

"fizz – to hiss" *Dinsdale* mid-Tees 1849; "fizzle – a faint crackling noise" *Wade South Moor* C20/mid. *Plus* "fizzer – a singing hinnie without spice" *Brockett* Newc & Nth 1829

flacker 1. to move or fly with a fluttering motion, 2. to flinch

1. "flacker – to flutter or quiver" *Bailey* Co.Durham 1810; "it [an owl] flakker'd oot at neets" *Allan's Tyneside Songs* p.311 1827; "flacker, flecker – to flutter, to vibrate... to quiver" *Brockett* Newc & Nth 1829; "flacker – to flutter" *Atkinson* Cleve 1868; "he [a bird] gies one flacker" *Wearside Tales* 1879 *EDD* distribution to 1900: Nth. [ME flakeren, ON flokra, MDu flackeren]
2. "he nivver flackered when I asked for a fiver" *IA* S'm 1950s,60s; "never flakkad" *Dodd* MS Tanfield Lea C20/2; "nivver flackered" (did not move) *JP* S'm C20/2; "flacker – to flinch or turn back; flackered – finished, unable to do any more" *Wade South Moor* C20/mid

fladge snowflake

"Fladges – snowflakes. Often called 'flatches'" *Palgrave* Hetton 1896; "fladge – snowflake" EP Southwick 2001 Q. *EDD* distribution to 1900: eD'm. [OE flacea (via Junius), ME flaw, Du sneflage]

flags flake, flag

"snow-flag – a snow-flake" *Atkinson* Cleve 1868" *Atkinson* Cleve 1868; "flags – pavement" *Dobson* Tyne 1973; "flags – square or rectangular paving-stones" *JB* Shildon C20/mid. [ON flaga]

flannen flannel

"Thor's a man o' mine, a hewer, / Weers a shirt o' flannen blue" *Barrass* Stanley 1892; ex. *Blenkinsopp* Teesdale 1931

flat assembly and transition point in pit

"flatt – in a coal mine, the situation where the horses take the coal tubs from the putters" *Brockett* Newc & Nth 1846; "flat – the station to which the putters take the full tubs, to be taken by the drivers to the engine plane or to the shaft" *Nicholson* 1880; "Flat – the station to which the 'putter' pushes the full 'tubs.' Here they are hitched together, and taken by the driver, ten or twelve tubs at a time, to the 'landing', which is a larger flat. From this flat they are drawn by the engine to the 'shaft'." *Palgrave* Hetton 1896; 'underground assembly point for vehicles' *Northumbrian III* 1990 re Backworth; "flat or pass-by – where pony transporters of tubs meet and change their loads over to each other" *McBurnie* Glebe Colliery C20/mid; "flat – marshalling point, underground tub standage" *Dodd* MS Tanfield Lea C20/2. *Plus* flats: 'sheets put on the floor of the seam when the floor is soft' *JM* Dawdon 1970s

flay to scare

"thai flowe (i.e. crows flew) away as thai wer flayde" *Cuthbert* C15/mid; "to hew aw'm not flay'd" *Marshall* G'head 1806; "flaid – frightened" *Bailey* Co.Durham 1810; "flay – a fright; to frighten: 'flaid to deeth'" *Pitman's Pay* G'head 1820s; "Aw's flayed" *Brockett* Newc & Nth 1829; "aw's kind o' flaid when aw cum te think o'... sailin' ower places where thor's ne bottom" *Allan's Tyneside Songs* p.401 C19/mid; "Aa wis flaid o' yor commin heym on a streker, killed or maimed" *Haldane* Newc 1879; "Fley – to scare: 'Lad, dinna fley the galloway'" *Palgrave* Hetton 1896; "flaid – afraid" *Dodd* MS Tanfield Lea C20/2. *EDD* distribution to 1900: Sco, Ire, Nth. [OE aflygan, ON fleyja]. See also **scarecrow**. *Plus* "the folks o' wor raw was aflaid" *Allan's Tyneside Songs* p.359 1849, "aflaid – afraid" Tanfield Lea 1960

flee to fly

"ane come fleand to him" (flying) *Cuthbert* C15/mid; "let flee!" *Errington* p.50, Felling/ Heworth re 1790s; "see the skemmies (pigeons) tiv his duckit flee" *MC* Tyne May 1881; "come fleein out" (rushing) *Hay* Ushaw Moor C20/1; "skin and hair wis fleein" (flying about) *Armstrong* Tanfield C19/2; "te flee throo the air" *Chater* Newc 1880; "fleein' aroond on me bike" MS North Shields C20/2; "fleein' aboot" eD'm 2001 Q. *EDD* distribution to

flee cont.

1900: general. [ON fleon]. *Plus* "flee – fly (an insect)" *JB* Shildon C20/mid. See also **dragonfly**

fleet net for trawling for herring

"About dawn next morning the net or 'fleet' is hauled in" *Coulthard* p.124 1934. *EDD* distribution to 1900: general

flesh-flies bluebottles

att. JO re High Thornley/Rowlands Gill, 1930s–1940s in *Nth Words. EDD* distribution to 1900: general

fligged fledged, feathered

"flig'd – young birds full feathered; "flig'd owr the doup" means that they flig'd or feather over the tail end" *Bell* MS Newc 1815; "the young birds have fliggied their nest or you fliggied when playing knocky nine doors" *JS* Easington C20/mid; "when chicks flew a nest we said they fliggied" *JR* Sacriston C20/2. *EDD* distribution to 1900: Nth, Mids. [note: though there is some similarity to / confusion with the verb 'flee', this seems to be a separate root]

flipe brim of a hat

"hats wivoot e flipe" (brim) *Armstrong* Tanfield C19/2; "flipe – the brim of a hat" *Atkinson* Cleve 1868, *Palgrave* Hetton 1896. [cognates in Du, Dan, Ice]

flit to remove from one house to another'

"thai walde nogt flytt" (depart) *Cuthbert* C15/mid; "flittyd that yere to Osworth" *Raine* MS Langley ca.1575; "flit – to remove: two flittings are as bad as one fire" *Grose* 1787; "flit – to remove from one dwelling to another" *Bailey* Co.Durham 1810; "And when we flit, the landlord stops Ma sticks [furniture] till a' the rent be paid." *Pitman's Pay* G'head 1820s; "flit – avoid rent collectors" *Dodd* MS Tanfield Lea C20/2. *EDD* distribution to 1900: Sco, Ire, Nth, Mids. [ON flyttja] *Plus* "flit, flitting – a removal from one place of residence to another" *Atkinson* Cleve 1868

flite to dispute, challenge

"me he'll never fash nor flyte" 'Bobby Shaftoe' C18; "flite – to scold, to make a great noise" *Brockett* Newc & Nth 1829; sim. *Dinsdale* mid-Tees 1849; "wad flite the colliery for a croon or twe" (offer to fight?) *MC* Tyne May 1881

flite cont.

EDD distribution to 1900: Sco, Nth, EMids. NE 2001: not in use. [ON flytja, OE flítan]

flithers limpets

"flithers – the common limpets" *Atkinson* Cleve 1868, *Hill* Flamborough 1970s; "flithers – limpets or anything similar used for bait" Amble via BG 2003. *EDD* distribution to 1900: Yx, Isle of Man

flittermouse bat

"flitter-mouse – the bat" *Atkinson* Cleve 1868. *EDD* distribution to 1900: general

flucker, fluck flounder

"'it's a fluiker' ki Dick" *Marshall* G'head 1806; "jenny flucker – a smal fluck or flounder" *Bell* MS Newc 1815; "fluck – a flounder, a small fish" *Bell* MS Newc 1815; "twas neither flucker, whale, nor king" *Oliver* Newc p.7 1824; "fluck, flucker, or jenny-flucker – a flounder" *Brockett* Newc & Nth 1829" *Brockett* Newc & Nth 1829. *EDD* distribution to 1900: Tyne. [OE floc, ON flóke]

flutter-by see **butterfly**

foal young putter

"foal – the youngest in the rank of putters in a coal pit" *Brockett* Newc & Nth 1829; *Brockett* Newc & Nth 1846; "foal – a little boy who was formerly employed to assist a stronger boy (called a headsman) to put; he pulled in front of the tub by a pair of ropes or traces called soams whilst the headsman pushed behind" *Nicholson* 1880. *EDD* distribution to 1900: N'd, D'm

foalfoot coltsfoot (wild plant)

"foal-foot – colt's-foot" *Atkinson* Cleve 1868, *Palgrave* Hetton 1896. *EDD* distribution to 1900: Nth, Mids

fog second growth of grass

"fogge – long grass remaining in pastures till winter" *Ray* 1674; "fog, fogg – the grass grown in autumn after the hay is mown – the second crop, or aftermath" *Brockett* Newc & Nth 1829. *EDD* distribution to 1900: general

foison, fusin abundance, etc.

"fusin – nourishment" *Bailey* Co.Durham 1810; "fusson, foison – freshness, moisture" *Bell* MS Newc 1815; "fusin, fuzzen – nourishment, abundance" *Brockett* Newc & Nth 1829

foison, fusin cont.

EDD distribution to 1900: general [AN fuison, foison 'quantity, abundance']

foisty musty

"corne will foyst with lyinge long in the garner" *Raine* MS EYorks 1641; "foist – fusty, musty" *Kennet* 1690s as Nth; *Dinsdale* mid-Tees 1849; "foistee – mildewed" *Dodd* MS Tanfield Lea C20/2; "foisty pies" *Dobson* Tyne 1970; "a foisty room, a foisty loaf, etc" *Graham* Geordie 1979; "foisty – damp: 'by it's foisty in heor'" *Leslie* Newc 1992. *EDD* distribution to 1900: Sco, Nth, EA. [?AN fust 'barrel']

folk people

"to preserve folks frome the farye" *Raine* MS Wallsend 16th century; "wark-folk – labourers" *Dinsdale* mid-Tees 1849; "men fokes en wumen fokes" *Armstrong* Tanfield C19/2; "fwoak" *Egglestone* Weardale 1870s; "deed folk" (the dead) *Embleton* Newc 1897; "Th' next time thi' folk gan shopp'n i' th' town, see if th' lucky enough t' gerron th' new trams" *CT* New Herrington C20/mid. *EDD* distribution to 1900: general. [OE folc]

fond silly

"fond – silly, foolish" *Bailey* Co.Durham 1810, *Dinsdale* mid-Tees 1849; "fond as a buzzom" (besom, brush) *Brockett* Newc & Nth 1829; "d'ye think aw'm fond [stupid], or tired of maw life?" *Allan's Tyneside Songs* p.461 1862; "dont' be so fond" *IA* S'm 1950s, 60s; "dinna taak se fond – do not be silly" *Dunn* B'p Auck 1950; "his nyen fond – not as daft as he looks" *Dunn* B'p Auck 1950; 'half-witted, silly' *Graham* Geordie 1979; "fond fool!" *Wood* Tees 2002; "That's a fond idea" Horden 2004 E; "brazen fond... impittent fond" (used especially about young boys) *JS* Easington C20/mid; "brazzen'd fond – cheeky" Marske C20/2 via *Wood*, "brazen-fond – forward, impudent" H'pool. 2001 Q; "impíttent fond – cheeky" *Dunn* B'p Auck 1950, *MB* Coxhoe C20/mid. *EDD* distribution to 1900: Sco, Nth, EA [ME fonned]

fondy simpleton

"foudy [sc. fondy] – an eccentric or half foolish person" *Bell* MS Newc 1815; "fondy – a fool, a simpleton, an idiot" *Atkinson* Cleve 1868; "thoo's a fondie" *Palgrave* Ho'ton 1896. *EDD* distribution to 1900: NE [ME fon 'a fool']

foonded cold

"I'm foonded" *RV* re Esh/Winlaton C20/mid. [?foundered]

footie the game of football

"footy – a game of football" NE 2001 Q; "Footie manager takes home advantage" *The Sun* 19 Sep 2003. NE 2001: in common use

forby as well as, besides

"forby – besides, over-and-above, moreover: 'forbi a' that...'" *Atkinson* Cleve 1868; "We've had lots o' good fortin forby" *Barrass* Stanley 1890s; "Forby – besides (accent as in 'besides'): 'There was other six forby me'" *Palgrave* Hetton 1896; "will dee ye the world o' good forbye" *Dobson* Tyne 1972; "forbye thon – as well as that" *Todd* Tyne 1977. *EDD* distribution to 1900: general. NE 2001: not in use

fore-elders ancestors

"he was a thief & wold be hanged, as all his fore ellers was" *Raine* MS via Durham 1567; "fore-elders – ancestors" *Atkinson* Cleve 1868. *EDD* distribution to 1900: Nth

fore-shift early shift

"when the fore shift wis gan in-by" *Haldane* Newc 1879; "the fore shift... meant going to work at 4 a.m. and returning at noon." *Hitchin* re Seaham 1910s p.62. See also **back-shift**

forky-tail see **earwig**

fornenst in front of, opposite and facing

"Borders or Frontiery(s)... of England foreanenst Scotland" *Raine* MS 1542; "fore-anent, fore-anens – over against, opposite to, in front of" *Atkinson* Cleve 1868; "Then Aa leuks strait forenenst me" *Other Eye* Newc, ca.1890; "Forenénst (fu:nenst) (accent on last syllable) – facing opposite. Of houses in a street: 'He lives right f'nenst us' Also metaph. 'They're not doing right forenenst me'" *Palgrave* Hetton 1896; "f'nest" Wheatley Hill C20/1 Q; "straight fornenst ye" *MR* S'm, re 1940s; "freninst" eD'm C20/mid Q; "to stand fornenced – to stand beside" *Crocker* Tees 1983. *EDD* distribution to 1900: Sco, Ire, Nth. NE 2001: not in use. See also **anenst**

forst first

"forst" (first) *Armstrong* Tanfield C19/2, Coxhoe 1916; "the man meant nothin by it, forst ter last" MS North Shields C20/2; "in fawst – morning shift

forst foot New Year visitor

"first-foot – the name given to the person who first enters a dwelling-house on New Year's Day" *Brockett* Newc & Nth 1829; "Footing, first – properly, the first person who enters one's doors on New Year's Day. This refers to the custom of going round to various houses on the morning of the New Year, soon after the old year has passed, and being regaled by those who humour the custom by keeping open house" *Palgrave* Hetton 1896; "Forst-futtin time is for us heor" *Dobson* Tyne 1972; "About ten to twelve, our father would set out, with some coals and sticks (kindling) with him – to make sure (on return) there would always be fire in your hearth for the coming year. All the family men would gather at the bottom of the street, and await midnight. The New Year would be signalled by the church bells ringing, and the ships in harbour would blow their whistles, the pits too, while we waited silent indoors for the first footer. This would be our own father of course." *MR* S'm 1920s

fortnith fortnight

"duen a fortnith's weshin'" *Wearside Tales* 1879; "fortneth" *Egglestone* Weardale 1870s; "fortnith" *Armstrong* Tanfield C19/2

foss, force waterfall

"forse – a cascade" *Bailey* Co.Durham 1810; "force – waterfall" *Dinsdale* mid-Tees 1849; "foss, force" *Atkinson* Cleve 1868. *EDD* distribution to 1900: Nth. [ON fors]. See also **linn**

fother a load, a measure

"fother or futher – in Newcastle, as many coals as a two-horse cart can carry" *Brockett* Newc & Nth 1846; "fother – a measure of coal, being one-third of a chaldron, or 17⅝ cwts" *Nicholson* 1880; "fother of coal – a cartload for delivery" *CT* New Herrington 1930s. *EDD* distribution to 1900: Sco,Nth, eMids. [OE foðer]

foumart polecat

"First got a foumart in a trap, & black cat" *Raine MS* Askham 1668/69; "foumart – a pole-cat" *Brockett* Newc & Nth 1829, *Dinsdale* mid-Tees 1849; "foulmart (pronounced fou'mmart or fummart) – the pole-cat" *Atkinson* Cleve 1868; "fulmart" *Smith* Weardale 1883. [ME fulmard]. *Plus* "i gown furr. cum fuynes" (polecat) *Raine MS* ?York 1391; "a gowne faced with fones" *Raine MS* Durham City 1558

fouth plenty

"fouth – abundance, plenty" *Pitman's Pay* G'head 1820s. *EDD* distribution to 1900: Sco, Nth

fouter (insult)

"fouter – an ill name or disrespectful name given to any person" *Bell MS* Newc 1815. *EDD* distribution to 1900: Sco, N'd

fower four

"for felling fower trees" Bolton/Barden C17/ult via Raistrick *Yorkshire Dales* ch.4; "fowa – four" *VIZ* 42, 1990s. [OE fower]

foy 1. pilot boat, 2. free for piloting, 3. to pilot

1. "Foy / foyst... meant a small pinnace or boat" *Nth Words* Blyth 1938
2. "pocketting the foy" *Wearside Tales* 1879; "the first tugboat is entitled to the 'foy' or 'fee'" *Nth Words* Northumberland 1938; "Shipbrokers and the Agents speak of charging a 'foy' or fee as payment for their work in clearing a ship and the ship's disbursements" *Nth Words* Blyth 1938
3. "...with glances at... the 'narrows' through which the vessels were being 'foyed'" *The Maister* p.38 re Shields 1800-1840; "In foying a ship the foymen moved ahead in a small boat, and at warp's length dropped a small kedge [anchor], which, being being hove upon by the ship's windlass, brought her up to a position nearly over it. The kedge was then... weighed, carried ahead again, dropped and hauled upon, the process being repeated until sufficient sea-way had been attained by the vessel." *The Maister* p.39 re Shields 1800–1840; 'perform services for larger shipping while it is near to shore or in harbour' *Hill* Flamborough 1970s. *EDD* distribution to 1900: East coast. *Plus* "foyboatman – a boatman who watches for boats coming into the Tyne in the hope of getting employment in mooring them" *Graham* Geordie 1979 (re past practice)

fozy spongey (of poor veg)

"fozy, fuzzy – light and spungy" *Brockett* Newc & Nth 1829; "a fozzy turnip" *Egglestone* Weardale 1870s; "fozy – soft and spongey, generally applied to frosted turnips" *Luckley* Alnwick 1870s; "Fozy – unsound, of vegetables. A 'fozy' turnip is a woolly one" *Palgrave* Hetton 1896. *EDD* distribution to 1900: Sco, Ire, Nth, EA. [compare Du voos, Norw. fos 'spongey']

fra, frae, frev from

"he come fra his awn lande" *Cuthbert* C15/mid; "we shemm'd the cheps fra Newcassel" *Marshall* G'head 1806; "frev a needle tiv an anchor" *Marshall* G'head 1806; "not far fra here" *Armstrong* Tanfield C19/2; "where Ah com fra" *Egglestone* Weardale 1870s; "frev clock makin tiv 'lectricity" *Haldane* Newc 1879; "fowks ... frev aal pairts o' the toon" *Barrass* Stanley 1890s; "Fray (frae) – from" *Palgrave* Hetton 1896; "he cam doon fra the gallery" Coxhoe 1916 [ON frá, OE fram]

fratch to quarrel

"fratch – to scold, to quarrel" *Brockett* Newc & Nth 1829; 'to squabble angrily' *Atkinson* Cleve 1868 "fratching – fighting" cen D'm 2001 Q. *EDD* distribution to 1900: Sco, Nth, Mids. *Plus* "fratch – a quarrel" *Graham* Geordie 1979

fratchy irritable, quarrelsome

"Fratchy – cross tempered. I have also heard 'fratch,' but these words are imported from Tyneside" *Palgrave* Hetton 1896; "fratchety" H'pool, D'ton Q 2001

fremd strange, alien, far off

"fremd, fremt – far off, not related to, strange, at enmity" *Ray* 1674; "a frem'd person – a stranger, as contradistinguished from a relation" *Bell* MS Newc 1815; "distant, fallen out, estranged from: 'ahse kin o' fremd wi thy wife'" *Embleton* Tyne 1897; "Fremd – strange. 'a frem'd body' (a stranger)" *Palgrave* Hetton 1896; 'strange' *Smith* Weardale 1883; 'stormy (of weather), strange' *Crocker* Tees 1983. *EDD* distribution to 1900: Sco, Nth, Mids. [OE fremde]. *Plus* "no-nation – strange, remote: 'a no-nation spot'" *Atkinson* Cleve 1868

fresh thaw or flood

"in the great freshes we have had of late" (floods) *Raine* MS Berwick-on-Tweed, 1647; "fresh – a thaw" *Bell* MS Newc 1815; "fresh – the swelling or overflowing of a river, a flood, a thaw" *Brockett* Newc & Nth 1829; "Fresh – a thaw. 'There's a heavy (or, thick) fresh on'" *Palgrave* Hetton 1896. *EDD* distribution to 1900: Sco, Nth

fret see **sea-fret**

fridge to rub

ex, *Dinsdale* mid-Tees 1849; "fridge – to rub up or chafe" *Atkinson* Cleve 1868. *EDD* distribution to 1900: D'm, Yx, Lx, Mids

froating stressful work

"froating – anxious unremitting industry" *Bailey* Co.Durham 1810, *Brockett* Newc & Nth 1829. *EDD* distribution to 1900: C'd, Shrops, Herts... obsolete. [AN froter 'to rub, to beat']

frosk a frog

exx. *Kennet* 1690s as Nth, *Brockett* Newc & Nth 1829 as D'm; "like frosks in a peat-pot" *Egglestone* Weardale 1870s. *EDD* distribution to 1900: Nth. [OE frosc, frogga, ON froskr]

frozzen frozen

exx. RM Norton C20/mid, *Dodd* MS Tanfield Lea C20/2. *EDD* distribution to 1900: Nth, Mids

frumenty a sort of porridge

"frumenty or frumity – a dish made of bruised wheat or barley, boiled with milk, and seasoned with sugar and spices" *Brockett* Newc & Nth 1846. *EDD* distribution to 1900: general. [OFr frumentée]

fullick blow at full strength

"fullock" [?unfair, sudden or jerky action] *Atkinson* Cleve 1868; 'a blow with great force' Wade South Moor, 1966. *EDD* distribution to 1900: N'd. [full plus lick]

funnin' practical joking, teasing

"he wis ony funnin" *Haldane* Newc 1879; "expectin that thor funnin wad be free" *Barrass* Stanley 1890s; 'joking' *Dodd* MS Tanfield Lea C20/2

fusin see **foison**

fuzzball puffball mushroom

"fusba' – fuzzball, a fungus... a puff-ball" *Brockett* Newc & Nth 1829. *EDD* distribution to 1900: general

gadgie bloke, old man, official

"gadger or gauger – an exciseman" *Brockett* Newc & Nth 1829; "gadgey – a tramp" *Blenkinsopp* Teesdale 1931; "night watchman (usually in a small open front hut with a coke fire, there all night guarding open workings)" *ER* M'bro. C20/2; "gadgie – old man" *Leslie* Newc 1992; "a proper roofing gadgie" i.e. expert *Wood* M'bro 2002; 'night watchman, park-keeper, etc." M'bro. 2001 Q; 'old man or any odd character' Upper Teesdale 2001 Q; 'a kind of minor authority figure like an a watchman or a park keeper" S'm 2000 Q. *EDD* distribution to 1900: N'd. NE 2001: in use. [Romany gorgio, gaujo 'non-gipsy' – as in the following 'set piece': "Deck at the gadgie wi' a shaun oni on jinkin roond the corner wi' a manniske on his airm and a jugal at his heel" (Look at the youth with a tall hat on, trotting round the corner with a woman on his arm and a dog at his heel) – ex. of Mugger (Romany) speech from N'd, *Nth Words* 1938] *Plus* "mister, bloke than gadgie, which more Sunderland" *JP* S'm C20/2; "watchie" *GP* S'm 1950s

gaff a theatre or cinema

"A theatre known as the 'Gaff'" *Hitchin* re Seaham 1910s p.28; "gaffe – cinema" eD'm 2001 Q plus "penny gaffe" (re 1930s?); "gaff – theatre" *Dodd* MS Tanfield Lea C20/2; "penny gaff" (cheap cinema matinee) *Graham* Geordie 1979; 'cinema or billiard hall' Ferryhill. 2001 Q. *EDD* distribution to 1900: Sco, Oxf, London – noted as slang. [C18 coining]

gaffor boss

"Ar' ye much warse off than yor gaffors?" *Barrass* Stanley 1890s; "Gaffer – a 'masterman' or foreman" *Palgrave* Hetton 1896; 'under-manager / overman' *Northumbrian III* C20/2 re Durham collieries; "gaffor – foreman" Tanfield Lea 1960; "gaffa – boss, old man" *Dodd* MS Tanfield Lea C20/2; "the petty chiefs or gafferz of the shipyards and factries" *Dobson* Tyne 1970. *EDD* distribution to 1900: general. [godfather]

gain near, direct

"gain – a Northumbrian expression... attached to other words to express a degree of comparison: 'gain quiet' pretty quiet; 'gain brave' – tolerably courageous" *Brockett* Newc & Nth 1829; "gainer way – nearer way" *Dinsdale*

gain cont.

mid-Tees 1849. *EDD* distribution to 1900: general. [ON gegn 'direct']

galloway pony

"Of galloways he was well stockt" Rothbury C18/2; "a man riding upon a pye bald gallaway" *Errington* p.31 Felling/Heworth re 1780s; "galloways, a small, but spirited, breed of horses, from Galloway, a district of country in Scotland, famed for rearing them" *Brockett* Newc & Nth 1829; "A pony became a 'gallowa'" *Hitchin* re Seaham 1910s p.70 sim. *JR* Seaham C20/1; *JM* Dawdon 1970s; "Galloway (gaal:u:wu) – pony. The only term in use. Pit-ponies are always spoken of as 'galloways'" *Palgrave* Hetton 1896; "efter yolkin me gallower" West Stanley C20/1; "rag and bone men's horses were always gallowas" *JS* Easington C20/mid; "the gambolling of the gallowa's" *Dobson* Tyne 1970. *EDD* distribution to 1900: Sco, Nth, Mids. [from place-name]

galluses braces

"gallowses – men's braces" *Atkinson* Cleve 1868; "galices – a pair of braces" *Nth Words* N'd 1938 "galusses" N.Shields C20/mid Q; "gallusis – braces" *Dodd* MS Tanfield Lea C20/2. *EDD* distribution to 1900: general. [Fr galloches? Eng. gallows?]

gam game, sport, fun

"you would have laugh'd had you seen the gam" *Collier's Rant* Newc C18/2; "maek gam of wor bur [i.e. letter 'R']" *Allan's Tyneside Songs* p.50 1812; "whe are ye myekin yor gam on?" *Allan's Tyneside Songs* p.337 C19/1; "gam – sportiveness, playfulness; mockery, ridicule: 'they did nowght but mak' gam' o' me'" *Atkinson* Cleve 1868; "drama-gam" *Barrass* Stanley 1890s; "whee's thee makkin gam on?" *Dunn* B'p Auck 1950. *EDD* distribution to 1900: in this pronunciation, Nth

gan, gang to go

"a cach (fishing boat) gangand on ye water" *Raine* MS York C15/1; "nouthir stande na gang" *Cuthbert* C15/mid; "gang – to goe or walk" *Ray* 1674; "I am gang hame – I am going home" *Kennet* 1690s as Nth "gang – to go, to walk: 'gang your gait'" *Grose* 1787; "if thee muther gans on this way" (carries on) *Bewick* Tyne 1790s; "time to gang to wark... off hame aw gans" *Allan's Tyneside*

gan cont.

Songs p.141 1816 "aw gans..." *Allan's Tyneside
Songs* p.222 1823; "gang – to go: 'Let us a'
gang to the hopping for there we'ill a' meet
our dearist'; 'You'd better gang to it than be
bang'd [forced] to it'" *Bell* MS Newc 1830s;
"they tell'd us a' to gang away" *Allan's Tyneside
Songs* p.194 1842; "a little lad... was gan a
bonny bool ti pitch" *Allan's Tyneside Songs*
p.355 1849; "t' gas gans oot" *MWN* 16 Nov
1861; "in gan te Blaydon Races" *Allan's
Tyneside Songs* p.451 1862; "are you ganging or
riding?" *Atkinson* Cleve 1868; "it's gan te rain"
MC Tyne Nov 1891; "gan wrang" *Barrass*
Stanley 1890s; "e's neetha cummin o' gannin"
(he doesn't know what he wants to be) *CT*
New Herrington 1930s; "gannin' is ends –
creating a fuss" *Dodd* MS Tanfield Lea C20/2;
"gannin stryts – courting with marriage in
view" *Dodd* MS Tanfield Lea C20/2; "what we
gan te de aboot the Picts?" *Dobson* Tyne
1970–71; "they're gan to clean the Central
Station" *Dobson* Tyne 1972; "worra wuz ganna
dee?" *VIZ* 48 1990s; "gan on then" (go ahead)
eD'm via BG 2000, 2004. *EDD* distribution to
1900: Sco, Nth. NE 2001: gan in use, gang
not used. [ON ganga, OE (Anglian) gangan]
noun formations: "good ganner – good goer"
Dinsdale mid-Tees 1849; "gangers – strollers,
as Gipsies, etc., famous for telling of fortunes,
news, etc., as 'a ganging man tell'd me a cure
for sair een'; 'a ganger scried my hand...'"
Bell MS Newc 1830s; "ganger – 'exciseman'"
Chater Newc 1885 p.18; "undergang – an
[underpass]" *Atkinson* Cleve 1868; "upgang –
a track up, an ascent" *Atkinson* Cleve 1868;
"down-gang – a means of descent" *Atkinson*
Cleve 1868; "Thor's a hawf-a-dozen gannins
at the flat that Aw'm at noo" (branches,
routes) *Barrass* Stanley 1890s; "canny gannen
– not bad" (re a miner's shift) Spennymoor
C20/mid; "all gas and gan-on – a person who
is pushing and voluble" *AK* Newc 1950s;
"gan-on – a fuss" *Graham* Geordie 1979;
"ganibil – passage or use possible" *Dodd* MS
Tanfield Lea C20/2; "klubganner" *Dobson*
Tyne 1969; "gisa gan" (give me a turn) *JS*
Easington C20/mid, *JP* S'm C20/2, also
Dawdon 2001 Q. See also **go**

ganny grandmother

"mi owld ganny" *CT* New Herrington 1930s;
"When I was a laddie / I lived with me
gannie" *BH* South Shields C20/1; "G'anny
Hen-wife's cottage' *S'd Echo* 17 Nov 1965 re
C20/1; "gannee" South Moor (Stanley) 2003
per BG. *EDD* distribution to 1900: C'd, Lx.
[variant of gammer from grandmère; or
godmother]. *Plus* "gammy" N'd 1995 (rural/
children); "where's your Nanna going to sit?"
EP S'm 2003

gansey a jersey or jumper

'a corruption of Guernsey... a style of knitting
a fisherman's sweater' *JS* Easington C20/mid;
'pullover' *ER* M'bro C20/2; "ganzee – jersey"
Dodd MS Tanfield Lea C20/2, sim. Tyne 2003
Q, NShields C20/mid Q; "a bonny ganzee"
(jumper) *Dobson* Tyne 1970; 'a thick woollen
jersey, especially worn by fishermen' *Graham*
Geordie 1979. *EDD* distribution to 1900:
Shetlands, Yx, Suff. [from Guernsey; but
Irwin suggests a Norse root]

gant to yawn

"?gaunt – to yawn" *Bell* MS Newc 1815; "she
put her jah oot wi gantin" *Embleton* Tyne
1897; "Yor gob wes ganting open" *Nth Words*
Seaton Sluice, 1938. *EDD* distribution to 1900:
general. [OE gánian]

gar to make (someone do something), compel

"the priour... gart make a grete bell" *Cuthbert*
C15/mid; "[I will] Gare her believe in me"
Noah's Ark Newc C15/16; "She gar'd saddle
him his horse" *RR* Weardale 1569; "Pride...
garr'd Tindaill lads begin the quarrel" *Reed
Border Ballads* C16; "gar – to oblige to do
any thing" *Bailey* Co.Durham 1810; "gar – a
Northumberland word, to force or compel"
Bell MS Newc 1815; "sic a dream as gar'd
me scart me lug" *Allan's Tyneside Songs* p.312
1827; "Steam gars wor boats and packets sail"
Pitman's Pay G'head 1820s; "yor looks gar
me shiver" (re a ghost) *Allan's Tyneside Songs*
p.300 1842; "mi fahther gar'd us gan to bed"
Egglestone Weardale 1870s; "Nance had garr'd
them aal te gurn" *Barrass* Stanley 1890s.
EDD distribution to 1900: Sco, Ire, Nth,
eMids. NE 2001: not in use. [ON gera]

garsel hedging material

"ledynge... garsell furthe of the woods to the... hegges" *Raine* MS York 1530/31; "hath cut down at pleasure ryse and garsell..." *Raine* MS Brancepeth 1615; "garsil – hedging wood" *Bailey* Co.Durham 1810; "garcil – small branches, cut for the purpose of mending hedges" *Brockett* Newc & Nth 1829. *EDD* distribution to 1900: Nth. [ON gerða 'fence']

garth yard, garden

"garth – yard or backside, a croft" *Kennet* 1690s as Nth; "garth – a small enclosure adjoining to a house" *Brockett* Newc & Nth 1829; "garth – an enclosure generally" *Atkinson* Cleve 1868; "applegarth, tettygrath, stag-garth (stackyard)" *Hull* MS wNewc 1880s; "'garth – paddock" *Blenkinsopp* Teesdale 1931. *EDD* distribution to 1900: Sco, Nth, eMids. [ON garðr; *OED* says obsolete in Sco]

gate 1. road, 2. route, course, way, 3. access to or right to pasturage

1. "thai come to the toune yate / thai lete thair oxen in the gate / a while standdand rest" *Cuthbert* C15/mid; "At the bryge end apon the gatt war many children revested of surpelez (surplices)" *The Maister* p.20, quoting document of 1503; "gait or gate – a path, a way, a street" *Bailey* Co.Durham 1810; "Gýét (from Gait, to walk) – a way, a path, a street, as Towngyet, a Town street" *Bell* MS Newc 1815; 'an underground roadway' (in pit) *Northumbrian III* 1990 re Backworth. *EDD* distribution to 1900: Sco, Nth, Mids. [ON gata 'road, way']. *Plus* "mothergate – in the workings of a colliery are the way by which the workmen first proceed" *Bell* MS Newc 1830s. 'the principal road of a coal-pit' *Brockett* Newc & Nth 1846; "mutha git / tail git – mothergate, tailgate, ends of [coal] face" *Dodd* MS Tanfield Lea C20/2
2. "we have a great sea-gate in a storme" *Raine* MS Scarborough, 1565; "gate – way or path " *Ray* 1674; "ga his gate" (went on his way); "algates – in any case" *Cuthbert* C15/mid; "'what gate are ye ganging?' *Brockett* Newc & Nth 1829; "also 'gang your gate'" – go [on] your way" 1846. *EDD* distribution to 1900: Sco, Nth, Mids
3. "gait for cattle – the going or pasturage of an ox or cow through the summer" *Bailey* Co.Durham 1810; "gate or gait – a right of pasturage for cattle through the summer"

gate cont.

Brockett Newc & Nth 1829; "cow-gate – pasturage for a single cow" *Atkinson* Cleve 1868; "gait – right or privilege of stray and pasturage for cattle etc.; pasturage for a specified time" *Atkinson* Cleve 1868. *EDD* distribution to 1900: Nth. See also **yet**

Gateshead

"Goatside" Bell Newc p.71 1812 re 1780; "Gyetsidd – Gateshead" *Dodd* Tanfield Lea C20/2; "aal the world and pairt of Gyetside" *Geeson* N'd/D'm 1969. [Bede: 'Ad Caprae Caput']

gavelock crowbar

"i gavelock" *Raine* MS Jarrow 1310; "gaveloke – an iron crow or lever" *Finchale* 1354; "gaveluk – an iron bar" *Kennet* 1690s as Nth; "gaivlick – an iron instrument about 4 feet long used by quarry men and builders to paize large stones, etc." *Bell* MS Newc 1830s; "gavelick (pronounced geavlick) – a strong iron crow, or bar, used as a lever, chiefly by masons and quarrymen" *Brockett* Newc & Nth 1846; "gavelick – crowbar" Upper Teesdale 2001 Q. *EDD* distribution to 1900: Sco, Nth, eMids, EA. [OE gafeluc, ON gaflak 'javelin']

gay, gey 1. considerable, 2. cheerful

"gay – tolerable: "he's a gay decent man"; also considerable: " a gay while – a considerable time" *Brockett* Newc & Nth 1829; "we hed a gay heartsome time on't" *Lakeland* re C'd 1901. *EDD* distribution to 1900: Sco, Nth. *Plus* "gaily – tolerable, pretty well" *Brockett* Newc & Nth 1829
2. "all hearty and gay" *Armstrong* Tanfield C19/2; "Whitley Bay's summer show 'Gay Parade'" *Newc Jnl* 12 Jun 1958

gear equipment, weapons, tools

"the stoutest men and best in gear" (military equipment) *RR* Weardale 1569; "my gear's a' ta'en" (stock, possessions) Reed *Border Ballads* C16; "gear – stock, property, wealth" *Bailey* Co.Durham 1810; "geer, set o' geer – pitmen's working tools: 'te get his geer sharp'd at the smiddy'" *Pitman's Pay* G'head 1820s; "gear – work-tools, consisting of picks, drills, maul and wedge, shovel, cracket, &c." *Nicholson* 1880; "sets of gears –collars, bridles, straps and chains" [for the ponies] *Hitchin* re Seaham p.66 1910s; "Maw workin' gear's the axe an'

gear cont.

saw" *Barrass* Stanley 1890s. *EDD* distribution to 1900: as tools, etc., Sco, Nth. [ON gervi]. *Plus* "The whole Gears [timber structure] at one loading place is called a Staith." *Bell* MS Newc 1830s; "obscenely, [as] "the great beast showed me a' his gear" *Bell* MS Newc 1830s

geck scorn, derision

"dinna ye mak you geck o' me" *Brockett* Newc & Nth 1846 as D'm

gee see **ghee**

Geordie 1. George, 2. King George, 3. a guinea, 4. a North East miner, 5. Tynesiders, 6. a pit lamp, 7. a collier brig, 8. Tyneside dialect

1. "Gwoardy" *Bewick* Tyne 1790s; "Geordy – George" *Pitman's Pay* G'head 1820s; "Twas like our Geordy in a battle" Wade *South Moor* C20/mid; "Young Geordie starts work" *Irwin* Tyne 1970
2. "It's James and George they were two lords/ And they've coosten out about the kirn, / But Geordie he proved the strangest loon, / And he's gart Jamie stand ahin'.' (from 'Kirn-Milk Geordie', a song of the 1715 rebellion); "tho' Cam'rons, bra' lads! took the gumples / An' wadna own Geordie ava' (at all)" *Marshall* G'head 1806; "Geordie Prince Rex" *Allan's Tyneside Songs* p.97 1814; "Geordie's Coronashun" *Allan's Tyneside Songs* p.238 1829; "aw seed the Queen, Caroline... wi' Geordy the third drinkin wine" *Ross* Tyne p.23 C19/1
3. [guinea] "the yellow letter'd Geordie" Burns 1784 via *Johnson*; "Wor Geordies now we thrimmel'd oot, an' tread a' Shiels sae dinny" *Marshall* Newc 1823. *EDD* distribution to 1900: Sco, N'd, D'm [from either the figure of St George on the reverse of various gold coins (see *Johnson* p.47), or the head of one of the Georges on the obverse of coins]
4. [pitman] "Geordie – George, a very common name among the pitmen... " *Brockett* Newc & Nth 1829; "a genuine Geordie" (pitman) *NWC* 19 Apr 1873; 'C.N.Davies in *Unorthodox London* (series 1 and 2, 1873–5) uses "Geordie" to mean a pitman' *Johnson* p.48; "Geordie (jau:di) – a miner" *Palgrave* Hetton 1896; 'pitman, or even a Tynesider in general' Embleton, Newc 1897; "He was a queer little chap from the 'Pits' and had the typical cap and neckerchief of the 'Geordie'" *Windows* Newc 1917 4/11; "My mother-in-law

Geordie cont.

from Byker also thinks the miners are 'the real Geordies' not the citizens of Newcastle." *Wood* re C20/2. *Plus* "Geordieland means Northumberland and Durham" *Dobson* Tyne 1973
5. [Tyneside] "Near akin to this Geordie [keelman] is the other – the pitman" *The Maister* p.36 re Tyneside, 1800–1840; "Geordie and Pee-dee" (as crew of a keel) *Allan's Tyneside Songs* p.216 1823; "A Geordie is born wthin the sound of the shipyards' buzzers" *Dobson* Tyne 1971; "some 'purists' insist that no man may claim legitimately the honourable name of 'Geordie' unless he lives close to that part of the river Tyne which is tidal' *Johnson* p.49. *Plus* 'Tynesiders' *Allan's Tyneside Songs* p.529 1863
6. [pit lamp] "The pitmen have given the name of Geordie to Mr George Stephenson's lamp in contra-distinction to the Davy, or Sir Humphrey Davy's Lamp." *Brockett* Newc & Nth 1829; 'The publication of the Northumberland and Durham Association, London, October 1947, maintains that in 1815 George Stephenson's lamp was called the "Geordie lamp" and that "Geordie" is a Scots word believed to have been carried across the Border by Scottish miners. The writer states that when a man came to work in a new place outside his own district it was said "A Geordie had come among them."' *Johnson* p.48 *EDD* distribution to 1900: NE... obsolete?
7. [collier brig] "towards the end of the 18th century the three-masted collier barques began to give way to the two-masted collier brigs which were often called 'Geordies'" *GS* Laird Clowes *The story of sail* 1936 via *Johnson* p.49; "south county people... gave all north country vessels the name of Geordies" Walter Runciman *Collier brigs and their sailors* 1926 re ca. 1860; 'You thought of the channel aswarm with just such vessels as she – Geordies deep with coal' WC Russell *Jack's courtship* 1884 via *Johnson* p.48; 'A North-country "Geordie" that was coolly snuggling down and outweathering the fierce squall' *Daily Mail* 13 Oct 1897 p.7; "A writer in a recent periodical supplies us with the curious information that 'Mariners term a vessel from the Tyne a Geordie, and from the Wear a Jamie." William Fordyce History of... the County Palatine of Durham (1857) vol.2 p.509, fn

Geordie cont.

8. [dialect] "Larn yersel' Geordie" *Dobson* Tyne 1969; "the Geordie language", "to speak Geordie" *Dobson* Tyne 1970; "Geordie lingo" *Dobson* Tyne 1972

gerse grass

"gers – grass" *Kennet* 1690s as Nth; "girse – grass" *Dinsdale* mid-Tees 1849; "as green as gers" *Egglestone* Weardale 1870s. *EDD* distribution to 1900: Sco, Nth. [OE gærs]

get to get, also to reach: 1. present tense, 2. past tense

1. "able to get – able to reach a place: 'Ah know n't an Ah sal be yabble te get'" *Atkinson* Cleve 1868; "Get – 'reach' (a place): 'I couldn't get'" *Palgrave* Hetton 1896; "if th' lucky enough t' gerron th' new trams" *CT* New Herrington 1930s; "let steam git ye hyem" *Dobson* Tyne 1972; "How'd ye gerron?" *VIZ* 72 (1995). *Plus* "cauld getting, but" *PG* H'pool C20/2
2. "he gate leue (got leave)" *Cuthbert* C15/mid; "horses I trow they gat" *RR* Weardale 1569; "he gat ower wet" *Marshall* Newc 1823 p.15; "Ah gat up", "Ah gat a ride" *Egglestone* Weardale 1870s "Bobby Shaftoe's getten a bairn" co.D'm C18/mid; "gitten" *Egglestone* Weardale 1870s; "tha wid awl geten bail" *Armstrong* Tanfield C19/2; 'he had getten converted' Coxhoe 1916. [ON geta]

ghee (to take) offence

"gee – out of humour" *Bell* MS Newc 1830s; "Tak the gee, pronounced ghee" *Hay* Moor re C20/1; "tak the ghee – become huffed" South Moor (Stanley) 2003 per BG; "taking the ghee – getting upset or annoyed" *AK* Newc 1940s; "gee (tak thi) – stubborn" *Dodd* MS Tanfield Lea C20/2. *EDD* distribution to 1900: Sco, N'd, C'd

gif see **if**

gill half pint

"a gill o' beer" *Bell* Newc 1812 p.10; "if I had another penny / I would have another gill" *Bell* Newc 1812 p.36 re Walker; "gill o' milk" (third-pint?) *GP* S'm C20/mid. *EDD* distribution to 1900: general

gill, ghyll ravine

"gill – a small valley or dell" *Bailey* Co.Durham 1810, 'a glen' *Bell* MS Newc 1815; 'small

gill cont.

ravine' *Dinsdale* mid-Tees 1849. *EDD* distribution to 1900: Sco, Nth, SE. [ON gil]. *Plus* "griff – a deep narrow glen or valley" *Atkinson* Cleve 1868

gilt young sow

"gilt – young female pig" Upper Teesdale 2001 Q. *EDD* distribution to 1900: Sco, Nth, Mids, EA. [ON gyltr]

gimmer young ewe

"gimmer-lamb – ew-lamb" *Ray* 1674; "gimmer – a female sheep from the first to the second shearing" *Brockett* Newc & Nth 1829; "the gimmers aye are short of milk" *Northumbrian Words III* re Kielder C20/mid; 'a young ewe; also a low woman' *Graham* Geordie 1979. *EDD* distribution to 1900: Sco, Nth, Mids. *Plus* gimmer – a Newcastle word for a low-bred woman" *Bell* MS Newc 1815 [ON gymbr]. See also **jimmer**

gin see **if**

girdle a griddle, a flat round of iron for cooking on

"girdle – a circular iron plate, with a bow handle, on which thin and broad cakes of bread are baked" *Brockett* Newc & Nth 1829; "spice hinnies on the gurdle fizz'd" *Allan's Tyneside Songs* p.379 1849; "girdle, gordle – a flat circular iron plate with handle which is used on the open fire for making singin-hinnies" *Graham* Geordie 1979 re past practice. *EDD* distribution to 1900: general. [AN grédil 'gridiron'] *Plus* "girdle-cake – thin household bread baked on a girdle" *Brockett* Newc & Nth 1829; "like a hen on a hot griddle" Ashington C20/mid

girn to grin, grimace

ex. *Kennet* 1690s as Nth, *Brockett* Newc & Nth 1829; "like a monkey he did gairn, man" *Allan's Tyneside Songs* p.327 C19/1; "girn or gurn – to grin…" 'the dog girned at me as if he was ganging to bite me', 'he girns like a sheep's head and a pair of tangs'" *Bell* MS Newc 1830s; "they gurn'd like cats" *Allan's Tyneside Songs* p.384 1849; "gen, girn, gern – to grin; to snarl" *Atkinson* Cleve 1868; "Nance had garr'd them aal te gurn" *Barrass* Stanley 1890s. *EDD* distribution to 1900: general. [OE grennian]. *Plus* "the tugboat-maister… kinda

girn cont.

gorned" *Allan's Tyneside Songs* p.534 1882; "gawn – make funny faces" *Dodd* MS Tanfield Lea C20/2

girth, gord hoop

"'Hoop'... we called it a 'girth' usually metal made at a coal mine and used by young and old. There was the story of 2 men who would run with their girths and stop at a pub to have a drink then go back home. One day they found their girths had been stolen and they wondered how they would get home." *JG* Annfield Plain 1930s; "gorth – iron hoop in boy's game" *Dodd* MS Tanfield Lea C20/2;" coin yer gord" *Dobson* Tyne 1969. [ON giðrð 'hoop'] See also **booler**

gis, guissy 1. pig, 2. call to a pig, 3. toes, 4. a policeman

1. "grice, grise – a pig" *Kennet* 1690s as Yorks; "gissy – a pig: 'a bit o' gissy's tripe'" *Pitman's Pay* G'head 1820s; "gissy-pig – a pig (child's term)" *Dinsdale* mid-Tees 1849, eD'm 2001 Q; "gissy-pig – a gluttonous person" *PG* H'pool C20/2; "an' blubbered sair / aboot her gissy's fate" *Allan's Tyneside Songs* p.375 C19/mid; "A couple o' coos, a few gissies, sum hens and ducks" *Irwin* Tyne 1970; "gissee – a pig" *Dodd* MS Tanfield Lea C20/2; "giss – a pig" B'd Castle 2001 Q. [ON gríss 'a pig']
2. "gyss – a call for swine: 'Gyss-gyss!'" *Bell* MS Newc 1815; "gissy – the call of pigs to their meat" *Brockett* Newc & Nth 1846; "Gis gis gis (gis:gis) – call to a pig" *Palgrave* Hetton 1896; "gis gis gis" (call to a pig) Roker C20/mid. *EDD* distribution to 1900: Sco, Nth. [compare Swed. gis, 'a call to a pig']
3. "gissies or gissie pigs – an infant's toes" *SO* ED'm. 1940s; "When I was very young my mother referred to our toes as 'gissies' or 'gissie pigs'. *SO* re Seaham 1940s
4. "1890: a few months of industrial trouble at Silksworth when some miners evicted. When bailiffs arrived to clear the houses, they were escorted by police and the women lined the road hissing 'gissie'." *SO* from family notes re Sunderland

give 1. present tense, 2. past tense

1. "gie" *Oiling* G'head 1826; "gie'd ti me" (give it) *Wearside Tales* 1879; "Give over (giv uw:u) – 'Don't!' 'Stop that!'" *Palgrave* Hetton 1896; "Giz a leg up so's a can see i' th' winda" *CT*

give cont.

New Herrington 1930s; "gizabroon" *Dobson* Tyne 1969; "gi ower!" Teesside C20/2 Q
2. "the howdy never gav ower (stopped) cryin (saying loudly)..." *Bewick* Tyne 1790s; "aboot seven aw gov owr warkin'" *Allan's Tyneside Songs* p.96 1814; "gov" (pret.) *Tyneside grammar* 1880s; "gav" Tanfield Lea, 1960; "geen, gien gi'n – forms of the preterite of gove" *Atkinson* Cleve 1868; "if he'd geen them a chance" *Armstrong* Tanfield C19/2

glaky awkward, etc.

"a glaick or glaicky – a silly awkward indiscreet girl" *Bell* MS Newc 1830s; "glaikee – irresponsible" *Dodd* MS Tanfield Lea C20/2; "glaky – slow witted" *Graham* Geordie 1979. *EDD* distribution to 1900: in form glaikit, Sco, Ire, Tyne

glead bird of prey

"glead – a kite, the fork-tailed falcon" *Brockett* Newc & Nth 1829; "gleid – a hawk" *Bell* MS Newc 1830s "glead, gled – the kite" *Atkinson* Cleve 1868; *EDD* distribution to 1900: Sco, Ire, Nth, Mids. [OE glida]

glede

"glede, gleed – a coal in a state of strong heat" *Brockett* Newc & Nth 1829. *EDD* distribution to 1900: Sco, Ire, Nth, Mids. [OE gléd]

glee(d) squint-eyed

"Gleed Will" *Marshall* G'head 1806; "glee eyed" (has a squint) New Herrington C20/mid; Tanfield Lea 1960; "glee-yd – cross-eyed" *Dodd* MS Tanfield Lea C20/2. *EDD* distribution to 1900: Sco, Nth, EA, USA. [ME gleyen (vb)]

gleg to glance

"gleg – to glance, or rather to look sharp; [adjective] quick, clever, adroit..." *Brockett* Newc & Nth 1829; "gledge – to look slily" *Gibson* C'd 1880; "gleg – [to] glance, look at" *JB* Shildon C20/mid. *EDD* distribution to 1900: Yx, Mids. [ON glegg 'quick-sighted'; Swed. glia 'a glance']. *Plus* "gisa gleg" (let me look) *JS* Easington C20/mid; "gleg – quick clever" *Pitman's Pay* G'head 1820s

glent to gleam, to glance

"glent – a glance" *Pitman's Pay* G'head 1820s; "glent – to look aside, to glance, to peep, to sparkle; [as noun] an indistinct or oblique

glent cont.

view" *Brockett* Newc & Nth 1829; "glent – to ricochet, glance off" *Dinsdale* mid-Tees 1849; "glent – to gleam" *Gibson* C'd 1880. *EDD* distribution to 1900: general. [compare Swed. glänta]

gliff 1. a fright, 2. a glance, a sight, 3. to cause a fright

1. "glif – a glance, a fright" *Bailey* Co.Durham 1810 "ye divent ken whatin a glif aw gat" *Bell* MS Newc 1830s; 'gliff – shock' RLS Scots 1891; "got a gliff – a fright" *Nth Words* N'd 1938; 'a fright or shock' *RV* Winlaton C20/2; 'fright, shock' Newc, Teesdale 2001 Q; *EDD* distribution to 1900: Sco, Nth. [compare Du glippen]
2. "a gliffe – a glance" *Kennet* 1690s as Nth; "A short gliff" *Marshall* G'head 1806; "A gliff o' me" *Pitman's Pay* G'head 1820s; "glif – glimpse" *Dinsdale* mid-Tees 1849
3. "that gliff'd me" *Allan's Tyneside Songs* p.498 1886; "Gliff – startle 'She gliffed me there'" *Palgrave* Hetton 1896; "gliff – frighten" *Dodd* MS Tanfield Lea C20/2

glime glance (noun and vb)

"Betty Kell gav her sic a gleyme" *Bewick* Tyne 1790s; "glymin' – looking slily" *Pitman's Pay* G'head 1820s; "glime – to look sideways" *Gibson* C'd 1880. *EDD* distribution to 1900: Sco, Ire, Nth

glishy, glisk bright

"glishy – bright (as of weather)" *Dinsdale* mid-Tees 1849. *EDD* distribution to 1900: N'd, D'm, Yx. "glisk – a transient light" *Brocket* Newc & Nth 1846. *EDD* distribution to 1900: esp. Sco. [compare OE glisian 'to shine']

glore to stare

"glore – glower" *Kennet* 1690s as Yorks; "glore – to stare" *Bailey* Co.Durham 1810; "it was sic a fine seet / Aw cou'd glower'd a' neet" *Allan's Tyneside Songs* p.98 1814. *EDD* distribution to 1900: NE, EA; glower – general. [ME glóran, ON glora 'to stare']. *Plus* "wi' sec a glower" (look of hatred) *Bewick* Tyne 1790s

gnarly rugged

"a great gnarly stone wall" *Dobson* Tyne 1970–71; "geet narly (even bigger!)" Gosforth C20/2 (Q); "two geet gnarly M.P.s" (military poliss) Oz in *Auf Wiederseshn Pet*, Ser.2, epi.2, 1992. *EDD* distribution to 1900: general

go

"Gae wash't and mak it clean" Reed *Border Ballads* C16; "we hand't gane far" *Street Piracy* Newcastle 1822; "went – for gone. Frequent in the North..." *Brockett* Newc & Nth 1829; "gae – to go... pret. gard, geed. also gan which is in much more continual use" *Atkinson* Cleve 1868; "what are ye gawn ti dee wi' that?" *Wearside Tales* 1879; "these dark days hev gyen" *Barrass* Stanley 1890s. [OE gán, imper. gá!, pret. éode; the verb gán is the West Saxon equivalent to gangan]. *Plus* "The TV has gone off" – broken down (of anything mechanical/electrical not working) D'ton C20/2. See also **yewd**

goaf, gove, gob the emptied sector of a pit

"goaf – a Tyneside term in pit working applicable to that part of the pit in which both the first wrought coal and the pillars are wholly gone" *Bell* MS Newc 1815; "goaf – the space remaining in a coal mine after the removal of the coal" *Brockett* Newc & Nth 1846; "goaf – the space from which the coal has been extracted. it is usually of dome-like form, resting upon the wreck which has fallen from the roof of the exhausted space" *Nicholson* 1880; "the gove gans thud! for thud" *Barrass* Stanley 1890s "the 'gob' fire, when certain worked-out sections of the pit filled with gas." *Hitchin* re Seaham 1910s p.60; "gob – part of mine forbidden entry" *JP* S'm C20/2; "waste ground behind the face" *JM* Dawdon 1970s; "and when the face had been advanced and the goaf lay on the ground / they stood there in amazement when they heard that awful sound" *JM* Dawdon 1970s. *EDD* distribution to 1900: N'd, D'm, Yx, Lx. [ON gólf a bay in a barn, a space between wooden supports']

gob 1. mouth, 2. to talk

1."gob – an open or wide mouth" *Kennet* 1690s as Nth "gob – the mouth" *Bailey* Co.Durham 1810 "gob – the mouth: 'T'set up yur gob' is to hold up impertinant conversation" *Bell* MS Newc 1815; "bauld Dolly Raw stopt his gob wi a cod fish" *Marshall* Newc p.15 1823; "gob and guts like a young craw" (of someone with a big appetite) *Brockett* Newc & Nth 1829; "born wi' silver spoons i' thor gobs" *Allan's Tyneside Songs* p.440 C19/mid; "aw've a greet moosetash abuve me gob" *Allan's Tyneside Songs* p.456 1862; "mair gob"

gob cont.

(ready speech) *Haldane* Newc 1879; "haud yor gob" *Barrass* Stanley 1890s; "'haad thee gob' means be quiet" *HP* South Gosforth C20/mid; "a bat on the gob (mouth)" Tanfield Lea 1960; "scadyagob", "Aalborst yagob" East Boldon, 1985. *EDD* distribution to 1900: general. NE 2001: in common use. [possibly from Gaelic or Irish gob 'beak, mouth'] *Plus* "gob-stick – a spoon" *Brockett* Newc & Nth 1829
2. "the fine things ye are gobbin about" *Marshall* Newc 1823; "foaks gob aboot drink" *Allan's Tyneside Songs* p.366 1849; "Jackey an' Jenny sat gobbin / about the fine things i' thor hoose" *Allan's Tyneside Songs* p.464 1860. *Plus* "gobby – saucy" *Robson* Tyne 1849; "gobby – talkative" D'ton C20/mid; "gobbed" (spat) *ER* M'bro C20/2

goggle staring

"a blakeymoor / wi' goggle eyes se queer" *Allan's Tyneside Songs* p.370 1849; "greet big goggle eyes" 'Lambton Worm' 1867; 'staring' *Graham* Geordie 1979. *EDD* distribution to 1900: general

gollan buttercup, etc.

"gollan, gowlan, gowan – a yellow flower, the daisy" *Brockett* Newc & Nth 1829. *EDD* distribution to 1900: Sco, Nth

goller to shout, yell

"gollar, goller – to shout, to speak in a boisterous or menacing manner, to storm" *Brockett* Newc & Nth 1829; "goller – to find fault or scold in a hasty manner: 'he gollered at him'" *Bell* MS Newc 1830s; "Maw marra ... gollers up wor garrot stairs " *Barrass* Stanley 1890s; "golla – loud growling shout" *Dodd* MS Tanfield Lea C20/2. [ON gaula]

golly unfledged wild bird

ex. *JB* Shildon C20/mid. *EDD* distribution to 1900: Yx

gome to heed

"He niver gomed me there" *Palgrave* Hetton 1896. *EDD* distribution to 1900: Sco, Nth, eMids. [ON gaumr 'attention' (noun)]

goniel fool

"thoo greet daft gonniel" *Cuddy Cairt* Newc 1917; "gonniel – a stupid person" *Irwin* Tyne 1970; "Ye greet gonniel!" (idiot) *Dobson* Tyne 1970–71

good as adverb: well

"My! you did that good" *PG* H'pool C20/2. *Plus* "good-like – well-favoured" *Brockett* Newc & Nth 1846; "good-like – handsome" Dinsdale mid-Tees 1849

goodbye 1. **tata, tara**, 2. other phrases

1. "so ta ta" *Allan's Tyneside Songs* p.408 1862; "ta, ta, ti pay; ta, ta, ti penshin" *Allan's Tyneside Songs* p.429 1862; "an' then taw-taw" *Chater* Newc p.8 1885; "ta ta [to child]" *Dodd* MS Tanfield Lea C20/2; "say taa taa te yor da" *Dobson* Tyne 1969; "Ta-ra. Ta-ra Dad. Ta-ra our Billy." *Cate* B'p Auckland area 1987; "tara" S'm 1990s via BG
2. "Good neet hinny" (*Brockett* 1829)…; "Can ganny... Tara weel..." *Chater* Newc p.8 1885; "Keep ahaad" (Johnny Handle on radio) 2001; "gan canny" Wheatley Hill 2002 Q; "keep had" Wheatley Hill 2002 Q; "keep a ganun youngun" (goodbye) Wheatley Hill 2002 Q; "tak care now" *Dunn* B'p Auck 1950; "seeya" S'm 2000 per BG

gooseberry 1. **grozer**, 2. **goosegog**, 3. **goosegob**, 4. **carberry**, 5. **berries**

1. "goose-berries or grosers" *Raine* MS 1648; "grosers" *Bailey* Co.Durham 1810; "grozer" *Bell* MS Newc 1815; "berries en grozers" *Egglestone* Weardale 1870s; "...a Leek Show, a Grozer Show" NM vol.1 p.181 1888, re Newcastle; "apple trees and peir trees and peiches and grosers" *Allan's Tyneside Songs* p.554 1891 re S'd; "she jumped at it like a cock at a grozer" *Embleton* Tyne 1897; "beef an' grosser dumplings" *Graham* Geordie 1979 re 1966. *EDD* distribution to 1900: Sco, Nth. [Fr groseille. *Scottish National Dictionry* p.xiv gives as from French 15–16C]
2. "goosegogs" *RM* Norton C20/mid; Gosforth C20/2 Q; "goosegog" Blyth, Wheatley Hill 2002 Q; "got catched pinchin' goosegogs" *Dunn* B'p Auck 1950
3. "goosegob" *JB* Shildon C20/mid, D'ton C20/2, cenD'm 2001 Q, Trimdon 2002 Q. *EDD* distribution to 1900: Ex, Mids, EA. NE 2001: in use
4. "carberries – gooseberries" *Atkinson* Cleve 1868. *EDD* distribution to 1900: Yx, obsol.
5. "berries – gooseberries, par excellence" *Atkinson* Cleve 1868

gord see **girth**

gorn to moan

"gornin' and glowerin'" *Other Eye* Newc ca.1890; "to gorn on – to moan on. Still in regular use." *RV* Winlaton 2003

Gotham a sort of City of Fools

"Gotham – the cant name for... Newcastle, and other places, containing a considerable proportion of inhabitants not endowed with 'absolute wisdom'" *Brockett* Newc & Nth 1829. [legends of the 'wise men' of Gotham first appear in the mid 15th century]

gotherly sociably, affably, in a friendly way

"the ewe is gotherly with its lamb" *Brockett* Newc & Nth 1829; 'sociable, familiar' *Dinsdale* mid-Tees 1849; "Aw... wawk'd gotherly in" *Barrass* Stanley 1890s. *EDD* distribution to 1900: N'd, D'm, Yx

gowdspink goldfinch

"goldspink" *Brockett* Newc & Nth 1829; "gowdspink" *Bell* MS Newc 1830s; "gouldspink" *Dinsdale* mid-Tees 1849. *EDD* distribution to 1900: Sco, Nth as 'goldfinch', Yx as 'yellowhammer'. [compare Swed. gulspink]

gowie see **chewing gum**

gowk 1. cuckoo, 2. fool

1. "gouk, gowk" *Kennet*, 1690s as N'd; "gowk – a fool, also a cuckoo" Grose, 1787; "gouk – a cuckoo" Bailey, Co.D'm 1810; "gowk – the cuckoo... In some parts of Yorkshire, it is cowk" *Brockett* Newc & Nth 1846; "gowk – the cuckoo; a fool" Atkinson, Cleveland, 1868; "gowk – cuckoo, fool" *Gibson* C'd 1880; *EDD* distribution to 1900: esp. Sco, Nth. NE 2001: not in use. ['gowk' meaning 'cuckoo' is derived from ON gaukr, though compare OE géac (pronounced yea-ak).] *Plus* "gowk-spit – cuckoo-spit" *Brockett* Newc & Nth 1846
2. "gowk – a fool, also a cuckoo" Grose, 1787; "ye're a gouck if ye din't knaw that..." *Allan's Tyneside Songs* p.48 1812; "town folks, whe se oft ca' us gowks" *Allan's Tyneside Songs* p.91 1812; "gowk – a fool or simpleton, also a cuckoo; April Gowk or April Fool" *Bell* MS Newc 1815; "Maister A'body has a heap o' the gowk in him yet" *MacDonald* Aberdeen C19/1; "gowk's errand – a fool's errand; 'What are ye gauping at, ye gowk?'" *Brockett*

gowk cont.

Newc & Nth 1829; "gawk [sic] – clown" *Robson* Tyneside 1849; "Gowk (guuwk) or 'gowkie.' A soft person. An April fool is often called 'April gowk'" *Palgrave* Hetton 1896; "gouk – silly, slight person" N'd via *Nth Words* 1938; "daft gowk – on Wearside is an expression of foolishness" *SMcD* 1990s; "ye daft gowk!" Sacriston 2004 E. *EDD* distribution to 1900: esp. Sco, Nth. Not listed in *SED* C20/mid. NE 2001: not in clear use. [extension of meaning from 'cuckoo']

gowk apple-core

"goke, gowk – the core of an apple, the yoke of an egg, the inner part of any thing" *Brockett* Newc & Nth 1825; "goke – the central portion of anything, as the core of an apple, the yolk of an egg" *Atkinson* Cleve 1868; "gowk is also the core of an apple" Palgrave, Hetton 1896; "gowk, gowky – the pith of a tree: 'that's ne wood that, its ower gowky'" *Bell* MS Newc 1830s; "goke / gowk – apple-core" *Blenkinsopp* Teesdale 1931; "giz thee gowk" *JS* E'ton 1950s; "giz yer gowk" *IA* S'm C20/mid, sim. East Boldon 1985; "gowk – apple core, silly person" *Dodd* MS Tanfield Lea C20/2; "gork [sic] – apple core" *Todd* Tyne 1977; "gowk – applecore" *Haswell* South Shields 2001 Q, *PC* Wallsend C20/2 Q, *RV* Winlaton 2003. *EDD* distribution to 1900: Nth. *OED* only has goke 'the core of a rope' 1800, in a maritime context. *SED* C20/mid gives only as 'core of a boil': Yx, D'm, C'd, W'd. NE 2001: in use (as applecore). [OE geolc (pronounced rather like, and meaning 'yolk') is the ultimate source, in what seems a northernised form] Note: in pronunciation, goke was likely influenced by gowk, and has now replaced the original meaning of gowk: "to children an apple core, to adults idiot or fool" *Lore and Language* re Ashington 1990s. *Plus* "gorker" *Wood* M'bro C20/2, *ER* M'bro C20/2, M'bro 2001 Q, "gowker – apple core" South Moor (Stanley) 2003 per BG; "a coggie – an apple core" *RM* Norton C20/mid

gowpen a handful

"goping – as much as both hands can hold, when joined together" *Bailey* Co.Durham 1810; "gowd -i'-gowpens – gold by handsful" *Pitman's Pay* G'head 1820s; "gowpen – the hollow of a hand formed to receive any thing, a handful; gowpens – both hands held

gowpen cont.

together inform of a round vessel" *Brockett* Newc & Nth 1829; "a gowpen – as much as your hands will hold: "a gowpen of meal" as an alms to the poor, also 'a gowpen or herbs' in medical prescriptions" *Bell* MS Newc 1830s; "ye cud ha gitten a gowken fu' fer a penny" *Egglestone* Weardale 1870s. *EDD* distribution to 1900: Sco, Ire, Nth. [ON gaupn]

goz, guzzle share of a drink

"giz a guzzle, giz a goz" *IA* S'm 1950s, 60s

grain branch

"up the East grane of Soulgill" *Raine* MS Wellrigg 1667; "grain of a tree – a branch" *Bailey* Co.Durham 1810; "grain – a separate linear portion of a thing, as the branch of a tree" *Atkinson* Cleve 1868. *EDD* distribution to 1900: general. [ON grein 'branch, division']

graith to equip, to work on

"he began the seiues [rushes] graythe" *Cuthbert* C15/midl "to grath(e) a hous or room – to deck it or dress it up neat and fine" *Kennet* 1690s as D'm; "graith – to clothe, or furnish with any thing suitable" *Brockett* Newc & Nth 1829; "graithed – equipped, furnished..." *Bell* MS Newc 1830s; "graith – to put into working condition, to service" *Dinsdale* mid-Tees 1849; "a well graithed table" *Atkinson* Cleve 1868. *EDD* distribution to 1900: Sco, Ire, Nth. [ON greiða]. *Plus* "graithly – decently, in order, mensefully" *Atkinson* Cleve 1868

grand fit, well

'he didn't feel ower grand' Coxhoe 1916

granfu grandfather

ex. *CT* New Herrington 1930s

grape see **gripe**

grassman officer for grazing land

"'grassman – an officer whose duty it was to take charge of and attend to the herbage of a parl and the cattle feeding on it" *Raine* MS C19 note

grave to dig

"grave – to dig, to dig up ground with a spade" *Brockett* Newc & Nth 1829; "grave – to dig, using a spade. pret. grove, p.p. groven, grovven" *Atkinson* Cleve 1868. *EDD* distribution to 1900: Sco, Nth, Lx. [OE grafan]

greasers mechanism for automatically greasing wheels

"the greaser was a tiny rectangular hole set between the rails, and as the trains of tubs, the 'sets' passed over it, the axles were automatically greased." *Hitchin* re Seaham p.66 1910s; "gan steady owr the greaser" Wheatley Hill 2004 Q. *Plus* "the greasers clatter loudly" (?wheels on man-riding train in pit) *JM* Dawdon 1970s; 'curved wheels' Crocker *Lore and language* re Maria Pit, Throckley C20/mid

great 1. **greet, gret,** 2. **girt, gurt,** 3. **git**

1. "vi [6] grett castelles" *Anderson* Newcastle 1568; "for a greet while" *Bewick* Tyne 1790s; "greet an' sma', fishwives an' a'" *Allan's Tyneside Songs* p.235 1829; "a grit big bird" *Wearside Tales* 1879; "greet surprise" *Armstrong* Tanfield C19/2; "the Greet North Road" *Dobson* Tyne 1972; "grit" *IA* S'm 1950s,60s, Peterlee, B'd Castle 2001 Q. *Plus* "wassen great" (huge) S'm via BG C20/2
2. "Girt and small" *Brockett* Newc & Nth 1829; "t'windows is gert big 'uns" *Egglestone* Weardale 1870s; "on th' girt grey horse" ?N'd, *NCM* 1900–1901. [metaphasis of 'r']
3. "git biggen" (any thing of great size) *JS* Easington C20/mid; "geet big gob" *Graham* Geordie 1979; "geet – great, big" *Dodd* MS Tanfield Lea C20/2; "git – really" Thornley. 2001 Q; "git – great" Trimdon 2002 Q; "He was a proper geet bloke". *Plus* "You're git thick, you" Charver 2000–2002. [?loss of 'r' after metaphasis]

gree to agree

"Law's costly; tak a pint and gree" *Brockett* Newc & Nth 1829; "gree – to agree" *Dinsdale* mid-Tees 1849. *EDD* distribution to 1900: general. [from agree, Fr agréer]

greet to weep

"the children gretand" (weeping) *Cuthbert* C15/mid; "Aws sure his muther grat mair at the dhael [funeral] than ony body" *Bewick* Tyne 1790s; "greet – Scotch for grief or weeping" *Bell* MS Newc 1830s; "greet – to cry, to weep, silently rather than with any great outcry. pret. gret or grat, p.p. grettan" *Atkinson* Cleve 1868; "greeting – weeping, crying, lamenting" *Smith* Weardale 1883; "greet – great, weep" *Dodd* MS Tanfield Lea C20/2. *EDD* distribution to 1900: Sco, Ire, Nth. [OE grétan]

greetings 1. **fettle**, 2. **cheor**, 3. **how**, 4. other

1. "What fettle noo?" *Allan's Tyneside Songs* p.576 ca.1890; "a salutation: 'Well, what fettle?', 'Oh, canny.'" *Palgrave* Hetton 1896; "whatfettletheday?" *Dobson* Tyne 1970; "what fettle lad? – how are you?" *Dunn* B'p Auck 1950; "What fettle the day, marra?"... "Not ower clivvor." *JS* Easington C20/mid; "What fettle"... "Fair to middling" nwD'm C20/mid Q

2. "What cheor, hinny!" (greeting) *Haldane* Newc 1879; "What cheer (chai:u, chae:u) commonest greeting of man to man, answered back in the same words" *Palgrave* Hetton 1896; "Wotcha" *CT* New Herrington 1930s; "Wot cheer!" N.Shields C20/mid Q; "Whatschai" (pit greeting) *JP* S'm C20/2; "wa chee-a – greeting" *Dodd* MS Tanfield Lea C20/2; *EDD* distribution to 1900: D'm, Yx. *Plus* 'Wotcha Geordie' (radio, 1950s)

3. "How dye?" *Bell* Newc p.40 1812; "How d'ye de?" "Aw's teufish," (toughish?) says as, "canny man, how are ye?" *Allan's Tyneside Songs* p.312 1827; "Wi, how is thou?" *Marshall* Newc p.10 1823; "How! How-marrow! – a favourite salutation among the pit-men" *Brockett* Newc & Nth 1829; "How there, lads, what cheer?" *Allan's Tyneside Songs* p.537 1886; "How there, marrah! – How there, Bob!" *Embleton* Tyne 1897; "hooyeganon?" *Dobson* Tyne 1970; "How there marra? followed by the reply, What cheer, hinney" *Graham* Geordie 1979

4. "Holloa!" *Wearside Tales* 1879; "hooz thoo haddin the day?" *Embleton* Tyne 1897; "Now then" *DO* D'ton C20/2; "Aareet?" S'm 1990s per BG; "hooz thoo haddin the day?" (how are you) *Embleton* Tyne 1897; "whahey!" [greeting] *VIZ* 72 (1995); "used to greet anyone: 'y'alreet workid?'" Charver 2000-2002

greybird thrush

exx. *Grose* 1787; *Palgrave* Hetton 1896. *EDD* distribution to 1900: general

grey-hen stoneware bottle

'stone bottle' *Pitman's Pay* G'head 1820s; "Greyhen – a jar in basket-covering, containing spirit" *Palgrave* Hetton 1896; "grai hen – stoneware bottle" *Dodd* MS Tanfield Lea C20/2. *EDD* distribution to 1900: Nth

grip small watercourse

"grip – a ditch, gutter" *Dinsdale* mid-Tees 1849. *EDD* distribution to 1900: general. [?OE grype]

gripe, grape agricultural fork

"v grapes, vi sholes" *Raine* MS Jarrow 1362; "grape – a three pronged fork for filling rough dung" *Bailey* Co.Durham 1810; "grape... sometimes pronounced grip" *Bell* MS Newc 1830s; "Grape... a kind of shovel (sometimes called 'gripe '), or huge fork-like implement used in filling coke, and by farmers for removing manure" *Palgrave* Hetton 1896; "a gripe was a fork with flattened tines like a spoonbill's beak used for lifting turnips and potatoes" *JS* Easington C20/mid; 'a garden fork' *CT* New Herrington 1930s, *Graham* Geordie 1979; "A gripe is strictly a three pronged farming fork but I've heard it used of an ordinary garden fork" *Wood* re Teesside C20/2. *EDD* distribution to 1900: Nth, Notts. [ON græip; compare OSwed greep, Dan greb 'fork']

groove a lead mine

"one groove work in the Helmeford" *Raine* MS Stanhope 1567; "Robert Rutter bur[ied]. He was hurt in a groove." *Raine* MS Stanhope 1625; "groove – a lead mine" *Bell* MS Newc 1830s. *EDD* distribution to 1900: Nth, Mids. [ON gróf 'pit' or via Du groeve; see also **grave** 'to dig'] *Plus* "groveman" (a lead-miner) *Raine* MS Marske 1635; "Robert Beck, a grover" *Raine* MS Ronald Kirk, 1670

grow-day a warm, moist day

ex. *Dinsdale* mid-Tees 1849

grozer see **gooseberry**

grund ground

"ground – pronounced grund or groond: 'gan to grund' (to relieve nature)" *Atkinson* Cleve 1868

grunge to grunt or growl

"th' little dogs il grunge en bark" *Armstrong* Tanfield C19/2; "Grunge – to grunt: 'They will show their teeth at you and grunge at you'" *Palgrave* Hetton 1896. *EDD* distribution to 1900: Sco, NE

guest ghost

"The streets of this Northern Metropolis [Newcastle]... haunted by a a mighty guest, which appeared in the shape of a mastiff dog" Brand via *Raine* MS "guest – a ghost or spectre" *Brockett* Newc & Nth 1829; "guest – ghost or spirit" *Bell* MS Newc 1830s. [OE gæst]. See also **barguest**

guiser someone in disguise eps. for fancy-dress party

"guizers... Christmas Masqueraders" *Bell* MS Newc 1815; "guisers – persons wo dance in masks, oe with their faces blackened, or discoloured, and in rustic disguise" *Brockett* Newc & Nth 1829; "guisers – fancy-dress revellers and competitors" *Dinsdale* mid-Tees 1849; "Voices called: 'Let the guysers in.' ...Men were dressed as women; women as men; some had black faces and other carried musical instruments... they sang songs and danced jigs in which all the family joined." (re Xmas Eve) *Hitchin* re Dalton-le-Dale p.24 1910s; "guizer – a masquerader" *Graham* Geordie 1979, S'm 1995 (re New Year) via BG. *EDD* distribution to 1900: Sco, N'd, D'm, Yx, Derbys. [OFr guise]. *Plus* "He's twisting his guiser, i.e. pulling a funny/miserable face" *RV* Winlaton 2002

guising costume performance or merry-making

"ther was dysgysyng, piping & dansyng" (*Durham* C16/2); "Guising (gaa:yzn) – play-acting by ' guisers' – men and boys in disguise (with blackened faces and paper caps), who go about performing a rough Christmas play" *Palgrave* Hetton 1896

guissie see **gis**

guizen to crack through dryness

"guisen'd – tubs that leak through drought" Ray Nth 1737; "ma thropple was ready to gizen" *Allan's Tyneside Songs* p.49 1812; "With parched tongues and gyzen'd throats" *Pitman's Pay* G'head 1820s; "to guizen, guizend – to be drie as a cask till the staves separate" *Bell* MS Newc 1830s; "Guisen (gaa:yzn) – to become dried and contracted, of rain-tubs or wooden cisterns, so that the water 'sipes' out" *Palgrave* Hetton 1896; "gizzend – thirsty, dry, overcooked" *Dodd* MS Tanfield Lea C20/2; "gi's a drink I'm gyezend" *Graham* Geordie 1979. [ON gisna (vb), gisenn (adj); compare OE wisnian] See also **kizzen'd**, **wizzen'd**

gully household knife

"gully – a knife... a common hous-knife" *Kennet* 1690s as Nth; "gully – a large knife" *Bell* MS Newc 1815; "gully – a large sharp knife used in farm-houses, principally to cut bread, cheese, etc., for the family; also used by butchers in killing sheep" *Brockett* Newc & Nth 1846; "gully – breadknife" *Dinsdale* mid-Tees 1849; "Gulley – carving-knife, bread-knife" *Palgrave* Hetton 1896; "gully – large (kitchen) knife" *JB* Shildon C20/mid; "gully – used by the fish man who came to the door; it had a unique shape" *JS* Easington C20/mid; "he took the gully knife out" *Cate* p.77 B'p Auck area 1987. *EDD* distribution to 1900: Sco, Ire, Nth. NE 2001: in use

gurn see **girn**

gut ?ravine, channel

"divided...by a deep gyut, wherein ran a little river" Reed *Border ballads* p.35 re 1547; "The Gut – River Team" C20/mid Q

guytrash a large brown dog of ill boding

"The Guytrash!... a great beast, brown and shaggy" ?N'd, *NCM* 1900/1901. *EDD* distribution to 1900: Yx

gwaak, gaak to stare

"gaak – stare" *Dodd* MS Tanfield Lea C20/2; "gwaak – stare foolishly, gawk" *LL* Tyneside 1974

haad, had, haud 1. to hold, 2. phrases

1. "as lang as storm hods" Coniston C17/ult via Raistrick *Yorkshire Dales* ch.11; "had up the low" *Collier's Rant* Newc C18/2; "Bill Shakspur... hadded horses for ha'pennies" *Allan's Tyneside Songs* p.368 1849; "ho'd – (hold)" *Atkinson* Cleve 1868; "Aa hadded" (I held) *Other Eye* Newc, ca.1890; "haad – hold" *LL* Tyneside 1974

2. "Now haud your tongue, my daughter dear!" Reed *Border Ballads* C16 "had thy wisht" *Marshall* G'head 1806; "had your tongue", 'had away!', "haud away!" (go away / hold on your way) *Brockett* Newc & Nth 1829; "tack haud" 1846; "aw was nowther to haud or to bind, man" (i.e. upset) *Allan's Tyneside Songs* p.359 1849; "aw mun haud mee jaw" *Allan's Tyneside Songs* p.396 C19/mid; "wad ta nobbit hot the tongue" (hold) *Egglestone* Weardale 1870s; "had thee watter" (be patient) *IA* S'm 1950s, 60s; "haddawy", "haddaway, man" ('well I never', 'you must be joking') *JG* Annfield Plain 1930s; "haad thee pipe" *JS* Easington C20/mid; "keep a had" (take care) *JS* Easington C20/mid; "had-away – get along" Tanfield Lea 1960; "haddaway an' buy yer aan" (go away) *Dobson* Tyne 1970; "get ahad on't" *Graham* Geordie 1979; "hadawai" *Dodd* MS Tanfield Lea C20/2; "hadaway" (get lost) Trimdon C20/2 (Q); "had on – wait" *Dodd* MS Tanfield Lea C20/2; "had thee gob, had thee wisht" *Dodd* MS Tanfield Lea C20/2; "hadaway'n sh..." ('you must be joking') East Boldon 1985; "fast haad" (stuck fast) *Northumbrian III* 1990 re Backworth; "A'm haddin on – doing nothing" Tyneside 2001 Q. *EDD* distribution to 1900: in this pronunciation Sco, Nth. See also **howay**

haaf half

"hofe-croons" *Egglestone* Weardale 1870s; "'he hesn't haaf some wool on' – needs a haircut" *Dunn* B'p Auck 1950; "hawf nowt – small quantity" *Dodd* MS Tanfield Lea C20/2; "nee hahfas – no sharing" *Dodd* MS Tanfield Lea C20/2

hack pit tool

"hack" (a hack or two-toothed pickaxe) *Raine* Finchale (1360); "Hack is a tool that Miners use like a Mattock" Derbyshire 1681; "hack – a pick-axe, a mattock made only with one end, and that a broad one" *Grose* 1787; "hack – a strong two-toothed pick-axe or hoe, much

hack cont.

used in agriculture" *Brockett* Newc & Nth 1829; "hack – a heavy pick, 18 inches long, and weighing about 7lbs., used in sinking or stonework" *Nicholson* 1880; "Hack – a heavy pick, weighing about 7lbs., with head about 18 in. in length. There are various kinds, e.g. Tommy hack (round head and chisel point), Jack hack (round head and sharp point), Pick hack (sharp head and chisel point)" *Palgrave* Hetton 1896; "coal cutter's hack – 2 [foot] 6 [inch] shaft with a head composed of one side, hammer, one side, pick... rolleywayman's hack had a 3 [foot] 6 [inch] shaft with a much heavier head, one side hammer, one side a flat curved blade... conveyor advancer's hack...was one side pick, one side axe." *Northumbrian III* C20/2 re Burradon Colliery. *EDD* distribution to 1900: general. [ME from late C13; compare OE haccian, Du hak, OFr hache]

hacky dirty

exx. *RM* Norton C20/mid, Trimdon 2002 Q, 'Tyneside slang for dirty' *Graham* Geordie 1979; "hakkee – dirty" *Dodd* MS Tanfield Lea C20/2; 'hack-mucky – needs a wash" *Dobson* Tyne 1969; "hack-mucky" Roker C20/mid (Q), *MB* Coxhoe C20/2. *EDD* distribution to 1900: eD'm. *Plus* "hack – filth, dirt: 'Aa canna get the hack off tha'" *Palgrave* Hetton 1896

haffit the temples

"haffit – the side of the head" *Pitman's Pay* G'head 1820s. *EDD* distribution to 1900: Sco, Ire, N'd, C'd, W'd. [OE he
alf-heafod]

haffle to falter

"haffle – to waver, to speak unintelligibly, to prevaricate" *Brockett* Newc & Nth 1829; "haffle – to stammer or hesitate in speech: 'to haffle and snaffle'" *Atkinson* Cleve 1868. *EDD* distribution to 1900: Nth, eMids. [Du haffelen]

hagberry bird-cherry

"hagberry, heckberry – the bird-cherry" *Brockett* Newc & Nth 1829; "hag-berry " *Atkinson* Cleve 1868; "heckberry" *Blenkinsopp* Teesdale 1931; "heck-berry – sloe" *Dinsdale* mid-Tees 1849. *EDD* distribution to 1900: Sco, Nth. [ON heggr; compare Dan hægge-bær-]. *Plus* "Hackaberries or Heckerberries" (inhabitant of Winlaton Mill) *KE* Winlaton C20/mid

haggis

"haggish – two kind of, a Scottish and Northumberland dainty, both made of minced mutton, etc., the one seasoned savoury with spices and the other with currans and raisons, etc., and called a spice haggish – and boiled up in the bagg of stomach of a sheep..." *Bell* MS Newc 1830s

hagworm adder

"to my surprise there was 2 hagworms 16 inches length" *Errington* p.33 Felling/Heworth re 1780s; "hagworm – the common viper" *Atkinson* Cleve 1868, *Gibson* C'd 1880; "hagworm – large brown worm" *Dinsdale* mid-Tees 1849. *EDD* distribution to 1900: Nth. [ON h'ggormr 'adder'] See also **worm, nedder**

hail haul a keel

"they would hail the keels in this manner right up to the Low Lambton staith" *Wearside Tales* 1879. [?variant of haul] Plus "hailers – ropes to haul keelboats upstream" *Wearside Tales* 1879

hain to protect, manage so as to conserve

"the tenants... ainciently hain'd & hirded the Fawside" (managed?) *Raine* MS Hexham 1664; "hain – to save, to preserve: 'haining wood', 'haining land', 'haining a new suit of clothes'" *Brockett* Newc & Nth 1829 *Brockett* Newc & Nth 1829; "Thor grass fields are a' hained for the cows to gan in" (reserved) *Luckley* Alnwick 1870s extra; "hain – to shield, exculpate" *Palgrave* Hetton 1896. *EDD* distribution to 1900: general. [ON hegna 'to save, protect']

hause throat

"hause, hose – throat" *Ray* 1674, 'the neck, the throat' *Brockett* Newc & Nth 1829, *Atkinson* Cleve 1868. *EDD* distribution to 1900: halse 'neck' Sco, Nth. [OE heals]

hame, 1. **hyem**, 2. **yem**, 3. home

1. "there is nane but women at hame" *RR* Weardale 1569; "I am gang hame – I am going home" *Kennet* 1690s as Nth; "hout lad, get hame" *Chicken* Benwell 1720s; "toddling hame" Bell Newc 1812 p.43 "hame aw gat, tired" *Allan's Tyneside Songs* p.98 1814
2. "at heame or away" *Bells* re Carlisle, 1802; "heam, h'yem – home" *Brockett* Newc & Nth 1829; "hi'am's hi'am!" *Egglestone* Weardale 1870s; "the pitman's humble hyem" *MC* Tyne

hame cont.

May 1881; "cairted hyem" *Barrass* Stanley 1890s; "in wor little hyems" Coxhoe 1916; "let steam git ye hyem" *Dobson* Tyne 1972; "just as he's comin ower hyem..." *Irwin* Tyne 1970/71; "heycm-coming" *Graham* Geordie 1979; "wa ganninhyeum" East Boldon 1985
3. "when we got yam" Alston 1992 per BG *Texts* p.96; "comin yem", "hees landed yem" *Armstrong* Tanfield C19/2; "Yam. The invariable pronunciation of 'home'" *Palgrave* Hetton 1896; "Aa wish aa was yairm" *NDN* 31 May 1919; "gerraway yem" *Hay* Ushaw Moor C20/1; "yem" *JR* Seaham C20/1, *Dodd* MS Tanfield Lea C20/2; "went yam" *Lakeland* re C'd 1934; "at yem" *VIZ* 40, 1990s. *EDD* distribution to 1900: heyem N'd, heeam, yam nYx, hoame wYx. [OE hám]

handfast

"handfast — a staple" *Blenkinsopp* Teesdale 1931

hansell 1. an advance; 2. to wear in

1. "hansel or handsel – the first money received for the sale of goods; an earnest given on hiring a servant" *Brockett* Newc & Nth 1829. *EDD* distribution to 1900: general. [OE handselen, ON handsal]
2. "handsel – to make of anything for the first time" *Atkinson* Cleve 1868; "We used to 'hansell' articles when we put them on for the first time" *Nth Words* Morpeth 1938; "you've hanselled the new kettle... to use or wear in a new item, inc. clothes" Morpeth C20/2 Q

hant habit

"hant – custom, habit: 'at your aud hants'" (at your old habits) *Brockett* Newc & Nth 1846; "Aa'd getten canny inte the hant o' weerin' me new blinker" *Other Eye* Newc, ca.1890; "'He has a nasty hant of doing that" *Palgrave* Hetton 1896. *EDD* distribution to 1900: N'd, C'd, Yx. [AN hant, haunt, 'haunt, practice']

hanted accustomed (to)

"to be haunted – to grow used to, or become accustomed: 'he got haunted to it by degrees'" *Atkinson* Cleve 1868; "Aa wan't reet hanted wid (with it)" *Other Eye* Newc., ca.1890; "pigeons were kept in the new loft or cree until they were hanted" *JS* E'ton 1950s. [F hanter 'to frequent'] See also **heft** hap

hap 1. to wrap, cover, 2. a covering

"digged a grave... and happ'd him the sod sae green" Reed *Border Ballads* C16; "happe – to cover for warmth" *Ray* 1674; "hap – to cover, by placing or heaping clothes, etc. upon: 'are you well happed?', 'all's white and happed up' (with snow)" *Atkinson* Cleve 1868; "hap up warm" Thornley 1940s Q; "happed up" (bandaged) *JP* S'm C20/2; "hap weel up; it's a caad neet" *Graham* Geordie 1979; "happed up – buried with stones" (in pit) *Northumbrian III* 1990 re Backforth. *EDD* distribution to 1900: Sco, Ire, Nth, Mids, EA. [ON source suggested by, e.g. Swed hypja 'to cover']
2. "hap – a cover of any kind of stuff, but generally applied to one of coarse material" *Brockett* Newc & Nth 1846; 'bed-cover, etc.' *Dinsdale* mid-Tees 1849; "haps – overclothes, rugs, shawls, great coats, etc." *Atkinson* Cleve 1868; "he has a good hap on" (coat) *Nth Words* Bensham 1938; 'overcoat' *GP* Seaham re 1940s; also Tyne, wD'm 2001 Q, 'topcoat' *AT* Co.D'm C20/mid. *Plus* "ii happins and a coverlett" Cockerton 1612 via *Atkinson* D'ton no.30; "bed-happings – bed-clothes" *Atkinson* Cleve 1868

happen to experience (trans. vb.)

"happen – to meet with, to incur: 'she's happ'n'd a misfot'n'"" *Atkinson* Cleve 1868; "aw happened an accident i' me back" *JA* Newc 1875; "ye'll be happenin something sum day" *Allan's Tyneside Songs* p.504 1891. *EDD* distribution to 1900: D'm, Yx, Lx. [ON happ]

hard up in poor health

"She's gey hard up" *Nth Words* Shotley Bridge 1938

hardlies scarcely, hardly

"hardleys – scarcely, hardly. Universal among the vulgar" *Brockett* Newc & Nth 1829, GP S'm C20/2, *Graham* Geordie 1979. *EDD* distribution to 1900: Sco, N'd, C'd, Yx

hare 1. mally, 2. wattie

1. "mally – a name for the hare (D'm)" *Brockett* Newc & Nth 1829
2. "wat or wattie is a hare: a man (or a woman!) may be dubbed a 'daft wattie' which really means as mad as a March hare" *Tyneside Grammar* 1880

harns brains

"she did take the axe & knocked her husband's harnes out, for he had done her a great injury & did deserve it" *Raine* MS Pickering 1671; "harns – brains" *Brockett* Newc & Nth 1829. *EDD* distribution to 1900: Sco, Nth. [ON hjarne]

har, harl rain-mist

"har – small rain" *Kennet* 1690s as D'm; "a harl – a mist" *Kennet* 1690s as Nth; "hare or harr – a mist or thick fog" *Brockett* Newc & Nth 1829; "harr – a strong fog or wet mist, almost verging on a drizzle" *Atkinson* Cleve 1868; 'a mist' *Graham* Geordie 1979. *EDD* distribution to 1900: haar – Sco, NE, Lx, Lincs; harl – ?Lincs

harring herring

"heerin, harrin – herring: 'four twopence caller harrin'" *Brockett* Newc & Nth 1829; "reed-harrin" *WM* Newc C19/2; "harrin" *Dodd* MS Tanfield Lea C20/2. [Du haring]

hather heather

"hether, hather or heath – a plant" *Bell* MS Newc 1830s; "In some parts of this country, the ordinary people make a good sort of ale called hather, that is, ling ale, by boiling the tips of the Hather plant to a wort" (and ferment it) *Wm Stukeley* 1776 vol.2 p.64. *EDD* distribution to 1900: in this pronunciation N'd, nLincs

haud see **haad**

haughs low ground

"haughs, holms – flat ground by the sides of rivers" *Bailey* Co.Durham 1810. *EDD* distribution to 1900: Sco, Nth. [OE healh 'corner, recess']

have 1. to have, 2. hed (have it), 3. to have to

1. "yeel hev" (you'll have) *Bewick* Tyne 1790s; "hez" *Marshall* G'head 1806, *Oliver* Newc p.8 1824; "aw've... aw hev" *Ross* Tyne p.4 C19/1; "henna, hanna – have not" *Brockett* Newc & Nth 1829; "if he'd hadden twee wooden legs" *Haldane* Newc 1879; "hev, heh" (have) *Armstrong* Tanfield C19/2; "hes", "hev", "hed" (have it), *Barrass* Stanley 1890s; "let me hae thee job" *Barrass* Stanley 1890s; "hed (had), hes (has), hev, hae (have)" Coxhoe 1916; "Aa hev – I have" *Dunn* B'p Auck 1950; "he' – have, hev before a vowel", "hevvent – haven't"

74

have cont.

Tanfield Lea, 1960; "ye'll hev" *Dobson* Tyne 1972

2. "we'll hed [have it] stuck on a pole" *Allan's Tyneside Songs* p.339 1843; "th' dog wadint hed" (have it) *Armstrong* Tanfield C19/2; "Ah suppu'as ye'll hed here a nee time" (have it) *Egglestone* Weardale 1870s

3. "it hesn't ti gan tiv his house" *Wearside Tales* 1879; "ye havn't to dee that" (must not) S'm 2000 via BG

haver oats

"a bowle of haver or oats" *Raine* MS Auckland 1572/73; "haver and hey" Rothbury C18/2; "haver – oats" *Ray* 1674 re C'd, *Bailey* Co.Durham 1810; "haver – (oat)meal" *Dinsdale* mid-Tees 1849; "haver (pronounced havver) – oats" *Atkinson* Cleve 1868. *EDD* distribution to 1900: Sco, Nth. [ON hafre]

haver-meal oatmeal

"haver-meal – oat-meal" *Bailey* Co.Durham 1810, *Bell* MS Newc 1830s; "grudge for haver-meal to pay / to make them crowdies once a day" *Bell* Newc p.51 1812. *Plus* "haver-bread, haver-cake – large, round, thin oaten cakes, baked on a gridle" *Brockett* Newc & Nth 1829; "haveridils – riddles for haver or oats" *Finchale* 1479-80

hawkey cow with white markings

"a reed whye stirke, being awked or whyte faced" *Raine* MS Bishop Auckland, 1585; "Haakie – pet name for a cow" *Dobson* Newc 1974; 'white faced cow' Graham Tyne 1980. *EDD* distribution to 1900: Sco, N'd, C'd

heald, hale, hell to pour out

"heald – to pour from a pot" *Ray* 1674; "to heald the pot" *Grose* 1787; "hell or hail – to pour" *Bailey* Co.Durham 1810; "hale – to pour or empty out" *Atkinson* Cleve 1868. *EDD* distribution to 1900: heald – Yx, Lx, Glos; hell – Nth, SW. [OE hieldan, ON hella]

heap, heapstead buildings or area round pit head

"heapstead – the elevated platform near the shaft above the surface upon which the tubs are landed and run to the screens" *Nicholson* 1880; "Aa wis waaking off the heap" i.e. going home from work. West Stanley C20/1; "heep – mine surface buildings" *Dodd* MS Tanfield Lea C20/2; "heap / heapstead – the pit head"

heap cont.

Northumbrian III Burradon Colliery C20/2; "See yi on the heap – a common quip when parting company at the Club" *Northumbrian III* 1990 re Backforth. *EDD* distribution to 1900: N'd

hear

"what news aw had hard" *Allan's Tyneside Songs* p.98 1814; "Aa's hard o' him afore" *Haldane* Newc 1879, sim. *Armstrong* Tanfield C19/2; "axin if aw'd heer'd the news" *Allan's Tyneside Songs* p.180 1824. sim. *Egglestone* Weardale 1870s, *Barrass* Stanley 1890s; "Aa hord" Coxhoe 1916

heave to lift

"Easter Monday is commonly known as 'heaving day'. The men heave or lift as many of the opposite sex as they can lay hands on before noon." *NWC* 18 Feb 1893, Sup, p.1. *EDD* distribution to 1900: general. *Plus* "heaving – crowded full" *GP* S'm C20/mid, S'd 2002 Q

heck part of door

"heck – the door...." *Grose* 1787; "heck – lower half of a door; interior door" Bailey D'm 1810; "heck – the upper part of a half-door or hatch-door" *Atkinson* Cleve 1868. [OE hec, pronounced hech]

heck-berry see **hagberry**

heckle coat of animal

"rough-hackled or smooth-hackled" (re skin of an ox) *Kennet* D'm 1690s; "hackle, heckle – feathers, wool, hair" *Atkinson* Cleve 1868; "ginger heckled" (hair colour) *Allan's Tyneside Songs* p.519 1872. *EDD* distribution to 1900: Eng. [OE hæcele 'cloak']

hedgehog a snarl up

"hedgehog – the strand of a wire rope having, broken is carried along the rope by coming in contact with the sheaves or rollers and forms a ravelled mass or ruffle on the rope which is then said to be hedgehogged" *Nicholson* 1880; "hedgehog – occurs on haulage rope when one or more strands of wire are broken... forming as mass of uncoiled strands around the rope" *McBurnie* Glebe Colliery C20/mid; "a snarl up on a steel haulage rope" *Northumbrian III* 1990 re Backforth.

See also **urchin**

heed head

"heaid" *Anderson* Newcastle 1628; "heeds" *Bewick* Tyne 1790s, sim. *Armstrong* Tanfield C19/2, Coxhoe 1916, etc.; "heeds and hearts" *Allan's Tyneside Songs* p.177 1824 Newc; "takken by t' heead – under the exciting influences of drink, passion, fancies, etc." *Atkinson* Cleve 1868; "dissent knaw whether thor heeds or thor heels are uppermost" *Chater* Newc 1880; "that curly heed" *Barrass* Stanley 1890s; "aa gov mesel an aaful crack on the back o' the heed" *Robson* Newc C20/1; "put yer eyes back in ya heed" *VIZ* 37. *EDD* distribution to 1900: in this pronunciation, Sco, Nth. [OE heafod]. *Plus* "hede-wark – headache" *Cuthbert* C15/mid; "slap-heed – idiot" 1990 eD'm via BG

heedways forwards

"heedways – head on, forward" *Tyneside Grammar* 1880s; "heedwis-end – headway, passages that lead to the crane or shaft" *Pitman's Pay* G'head 1820s; "headways – excavations in a coal pit at right angles to the boards, for the purposes of ventilating and exploring the mine" *Brockett* Newc & Nth 1846

heessel, hissel himself

"heessel" *Allan's Tyneside Songs* p.453 1862; "hees sel" (himself) *Armstrong* Tanfield C19/2; "hissel" Coxhoe 1916

heffering loud laughter

ex. *Nth Words* N'd 1938. *EDD* distribution to 1900: N'd

heft 1. haft, 2. accustomisation

1, "heft – knife-handle" *Dinsdale* mid-Tees 1849; "heft – a handle; a pretext or excuse" *Atkinson* Cleve 1868. *EDD* distribution to 1900: general. [variant of haft]
2. "heft – a haunt" *Bailey* Co.Durham 1810; "heft… in the passive, to become accustomed to" *Atkinson* Cleve 1868. *Plus* heffed/heft – of sheep having to learn new territory. *TP* re Alston Moor 2003. *EDD* distribution to 1900: Sco, D'm, C'd

hell see **heald**

hemmel outbuilding

"a long helme with propes, overthwartes, sidetrees & skelbourses, with a heck" (i.e. a barn) *Raine* MS ?York 1626; "a hemble or

hemmel cont.

helme – a hovel or house [Yorks], And in Dunelm. any place covered over head and open on both sides is call'd a hemle or hemble" *Kennet* 1690s; "hemmel – a shed for cattle, &c." *Bailey* Co.Durham 1810; "hemmels – originally, a thatched shed, stable, or byre; now the same, though seldom thatched. The word, although still understood, is going out of use" *Palgrave* Hetton 1896; "hemmels – the outbuildings of a farm" Spennymoor C20/mid. *EDD* distribution to 1900: Sco, Nth. [?OE helm 'protection'; ON heimile 'homestead']

hempy mischievous

"hempy – mischievous" *Brockett* Newc & Nth 1829; "'a hempy dog' – a youth disposed to practices which may end in the hangman's hemp" *Atkinson* Cleve 1868; "hemps" children – *Other Eye* Newc, ca.1890; "hempy – up to tricks and pranks, mischievous" *Palgrave* Hetton 1896; "hempee – troublesome child" *Dodd* MS Tanfield Lea C20/2. *EDD* distribution to 1900: Sco, Nth. [more likely from imp than hemp]. *Plus* "the yung imp" *Allan's Tyneside Songs* p.510 1872; "imp – mischievous child" *Dodd* MS Tanfield Lea C20/2

heor here

ex. *Graham* Geordie 1979, etc.

heronsew heron

"heronsew, heronseugh – a heron" *Brockett* Newc & Nth 1829; "heron-sew, hern-sew – the common heron" *Atkinson* Cleve 1868. [AN herouncel 'young heron']

hesp hasp

"hesp – a clasp or fastening, especially to doors or windows" *Atkinson* Cleve 1868. *EDD* distribution to 1900: variant of hasp in use in Sco, Nth, Linx. [OE hæpse, ON hespa]

het hot

"as hett as pepper" *Bell* MS Newc 1830s; "scaddin' het tea" *Allan's Tyneside Songs* p.395 C19/mid; "skeeding het – scalding hot" *Dunn* B'p Auck 1950; "mad het – very hot" *Dodd* MS Tanfield Lea C20/2; "reed-hot" *Graham* Geordie 1979. *EDD* distribution to 1900: het — Sco, Nth; heeat, yet nYx

hetter keen

"hetter – eager, earnest, keen" *Brockett* Newc & Nth 1829. [ME het(t)er] *Plus* "hettle – hasty: 'he was hettle'" *Pitman's Pay* G'head 1820s

heugh prominence

"yuff – heugh, steep hill or cliff" *Dodd* MS Tanfield Lea C20/2. *EDD* distribution to 1900: Sco, Ire, Nth [OE hó]

hetch hatch for loading coal from back lane into coal shed

"the coal-house hetch was open" *JM* Dawdon 1970s. *EDD* distribution to 1900: in this pronunciation neYx

hev see **have**

hew to cut coal

"a man thit hes te yew coals" *Armstrong* Tanfield C19/2. [OE heawan]

hewer coalface worker

"hewers – the men who work the coals in a coal pit" *Brockett* Newc & Nth 1846; "Thor's a man o' mine, a hewer, / Weers a shirt o' flannen blue..." *Barrass* Stanley 1890s; "yewer" *GP* S'm 1950s; "kohl yoo-a – coal hewer" *Dodd* MS Tanfield Lea C20/2; 'man who cuts the coal' *JM* Dawdon 1970s. *EDD* distribution to 1900: N'd, D'm, Lx

hewy bilious

"billious, ready to vomit" *GP* S'm C20/mid

hidey hide-and-seek

ex. *HP* South Gosforth C20/mid

hike 1.to swing, 2. a free lift

1. "a bairn... for to hike on his airm" 'Bobby Shaftoe' C18; "the heykin myed me vurry wauf" (the movement of the boat) *Allan's Tyneside Songs* p.53 1823; "hike – to swing, to put in motion: a nurse hikes her child when she tosses it up and down in her arms. There is also the hiking of a boat" *Brockett* Newc & Nth 1829; "hikey seas" *Allan's Tyneside Songs* p.409 C19/mid. *EDD* distribution to 1900: NE
2. "hike – to ride in a coach or cart; 'hike me' or 'De'il hike me', [a] common asseveration; also a saying 'he that borrows and pays not again shall surely have a hike in the Devils wain'" *Bell* MS Newc 1830s; "let's go hikey on the buntin's" *Brockett* Newc & Nth 1846. *EDD* distribution to 1900: general

hills an' howls the ploughed profile of a field

ex. *CT* New Herrington 1930s; "hilly-howly – undulations in a field" *FS* Shotton Colliery 1930s

hind farm-worker, supervisor

"the hynde or steward to Mr Butler" *Raine* MS Tynemouth 1680/81; "hind – an husbandry servant" *Grose* 1787; 'a servant or bailiff in husbandry' *Brockett* Newc & Nth 1829; 'an agricultural servant, hired by the year or term' *Atkinson* Cleve 1868; 'a yearly farm servant' *Luckley* Alnwick 1870s extra; "Hind (the 'i' long) – a farm-labourer (The only term in use)" *Palgrave* Hetton 1896; "wen th' hind wis it wark wi his horses and plue" *Armstrong* Tanfield C19/2. *EDD* distribution to 1900: farm-worker esp. Sco, steward Nth. [OE híne 'servant']

hing to hang

exx. *Brockett* Newc & Nth 1829, *Dinsdale* mid-Tees 1849, *Palgrave* Hetton 1896; "to walk in an' hing up me hat" *Allan's Tyneside Songs* p.408 1862; "ther hair hingin' down their backs" *Egglestone* Weardale 1870s; "a hoose, the Blue Bell... that hings oot its sign at the fut o' Sheel Raw" *Barrass* Stanley 1890s; "hinging" (intrans) Coxhoe 1916. *EDD* distribution to 1900: in this pronunciation Sco, Ire, Nth, Mids. [ON hengja]

hing on to get underway

"hingin' on – hanging on, the time the pit begins to draw: "Frae hingen on till howdy ma" *Pitman's Pay* G'head 1820s; "The wark's hung on" (the project's underway) *Barrass* Stanley 1890s; "hing-on or hang-on – a call from the banksman to the onsetter after any stop (the cause of which has been at bank), meaning recommence coal work" *Nicholson* 1880; "'Hang on'... was the signal to resume normal working" *Hitchin* re Seaham 1920s p.79; "hang on – start loading tubs onto haulage rope" *Northumbrian III* C20/2 re Durham collieries. *EDD* distribution to 1900: N'd, D'm

hinny honey, sweetheart, friend

"hinny – my honey, a term of endearment: 'my honey bairn'" *Grose* 1787; "Come come maw hinny..." (mother to daughter) *Bewick* Tyne 1790s; "Where hez t' been, maa canny hinny?" *The Maister* p.46 Tyneside song

hinny cont.

ca. 1800; "come listen, my honies, a while" *Marshall* G'head 1806; "Ma hinny" (to a girl) *Marshall* G'head 1806; "Ah hinnies! about us the lasses did loup" *Allan's Tyneside Songs* p.49 1812; "those married jog on with their hinnies" *Bell* Newc p.39 1812; "hinny – a favourite term of endearment, a corruption of honey: 'hinny maisters'" *Pitman's Pay* G'head 1820s; "hinny or hinney – a favourite term of endearment, expressing of great regard. A mispronounciation of honey – used with much effect by the Irish" *Brockett* Newc & Nth 1829; 'Come, hinny Barty, lens a hand *Pitman's Pay* G'head 1820s – workman to workman; "hinney – my honey, dear, or sweet; Alderman Cocke of Cockes Chare on the Quay called his daughter his "canny hinneys" *Bell* MS Newc 1830s; "Oh hinny Jack" (so addressed by his wife) *Allan's Tyneside Songs* p.275 1854 (T Wilson); "Noo, Geordy hinny..." (dear friend) *Haldane* Newc 1879; "O, hinney, put the led un in!" (to workmate) *Barrass* Stanley 1890s; "hinny" (friend: of man to man) Coxhoe 1916; 'used of woman or man' – *BL* re Blaydon 1950s; (to any money-collector) "karlbach themorrerhinny"; (starting a letter) "Esteemed hinny..." *Dobson* Tyne 1972. *EDD* distribution to 1900: Sco, N'd. C'd, D'm. NE 2001: in use. (doubtless from 'honey', but it is worth noting the Scots hen 'old woman' e.g. "In Glasgow, 'hinnie' becomes 'hen'" *Geeson* N'd/D'm '1969' p.38) *Plus* "honey – a term of endearment: 'honey-bairn'" *Atkinson* Cleve 1868

hint end back end

"hintend – end not front" *Dodd* MS Tanfield Lea C20/2; 'rear part of a machine, etc.' *Northumbrian III* 1990 re Backworth; "frostbite in the hint end" (backside) *Dobson* Tyne 1972; "hint end – backside, bottom" Newcastle/Chester-le-Street 2001 Q. *EDD* distribution to 1900: N'd, C'd, Northants, Suff. *Plus* "hinder-ends – the refuse of anything" *Brockett* Newc & Nth 1829

hint ways backwards

"Aa wayses, fore ways, side ways, hint ways" *Other Eye* Newc, ca.1890

hip to hop

"hipping and skipping" *NChorister* D'm, C18/2. *EDD* distribution to 1900: Sco, Nth

hipe to gore

"to see whether the oxe had hiped or goared her behinde" *Raine* MS Easby, Cleveland; 'to rip or gore with the horns of cattle' *Bailey* Co.Durham 1810; 'to push or strike with the horns, as cattle do' *Atkinson* Cleve 1868. *EDD* distribution to 1900: W'd, Yx, Lx, eMids. *Plus* "to hipe – to find fault with as 'what do you mean to be allways hiping at me for?'" *Bell* MS Newc 1830s

hippin' nappy

"hippings – clouts for infants" Grose 1787; "hippen or hipping – a cloth for an infant" *Brockett* Newc & Nth 1829; "hippings – napkins (for infants)" *Atkinson* Cleve 1868; "e bairns' hippin" *Armstrong* Tanfield C19/2; "Aa warrant thoo hasn't got thee hippins off yet" (of a boastful child) *JS* Easington C20/mid; "hippins – nappies" *Dodd* MS Tanfield Lea C20/2. *EDD* distribution to 1900: Sco, Nth, EA. [from covering the hips]

hirple to limp

"hirplen' – walking lamely: 'hirplen cross the floor'" *Pitman's Pay* G'head 1820s; "hirple or hipple – to halt, to go lame, to creep, to limp in walking" *Brockett* Newc & Nth 1829; "hirple – to shrug or stick up the back; to be dull [and slow], to creep" *Atkinson* Cleve 1868; "hirple – to limp" *Gibson* C'd 1880. *EDD* distribution to 1900: Sco, Ire, Nth, eMids

hirsel, hairsel sheepland

'the piece of land that hill farmers allotted to their shepherds' *Northumbrian III* C20/mid re Kielder. *EDD* distribution to 1900: Sco. N'd. [ON hirzla 'safe-keeping']

hit it

ex. *Tyneside grammar* 1880s; "hit – once common as in 'That's hit noo'" *Graham* Geordie 1979. [likely an extra initial 'h', but note the equivalent OE pronoun is 'hit']

hitch 1.to skip, 2. fault in strata

1. "hitch – to hop" *Dinsdale* mid-Tees 1849; "hitching is skipping, as in a dance step" *HP* South Gosforth C20/mid. *EDD* distribution to 1900: general. [ME 'to move jerkily']
2. "hitch – a small 'trouble' or dyke, in coal-mines, generally limited to a few inches' dislocation" *Brockett* Newc & Nth 1829

hitty-missy at random

ex. *Graham* Geordie 1979, S'm via BG 2002; "hittee-missee – at random" *Dodd* MS Tanfield Lea C20/2. *EDD* distribution to 1900: Sco, Nth, EA

hob 1. fire grate, or part you can rest things on, 2. elf

1. 'the iron bars in front of a fire' *Graham* Geordie 1979; "as hard as the hobs o' Hell" *GP* S'm C20/mid. *EDD* distribution to 1900: general
2. "hob – a spirit or being of elf-nature" *Atkinson* Cleve 1868. *EDD* distribution to 1900: D'm, Yx. [Robert]

hobbas hobnail boots

ex. *Northumbrian III* 1990 re Backforth

hobby 1. goose, 2. young colt, 3. a tool

1. "hobby – goose (child's term)" *Dinsdale* mid-Tees 1849. *EDD* distribution to 1900: D'm. [?OFr hobet 'a hawk']
2. "O maw Bobby! maw laddie, maw lover, maw hobby!" *Barrass* Stanley 1897 (here as nickname for a putter). *EDD* distribution to 1900: 'colt' Yx, EA
3. "hobby – caulker's or riveter's tool" Newc 2001 Q. *EDD* distribution to 1900: N'd

hockle to spit

ex. Ferryhill 2001 Q

hog a young sheep

"hogg – a young sheep before it be shorn" *Bailey* Co.Durham 1810; "hog – a sheep in its state from a lamb to its first shearing; after which it is a dinmont if a wedder, and a gimmer if a ewe" *Brockett* Newc & Nth 1829; "hog – a male of the pig kind; a sheep of a year old" *Atkinson* Cleve 1868. *EDD* distribution to 1900: general

hogger(s) 1. hosepipe, 2. shin-guards, 3. work shorts

1. "hogger – a wide leather pipe used to deliver water into a cistern" *Nicholson* 1880; "Hogger – hose-pipe" *Palgrave* Hetton 1896, *CT* New Herrington 1930s, *Northumbrian III* 1990 re Backforth, *PM* S'm 2000; "the hogger – a wire-covered rubber hose-pipe through which the compressed air passed to the engine..." *Hitchin* re Seaham 1920s p.101; "air hose" [in pit] *GD* Co.D'm. *EDD* distribution to 1900: N'd, D'm

hogger cont.

2. "there is my hoggars, likewise my half shoon" *Collier's Rant* Newc C18/2; "hoggers – stockings with the feet cut off" *Pitman's Pay* G'head 1820s; 'old stockings with the feet cut off, used as gaiters – riding stockings' *Brockett* Newc & Nth 1829; 'stockings without feet, chiefly used by the putters' *Nicholson* 1880; "The coal-hewer formerly wore his stockings with the 'feet' cut off [i.e. separate], so that when small coals got into the stocking-foot, he had only to pull off this, and not the whole stocking; consequently his ankles were bare, while the stocking-leg covered his calf" *Palgrave* Hetton 1896. *EDD* distribution to 1900: Sco, Nth
3. "knee britches tied or open at the knee called pit hoggers" *Wade* Annfield Plain re pit working clothes, 1890s; "pit-hoggers or drawers" (as a child's swimming costume) *Hitchin* re Seaham 1910s p.35; "at the face they generally wore a body shart (sleeved vest) and pit hoggers (cotton pants fastened below the knee with tape)" *Northumbrian III* C20/mid re Winlaton/Marley Hill; "underpants – as yer knar most fyes wurkers stripped down or did when coals kyem off the showlder... worn by aarl fyes wurkers except cutters whe used te keep their trousers on" *GD* Co.D'm C20/mid; "with your hoggers and your vest" *JM* Dawdon 1970s; "hoggers" 'shorts', *Dobson* Tyne 1974

hoit term of disparagement

"hoit – an awkward boy" *Grose* 1787; "hoyt – an awkward ill-bred youth, a lazy idle fellow" *Brockett* Newc & Nth 1829; "hoit – to play the fool; [noun] a simpleton, a fool" *Atkinson* Cleve 1868; "Hoit – slut: 'Ye mucky hoit!'" *Palgrave* Hetton 1896; 'person of no account' *Dodd* MS Tanfield Lea C20/2; 'wrong-doer' Ferryhill 2001 Q; "ye little hoits!" (something shouted at bad children) eD'm. 2001 Q. *EDD* distribution to 1900: Sco, Nth

hollin holly

"holyn in Werfdale" *Raine* MS 1368; "the grene hollin" *Reed Border ballads* C16; "hollin – the holly tree" *Brockett* Newc & Nth 1829, etc. *EDD* distribution to 1900: Sco, Nth, eMids. [OE holegn]. *Plus* "hollin – the breakthrough of one working into another" *Northumbrian III* 1990 re Backforth

holm islet or river-land

"haughs, holms – flat ground by the sides of rivers" *Bailey* Co.Durham 1810; "holm – low flat land caused by alluvion – a small island" *Brockett* Newc & Nth 1829; "holme – a low field, skirted by a river; esp. south side of Tees above Barnard Castle" *Dinsdale* mid-Tees 1849. *EDD* distribution to 1900: esp. Sco, Nth. [ON holmr 'islet']

hoo see **how**

hookie mat home-made mat

"a hookie mat [was] made with narrower clippings which were as long as the cloth would allow and a progger with a barbed point to pull the clippings through the harn or hessian backing" *JS* Easington C20/mid; "hookee mat – home-made rug" *Dodd* MS Tanfield Lea C20/2; 'a mat made from rags and clippings' *Graham* Geordie 1979.
See also **clooty, proggie mat**

hoop, hope 1. a hollow or valley, 2. a ring

"Great floods shall... run over hoope and hill" *Noah's Ark* Newc C15/16. *EDD* distribution to 1900: Sco, NE, SW. [OE hop 'enclosed land', ON hóp 'landlocked bay']
2. "hoop – a ring, generally used of the wedding ring and still in common use" *Raine* MS re C19/2

hoose house

exx. *Marshall* G'head 1806. Coxhoe 1916; "there's nae gud luck about the hoose" C19/1 song. [OE hús]

hoot/s (exclamation)

"hout lad, get hame" *Chicken* Benwell 1720s; "Houts muther..." *Bewick* Tyne 1790s; "hout – an exclamation of disappointment or dissent" *Pitman's Pay* G'head 1820s; "hout! – an exclamation of disapprobation, or disbelief... now used only by the vulgar" *Brockett* Newc & Nth 1846; "hoots, man!" *JA* Newc C19/mid; '[expressing] impatience or contempt' *Tyneside Grammar* 1880s; "Hoats, lad!" (Hush!') *Palgrave* Hetton 1896. *EDD* distribution to 1900: Sco, Ire, Nth

hopping a dance, fair

"Sunday feasts, meetings, hoppings and drinkings" *Raine* MS Lanchester, 1575 via Durham; "O' the hoppen day" *Marshall* G'head 1806; "hoppen, hopping – a country

hopping cont.

wake or rural fair" *Brockett* Newc & Nth 1829; "Last hoppin' thou wun up my fancy / Wi' thy fine silken jacket o' blue." *Crawhall* Newc 1888; "the Hoppins – the Temperance Festival on Newcastle Town Moor" *Dobson* Tyne 1969; "the hoppin's fer bairns, man" *VIZ* 37, 1990s. *EDD* distribution to 1900: NE. [used in this sense since C14]

hopscotch 1. **hopscotch**, 2. **hitchie**, 3. **(h)itchie-dabbers**, 4. **(h)itchy-bay**, 5. **bays**

1. hopscotch – *FS* Shotton Colliery 1930s
2. "hitchie is the word we used for hopscotch" *AK* Newc 1950s
3. "hitchy-dabbers" *CT* New Herrington C20/mid, "itchy dabber" *Wood* re Trimdon 2002. *EDD* distribution to 1900: hitchy dabber N'd, D'm. [hitch – to hop]
4. "Hitchy-bay – the game of Hopscotch. Properly speaking, 'hitchy-bays' are the courts marked out. The square bit of wood is called the 'hitchy-dabber'" *Palgrave* Hetton 1896; "itchy bay" *Wood* re Teesside/H'pool, 2002, *RM* Norton C20/mid. *EDD* distribution to 1900: hirchy-bays eD'm [bay "the starting place or place of refuge in a game" *Hull* MS wNewc 1880s]
5. "bays" *CT* New Herrington, C20/mid, "bays" *Wade* South Moor C20/mid

hor her

exx. *Armstrong* Tanfield C19/2, *Barrass* Stanley 1890s; "horsel – herself" Tanfield Lea 1960

horn-book learning book for children (ABC display with thin horn covering)

ex. Dinsdale mid-Tees 1849; "iv a hornbuik position aw stuid" *Street Piracy* Newcastle 1822. *EDD* distribution to 1900: general but uncommon

horn-top snail

"Horntop – only heard in the simile, 'as slaa (slow) as a horntop'" *Palgrave* Hetton 1896. *EDD* distribution to 1900: eD'm, nYx

horse-gog plum

"horse-gogs – a fair-sized but highly astringent blue plum" *Atkinson* Cleve 1868, Morris *Yorkshire Folk Talk* 1911

hotter to shake

"hatter/hotter – to shake, to harass, to weary: 'I'm all hottered to pieces', said of a jumbling

hotter cont.

ride in an uneasy vehicle" *Brockett* Newc &
Nth 1829; "hotter – to shake, or even jolt:
'we went hotterin' in the cart'" *Atkinson* Cleve
1868. *EDD* distribution to 1900: Sco, Nth.
[only in ModE 1800 plus, so perhaps from
Du hotten 'to shake']. *Plus* hottery – shakey
Lore and language NE C20/2

hough, huke thigh, ham

"a tough sinew in an old wife's hough" ('back
part of the thigh above bend of knee') *Raine*
MS Morpeth 1673; "the hough — the ham or
upper joint of the leg" *Kennet* 1690s as Nth;
"cruck yor hough" (sit down) *Allan's Tyneside
Songs* p.49 1812, "Draw in a seat and crook
thy hoff" *Pitman's Pay* G'head 1820s; "cruick'd
wor houghs" *Allan's Tyneside Songs* p.299 1831;
"the warst o' meat, Bad bullock's liver –
houghs and knees " *Pitman's Pay* G'head
1820s; "huke – the hip", "to crook huke – to
sit down" *Atkinson* Cleve 1868; "ahl cruk me
hough a bit" (sit down) *Embleton* Tyne 1897.
EDD distribution to 1900: general. [OE hóh
'heel']

how, hoo 1. call for attention, 2. in what way,
etc. (conj.)

1. "How! mind my legs!" *Allan's Tyneside Songs*
p.131 1813; "Ki' Geordy, How! where are ye
gannin?" *Marshall* G'head 1806; "how, man,
speak of the devil" *VIZ* 51, 1990s; "hoo man –
excuse me" Charver 2000–2002. [OE hú, also
used as interjection] See also under **greetings**
2. "hoo te get te heaven" *Allan's Tyneside Songs*
p.460 1862; "hoo" Coxhoe 1916; "hoo aboot
a raffle...?" *Dobson* Tyne 1972; "How's that
then?" (what do you mean?) S'm 2003 via BG

howay term of encouragement, signal for
action, etc.

"Ho'way hyem" *Marshall* G'head 1806; "Ha
woy – a call to horses to come to the left or
'near' side" *Palgrave* Hetton 1896; "Ha'way,
Jack!" *JR* Seaham C20/1; "howee out to play"
JS Easington 1950s; "howway – come along"
Tanfield Lea, 1960; "howwaydoon tuthe
chippy" *Dobson* Tyne 1970; "Howay the lads"
Graham Geordie 1979; "howawiwi" East
Boldon 1985; "howee – come on!" Thornley
2001 Q; "Haway back to my place" *VIZ* 72
1995; "Howay man Sid" *VIZ* 34 1989; "haway-
man – come round to my way of thinking"
Trimdon 2002 Q ['Howay... is a corruption of

howay cont.

hadaway' *Graham* Geordie 1979, compare
"cow-wa – come away" *Bailey* Co.Durham
1810]

howdy midwife

"M[ar]gery the Howdy" *Bewick* Tyne 1790s;
"the parish howdy" *Bells* nC'd 1815; "howdy –
a midwife; in Scotch, howdie" *Bell* MS Newc
1815; 'midwife' *Pitman's Pay* G'head 1820s,
Atkinson Cleve 1868, *GP* Seaham 1950s;
"howdy, howdy-wife – a midwife" *Brockett*
Newc & Nth 1829; "Thoo's niver been weshed
since the howdie weshed th'." *Palgrave* Hetton
1896. *EDD* distribution to 1900: Sco, Nth.
Plus "grace-wife – a midwife" Durham
1929/30, sim. York 1561/62

howdy-maw end of work

"howdy-maw – the conclusion of the day's
labour, the last corf: 'Frae hingen on till
howdy ma' *Pitman's Pay* G'head 1820s. *EDD*
distribution to 1900: N'd, D'm

howk 1. to scoop out, dig, 2. to hit

1. "she's howket a grave" *Reed Border Ballads*
C16; "kild yesterday at ye Black middens by
ye bank & a great stone yt fell down upon
him when he was houcking for coales" *Raine*
MS Tynemouth 1681; "holkit – made a way by
digging or otherwise" *Kennet* 1690s; "howk –
to dig imperfectly, to scoop" *Brockett* Newc &
Nth 1829; "goold's better far than howkin'
coals" *Allan's Tyneside Songs* p.363 1849; "hoke
– to scoop a hole" *Dinsdale* mid-Tees 1849;
"we'll find Sir John Franklin if we howk throo
the ice" *Allan's Tyneside Songs* p.399 C19/mid
"the big dredgers that howcks oot the muck
[from the Tyne]" *Haldane* Newc 1879; "Howk
– to dig or hew out: 'He's howked all the
flowers up'" *Palgrave* Hetton 1896; "hoke (not
howk) – to dig out" *Blenkinsopp* Teesdale 1931;
"the dentist will howk that tooth out" *IA* S'm
1950s,60s; "drag, poke or dig out – 'howked
the wax oot his ears'" *Irwin* Tyne 1970;
"Certificated Tettie-Howker" *Dobson* Tyne
1972; 'to dig' *Northumbrian III* 1990 re
Backforth; "howk your powk – pick your
nose" Newc., Ch-le-St 2001 Q; 'dig or pull
out' Wheatley Hill 2004 Q. *EDD* distribution
to 1900: general. NE 2001: in use. [nME holk;
Swed. halka, Frisian holka; OE holc 'cavity']
2. "githa a good howk'n" (beating) *CT* New
Herrington 1930s; "howk – dig out, assault"

howk cont.

Dodd MS Tanfield Lea C20/2; "howk – to beat: 'give someone a good howking'" eD'm 2001 Q

howl-kite see **kite**

howlet owl

"howlet – an owl. Northumberland is jinny howlet" *Bell* MS Newc 1815; "Jack's hoolet e'en" *Pitman's Pay* G'head 1820s; "howlet – the barn or white owl" *Brockett* Newc & Nth 1829; "hoolit – owl" *Dodd* MS Tanfield Lea C20/2; "houlet" *Graham* Geordie '1979. *EDD* distribution to 1900: general. See also **jenny howlet**

hoy 1. to cast, throw, chuck, lob,
2. verb phrases, 3. noun formations

1. 'to heave or throw, as a stone' *Brockett* Newc & Nth 1825; "his backers they hoy'd up the sponge" (re boxing) *Allan's Tyneside Songs* p.407 1862; "hoy hor off" (cast her off) Oliver Heslop in *NWC* 1882; "a similor storm com' on / An' hoy'd us back as far as ivor" *Barrass* Stanley 1890s; "Let's see wee'll (who will) hoy the far-est" *Palgrave* Hetton 1896; "hoy a happny out / me father's in jail / and we cannot get him out" PHm S'd C20/1; "het watta... t' hoy it ower th' ice i' th' yard" *CT* New Herrington 1930s; "hoy clemmies" *BF* Billingham C20/mid; "hoyin' snaa-baals at yan another" *Dunn* B'p Auck 1950; "hoyed himself into the Wear" *Dobson* Tyne 1970; "hoy – to throw: 'Hoy it arriz.'" Charver 2000–2002. *EDD* distribution to 1900: N'd, D'm, C'd, with exx. exclusively from Tyneside and eD'm. *SED* (C20/mid) records as D'm and older respondents from N'd. NE 2001: in common use. [The Scots form of 'hoy' means 'to expel, to drive out with noise', almost literally to shout 'Hoy!' (see *OED*.) This seems an unlikely origin for our word. The *Scottish National Dictionary* gives 'hoy' as a reduced for of hoise, which points to the Dutch hijschen as a possible source. ("hyse – a hyse in prices" Aberdeens., 1993, "heeze – to hoist" *Gibson* C'd 1880.). See also *OED* entry for 'hoick'. Most feasible perhaps is a source in the Dutch vb gooien. "The g is gutteral, but in some parts of the Netherlands it becomes h" Peter Cain (E)]
2. "hoying it down whole watter" *JP* S'm C20/2; "hoi-a-oot – doorman checking visitors" *Dodd* MS Tanfield Lea C20/2; "hoi-in

hoy cont.

oot tym – 'last orders'" *Dodd* MS Tanfield Lea C20/2; "a hoy out – following a church wedding... the father of the bride would throw a handful of copper/silver towards the public and the waiting children" *TC* New Herrington C20/mid; "hoy oot – we used to go to the church when a wedding took place and call to the bridegroom when the couple were in the bridal carriage. He would throw pennies out and we all scrambled for them!" *HP* South Gosforth C20/mid; "hoi-in skyul – pitch and toss" – *Dodd* Tanfield C20/2; "hoyahama-owaheor" (Nissan joke) East Boldon 1985
3. "the hoy" – game of pitch n toss *LG* S'm C20/mid; "the hoyer" thrower in pitch n toss; "hoyers" (loose change) *GP* S'm C20/2; *TC* S'm C20/2; Stanley 2002 Q; "to get the hoyers" (to be jilted) *Viereck* re Gateshead 1966; "on the hoy" (drinking spree) S'm 1990s; "hoy – to go on the piss: 'Am gan on the hoy – y'cummin?'" *Charver* 2000/2002. See also **pitch n toss**

hubby-shew a mess, confusion

"fecit unam brawl voc. a hubbylshew" *Raine* MS ?Knaresborough, 1520s; "hubbilschow, hobbleshow – a hubbub" Jamieson *Scots Dictionary* 1808; "hubby-shew... a disturbance, a noise, a state of confusion" *Brockett* Newc & Nth 1829; "hubble-shew, hubble-shoo – tumultuous... crowd; a state of commotion or disturbance" *Atkinson* Cleve 1868; "a proper hubby-shew" *JO* re High Thornley/Rowland's Gill, 1930s,1940s in *Nth Words*. *EDD* distribution to 1900: hobble-show Sco, Nth

hud hood

"hud – the side, or rather the covering of the top of the side, of a fire-place" *Brockett* Newc & Nth 1829; "hud ni'ak – chimney nook" *Egglestone* Weardale 1870s

huddock covered part of boat

"The skipper luik'd oot o' the huddock" *Allan's Tyneside Songs* p.27 1805; "huddock – the cabin of the keels on the River Tyne" *Bell* MS Newc 1815; "huddick, or huddock – the cabin of a keel or coal barge" *Brockett* Newc & Nth 1829; "Then into th' huddock they gat / And th' flesh they began to fry" *Allan's Tyneside Songs* p.28 1805; sim. *Marshall* G'head 1806; "The cabin of the keels was called the 'huddock' or 'hurrick'" *Mitcalfe* p.4 re 1822; "as stale as swipes (drink) kept ower lang i' the

huddock cont.

huddock" *Allan's Tyneside Songs* p.188 1824;
"So the men an' their skipper each sat on
their buttock / An' a council they held, wi'
their legs down the huddock" *Allan's Tyneside
Songs* p.220 1842; "keel bullies... snug in their
huddocks" *Allan's Tyneside Songs* p.300 1842;
"wor merry lads lay snorin' on the huddock's
hard bed" *Allan's Tyneside Songs* p.151 1849.
EDD distribution to 1900: N'd, D'm. *Plus*
"hud" *C/GR* Amble C20/2. See also **cuddy,
dodger**

hug to carry, manhandle

' to carry' *Brockett* Newc & Nth 1829,
Blenkinsopp Teesdale 1931; 'to carry [esp. in
the arms]' *Atkinson* Cleve 1868; "roond the
raws ... the youngsters hugg'd the teup"
Barrass Stanley 1890s. *EDD* distribution to
1900: Nth

huly fretful

"huly – peevish, fretfull. When a man is not
easily pleas'd or seems captious and forward,
then is said to be 'huly', and a 'huly man'"
Kennet 1690s as D'm; "yulley – whimpering"
Blenkinsopp Teesdale 1931. *EDD* distribution to
1900: hooly – N'd, D'm. [?ON hófligr
'moderately']

humble 1. de-awning, 2. de-horning

1. "humbling barley – breaking off the awns
(beards), with a flail or other instrument"
Bailey Co.Durham 1810
2. "a white humble ewe with her lambs"
(without horns) *Raine* MS Coniscliffe 1616;
"mild as a humblick" (i.e. dehorned cow) *GP*
S'm re C20/1

humblick hemlock

"humlick – the Northern pronunciation of
hemlock" *Brockett* Newc & Nth 1846. *EDD*
distribution to 1900: NE. *Plus* "that scene in
Hamlick" *Allan's Tyneside Songs* p.439 C19/mid

hunkers haunches

"down o' my hunkers" *Marshall* Newc
1823; "hunkers – haunches... used by the
Northumbrian vulgar only in the sense of
'sitting on the hunkers'" *Brockett* Newc & Nth
1829; "hunkers – to sit on ones hunkers is to
sit with the hams resting on the calves of the
legs" *Bell* MS Newc 1830s; "hunkers – sitting
on the hunkers – sitting on the toes with the
thighs resting on the calves of the legs, a

hunkers cont.

manner of sitting peculiar to pitmen"
Nicholson 1880; "Sitting on the hunkers means
squatting, as miners do in the streets" *Palgrave*
Hetton 1896; "on your hunkers" nwD'm
C20/mid Q; *HP* South Gosforth C20/mid;
"miners on thor hunkers sit" *Dobson* Tyne
1972. *EDD* distribution to 1900: general.
[?ON húka, Du hukken, OFr hanche]

hupstick now and again

"Every hupstitch – every now and again: 'she
bakes every hupstitch'" *Palgrave* Hetton 1896.
EDD distribution to 1900: eD'm. *Plus* "whup-
while – at short periods, frequently" *Pitman's
Pay* G'head 1820s

huse a cough

"hauste, hoste – a dry cough" *Ray* 1674 Nth;
"huse – a short cough" *Bailey* Co.Durham
1810

hyem see **hame**

hyrd shepherd

"he being hyrd, or keper of cattell" *Raine*
MS Durham, 1634; "herrud – shepherd"
Ashington C20/2. *EDD* distribution to 1900:
herd – general; herid – N'd

icicles 1. **ice-shoggle**, 2. other

1. "ice shoggle — an icicle" *Bell* MS Newc 1815, *Brockett* Newc & Nth 1829; "ice-shoccle" *Dinsdale* mid-Tees 1849; "ice-shoggles, ice-shoglins" *Atkinson* Cleve 1868; "iceshogils" *Armstrong* Tanfield C19/2; "ysikel, yss-shogil – icicle" *Dodd* MS Tanfield Lea C20/2. *EDD* distribution to 1900: Sco, Nth. [compare Dan isjokkel]
2. "ickles" *Atkinson* Cleve 1868; "can-kils" *Luckley* Alnwick 1870s extra; "tinkle tankle" *Luckley* Alnwick 1870s

if

"gif" *Allan's Tyneside Songs* p.99 1814; "gin I be not fair" *NChorister* D'm C18/2; "gin – if, in case, even if, although (?p.p. of give)" *Atkinson* Cleve 1868; "kin: 'yammering and shouting as kin yen was deef'; 'as kin howse (anything) had happend'" *Bewick* Tyne 1790s

ignorant rude

"higarent – bad mannered and stupid" *CT* New Herrington 1930s; "without care or consideration for other people or things" *PG* H'pool C20/2. *EDD* distribution to 1900: in this sense, Sco, Ire, Mids

ilk each, every

"on ilk halfe" *Cuthbert* C15/mid; "of ilk a thing" *Noah's Ark* Newc C15/16; "I saw him ilk other day" *Atkinson* Cleve 1868. *EDD* distribution to 1900: Sco, Ire, Lakes, Glos, Som. NE 2001: not in use. [OE ilca]

impittent cheeky, impudent

exx. *FS* Shotton Colliery 1930s, *Viereck* re Gateshead, 1966; "impitant – impudent" *Dodd* MS Tanfield Lea C20/2; "impitent – impudent (of a child)" D'm. 2001 Q. *EDD* distribution to 1900: only as 'in good spirits' C'd. *Plus* "impittance" *JO* re High Thornley/Rowlands Gill, 1930s,1940s in *Nth Words*. See also **fond**

in, iv, i' in

"suon ee mworning" *Bewick* Tyne 1790s; "iv a byre" *Allan's Tyneside Songs* p.238 1829; "iv – in; intiv – into. So pronounced by country people" *Brockett* Newc & Nth 1829; "i', iv (before a vowel) – in" *Dinsdale* mid-Tees 1849; "iv oor hoos" *Atkinson* Cleve 1868; "i' this hoose" *Barrass* Stanley 1890s; "plunged... iv a torrible fray", "iv his nest" *Barrass* Stanley 1890s; "Aa's iv a horry" *Graham* Geordie 1979. *EDD* distribution to 1900: iv as Nth. *Plus* "it

in cont.

nuze" (in the news) M'bro *MWN* 28 Jan 1860. See also **into**

inbye 1. towards the interior, 2. in mining, towards the work face

1. "in-by – in general applied to the inner chamber of a house: 'Had away in-by, man, an' hev a few broth' *Luckley* Alnwick 1870s; "in-by – the inner chamber of a house" *Brockett* Newc & Nth 1846; "inbye – near as opposed to far from the farm" Teesside 2001 Q; "inbye / outbye – comands to a sheepdog" Barnard Castle. 2001 Q
2. "in-bye – in the workings, or in any direction away from the shaft" *Nicholson* 1880; "Frae what they craft aboot the shaft, te what they de inbye" *Barrass* Stanley 1890s; "I knew what in-bye meant. It signified in or approaching the working area." *Hitchin* re Seaham p.66 1910s; "walking in by, i.e. from the shaft to the coal face" *BW* West Auckland C20/mid; 'from shaft bottom into the workings' Wade *South Moor* C20/mid; "going towards the face, away from the shaft" *JM* Dawdon 1970s; "at the face; the direction away from the shaft" (in a pit) *Northumbrian III* 1990 re Backforth. *EDD* distribution to 1900: N'd, D'm, wYx

ing meadow, pasture

"another child found in the ings; [to be] bur[ied]" *Raine* MS Wakefield, 1662; "ing – a common pasture or meadow" *Grose* 1787; "ings – low wet grounds" *Bailey* Co.Durham 1810; "ing – a meadow, a pasture" *Brockett* Newc & Nth 1829, *Blenkinsopp* Teesdale 1931. *EDD* distribution to 1900: general. [ON eng 'grassland']

ingate way in

"ingate – the entrance or inlet (at a coal-mine)" *Brockett* Newc & Nth 1846; "ingate – the means of entrance" *Atkinson* Cleve 1868. *EDD* distribution to 1900: Sco, Nth. See also **gate**

ingle fire, flame

"ingle – a fire or flame" *Brockett* Newc & Nth 1829, 'fire, flame; fireside' *Atkinson* Cleve 1868. *EDD* distribution to 1900: Sco, Nth, Linx. [?Gaelic aingeal 'fire'] *Plus* "inglenook" (corner by the fire) *Eggleston* Weardale 1877

inonder under

"inonder, ininonder – under' *Embleton* Newc.
1897. *EDD* distribution to 1900: Sco, N.I.,
wYx

insense to explain

"insense – to make to understand, to inform
or impart knowledge" *Brockett* Newc & Nth
1829; 'make to understand' *Palgrave* Hetton
1896. *EDD* distribution to 1900: general.
[OF ensenser]

into, intiv

"intiv a field" *Armstrong* Tanfield C19/2; "intiv
(before a vowel) – into" *Dinsdale* mid-Tees
1849; "inted toon" (into the town), "intev a
ki'ak shop" *Egglestone* Weardale 1870s; "Aw
went intiv a hoose" *Barrass* Stanley 1890s;
"inte… intiv before a vowel" Tanfield Lea
1960. See also **in**

inwiver a rail on a coble

"Inwire – inwyver, the riser or stringer
supporting the tofts (thofts)" *Hill* Flamborough
1970s; "inwiver – inner rail, compare
'toe-rail'" *C/GR* Amble C20/2; "inwiver"
FT Cullercoats 2003. *EDD* distribution to
1900: N'd

Ironopolis Middlesbrough

ex. 1890s. *Plus* "Boro"

it (in contractions)

"she let Geordie hed" (have it); "Twiz" (it was),
"twad" (it would), "hed" (have it), "nyen cud
did" (none could do it), "when we get tid"
(to it) *Barrass* Stanley 1890s; "weed" (with it)
Rothbury C18/2

itchy-dabber see *hopscotch*

ite eight

"hite" (eight) *Armstrong* Tanfield C19/2. *Plus*
"hiteen" (eighteen) *Armstrong* Tanfield C19/2;
"yteen – 18" *Dodd* MS Tanfield Lea C20/2

iv of

"pack iv yelpin' curs" *Allan's Tyneside Songs*
p.236 1829; "men iv science" *Allan's Tyneside
Songs* p.241 1829. See also **in**

ivin ivy

"ivin – the common ivy" *Atkinson* Cleve 1868.
EDD distribution to 1900: Nth, eMids

ivvor ever

"iver see big" *Egglestone* Weardale 1870s;
"ivor" *Barrass* Stanley 1890s; "ivvor" *Graham*
Geordie 1979. *Plus* "ivvery" (every) *Allan's
Tyneside Songs* p.411 C19/mid; "ivory"
Armstrong Tanfield C19/2; "ivvory – every"
Tanfield Lea 1960

ivvorybody everybody

"ivvorybody" Coxhoe 1916. *Plus* "ivery yan"
Moore Weardale 1859, *Tyneside grammar* 1880s
(as 'each')

jacky gin

'English gin' Bell 1812 p.89; "we'd Jackey an' fine ginger pop" *Allan's Tyneside Songs* p.139 1816. *EDD* distribution to 1900: N'd, Suff – 'slang'

jacky blue-cap blue tit

ex. *JB* Shildon C20/mid

jagger 1. pedlar. 2. his pony

1. "jagger, in the Scottish language, means a pedlar – jagger-galloway, a pedlar's pony" *Brockett* Newc & Nth 1846
2. "jagger – pony or galloway" *Blenkinsopp* Teesdale 1931; "jagger – pony" Middleton in Teesdale 2001 Q. *EDD* distribution to 1900: jagger-galloway – N'd, C'd, W'd

jaistering swaggering

ex. *Dinsdale* mid-Tees 1849; 'swaggering or bragging' *Blenkinsopp* Teesdale 1931. *EDD* distribution to 1900: N'd, D'm

jalup, jollup a purgative

"a pennorth o' Jalup we put iv his bottle" *Allan's Tyneside Songs* p.411 1862; "jollup, jalap – the powder of the dried tubercles of *Exogonium purga* – a purgative" *Embleton* Newc 1897; "jallup... openin medicine" *Hay* Ushaw Moor C20/1. *EDD* distribution to 1900: Edin, Tyne. [F jalap from Aztec Xalapan] *Plus* "Aw've jollop'd [dosed] the drivers that's stolen me bate" *Barrass* Stanley 1890s

Jamies inhabitant of Sunderland

"Sunderland Jammy's Lamentation" (song re cholera of 1831); "A writer in a recent periodical supplies us with the curious information that 'Mariners term a vessel from the Tyne a Geordie, and from the Wear a Jamie." William Fordyce *History of... the County Palatine of Durham* 1857 vol.2 p.509, fn. [Jamies and Geordies might then refer back to sides in the C18 Hanoverian/Stuart rivalry]
See also **Mackem, Geordie**

jannock, jannick fair, straight, etc

"jannick – staunch, firm (Yorkshire)" *Brockett* Newc & Nth 1846; "jannock – behaviour that is all fair and straightforward" *Dinsdale* mid-Tees 1849; 'even, level; fair, equitable: 't cloth deean't lig jannock", "that now is not jannock'" *Atkinson* Cleve 1868; "jannock – square, honest" *Blenkinsopp* Teesdale 1931

jannock cont.

EDD distribution to 1900: general; *OED* says not Sco

jarble to spatter

"jarble – to bedraggle" *Blenkinsopp* Teesdale 1931; "jarbled – wettened, e.g. trousers by grass" *Dinsdale* mid-Tees 1849. *EDD* distribution to 1900: Nth

jaup, jarp 1. to joggle, 2. to strike eggs at Easter

1. "jaup – to move liquid irregularly – to splash: 'The water went jauping in the skeel'" *Brockett* Newc & Nth 1829; "jawp – to shake liquid" *Bell* MS Newc 1830s; "jap – to splash with a liquid; to agitate a fluid in a vessel" *Luckley* Alnwick 1870s. *EDD* distribution to 1900: general
2. "jaup – to strike, to chip or break by a gentle though sudden blow. Jauping paste-eggs at Easter is a youthful amusement in Newcastle and the neighbourhood. One boy, holding an egg in his hand, challenges another to give blow for blow. One of the eggs is sure to be fractured in the conflict, and its shattered remains become the spoil of the conqueror" *Brockett* Newc & Nth 1829; "Jawping eggs' – a gambling game with eggs at Easter" *Bell* MS Newc 1830s; "thor eggs wad jawp an' var-ny crack a styen" *MC* Tyne May 1881; "the champion times aa've hed at Easter jaapin' an' boolin' me eggs" *Robson* Newc C20/1; 'we decorated hard boiled eggs and went out "jarping", banging the ends of the boiled eggs – the winner taking over the loser's egg' *JG* Annfield Plain 1930s; 'One holds an egg and challenges anyone to strike it with another egg. The first broken egg is the spoil of the conqueror' *Graham* Geordie 1979. *EDD* distribution to 1900: NE

jee-wye out of true, crooked

"Gee-y – crooked, twisted: 'It's all a-gee-y' [u:jae:waay)" *Palgrave* Hetton 1896; "all jee-wye" Newc 1940s via AK, *Wingate* Tyneside 2001 Q; "arl gee wye" (out of trim/order) *CT* New Herrington 1930s; "jee-wye" Teesdale, Thornley, S'd. 2001 Q; "all gone gee-why – gone wrong" Horden 2004 E. *Plus* "jee – crooked, awry" *Brockett* Newc & Nth 1829.
See also **ajee**

jells wooden planks

'...to cover or divide the hold of a keelboat' *Mitcalfe* re 1822; 'piece of wood' *GP* S'm C20/mid; "dyell – wood" *Dodd* MS Tanfield Lea C20/2. [same as deal, first noted ca. 1400]

jelouse to suspect

"jealous – to suspect" *Brockett* Newc & Nth 1846; "the byukmaker wad nivvor jealous onything" Coxhoe 1916; "jealoused – guessed or suspected rightly" *JO* re High Thornley/ Rowland's Gill, 1930s, 1940s in *Nth Words*; "my Aunt would use the word after someone knocking on the door and enterng her house: 'I jaloused it was thoo'" *IL* Sunnybrow C20/2. *EDD* distribution to 1900: Sco, Nth, eMids. [FR jalouser]

jenkin term in hewing

"jenkin – a narrow place driven up the middle of a pillar of coal when it is about to be excavated" *Brockett* Newc & Nth 1846. *EDD* distribution to 1900: N'd, D'm

jenny howlet owl

"an au'd Jenny Howlet" (rhymes with 'foot it') *Allan's Tyneside Songs* p.217 1823; "jenny-howlet – the tawny owl" *Brockett* Newc & Nth 1829' "jenny-howlet (pronounced jinny-hullot) – the tawny owl" *Atkinson* Cleve 1868; "Geordy's feyce just as solemn like as a jenny hoolet" *Haldane* Newc 1879; "jinny howlets" *JO* re High Thornley/Rowlands Gill, 1930s, 1940s in *Nth Words*. *EDD* distribution to 1900: Nth, usually as 'barn owl'. See also **howlet**

jimmers a twinned pair, e.g. hinges

"gimmers – door-hinges" *Kennet* 1690s as D'm; "jimmers esp. of a pair of doors" *Kennet* 1690s; "a gimmer tree – a tree that grows double from the root" *Kennet* 1690s as D'm; "jimmer – a small hinge for a closet door or desk" *Brockett* Newc & Nth 1829. *EDD* distribution to 1900: Nth, EA. [AN gemel, jomel 'twin']

jinny spinner cranefly

"jinny-spinner – a very long slender-legged fly" *Brockett* Newc & Nth 1829; 'daddy-long-legs' *Dinsdale* mid-Tees 1849; "jenny spinner – an insect; a feathered seed of the dandelion tribe, flying about" *Luckley* Alnwick 1870s; "jinny-longlegs" Sherburn. 2001 Q; "ginny, ginny-longlegs – cranefly" *Wood* Cleve C20/2;

jinny spinner cont.

"johny-spinner" Ashington. 2001 Q. *EDD* distribution to 1900: Sco, Nth. [Jeanie i.e. female]

joggly unsteady

"joggly – unsteady; rough, of a road" *Atkinson* Cleve 1868

jollop see **jalup**

jonker pit electrician's term

'coupling box for electric cables' Ho'ton 2001 Q

jook see **dook**

jowl to strike in order to cause a sound

"When a signal is to be made to some distance, it is done by beating on the rails or posts, five beats, the first two slow, the other three quick, and this is repeated several times. The same signal is used in the Newcastle coal mines, where it is denominated 'jowling'" *Alston* 1833; "Pitmen ascertain, by jowling against the coal, the probable thickness and direction of two approaching workings. 'Gan and gie us a jowl to see if she's fair on.'" *Brockett* Newc & Nth 1846; "jowl – a sort of "tattoo" beaten alternately upon the face of two places or drifts near holing, or intended to hole into each other, by a person in each place, for the purpose of ascertaining by the sound their relative positions" *Nicholson* 1880; "Jowl, jowl, and listen, lad!" *Lloyd* re Low Fell 1962; "jowling – a means of communicating through the mine. particuly after roof falls (knocking on walls etc)" *IL* Tow Law C20/mid. *EDD* distribution to 1900: N'd, D'm, Yx. *Plus* "A'l jowl tha" Wade, South Moor 1966

jud section of coalface ready for taking down

'a piece of coal ready for taking down, either by wedges or powder' *Pitman's Pay* G'head 1820s; 'the portion of the coal about to be removed by blasting' Brockett Newc & Nth, 1846; 'a portion of the seam, kirved, nicked, and ready for blasting; also, a portion of a pillar in course of being worked away in the broken mine' *Nicholson* 1880; "Crack gans the timmor i' maw jud" *Barrass* Stanley 1890s. *EDD* distribution to 1900: N'd, C'd, D'm, Yx

jumly muddy

"Jumly water" *Palgrave* Hetton 1896. *EDD* distribution to 1900: Sco, NE

ka— see also under **ca—**

kale 1. cabbage, 2. broth
1. "kail – cabbage, greens; broth or pottage" *Brockett* Newc & Nth 1829; "keal – broth, cabbage" *Gibson* C'd 1880. *EDD* distribution to 1900: Sco, Ire, Nth, Glos. [ON kál, OE cáwel] *Plus* "kail-garth – a kitchen-garden, a cabbage garth, though often adorned with a profusion of flowers" *Brockett* Newc & Nth 1829; "corly-greens" wNewc 1880s
2. "cole, keal – potage made of colewort" *Ray* 1674; "kale, kyel – broth, soup: 'Splash gan the spuins amang the kyell'" *Pitman's Pay* G'head 1820s; "kail, kyel – broth or soup, especially when made with potatoes or fish: 'Will ye hev a few tatie kail...?'" *Luckley* Alnwick 1870s

kale-pot stew pot
"kail-pot – large metal cooking pot" *Dinsdale* mid-Tees 1849; "kale-pot – a pottage-pot... a large semi-globular or full-bottomed iron pot on three spiky legs" *Atkinson* Cleve 1868; "The kail-pot's callin' the yetlin' smutty (common proverb)" *Palgrave* Hetton 1896; "heed like a kail-pot – big-headed, swankey" *Dunn* B'p Auck 1950

kavel to struggle
"to struggle, be in great difficulty" *MG* Teesdale C20/2. See also **cavel**

kedge to stuff
"kedge – to fill, stuff full, esp. [re] eating" *Atkinson* Cleve 1868; "As kedged – full up" *Dunn* B'p Auck 1950. *EDD* distribution to 1900: Sco, Nth. *Plus* "kedge-belly – a large protuberant body, a glutton" *Brockett* Newc & Nth 1829

kee the quayside, esp. Newcastle
"wor Keeside" *Allan's Tyneside Songs* p.189 1824; 'The Fire on the Kee' – Billy Purvis' recitation about the great fire of 1854

keek 1. to peep, 2. a peep
1. "thro' all the world aw wisht to keek" *Allan's Tyneside Songs* p.51 1823; "keek – to peep, to look with a prying eye, to view slyly" *Brockett* Newc & Nth 1829; "keek'd through their glasses at us" *Oiling* G'head 1826; "Forst Aa keeked this way then Aa keeked thay way, then Aa torn'd half roond an' tries to keek ower me showlder." *Other Eye* Newc ca.1890. [ON kíkja 'to pry', Du kijken]

keek cont
2. "we'd a keek at the Monument" *Marshall* Newc 1823; "down every quayside Chare there's such a glorious keek" (view) *Allan's Tyneside Songs* p.194 1842

keeker inspector, mine official
"keeker – in Northumberland and Durham Collieries it is a sort of overlooker, or spy, on the pit heap of the Colliery" *Bell* MS Newc 1830s; "keeker – in coal mining, a person employed to see that the coals are sent to bank in a proper state" *Brockett* Newc & Nth 1846; "keeker" (surface official who checked hewers' tubs) *Armstrong* Tanfield C19/2; "keeka – pit surface foreman" *Dodd* MS Tanfield Lea C20/2. *EDD* distribution to 1900: N'd, D'm, nYx

keel boat esp. lighter in coal trade
"tribus ut lingua eius exprimitur cyulis" (three 'keels' as it is called in their tongue) Gildas 564 AD re arrival of Anglo-Saxons; "for a kele with the wool from Newcastle" records re Gateshead 1329/30 via *Mitcalfe*; "weel may the keel row..." *Ritson* N'd 1793; "Aw was setten the keel..." *Marshall* G'head 1806; "The keels transported the coals from the riverside staiths to the ships were they lay in the river" *Mitcalfe* p.4 re 1822; "for as lang as keel gans down river Tyne" *Oliver* Newc p.1 1824; "keel – a low, flat, [clumsy-looking 1846] vessel or barge..." *Brockett* Newc & Nth 1829; "keel – a vessel on the River Tyne about 50 feet long and 20 feet broad and carries 8 Newcastle or 15 London chaldrons of coal, or 21 tons 13 cwt. [It] is navigated by a skipper, 3 men and a boy, who is called the Pee dee... Keels are navigated three different ways on the Tyne, viz by sail, by rowing (with oar and swape) [and] by putting which is done with a puuy or puvy, a pole about 25 feet long with an iron fork on the end. [The] Pee dee, the boy, takes care of the huddock or cabin of the keel, or fetches and carries as the keelmen and skipper direct." *Bell* MS Newc 1830s; "keel – a vessel used to carry coals from the staithes on the Tyne or Wear, to ships lying about Shields or Sunderland. Keels are broad, flat vessels, sharp at each end, and carry eight Newcastle chaldrons" *Nicholson* 1880. *EDD* distribution to 1900: E coast. [ON kjʔlr, OE ceol 'boat']

keelmen, keelers etc. crew of the keels (coal tenders)

"kelers" re Tynemouth C14, via *Mitcalfe*; "The 'Kelers' [sic] of Tynemouth were a recognized class away back in the days of the early charters, and, in the year 1700, numbered some sixteen-hundred, with a fleet of four hundred keels." *The Maister* p.35; "keel-bully" *Marshall* G'head 1806; "the North Shore for keelers" *Allan's Tyneside Songs* p.30 1812; "the mony keel lads o' Coaly Tyne" *Allan's Tyneside Songs* p.45 1812; "but last I married a keelman / and my good days are done" *Allan's Tyneside Songs* p.152 1812; "he and his 'marra' had to 'cast' – that is, shovel – [the coal] from the keel into the hold of the vessel being loaded" *The Maister* p.35 re Tyneside 1800–1840; "keel dighter – a woman who scrape[s] or clean[s] out the floor of the keels, and get what small coals may have been left after the delivery of the keel" *Bell* MS Newc 1815; "The keels were generally manned by the skipper, two keel bullies and a boy known as the 'pee-dee'" *Mitcalfe* p.3 re 1822; "keelmen – the watermen who mavigate the keels; an exceedingly hardy and striking race of men" *Brockett* Newc & Nth 1829; "the city was hush, save the keel bullies snoring" *Allan's Tyneside Songs* p.299 1842; "keel-bullies – the keelmen, or crew of the keel – the partners or comrades in the vessel" *Brockett* Newc & Nth 1829, "keel-brothers" 1846; "brave keel-laddies" *Allan's Tyneside Songs* p.381 C19/mid

keggy lump

"keggy – a lump on the face after a fight" *Wood* Tees 2002; "keggy-eyed – having a black eye" *Wood* Redcar 2002

keks, kegs trousers, pants

"kegs" *JS* re Blackhall C20/mid, Gateshead 1986 per BG; "keks, kegs, underkegs" *JP* S'm C20/2 keks – tousers Q 2001 Tyne, D'm; "keks – underwear" Ashington. 2001 Q; "swimmin kex" *VIZ* 40 (1990s). See also **breeks, trousers**

kellee see **tadger**

kelk a blow

"I gave him two or thee good kelks" *Grose* 1787; "kelk, kelker – a severe blow" *Brockett* Newc & Nth 1829; "kelk – a blow" *Blenkinsopp* Teesdale 193. *EDD* distribution to 1900: Nth, Lincs

kelk the hemlock

"kelk – a term commonly used for the ordinary field hemlock" *Brockett* Newc & Nth 1829; 'a small specie of hemlock' *Dinsdale* mid-Tees 1849. *EDD* distribution to 1900: general

kelks salmon

"kelks – the salmon in the river Tyne after it has spawned" *Bell* MS Newc 1830s

kellick unfledged bird

"Kellick – unfledged bird" *Palgrave* Hetton 1896; "raw kellick" *GP* S'm 1950s. *EDD* distribution to 1900: eD'm. *Plus* "a new kelk" Brockett Newc & Nth 1846 as D'm

kelpie water sprite

"the Spirit of the Waters, known by the name of Water Kelpie in Scotland" *Marshall* G'head 1806. *EDD* distribution to 1900: Sco

kelter 1. riches, money, 2. rubbish, odds and ends

1. "the blythe morning [pay day] comes... when kelter makes colliers sing" *Bell* Newc p.38 1812; "show'd her the kelter aw had won" *Allan's Tyneside Songs* p.141 1816; "that brag o' birth and kelter" *Oiling* G'head 1826; "a cheppy tuik kelter as fast's he was yeble / there war gan for ti raffle aud Jack's wooden leg" *Allan's Tyneside Songs* p.489 1862
2. "kelter – rubbish" *Blenkinsopp* Teesdale 1931; "kelter – rubbish, heap of unsorted objects" *JB* Shildon C20/mid; 'rubbish or clutter' M'bro 2001 Q. *EDD* distribution to 1900: sD'm, Yx, Notts, Linx

kelterment small worthless things

"kelterments – odds and ends" *Atkinson* Cleve 1868; "odds and ends... the sort of thing you find on the floor" *GP* S'm C20/mid *EDD* distribution to 1900: Nth. *Plus* "toffer, tofferments – odds and ends, 'rubbish'" *Atkinson* Cleve 1868

kemp to compete

"kemping – to strive against each other in reaping corn" *Bailey* Co.Durham 1810; "kemp – to strive in order to outdo a competitor" *Atkinson* Cleve 1868. *EDD* distribution to 1900: Sco, Ire, Nth, Suff. [ON keppa, OE campian]. *Plus* "kempers – the competitors" *Brockett* Newc & Nth 1829; "cample – to argue" *Brockett* Newc & Nth 1829

ken to know

"he kenned thair synnes" *Cuthbert* C15/mid; "he kend not his owne father" *Raine* MS ?Durham 1573; "Aw ken weel enough" *Bewick* Tyne 1790s; "ken – to know" *Bailey* Co.Durham 1810; "ye mebby ken best" *Allan's Tyneside Songs* p.150 1827; "I dinna ken yor nyme" *Stobbs* Woodhorn, C19/mid; "he kens biv his nose / when a pick-pocket's near" *Allan's Tyneside Songs* p.309 1862; "aw ken... whe thoo is" *Armstrong* Tanfield C19/2; "nebody kens" *Parker* Tyne Valley p.88 1896; "Of recognizing, or being acquainted with, people: 'aa kenned 'im' (universal). /Aa: din:u ken/ common about Auckland, is not so common around Hetton as /aa:din:aa/ or more strictly /aad:i:naa/ (I don't know)" *Palgrave* Hetton 1896; "Aa kens Harry and Jake" Coxhoe 1916. *EDD* distribution to 1900: general. NE 2001: occasional use, esp. of knowing a person. [ON kenna, OE cennan]

ken home

"ken – Charver's home" *Charver* 2000–2002. [Romany 'ken' a house, a nest]

kennor signal to end work (in pit)

"kenner – an expression signifying time to give up work, shouted down the shaft by the banksman where practicable, and where not, signalled and conveyed into the workings from mouth to mouth or by further signalling" *Nicholson* 1880; "Till kennor's call'd" *Barrass* Stanley 1890s; "Kenner – time to cease work. The common expression is 'lowse' (vb.)" *Palgrave* Hetton 1896; "its vennigh kennor – near knocking off time" *Dunn* B'p Auck 1950. *EDD* distribution to 1900: N'd, D'm

kenspecked / -speckled conspicuous

"kenspecked – marked or branded" *Ray* 1674; 'markt or branded with spots or speckles' *Kennet* 1690s as Nth; "kenspeckled – particularly marked, so as to be easily known" *Bailey* Co.Durham 1810; "Kenspreckled – well known, marked" *Palgrave* Hetton 1896; "kenspeckled – very fancy" Weardale, Teesdale 2001 Q. *EDD* distribution to 1900: general. [ON kennespeke 'recogniton']. *Plus* "kenmark – mark to show owner's identity" *FS* Shotton Colliery 1930s

kep to catch

"kep – to catch, to receive anything in the act of falling" *Brockett* Newc & Nth 1829; "he cuddint kep the ball" *Luckley* Alnwick 1870s; 'to catch in your hands' *JO* re High Thornley/ Rowlands Gill 1930s, 1940s in *Nth Words*, *MB* Coxhoe C20/mid; "kep thattun! – cry of victory" *Dobson* Tyne 1970–71. *EDD* distribution to 1900: Sco, Nth. [OE cepan 'to lay hold of, keep', ON kippa 'to snatch']

keps retractable blocks on which cage rests in pit shaft

"keps or keeps – movable frames or supports of iron, which, if left free, project about 1.5 inches into the shaft top at each side, immediately beneath the level of the settle boards. Their use is to support the cage containing the tubs of coals when drawn to the surface, the cage rising between the keeps and forcing them back; but when the cage is drawn above the keeps they fall forward to their places, forming a rest for the cage until the full tubs are replaced by empty ones. the keeps are then drawn back by a lever by the banksman or shover-in and the cage allowed to return down the shaft" *Nicholson* 1880; "the banksman put in his 'keps', and, as the cage rested on these iron protrusions, the chains that suspended it went slack." *Hitchin* re Seaham p.64 1910s; "no matter what weight you put on it it cannot dislodge the keps" *GP* S'm C20/mid; "keps – safety chocks for mine cage" Newton Aycliffe 2001 Q

kern see **kirn**

kersen to christen

"kersen, kirsen, kursen – to christen" *Brockett* Newc & Nth 1829; "kirsen" *Dinsdale* mid-Tees 1849; "kess'n" *Atkinson* Cleve 1868; "kersent ed church" *Egglestone* Weardale 1870s. *Plus* "krissnin" *Allan's Tyneside Songs* p.480 1869

Kersmas Christmas

"Kersmas, Kirsmas, Kursmas" *Brockett* Newc & Nth 1829; "Curstmis" *Allan's Tyneside Songs* p.416 1862; "Kirsmas" *Dinsdale* mid-Tees 1849; "Kess'mas, Kess'nmas" *Atkinson* Cleve 1868; "Kersenmiss" *Luckley* Alnwick 1870s; "Krissmiss" *NM* vol.1 p.197 1888 re Newcastle; "Cursamus" *Embleton* Newc 1897; "Kersmas" *Lakeland* re C'd 1922. See also **yule**

kerve, kirve to undercut coal

"kirving – hollowing out the bottom of the coal in the workings of a colliery so as to let what is above to easily fall down without making much small coal" *Bell* MS Newc 1830s; "kerve – the first operation in preparing a jud in a coal mine, for blasting, is the removel of a large portion of the foundation of the block" *Brockett* Newc & Nth 1846; "kirving – a wedge-shaped excavation, made by the hewer with his pick at the lower part of the seam previous to blasting" *Nicholson* 1880. *EDD* distribution to 1900: esp. NE. [OE ceorfan]. *Plus* "the cut itself would become choked with dust which we called 'curvings'" *Hitchin* re Seaham p.98 1920s

keslop rennet

'a calf's stomach salted and dried to make rennet' *Bailey* Co.Durham 1810; "keslip, keslop – rennet; also cheese-lop, cheslip, cheslop" *Atkinson* Cleve 1868. *EDD* distribution to 1900: Sco, Nth, Lincs. [OE cese-lyb 'cheese-chemical']. *Plus* "yerning – rennet" *Bailey* Co.Durham 1810

kessen see **cast**

ket offal, rubbish

"cadavera, Anglice kett" (carrion) *Raine* MS Howden, 1589; "ket – carrion, filth, useless lumber" *Brockett* Newc & Nth 1829; "ket – carrion; tainted meat" *Atkinson* Cleve 1868; "offal or poor quality meat" *Wood* re Whitby C20/2 (not used M'bro); "it it's a load a' ket (rubbish)" *IA* S'm 1950s,60s; "they're just ket" *KH* Stockton C20/2; "ket – rubbish, trash" *JB* Shildon C20/mid; "stop eating ket" (rubbish food) *Wood* D'ton 2002. *EDD* distribution to 1900: Sco, Nth, EA. [ON kjöt 'flesh']. *Plus* "ketment – a dirty mixture, any sort of filth" *Brockett* Newc & Nth 1829; "ketty – nasty" *Grose* 1787; "ketty – putrid" *Atkinson* Cleve 1868

ket, kets sweets

"ket – sweets" Lanchester 2002 Q; "giz a ket (sweet)" *IA* S'm 1950s,60s; "sweets are ket not kets" *MB* Coxhoe C20/mid; "dolly mixtues, jelly babies, lickrish torpedoes were 'kets'" *JS* Easington C20/mid; "kets" Ch-le-St 2002 Q; "ket – kiddies' confectionery" Charver 2000–2002. NE 2001: in use. [?from ket in sense of sweetmeat; the plural form ay only have been introduced ca.1960]. *Plus* "when I was at

kets cont.

school, we called sweets 'ebs'" *PG* H'pool C20/2; "bubus" Hetton-le-Hole, 1950s via BG

kevel large hammer

"kevcl – a large hammer" Finchale 1367; "one great Kevell" *Raine* MS York 1580s; "Bob canted the form with a kevel" *Bell* Newc p.42 1812; "kevel – a large hammer for quarrying stones" *Brockett* Newc & Nth 1829. *EDD* distribution to 1900: N'd, D'm, nYx
See also **cavil**

ki, kiv sez, etc.

"kive I – quoth I" *Grose* 1787; "kih she" plus "oh, kiv aw..." *Bewick* Tyne 1790s; "ki Dick... kiv aw" *Marshall* G'head 1806; "ki – quoth; kiv-Aw. kiv-I – quoth I" *Brockett* Newc & Nth 1829. *EDD* distribution to 1900: Tyne. [same as quoth?]

kibble large tub

"kibble – a wooden tub, usually square, and of the capacity of about 20 gallons, used in conveying rubbish from one place to another: it is placed upon a tram" *Nicholson* 1880; "Kibble – a big iron tub, for filling with rubbish, in sinking a shaft" *Palgrave* Hetton 1896; "kibbil – carries stone in mine" *Dodd* MS Tanfield Lea C20/2. *EDD* distribution to 1900: Nth, Derbys, SW – note mining link. [German Kübel]

kicky-can game of tag with a base

ex. *JP* S'm, C20/2; "kicky-can, kicky-tin" D'm. 2001 Q; "cannon than kicky-can" Gosforth C20/2 Q. See also **tiggy**

kiddar 'kid

"kidder – youngster, younger brother" *JB* Shildon C20/mid; 'a friendly term of address applied to children' *Graham* Geordie 1979; "kiddar – friend" *Leslie* Newc 1992; "gan on kidda" (to adult) *VIZ* 40, 1990s

(out of) kilter unlevel, unbalanced, etc.

"kelter – frame, order, arrangement, condition..." *Brockett* Newc & Nth 1829; "kelter – condition, case, circumstances; 'that drill is out o' kelter', 'in good kelter' (all right, sound)" *Atkinson* Cleve 1868; 'of machine being maladjusted' D'ton 1940s Q; 'out of step/line' D'ton C20/2; 'out of sorts, condition' *GP* S'm 1950s; 'not properly aligned' *KH* Stockton C20/2; "kelter is what we said" *HP* South Gosforth

(out of) kilter cont.

C20/mid. *EDD* distribution to 1900: kelter 'condition' – general

kincough whooping cough

"kink-cough" *Brockett* Newc & Nth 1829; "kin'-cough" *Atkinson* Cleve 1868. *EDD* distribution to 1900: NE, eMids

kinks laughter, fit

"kink – laughter; to kink, as spoken of children when their breath is long stopped, through eager crying or laughing. Hence the kink-cough" *Grose* 1787; "kink – to laugh immoderately, to labour for breath as in the hooping cough" *Brockett* Newc & Nth 1829; "gan in a kink – become hysterical" *Dunn* B'p Auck 1950; "he was in kinks" (a fit of laughter) *Viereck* re Gateshead 1966. *EDD* distribution to 1900: Scot, Nth, eMids. [OE cincung 'heavy laughter']

kip place in pit

'incline in pit' *JR* Seaham C20/1; 'raised platform' *GC* Seaham C20/1; "the landing place at the shaft bottom for the full tubs" *McBurnie* Glebe Colliery C20/mid

kirk church

"kyrk" *Anderson* Newcastle 1508; "kyrk" *Grose* 1787; "aud-fashion'd Jarrow kirk" *Allan's Tyneside Songs* p.228 1826; "An' went off te the kirk, as the Scotchman wad say" *Barrass* Stanley 1890s; "kork" Embleton, Newc 1897. *EDD* distribution to 1900: Sco, Nth, eMids. [OE cyrice]. *Plus* "kirk-garth – a church yard" *Brockett* Newc & Nth 1829; "kork-hole – grave" *LG* S'm C20/2; "chorch" *Graham* Geordie 1979

kirn, kern churn

"kyrne – a churn" *Raine* Finchale (1479–80); "kirnes... in the mylke-house" *Raine* MS ?York, 1559; "one kirne with a kirnstaf" Darlington 1610 via Atkinson no.25; "kirn or kurn – a butter churn" *Bell* MS Newc 1815; "kerran – butter churn" *MG* Teesdale C20/2. *EDD* distribution to 1900: Sco, Nth. [ON kirna] *Plus* "an kirn'ed ed Fridays" *Egglestone* Weardale 1870s

kirn supper end of harvest celebration

"kirn or kurn – the harvest home in Northumberland, at which there is generally a Supper, called the Kirn Supper" *Bell* MS

kirn supper cont.

Newc 1815; "kern-supper – a supper given to the working people by the farmer on the completion of shearing or severing the corn" *Atkinson* Cleve 1868; "kirn supper" *Lakeland* re C'd 1901. *EDD* distribution to 1900: N'd, C'd, nYx, Lx. *Plus* "kern-baby – an image dressed up with corn, carried before the reapers to their mell-supper or harvest-home" *Grose* 1787; "churn-supper, corn supper, the Northumberland festival on conclusion of harvest" *Bell* MS Newc 1830s.
See also **mell-supper**

kirtle dress

"coming owte of the chambre in her pretty-cot and slyving her kertil over her hed" *Raine* MS Adlingfleet, 1536; "kirtle – one-piece dress" B'd Castle 2001 Q. *EDD* distribution to 1900: kirtal 'loose jacket' nYx. [OE cyrtel, ON kyrtill 'tunic']

kirve see **kerve**

kist chest, box

"the reliks kyst" *Cuthbert* C15/mid; "the key of the said...kist" *Raine* MS ?Durham, 1570; 'linen box' *Nth Words* N'd, 1938; "kistful of paper" *Bell* Newc p.105 1812; "siller...to put i' wour kists" *Bell* Newc p.105 1812; "kist – a box in which servant girls keep their clothes etc." *Bell* MS Newc 1815; "kist – chest (less frequently used than chist)" *Dinsdale* mid-Tees 1849; "kist – a chest, of whatsoever kind" *Atkinson* Cleve 1868; "kist – a chest; commonly applied to a large box holding clothes" *Luckley* Alnwick 1870s; "a chest of drawers is a 'kist'" *Palgrave* Hetton 1896; "A kist was a tool-chest used by the deputy" *Hitchin* re Seaham p.70 1910s; "kist – tool chest [sic] which, when cleaned and polished, was turned into a linen chest" Spennymoor C20/mid; "kist – chest for clothing" Barnard Castle 2001 Q. *EDD* distribution to 1900: Sco, Ire, Nth, EA, SW. [ON kista, OE cist (pronounced chist)]. *Plus* "one old arke" Blackwell 1622 via Atkinson no.52; "ark – a large chest or coffer in farm houses, used for keeping corn or meal" *Brockett* Newc & Nth; "hutch means a chest for various uses, as the Towns' Hutch means the Treasure Chest at Newcastle" *Bell* MS Newc 1830s. See also **chist, deputy's kist**

kit small tub

"kit – a milking pail, like a churn, with two ears and a cover" *Grose* 1787; 'properly a covered milking pail with two handles, but often applied to a small pail of any sort' *Brockett* Newc & Nth 1829; "kit – a small wooden vessel, generally with one handle but often without: 'Put the weshins int' the kit'" *Luckley* Alnwick 1870s; 'a small tub for washing in, used by pitmen' *Palgrave* Hetton 1896. *EDD* distribution to 1900: general. [MDu kitte 'jug, pitcher']

kite belly

"kite – the belly" *Ray* 1674 re C'd; "a kite or kyte – a belly or womb" *Kennet* 1690s as Nth; "he'll never run to kyte" (i.e. become fat) 'Bobby Shaftoe' C18; "kite – the belly" *Bailey* Co.Durham 1810; "their kites were byeth empty an' sair" *Allan's Tyneside Songs* p.186 1824; "with his kite full o' yell" *Allan's Tyneside Songs* p.394 C19/mid; "…hand in hand toddled hyem / Varry oft wi' howl kites (empty bellies) an' torn duds" *Crawhall* Newc 1888; "fill yer kite" *IA* S'm 1950s,60s; "a pain in the kyte" *Graham* Geordie 1979. *EDD* distribution to 1900: Sco, Nth, Worcs. NE 2001: in low use. *Plus* "hungry kited" *Marshall* Newc p.23 1823

kittle 1. to tickle, 2. ticklish, tricky

1. "me Nancy kittled me fancy" Reed *Border Ballads* ca1800; "kittle – to tickle" *Bailey* Co.Durham 1810; "kittle – to tickle, to enliven" *Brockett* Newc & Nth 1829; "Many's the time I've kittled ma hinny" *Bell* MS Newc 1830s; "to kittle the fire" *GP* S'm 1950s; "kittle – tickle, ticklish" Tanfield Lea 1960. *EDD* distribution to 1900: general. [ON kitla]
2. "if an ewe be kittle on her yower" (sensitive) *Raine* MS EYorks 1641; "kittle – ticklish, hard, difficult: 'kittle wark', 'kittle weather', 'a kittle question', 'a kittle horse'" *Brockett* Newc & Nth 1829; "the times are kittle and we have little" Durham 1839; "kittle – ticklish, excitable; requiring delicate or judicious handling or management; uncertain, difficult" *Atkinson* Cleve 1868; "ah was as kittle and fresh as ah ivver was i' ma life" (lively) *Parker* Tyne Valley p.73 1896; "she's kind o' kittle i' the temper, whiles" *Embleton* Tyne 1897; "At sic a kittle time, ye knaw, Yen tells ye ony thing to please" *Pitman's Pay* G'head 1820s

kitty jail, holding cell

"they were handed off to the Ketty for the asolt" *Errington* p.71, Felling/Heworth re 1800s; "Kitty – a Newcastle word for the House of Correction" *Bell* MS Newc 1815; "Kitty – [a name formerly given to – 1846] the house of correction in Newcastle" *Brockett* Newc & Nth 1829; "shut up.. or aw'll wawk ye byeth off ti the kitty" *Allan's Tyneside Songs* p.444 1862; "Kitty – policeman's lock-up" *Palgrave* Hetton 1896. *EDD* distribution to 1900: N'd, D'm, nYx

kizzen to dry out, shrink

"kizzen – any thing in cooking which has got burnt and dried" *Bell* MS Newc 1815; "kizoned or kizzened – parched or dried: 'kizzened meat' – meat too much roasted" *Brockett* Newc & Nth 1829; "kizzen – to overbake" *Blenkinsopp* Teesdale 1931. *EDD* distribution to 1900: Sco, Nth.
See also **guizen, wizzen'd**

knaa to know

"Aw knaw it weel" *Brockett* Newc & Nth 1829; "whie, dinnet ye knaw..." *Allan's Tyneside Songs* p.352 C19/mid; "aw divn't knaw" *Wearside Tales* 1879 ; "a storee aw naw to be true" *Armstrong* Tanfield C19/2; "de ye not knaa?" Coxhoe 1916; "if he had knaad" Coxhoe 1916; "A din knaa" *Dunn* B'p Auck 1950; "dinaa" (don't know) *IA* S'm 1950s, 60s; "dive'nt naa" Roker C20/mid; "A divvent knaa" *VIZ* 37 ca.1990. *EDD* distribution to 1900: esp. Sco, Nth. NE 2001: knaa and dinaa, both in use. [OE cnáwan]

knack to speak affectedly

"to knack or nack – to speak finely or affect a fine soft pronunciation. applied to those who speak in the Southern dialect" *Kennet* 1690s as Nth; "knack – to speak finely, or affectedly" *Grose* 1787; "knack – to speak affectedly, to ape a style beyond the speaker's education" *Brockett* Newc & Nth 1829. *EDD* distribution to 1900: Nth. *Plus* "the Nack Pit" Seaham C19/mid (perhaps after affectations of 3rd Marquis of Londonderry, its owner)

knack to hurt

"Ow that knacks" (when something hurts considerably) *DS* Stockton C20/2. *Plus* "knacked – tired out" Trimdon 2002 Q

knack-kneed knock-kneed

> "knack-knee'd Mat" *Marshall* G'head 1806; "knack-knee'd – in-knee'd" *Brockett* Newc & Nth 1829. *EDD* distribution to 1900: Tyne

knoop see **cloud-berry**

knowl see **nool**

kranky see **cranky**

krissnin see **kersen**

kye cattle

> "kye – cows" *Ray* 1674; "kye or kie – the plural of cow" *Brockett* Newc & Nth 1829; "milk t'kye" *Egglestone* Weardale 1870s. *EDD* distribution to 1900: general.
> [OE cý pl. – for sg. see **coo**]

kyek cake, any round shaped loaf or cake

> "it's a bonny fight fer a bit kyek – hard to make a living" *Dunn* B'p Auck 1950.
> See also **stotty-kyek, spice-kyek**

kyevil see **cavil**

kytle light jacket

> ex. Teesside 2001 Q. *EDD* distribution to 1900: esp. Nth [compare Norw. kitte, Gm Kittel]

laa 1. low, 2. law

1. "the law end e the toon what the caw Irlind" *D'm Chron* 28 Apr 1865 re Trimdon; "he wiz varry laa doon" (in very low spirits) *Graham* Geordie 1979. *EDD* distribution to 1900: in this pronunciation C'd, W'd, N'd 2. "laa – law, low" *Dodds* Tanfield Lea C20/2

labber to splash about

"splashing and labbering aboot i' the tide" *Marshall* G'head 1806; 'floundering, struggling, or labouring in water' *Brockett* Newc & Nth 1829; "labber – to dabble in water" *Dinsdale* mid-Tees 1849. *EDD* distribution to 1900: Nth, Som

lace to wallop, lash

"if he says that again I'll lace him" *IA* S'm 1950s, 60s; "also meant heavily defeated at football or cricket; we got laced or we laced them" *JS* Easington C20/mid; 'to belt s.one' Tyneside C20/mid Q; "lace into s.one – attack" Newc 2001 Q. *EDD* distribution to 1900: general. NE 2001: in use. [OFr lacier]. *Plus* "lacing – a good beating" *Brockett* Newc & Nth 1829

lad boy

ex. *Brockett* Newc & Nth 1829; "lad – a male sweetheart: 'Tom Cubberson's maw lad'" *Luckley* Alnwick 1870s; 'boy, youth' *Palgrave* Hetton 1896; [plural] 'a group of comrades, not always young people – Hawk's Lads, etc' *Graham* Geordie 1979; "lads – Newcastle United, comrades" *Dodd* MS Tanfield Lea C20/2; "Oh lad!" (mild expletive) S'm 2003 via BG. *EDD* distribution to 1900: general. [ME ladde]

ladgeful bad

"ladgeful – used for expressing how bad something is: 'She's f***in' ladgeful hor, man'" Charver 2000–2002

laid in not working

"'laid in' – in a colliery is when it [had] given up working" *Bell* MS Newc 1830s; "wor pit was laid in" *Allan's Tyneside Songs* p.294 1842; "laid-in – a pit that has ceased working for an indefinite period" *Nicholson* 1880; "Laid off – discontinued. The invariable description of a pit which is not working is 'laid off' or 'laid in'" *Palgrave* Hetton 1896; "laid in – pit closed, e.g. coal exhausted, uneconomic" *Dodd* MS Tanfield Lea C20/2. *EDD* distribution to 1900: eD'm

laidly loathsome

"laidly, laithly – foul, loathsome, disgustingly ugly" *Brockett* Newc & Nth 1829; 'The laidley worm of Spindleston-Heugh' poem in Ritson 1809 (N'd). *EDD* distribution to 1900: Sco, N'd. [loathly]

laggans

'staves of a tub' *Palgrave* Hetton 1896; "black laggie – wooden dish with handle, for children" C19 D'm. [ON lǫgg]

lake 1. to play, 2. game(s)

1. ex. *Ray* 1674, *Bailey* Co.Durham 1810; "laking – playing, or playful games" *Bell* MS Newc 1815; "laik – to play" Upper Teesdale 2001 Q. *EDD* distribution to 1900: Sco, Nth, eMids. [OE lácan, ON leika] 2. "leeve thi laykes and lightnes" *Cuthbert* C15/mid; "lakes – sports, games" *Dinsdale* mid-Tees 1849. *Plus* "laker – a person engaged in sport" *Brockett* Newc & Nth 1846; "laking, baby-lakin – a child's toy, a plaything" *Brockett* Newc & Nth 1829; "Playlaking – a simpleton" *Palgrave* Hetton 1896

lalock, laylock lilac

"iv her brite lalock frock" *Allan's Tyneside Songs* p.562 1879; "laylock" *JO* re High Thornley/Rowlands Gill, ca.1900 in *Nth Words*. *EDD* distribution to 1900: general

lames injuries

"he's got his lames – had his share of pit injuries" *EP* Southwick C20/2. *EDD* distribution to 1900: Sco, Ire, Nth

landing area of pit

'a stopping place on the engine plane' *Nicholson* 1880; "landin' – pit tub standage" *Dodd* MS Tanfield Lea C20/2. *EDD* distribution to 1900: N'd, D'm

languij fine language

"languij – language esp. flowery" *Dodd* MS Tanfield Lea C20/2

lant urine

ex. *Brockett* Newc & Nth 1829. *EDD* distribution to 1900: W'd, Yx, C'd, Lx, Ches, Dev, Shr. [OE, ON hland]

lap to wrap

"a clathe samen lapped" (folded together) *Cuthbert* C15/mid; "lapt in a coverlet" *Raine* MS Newcastle, 1610; "he craaled away an

lap cont.

lapped he's tail / ten times roond Pensher Hill' 'Lambton Worm' 1867; "lapped up in a puddin' clout – wrapped" *Dunn* B'p Auck 1950; "lap – wrap, perimeter, water, seat above knees of sitter" *Dodd* MS Tanfield Lea C20/2. *EDD* distribution to 1900: general. [MDu lappen; ?influenced by Fr vloper]

lap leapt

"...the keel went bump 'gainst Jarrow / An' three o' th' bullies lap oot" *Allan's Tyneside Songs* p.27 1805; "lap – preterite of leap: 'the horse lap the wall'" *Brockett* Newc & Nth 1829. *EDD* distribution to 1900: Sco, Nth. *Plus* "Up lup awd Frank" (pret.) *Marshall* G'head 1806. *EDD* distribution to 1900: N'd. *Plus* "young bairns lapt fra their bed asleep" *Marshall* Newc p.17 1823. *EDD* distribution to 1900: Sco. [OE hléapan]. See also **lowp**

lare learning

"aw'd pick'd up some bits o' lare" *Pitman's Pay* G'head 1820s; "the corner-styen of a' wor lare" *Allan's Tyneside Songs* p.274 1843 (T.Wilson). *EDD* distribution to 1900: Sco, N'd, Yx. [OE lár]

larn to teach

"no man of the crafte learne his wife, his daughter, or anye woman to weave" *Raine* MS York 1607; "the [school] mistress larned me to wright" *Errington* p.32 Felling/Heworth re 1780s; "lairn them aul ye can" *Armstrong* Tanfield C19/2; "to larn the children" Coxhoe 1916. 'to teach, to learn' *Graham* Geordie 1979. *EDD* distribution to 1900: general. [OE leornian, 'to learn', 'teach']

lass young woman, sweetheart, wife

"lasse" (a working girl) *Cuthbert* C15/mid; "When bigger I grew / I cuddled the lassez" *Marshall* G'head 1806; "May... each lass her laddy cherish" *Allan's Tyneside Songs* p.46 1812; "Till he gets away hyem tiv his lass an' the news" *Barrass* Stanley 1890s; "'wor lass' – his lawful wedded wife, but sometimes this a union unblessed by the church" *Dobson* Tyne 1969; "wor lass – my wife" South Shields C20/2 (Q), *Graham* Geordie 1979. *EDD* distribution to 1900: esp. Sco, Nth. [ON *lasqa 'unmarried']

late to seek

"late" *Ray* 1674 re C'd; "late or lait" *Bailey* Co.Durham 1810; "lait, late – to seek, search for a thing: 'lait it while you finnd it'" *Atkinson* Cleve 1868. *EDD* distribution to 1900: Sco, Nth. [ON leita]

latt a lath, a thin piece of wood

ex. *Palgrave* Hetton 1896; "as thin as a latt" *Embleton* Tyne 1897; *RM* Norton C20/mid. *EDD* distribution to 1900: general. [lath]

law a hill

"lauue – a hill" Finchale (und., C14th?); "law – a hill or eminence, whether natural or artificial" *Brockett* Newc & Nth 1829. *EDD* distribution to 1900: general. [OE hláw]

laylock see **lalock**

lea a scythe

ex. Upper Teesdale 2001 Q. *EDD* distribution to 1900: Sco, Nth. [ON lé]

leach hard work

"leach – hard-work, great fatigue, a word frequent among the miners in the North" *Kennet* 1690s. *EDD* distribution to 1900: obsol.

lead to conduct, transport

"ledynge... garsell furthe of the woods to the... hegges" *Raine* MS York 1530/31; "lead – to carry or cart: in the North they lead coals" *Brockett* Newc & Nth 1829; "lead – to carry, harvest: 'leadin' cwols'" *Luckley* Alnwick 1870s; "To lead a horse and cart; practically 'leading' is equivalent to 'hauling'" *Palgrave* Hetton 1896; "lead – [to] carry esp. on horse-pulled cart" *JB* Shildon C20/mid. *EDD* distribution to 1900: Sco, Nth, Mids

leam a flame

ex. *Bailey* Co.Durham 1810. *EDD* distribution to 1900: Sco, D'm. [OE léoma]

leamers ripe nuts

"lemurs – ripe nuts that separate easily from the husk" *Bailey* Co.Durham 1810; "brown-lemur – a ripe brown hazel-nut" *Brockett* Newc & Nth 1829. *EDD* distribution to 1900: Sco, Nth, Mids

leazes pasturage

"leazes – common pasture belonging to the freemen of Newcastle" *Brockett* Newc & Nth 1829; "leazes – gently sloping fields" *Dinsdale*

leazes cont.

mid-Tees 1849. *EDD* distribution to 1900: general. [OE læligacutes]

led un spare tub (at coal face)

"led – in coal mining [of] any spare article: 'a led prop', 'led trams'" *Brockett* Newc & Nth 1846; "led-tub – a led tub means a spare one for the putter to leave empty with the hewer whilst the full one is being put to the flat; the empty one being filled by the hewer against the return of the putter with another empty one" *Nicholson* 1880. "O, hinney, put the led un in! / An' let's hed [have it] full!" *Barrass* Stanley 1890s

lee 1. to lie, fib, 2. a lie

1. "G—d forgih mih for leeing" *Bewick* Tyne 1790s; "If wark's ignoble, Ruskin lees" *Barrass* Stanley 1890s "lee – lie" *Tanfield Lea*, 1960. *EDD* distribution to 1900: in this pronunciation Sco, Nth. [OE léogan]. *Plus* "wor preacher he's nee leer" *Allan's Tyneside Songs* p.422 1862; "he's an aaful leear when he starts" *Irwin* Tyne 1970

2. "it was nowt but lees he teld him" *Marshall* Newc p.19 1823; "without a word ov a lee" *Wearside Tales* 1879; "th' biggest lee" *Armstrong* Tanfield C19/2; "ah canna tell a lee" *Irwin* Tyne 1970

lee urine

ex. *Raine* MS att. York 1649/50. *Plus* "Chemmerly – urine kept in a large stone bottle and used for washing clothes" *Palgrave* Hetton 1896. [lye from OE léag]

leet 1. light (noun), 2. to alight, 3. light in weight

1. "the leet of anithor day" Coxhoe 1916; "atween the twee leets" (at twilight) *Embleton* Newc 1897; "giv us a leet" *Dodd* MS Tanfield Lea C20/2. *EDD* distribution to 1900: in this pronunciation, esp. Nth

2. "let on the pavement" *Errington* p.50 Felling/Heworth re 1790s; "the great black owl that's let on Cappy's hearth" *Allan's Tyneside Songs* p.310 1827; "fore they can leet [from a train]" *Allan's Tyneside Songs* p.350 C19/1; "letten – p.p. of to let, or to light" *Atkinson* Cleve 1868

3. "as leet as a fethor" *Chater* Newc 1880

left-handed 1. **cuddy-handed**, 2. **cuddy-wifted**, 3. **cowie-handed**, 4. **car-handed**, 5. **cack-handed**

1. "'Cuddy-handed' is left-handed" *Palgrave* Hetton 1896; exx. *JS* E'ton, 1950s; *MB* Coxhoe C20/mid

2. "cuddy-handed was used in Easington – cuddy-wifted in Ryhope/Silksworth" *JS* Easington re 1950s; "cuddy wifter – anyone who is left-handed" *ER* M'bro C20/2, M'bro, S'd, B'p Auck 2001 Q, eD'm C20/2 Q

3. "kow paw – left-handed" *Bell* MS Newc 1815; "cowie handed" nwD'm C20/mid Q, Blyth 2002 Q; "cowie" Dinnington 1950s Q; "cow-handed/cowie-handed/cack-handed – left-handed" *Irwin* Tyne 1970.

4. "car-handed – left handed" *Brockett* Newc & Nth 1829, *Luckley* Alnwick 1870s. *EDD* distribution to 1900: Sco, N'd, Ches.

5. "cack-handed" (left-) S'd 2002 Q. *Irwin* Tyne 1970

leish see **lish**

let wi't let on

"let wi't – make known, let on: 'ye mun nivver let wi't'" *Dinsdale* mid-Tees 1849

letch ditch or gutter

"unto the full letch or sike of the said more" *Raine* MS Winston, 1606; "a leak or leche – a gutter" *Kennet* 1690s as D'm; "letch – a swang, or marshy gutter" *Bailey* Co.Durham 1810; "letch – a ditch or gutter through which water runs" *Bell* MS Newc 1815. *EDD* distribution to 1900: lache – Nth, C18. [?OE leccan 'to wetten']

lib to castrate (an animal)

"one man is to holde them [i.e. lambs]... whiles they are libbed" *Raine* MS EYorks 1641; "lib – to castrate" *Bailey* Co.Durham 1810, *Bell* MS Newc 1830s, *Atkinson* Cleve 1868. *EDD* distribution to 1900: Sco, Nth. [OE lib 'doctoring', Du lubben 'to geld']

library a library book

"Library (laay:bu:ri) – a book got from a library (always used): 'Hes thoo getten a lib'ry?'" *Palgrave* Hetton 1896; *GP* S'm 2000. *EDD* distribution to 1900: D'm, Yx, Lincs, Oxf, Essex

lick 1. to beat, to overcome, 2. a beating (plural noun)

1. "to lick – to beat" *Bell* MS Newc 1830s; "he

lick cont.

lick'd them all se fine" *Allan's Tyneside Songs* p.449 1862; "he cud lick aad Bobby clean away" *MC* Tyne May 1881; "Aw lick'd him te the flat" *Barrass* Stanley 1890s. *EDD* distribution to 1900: general. [OE liccian] 2. "licks – a sound beating, a severe chastisement" *Brockett* Newc & Nth 1829. *Plus* "fullick – a forceful blow" *Wade* South Moor 1966; "fullikin – cheating at marbles" *Dodds* Tanfield Lea C20/2

lig to lie (down)

"lig – to li" *Ray* 1674, *Bailey* Co.Durham 1810; "lig – to lie down, to rest the limbs" *Brockett* Newc & Nth 1829; "lig a bit langer" *Lakeland* re C'd 1856; "it ligs very fair for t' sun", *Atkinson* Cleve 1868; "where does she lig?" *NCM* N'd 1900–1901. *EDD* distribution to 1900: Sco, Nth, Mids. [OE licgan, ON liggja]

liggies 1. quoits. 2. testicles

1. "ligger or lignie – a carved wooden lignum vitae coit for playing at doddart, or the game of trippit and coit" *Brockett* Newc & Nth 1829; "Lignies – quoits made of lignum vitae wood, used in the game 'Spell and Nur'." *Palgrave* Hetton 1896. [lignum vitae]. See also **marbles** 2. ex. *MW* Tyneside 1960s, *Dobson* Tyne 1973

like used as emphatic at end of phrase, esp. a question

"How's that, like?" S'm per BG 2003

likeness photograph

ex. Coxhoe 1916; Spennymoor C20/mid; "getten his likeness tyun – photo taken" *Dunn* B'p Auck 1950. *EDD* distribution to 1900: Sco. Yx, Norf. *Plus* "Ars ganna hev mi photeens tuk" *CT* New Herrington 1930s

limmer rascally

"[calling him a] hold eeyd limber theiff" *Raine MS* ?D'm 1566; "limmer thieves" *RR* Weardale 1569; "limmer – a person of loose manners, a worthless idle person" *Brockett* Newc & Nth 1846. *EDD* distribution to 1900: Sco, Nth

limmers, limbers wagon shafts

"limmer, limmers – the shaft or shaftes of a cart: 'she's a lang limmer' a tall unsightly female" *Bell MS* Newc 1815; "limmers or limbers – the shafts by which a horse or pony

limmers, limbers cont.

is attached to the tubs" *Nicholson* 1880; "I was able to yoke a pony into his portable shafts, called 'limbers'" *Hitchin* re Seaham p.70 1910s; "limbers provided rigid coupling so that the pony could 'hold back' on undulating ground" *Northumbrian III* C20/2 re Burradon Colliery. *EDD* distribution to 1900: general. [AN limon 'shaft' (of cart)]

ling heather

"lynge – ling, used for covering the mill at Baxtanford" Finchale (1480); "ling – heath (*erica vulgaris*)" *Bailey* Co.Durham 1810; ex. wD'm 2001 Q. *EDD* distribution to 1900: Sco, Ire, Nth, Mids. [ON lyng]

lingey fit, active

"lingey – active, strong, and able to bear great fatigue" *Bailey* Co.Durham 1810; "lingy – active, strong, able to bear fatigue – also in the sense of tall, athletic, vigorous" *Brockett* Newc & Nth 1829. *EDD* distribution to 1900: esp. Nth. [OFr linge 'supple']

linin's winter underpants

'long fleecy underpants' *JO* re High Thornley/ Rowlands Gill, 1930s-1940s in *Nth Words*; "Linings – pitmen's drawers, fastened at the knee by strings" *Palgrave* Hetton 1896; "langlininz – long johns" *Dobson* Tyne 1972; 'underpants' *Graham* Geordie 1979

linn waterfall

"linn – a cascade" *Bailey* Co.Durham 1810; "lin, linn – a cascade (D'm and N'd)" *Brockett* Newc & Nth 1829; *Smith* Weardale 1883. *EDD* distribution to 1900: Sco, N'd, C'd, Lx. [OE hlynn, Gaelic linne]. See also **foss**

linty linnet, wren

"linties – linnets" *Pitman's Pay* G'head 1820s, *JO* re High Thornley/Rowlands Gill 1930s, 1940s in *Nth Words*; "as active as a lintie" *Graham* Geordie 1979. *EDD* distribution to 1900: Sco, Ire, N'd, Yx. [lint-white]

lippen to depend on

"I lippened on you to join me" *Brockett* Newc & Nth 1829; "I lippen on him doing it" *Palgrave* Hetton 1896. *EDD* distribution to 1900: Sco, Ire, Nth. *Plus* "to lippen – close your finger over your thumb (as a magical sign)" *Bell MS* Newc 1830s

lish nimble, active

"Whe's like my Johnny, / Sae leish, sae blithe, sae bonny?" *Allan's Tyneside Songs* p.45 1812; "leish, lish – nimble, strong, active, stout, alert, lithe" *Brockett* Newc & Nth 1829; "gan oot tiv his wark, leesh an' fresh" (fit) *Haldane* Newc 1879; "lish – strong and active" *Dodd* MS Tanfield Lea C20/2; "whilst t' auld 'uns wished th' waur a bit lisher" *Lakeland* re C'd 1901. *EDD* distribution to 1900: Sco, Nth

lisk groin

"a browne quie with a whit liske" *Raine* MS Haydon Bridge 1579; "lisk – that part of the side which is between the hips and the short ribs" *Kennet* 1690s as Yx; "a pain in the lisk" *Brockett* Newc & Nth 1829; 'the flank, the groin' *Atkinson* Cleve 1868; 'thigh' *Palgrave* Hetton 1896; 'the toppermost part of the leg on the inside or groin; the muscle or sinew at this part of the leg' *DO* D'ton C20/2; 'groin' Wheatley Hill 2002 Q; "he's ruptured his lisk area" Cockfield 2004 E. *EDD* distribution to 1900: Sco, Ire, Nth. [ON lióske; compare Dan. lyske]

list inclined, eager

"List – desire, energy: 'I haven't list to gan across', 'He hesn't list to did' (do it)" *Palgrave* Hetton 1896; "isn't list to do nowt – can't be bothered" *Dunn* B'p Auck 1950. *EDD* distribution to 1900: Nth. [OE lystan (vb), ON lysta]. *Plus* "it maks me narvish an unlisty" *Embleton* Tyne 1897

loggerheed a moth, etc.

"Loggerhead – a coloured butterfly. Large moths are also sometimes called 'logger-heads.'" *Palgrave* Hetton 1896; "loggerheed – large butterfly or moth" South Moor (Stanley) 2003 per BG; "A've been doon the born coppin loggerheeds" (response to the question "Wheor hev yee been?" – meaning "Mind your own business") *ED* Benwell C20/1; 'large moth' *Dodd* MS Tanfield Lea C20/2, Ch-le-St 2002 Q. *EDD* distribution to 1900: in this sense, N'd, D'm, C'd. *Plus* "logger – moth" S'd, Dawdon 2001 Q. See also **butterfly**

lolly the tongue

"oppen thy gob hinny and put out thy lolly" *Graham* Geordie 1979

lone, loan lane

"stannin at the lown end" *Bewick* Tyne 1790s; "lone, loan – a lane, a narrow passage" *Atkinson* Cleve 1868; "loan – a place for milking cows: 'the cow loan'" *Luckley* Alnwick 1870s; "back-lon" *Palgrave* Hetton 1896. *EDD* distribution to 1900: N'd, C'd, Yx. [OE lane]

lonnin lane

"the amendinge of Newbridge lonninge" *Raine* MS Newbottle 1581; "Haughton loning leading from Sunderland-by-sea to Darlington" *Raine* MS 1673; "the fiend gea down the loaning with her" Rothbury C18/2; "gallop away down the lonnon" *Green* Wearside 1879 re C19/1; "loaning, lonnin – a lane or bye-road" *Brockett* Newc & Nth 1829; "a lang lonnen wuv hooses en shops on bi'ath sides" *Egglestone* Weardale 1870s; "the lads an' the lasses i' t' lonnin" *Lakeland* re C'd 1901. *EDD* distribution to 1900: loaning – Sco, Ire; lonning – Nth. [little lane]

loof, leuf the palm of the hand

"leuf, luff, luif – the palm of the hand: 'If ye'll scart maw leuf, I'll claw yur elbow'" *Brockett* Newc & Nth 1829; "the gipsey... crumpled weel my liuf and glowered sair at it" *Bell* MS Newc 1830s; "loof, lufe – the open hand or palm" *Atkinson* Cleve 1868. *EDD* distribution to 1900: Sco, Ire, Nth. [ON lófe]

look, lowk to weed

"lowk – to weed corn" *Ray* 1674; "for 3 days looking corn, 1 s." *Raine* MS Appleton Roebuck 1692; "look – [to] weed esp. in corn-field" *JB* Shildon C20/mid. *EDD* distribution to 1900: Nth, parts Mids. [OE lúcan, ON lúka]

looksta, etc.

"there's a canny little lad gawn up the riggin, look 'e" *JS* South Shields C19/mid; "looks-t'ee – look you!" *Atkinson* Cleve 1868; "why, lucks thee..." *Wearside Tales* 1879; "lucka! / Lucks-ta!" (take note) *Tyneside Grammar* 1880s; "Looks-tha – an expression to gain attention" *Palgrave* Hetton 1896; "lukstha klip o that" (look at the state of that) *JS* Easington C20/mid, *JP* S'm C20/2; "lucksta – look thou" Tanfield Lea 1960

lop flea

exx. *Ray* 1674, *Bailey* Co.Durham 1810; "as whick as onny lop" *MC* Tyne May 1881; "she's

lop cont.

as peert [lively] as a lop" *Embleton* Tyne 1897, *Cuddy Cairt* Newc 1917; "he's got mair in his heid thin lops" (is clever) Ashington C20/mid; "only 'fit as a lop'" *PG* H'pool C20/2, D'ton C20/mid, *Graham* Geordie 1979; "lop – a small domestic insect... widely used in the cinema trade in the early days" *Dobson* Tyne 1972. *EDD* distribution to 1900: Nth. NE 2001: in use. [ON *hloppa, cf. Swed. loppe]. *Plus* "loppy – flea-ridden" *JB* Shildon C20/mid; "penny loppy" (a cheap cinema) *DB* G'head 1950s; sim. "the penny lop" *Graham* Geordie 1979

lopper to curdle

"lopper – to coagulate; loppered milk – milk that sours and curdles without the application of an acid" *Brockett* Newc & Nth 1829; "lopperd – putrified, as lopperd milk" *Bell* MS Newc 1830s; "loppered milk" (curds) *Embleton* Newc 1897; "Loppit – sour milk, curd milk" *Palgrave* Hetton 1896. *EDD* distribution to 1900: Sco, Ire, Nth, EA. [ON hløypa]. *Plus* "earn (pronounced yearn) – to curdle milk or cause it to coagulate" *Atkinson* Cleve 1868

loss to lose

"we'll niver loss seet o' Johnny" *Allan's Tyneside Songs* p.460 1862; "throo lossen th' tranes" (missing) *Armstrong* Tanfield C19/2; "Ryenhats! She losses them on piece!" (from piecework i.e. encouragement to do s.thing faster) *AK* re Newc C20/2; "A've loss that!" S'm 1990 per BG, sim. *Wood* Tees 2002. *EDD* distribution to 1900: in this pronunciation Sco, Ire, Nth, SW

loup see **lowp**

low (rhymes with 'how') 1.a flame, a light, 2. to flare, to burn

1. "the house had been in brynnande low" *Cuthbert* C15/mid; "had up the low" *Collier's Rant* Newc C18/2; "[the gas] was just coming... he called to all men and boys to put out their lows" (candles) *Errington* p.59 Felling/Heworth re 1800s; "the toon's iv a low" (aflame with gossip) *Allan's Tyneside Songs* p.273 1843 (T.Wilson); "'trying the lowe' an operation by which gas is detected in a coal mine" *Brockett* Newc & Nth 1846; "jillusey's crewl ast graave: t'cwols ont er cwols uv fire, whilk hes a maist tremendous lowe" *Moore* Weardale 1859; "shine a low – to direct the light of a lamp or candle in a required

low cont.

direction" *Nicholson* 1880; "if luck wad shine the lowe" *Barrass* Stanley 1890s; "While ye toast yor shins afore the lowe" (fire) *MC* Tyne May 1891; "Low (luw) – a flame, hence 'low-rope,' hempen rope steeped in tar, to burn as a torch" *Palgrave* Hetton 1896; 'a flame' Tanfield Lea 1960, *Viereck* re Gateshead 1966; "Gi'us a low" *Wade* South Moor 1966. *Plus* "lillilow – a bright flame, a blaze" *Atkinson* Cleve 1868. *EDD* distribution to 1900: Sco, Ire, Nth, eMids. NE 2001: not in use. [ON loge]
2. "to low – to flame, to blaze" Jamieson *Scots Dictionary* 1808; "doon dunny Tynside the fornaces lowe" *Allan's Tyneside Songs* p.537 1886; "lowe – flame, vb. to flame" *Ray* 1674; "low – to flame in Yorksh, as the fire lows" *Kennet* 1690s

lowie money

"lowie" Charver 2000-2002; "lower" Wheatley Hill 2003 Q. [Romany 'luvvo']. See also **brass, wedge, butterfly**

lowp, loup to leap

"lope – to leap" *Ray* 1674; "An' lowp se clever" (dance) *Marshall* G'head 1806; "fit to loup a yett or stile" *Pitman's Pay* G'head 1820s; "loup – to leap, bound, jump" *Atkinson* Cleve 1868; "They dore just as seun lowp frae the land above the meun" *Barrass* Stanley 1890s; "Aw lowpt clean ower the stock" *Barrass*; "'See we can lowp the far'est", "When I was young and lusty, I could lowp a dyke" *Palgrave* Hetton 1896; "we lowped over walls and fences" *JS* Easington C20/mid; "cracket-lowping" (jumping over) *Dobson* Tyne 1972; "Lowp oot fer the Central" (alight...) *Dobson* Tyne 1969; "lowp – to jump over" Wheatley Hill 2002 Q. *EDD* distribution to 1900: general. NE 2001: in common use. [ON hløupa]. *Plus* "lad-louper – a forward girl" *Atkinson* Cleve 1868; "a loup – a leap" *Bell* MS Newc 1830s. See also **leap, dyke**

lowse 1. loose, free (adj), 2. to set free, unyoke, loosen, 3. end of work

1. "louse – to unbind, to release, to leave of work" *Brockett* Newc & Nth 1829; "At neets, when frae wark aw get lowse" *WM* Newc C19/2; "th' lowse wheel" (loose) *Armstrong* Tanfield C19/2; "the evil beast that's brokken lowse" Coxhoe 1916; "thoos lowseitheheed"

lowse cont.

(demented) *Dobson* Tyne 1972; "lowz flatoot – expression of anger" *Dodd* MS Tanfield Lea C20/2; "the sneck's lowse" East Boldon 1985. *EDD* distribution to 1900: Sco, Ire, Nth, wMids [ON lauss 'free, loose']
2. "in about 10 minutes, they lowsed the seesing (cause of stoppage) and lowered (us) to the botum" *Errington* p.61 Felling/ Heworth re 1800s; "lowse – to make loose, untie" *Atkinson* Cleve 1868; "she lows'd her hat" (unpinned) *Armstrong* Tanfield C19/2; "Aw cud yoke'm or lowse'm " (pit ponies) *Barrass* Stanley 1890s; "es pictures lowsed out yit? – have they come out from the cinema?" *Dunn* B'p Auck 1950; "lowse – loose hold of it" *Dobson* Tyne 1973; "Aa'll lowse you out" [of baby from pram] Seaham 2003 via BG
3. "frae gannen doon te lowse", "quiet noo, for lowse is call'd " *Barrass* Stanley 1890s; "What time diz thoo louz?" *Palgrave* Hetton 1896; "pleeze sir izit varni lowse?" (end of schoolday) Ashington C20/1 Q; "loose or kennah – defines end of shift of work" *McBurnie* Glebe Colliery C20/mid; "we got an 'early lowse' – finished early" *JS* E'ton, 1950s; "Lowse was caaled at ten o'clock" (closing time) *Grieves* Tyne 1975; 'time to knock off or finishing time' *JM* Dawdon 1970s; "howway lads, it's lowse – time gentlemen" *Graham* Geordie 1979. [from the unyoking of ponies at the end of a shift in the pit]

lug ear

"luggs – ears" *Kennet* 1690s as Nth; "the horses cock their lugs" *Oiling* G'head 1826; "a word i' yor lugs" *Allan's Tyneside Songs* p.245 1827; "lug – the ear, of man or animal, or a pitcher..." *Atkinson* Cleve 1868; "little jugs hes lang lugs" (re children) *Tyneside grammar* 1880s; "the galawae lade hees lugs back" *Armstrong* Tanfield C19/2; "Ahlthumpyalug" East Boldon 1985. *EDD* distribution to 1900: Sco, Ire, Nth, eMids, EA. NE 2001: in use. [ON lugg 'a handle, s.thing to pull']

lum chimney

"a loom or lumm a chimney" *Kennet* 1690s as D'm; "as black as the lume" *Bell* MS Newc 1815; "as the snaw drops doon the lum"

lum cont.

Allan's Tyneside Songs p.399 C19/mid; "lum – the chimney of a cottage" *Brockett* Newc & Nth 1829; "Thou's as black as the lum" *Palgrave* Hetton 1896. *EDD* distribution to 1900: Sco, Ire, Nth. NE 2001: not in use. [OFr lum 'light', Welsh llummm 'chimney']. *Plus* "Chimla – chimney. Hence 'chimla-piece.'" *Palgrave* Hetton 1896

lumper a work practice

"a specific job could be a lumper or lumba, meaning if it was finished before time you could go home early" *JS* Easington C20/mid

lyke wake the watching of a dead body during the night

"I will that ther shall be no yong folkes at my lyke waike but onlie xiii wydowes" *Raine* MS Richmond 1558/59; "The night it is her low lyke wake / The morn her burial day" *Reed Border Ballads* C16; 'Lyke Wake Dirge' Title attributed to poem from Cleveland, of perhaps C15/16; "lake-wake or lyke-wake – the watching of a corpse previous to interment" *Brockett* Newc & Nth 1829; "Lake Wake or Late Wake – sitting up with the dead from the death till the burial" *Bell* MS Newc 1815. [OE líc 'dead body', ON lúk]

maa see **my**...

Mackem see Makem

macky mackerel

ex. *DP* S'm 1990s

maddle 1. to be fond of, 2. to be confused

1. "to maddle – to be fond of, to doat upon as, she maddles of this fellow" *Kennet* 1690s as Nth; "she maddles after that fellow"'*Grose* 1787
2. "maddled – confounded, distracted" *Bell* MS Newc 1815; "maddle – to wander, to talk inconsistently, to forget or confound objects..." *Brockett* Newc & Nth 1829. *EDD* distribution to 1900: nYx. [from mad]

mafted stifled

"mafted – stifled, overdone with heat and closeness" *Atkinson* Cleve 1868; "mafted – tired, knocked back, gassed, etc." *Blenkinsopp* Teesdale 1931; "overcome by heat and/or lack of air" *PG* H'pool C20/2; "mafted – hot" B'd Castle, Weardale, Teesdale 2001 Q; 'hot and bothered' Teesdale 2001 Q; 'overheated, flushed' Teesdale 2001 Q; NE 2001: in use (Tees). *EDD* distribution to 1900: nYx, eYx. *Plus* "it's mafting in here" (of a hot airless room) Tees 2000 Q. See also **scumfish**

maggies 1. magpies, 2. Newcastle football supporters, 3. turnip lamp

1. "maggy – a provincial name for a magpie" *Brockett* Newc & Nth 1829. *EDD* distribution to 1900: Sco, N'd, W'm, Lx. NE 2001: in use. See also **piots**
2. NUFC supporters – 'the name was noted as far back as 1895. It may be significant here that the familiar black-and-white stripe shirts were first adopted in 1894' *AK*
3. "'candle in a jamjar' [used in game] 'Jackie shine the maggie'" Dinnington 1950s Q, sim. Wade *South Moor* C20/mid, *JR* Sacriston C20/2; "a greet big turnip, holler it oot, put in a candle, an' mek it into a maggie" *BL* Winlaton 1950s; "a Halloween lamp made from a turnip was a maggie as in [the game] 'Jack shine yor maggie'" *JS* Easington C20/mid; "moggie – pit lamp" *Lore and language* re Maria Pit, Throckley C20/mid. See also **midgey**

mair more

"ne mare oh that!" *Bewick* Tyne 1790s; "mair wise than a king" *Allan's Tyneside Songs* p.187

mair cont.

1824; "a few mare" *MWN* M'bro 28 Jan 1860; "mair ar eight" (more than – literally over – eight) *Smith* Weardale 1883; "Wor spendin nee mair" *Irwin* Tyne 1970; "neemair" East Boldon 1985. *EDD* distribution to 1900: in this pronunciation Sco, N'd, Yx. [OE mára]

mairt meat

"mairt – a cow or ox slaughtered at Martinmas, and salted for winter store. The custom of salting meat to last throughout the inclement months was universal among our ancestors. Though less frequent, since the extensive cultivation of turnips, it still partially prevails in Northumberland..." *Brockett* Newc & Nth 1846. *EDD* distribution to 1900: mart – Sco, N'd, D'm, C'd. [Gael. mart]

maist 1.most, 2. almost

1. "a myest horrible din" *Barrass* Stanley 1890s. *EDD* distribution to 1900: in this pronunciation Sco, N.I., Nth. [OE mæst]
2. "till maist yen o'clock" *Haldane* Newc 1879

maistor pit-owner

"wor maistors, an' viewers, an' sinkers" *Allan's Tyneside Songs* p.350 C19/1; "just te vext th' maistors" (pit owners, bosses) *Armstrong* Tanfield C19/2; "Te risk such dangers for such pay / Wad turn the maistors blue!" *Barrass* Stanley 1890s; "maistas – coal owners" *Dodd* MS Tanfield Lea C20/2. *EDD* distribution to 1900: general

mak, myek 1. **mak** forms, 2. **myek** forms, 3. type, variety, 4. match, equal

1. "paied for the mackinge of his clothes" *Anderson* Newcastle 1616; "div'nt ye mak' sic a rout" *Allan's Tyneside Songs* p.47 1812; "I'll mak' a cwot (coat) wi onny other man" *Stobbs* Woodhorn C19/mid; "mack" *Moore* Weardale 1859 ; "it mack it leak respectable like" *MWN* 18 Feb 1860; "med" (made) *Haldane* Newc 1879; "makkin things worse" *Hay* Ushaw Moor C20/1; "what's th' mak on 'im – what do you make of him" *Dunn* B'p Auck 1950; "th's just mak'n on" (pretending, exaggerating) *CT* New Herrington 1930s; "maks nae odds" S'm, 2000; "mak" Trimdon 2002. *EDD* distribution to 1900: mak – Sco, D'm, sW'd, wYx, nYx, C'd; mek – C'd, wMids. NE 2001: in use. [OE macian]

mak, myek cont.

2. "meayke heayst!" *Bewick* Tyne 1790s; "I'll meak ye a bow" *Marshall* G'head 1806; "myek a voyage" *Allan's Tyneside Songs* p.51 1823; "aw myed wour bairns cry" *Marshall* G'head 1806; "to myek me happy" *Pitman's Pay* G'head 1820s; "Myek up yor sivoral minds" *Barrass* Stanley 1890s; "aw'd myek a poor moothful for a wild beast" *Allan's Tyneside Songs* p.404 C19/mid; "myek us a booler mister" *JS* Easington C20/mid; "myek – make", "myed – made" Tanfield Lea, 1960; "mekkin' whisky" *Dobson* Tyne 1970-71; "mek some noise!" *VIZ* 37 (1990); *EDD* distribution to 1900: N'd (i.e Newc?). [from southern pronunciation, early exx. esp. on Tyneside]
3. "mony a mack of greedy kite" Rothbury C18/2; "'a' mak's an' manders' varieties, different sorts" *Atkinson* Cleve 1868; "a' maks en manners o' things" *Egglestone* Weardale 1870s
4. "mack – a match: "I believe he or she has not a mack" *Bell* MS Newc 1830s; "mackless – matchless, unequaled" *Bell* MS Newc 1830s

Makem inhabitant of Sunderland or Wearside

"There were more shipyards in this one town of Sunderland than anywhere else. Likewise there were more sailors and crew to take the vessels to sea." *BS* N.Shields C20/2 i.e. the shipyard workers 'mak' the ships, the crews 'tak' them to sea, and thus Mackems and Tackems are (or were) two important and populous local groups. "The first time I heard the expression was when my daughter went to work at Swan Hunters Shipyard, Newcastle, in the five years before folding. I had worked at Doxford Shipyard, Sunderland for one year in 1968 and never heard the expression. However 'you makem / we takem' is obviously a superior remark as most ships built at Sunderland were transfered to the Tyne to have the engine installed." *CT* New Herrington. "They come from the shipyards" www.urbanDictionary.com 2003; "Makem – I thought this meant anyone from Sunderland" *SM* H'pool 2003. [the implication of 'mak 'em n tak 'em' may be no more than a comment on Sunderland (traditional) pronunciation as against Newcastle 'myek' – see previous entry] See also **Jamies**

malacise do harm to

"if your ma finds out...she'll malacise you, i.e. bray the living daylights out of you" *JS* Easington C20/mid. [?malison 'a curse', malacissant 'softening']

mall/y

1. "Mall – Mary" *Bell* MS Newc 1815; "Mally – a girl's name" (Mary) *Brockett* Newc & Nth 1829. See also **hare**

mam see **mother**

man of any person

"Man, Bob, but Aa tell the'" *Haldane* Newc 1879; "Man, father..." *Dobson* Tyne 1970; "Man. As throughout North, used in exclamations: 'Eh, mon, aa din-aa' (Indeed, sir (or, mate), I don't know). Also used irrespective of sex" *Palgrave* Hetton 1896; "it's flat, man, Bob" *VIZ* 37, ca.1990. [OE monn – any person, male or female]

mang 1. to mix, 2. a mix

1. "mang – to mix up, to intermingle (esp. food stuffs): 'nobbut a manged oop mess'" *Atkinson* Cleve 1868. *EDD* distribution to 1900: general. [OE gemang 'mixture']
2. "mang – barley or oats ground with the husk, for dogs and swine meat" *Bailey* Co.Durham 1810; "mang – a mash of bran, malt, etc." *Atkinson* Cleve 1868

marbles 1. **marvils**, 2. **muggles**, 3.**alleys**, 4. **boodies**, 5. **glassies**, 6. **liggies**, 7. **parper**, 8. **penker**, 9. **scudder**, 10. **taw**

1. "play at marvils" *JA* Newc C19/mid
2. "Muggles... were marbles. They were also called glass allys but this expression was not frequently used." *CT* New Herrington 1930s; "we called marbles 'muggles'" *SO* re Seaham 1940s; "the world of marbles, properly known as muggles... the object was to hit your oponent's muggle" *JS* E'ton 1950s; "muggels – marbles" *Dodd* MS Tanfield Lea C20/2. "muggies" Thornley 2001 Q, *TR* Deneside 2004. NE 2001: in use
3. "a marble made of alabaster is... called an Alley" *Brockett* Newc & Nth 1846; 'a marble made of alabaster' *Luckley* Alnwick 1870s; "glass alley" *FS* Shotton Colliery 1930s, *JS* Easington, 1950s; "'alley' for a marble... 'blood alley' for the marble with red in it" *SO* re Seaham 1940s, *RC* Dawdon C20/mid (as main word); "blood alley – glass marble with red

marbles cont.

glass in it; snot alley – glass marble with white glass in it" *ER* M'bro C20/2; "blood alley – glass marble with red in it" Teesside 2001 Q; "pop-alley – pop-bottle stopper as marble" Gateshead 2001 Q. NE 2001: in use, esp. eD'm [alabaster]
4. "boodies – a clay type marble" *JG* Annfield Plain 1930s. [clay marbles seems to have been typical of the C18]
5. "glassies were used when playing to knock out marbles from a marked circle" *JG* Annfield Plain 1930s; "glassies – cheap Woolworths marbles" *RC* Dawdon C20/mid
6. "liggies" Tyneside. 2001 Q. See also **liggies** [lignum vitae]. NE 2001: in low use, e.g. Tyne
7. "sometimes a glass alley, usually marbled white and a colour, was called a parper" *JS* Easington 1950s
8. "The 'panker' or 'penker' is a large marble, made of stone or iron" *Palgrave* Hetton 1896; "Wor Geordie's lost 'is penker" (song, C20/1); "penker – large marble" *FS* Shotton Colliery 1930s; "the first boy threw a penker – much larger than the other marbles (boodies) – the next boy tried to hit it" *JG* Annfield Plain 1930s; "pot penkers – larger again, not of glass but of earthenware/china clay" *CT* New Herrington 1930s; "pengka – very large marble half-two inch diameter, usually thrown" *Dodd* MS Tanfield Lea C20/2; "penker or benker" Roker C20/mid; "penker – stone marble" cenD'm 2001 Q; "an old ball-bearing" *JS* Easington, 1950s; "iron benger – steel ball bearing" *RC* Dawdon C20/mid; "iron benker" S'd 2001 Q; *EDD* distribution to 1900: panker/penker – eD'm. NE 2001: in use
9. scudder (the shooting marble): "me best scudder" *JS* Easington, 1950s
10. "taw – the shooting marble" *Dinsdale* mid-Tees 1849, *Hitchin* re Seaham p.55 1910s; "tawry – the name of a favourite marble... called taw in the south" *Luckley* Alnwick 1870s; "hoo'll tyek the taws" (special marble, prize) *Barrass* Stanley 1890s; "Taw (taa:). A boy in playing marbles always has his fancy marble to shoot with: this he calls his 'taw'" *Palgrave* Hetton 1896; but... "we never used the word 'taw' for the 'shooting' marble" *JS* Easington 1950s. *EDD* distribution to 1900: general

mare see **mair**

marra, marrow 1. workmate, close associate, 2. one of pair, a match, an equal, 3. to match

1. "O stay at hame, my marrow!" (wife to husband) Reed *Border Ballads* C16; "marrow – a companion or fellow" *Ray* 1674; "a marrow – in Yorkshire, a fellow or companion..." *Kennet* 1690s; "me and my marrow was ganning to wark" *Colliers Rant* Newc C18/2; "marrow – a companion, a fellow, an associate" Jamieson *Scots Dictionary* 1808; "...seeing the dog upon his marrow, evaded me to rescue the other" *Errington* p.91 Felling/ Heworth re 1810s; "he and his 'marra'" *The Maister* p.34 re keelmen on the Tyne, 1800–1840; "Marrow – an old word signifying brother but still used about Newcastle, as the name of a companion or acquaintance..." *Bell* MS Newc 1815; "marrow – a mess-mate, companion, or associate – an equal" *Brockett* Newc & Nth 1829; "Jim, like his marrows, drunk nowt but beer" *Allan's Tyneside Songs* p.483 1870; "...men term each other as their marrow when working in the same shift together. They term the men following them at the same work in the next shift their cross-marrows" *McBurnie* Glebe Colliery, C20/mid; "marra – workmate, friend" *Dodd* MS Tanfield Lea C20/2; "workin' marras in the pit" *Grieves* 1975; "cheers, marra" S'm 2003 (youth to bus-driver). *EDD* distribution to 1900: esp. Scot, Nth. [ON margr 'friendly'] NE 2001: in common use. *Plus* "half marrow – one of two boys who manage a team, of about equal age" *Pitman's Pay* G'head 1820s; "half-marrow – a middle-sized lad, two such being required in a coal-pit, to put a corf of coals equal to a man" *Brockett* Newc & Nth 1846; "yor mates at Sunderland" *Allan's Tyneside Songs* p.494 1871. See also **billy**
2. "...the relative term in pairs, as one glove or shoe is not marrow to another" *Kennet* 1690s; "this pair of gloves or shoes are not marrows" Grose 1787; "marrows – fellows; two alike, or corresponding to each other; as a pair of gloves, a pair of stockings, a pair of shoes" *Brockett* Newc & Nth 1829; "marrows – two alike, a pair" *Dinsdale* mid-Tees 1849; "T' ane's t' very marrow o' t'ither" *Atkinson* Cleve 1868; "Nanny bowt a pair o' stockings an; they warrent marrows" *Luckley* Alnwick 1870s. *EDD* distribution to 1900: Sco, Nth

marra, marrow cont.

3. "bad him match him with his marrows" (in combat) Reed *Border Ballads* C16; "marrow me that" is a Newcastle term for any thing good" *Bell* MS Newc 1815; "the fine things... we can marra iv Canny Newcassel" *Marshall* Newc 1823; "the Butcher Bank is bad (hard) to marrow" *Allan's Tyneside Songs* p.194 1842; "thor isn't a hoose ony way can marrow 't" *Haldane* Newc 1879; "An' smash! if thor Newcassel lyeddies / Coul'd marra the curls o' thy brow" *Crawhall* Newc 1888

mask to infuse

"mask – to infuse: 'mask the tea'" *Brockett* Newc & Nth 1829, *Atkinson* Cleve 1868; "ah hennot masked the tea yit" *Embleton* Tyne 1897; "mask the tea thin am clammin!" *Dobson* Tyne 1970–71. *EDD* distribution to 1900: Sco, Nth. [Nth form of mash? Dan. maske] *Plus* "maskfat – mashing vat, for brewing" *Finchale* 1837. See also **mast**

maslin, masselgem mixed grain

"myxtilio – maslin. A mixture of wheat and rye" Finchale 1303; "Wheat sold from 56s to 66s. Maslin 44s to 52s." *Newc Courant* 6 Sep 1828; "massilgam – maslin: wheat and rye ground together and generally baked with leven" *Bell* MS Newc 1830s; "masselgem – mixed meal" *Luckley* Alnwick 1870s. *EDD* distribution to 1900: maslin – general; masselgem – NE. [AN mestilon 'mixed grain', OE mæstling 'brass' (i.e. alloy), in MidE used of anything mixed components]. *Plus* "this silly and affected massiljim, intelarding [the Newcastle dialect] with low cockneyisms and what they consider fine words" *Chater* Newc 1880 p.13

mast, mass to mash, infuse

"our family has used 'mast the teas' for years" *JS* Easington C20/mid; "mash" *ER* M'bro C20/2; "mass" *KH* Stockton C20/2; "mass or mast – infusing tea" *Dodd* MS Tanfield Lea C20/2; "mast" *Todd* Tyne 1977, Trimdon 2002 Q; "wor lass's ganna mask the tye (tea)" *Graham* Geordie 1979. *EDD* distribution to 1900: mass – C'd, wYx; mesh – wYx; meysh – Lx. See also **mask**

maugh brother-in-law

"meaugh – my wives brother or sisters husband" *Ray* 1674; "maug, meaugh – a wive's

maugh cont.

brother" *Kennet* 1690s as D'm; "maugh – a brother-in-law" *Bailey* Co.Durham 1810; "maff or my maff is used to express the relation between such as marry two sisters" *Bell* MS Newc 1830s. *EDD* distribution to 1900: D'm, Yx but obsol. [ON mágr]

maum/y well ripe

"maumy – mellow and juiceless" *Bailey* Co.Durham 1810; "maum – mellow, possessing the softness of maturity or ripeness" *Atkinson* Cleve 1868. *EDD* distribution to 1900: malmy – Sco, NE [OE mealm-, ON malmr]

maunder to wander, esp. in the mind

"maunder – to wander about in a thoughtful manner; to be tedious in talking, etc." *Brockett* Newc & Nth 1829; "maundering – listless, idle" *Dinsdale* mid-Tees 1849; "maunder – to think, talk or act dreamily" *Gibson* C'd 1880; "if you're up in the early hours of the morning when everyone else is abed, you're a 'midnight maunderer'" *PG* H'pool C20/2. *EDD* distribution to 1900: general

mawk maggot

"there will malkes breede" *Raine* MS EYorks 1641; "mawks – maggots" *Kennet* 1690s as Yx; "mauk, mawk – a maggot" *Brockett* Newc & Nth 1829; "mawk – a maggot, the lava of a flesh-fly" *Atkinson* Cleve 1868; "maaks – maggots (as on sheep's back in summer)" *JB* Shildon C20/mid; "mawk – a miserable person" *Wood* Tees 2002. *EDD* distribution to 1900: Sco, Nth, eMids. [ON mǫkr]

mawky magotty

"maakee – magotty" *Dodd* MS Tanfield Lea C20/2, "maaky" *Graham* Geordie 1979; "marky – flea-ridden" cen D'm 2001 Q; "In Teesside 'mawky' is used to describe a miserable, depressing person. In fact they can be called a mawk. I've heard a colour scheme described as 'mawky'." *Wood* M'bro 2002

maybe

"mavies" *Allan's Tyneside Songs* p.45 1812; "mebby, maybees, mavies – perhaps, probably" *Brockett* Newc & Nth 1829; "mavies – short for 'may be'" *Bell* MS Newc 1830s; "maybees I may, maybees I may not" *Bell* MS Newc 1830s; "they'll mebby git browght doon a peg" *Egglestone* Weardale 1870s; "mevies" *Wearside Tales* 1879; "mevvies, mebbe, mevvy" *Haldane*

maybe cont.

Newc 1879; "mevvies" *Barrass* Stanley 1890s; *JO* re High Thornley/Rowlands Gill, 1930s-1940s in *Nth Words*; "mevvee – maybe" *Dodd* MS Tanfield Lea C20/2; "mebbes, mevvies – perhaps" Tanfield Lea, 1960; "maybies aa wull gan" *Graham* Geordie 1979; "mebeez – maybe" *VIZ* 37 ca.1990. *EDD* distribution to 1900: in varous similar forms, Sco, Nth

mazer someone impressive or weird

"Nanny's a maisor" (a phenomenon) *Armstrong* Tanfield C19/2; "leuked... astonished to see us such a mashor" *Robson* Newc C20/1; 'strange, amazing person' Dinnington 1950s Q; 'a wonder, an eccentric' *Graham* Geordie 1979; "maiza – a wonder" *Dodd* MS Tanfield Lea C20/2. *EDD* distribution to 1900: N'd

mazzled confused

"I'm just mazled with thinking on it" (confounded) *Bell* MS Newc 1830s; "maiz't, maizelt – stupified" *Gibson* C'd 1880; "The word mazzled (rhymes with dazzled) means all churned up/mixed up in the mind / head in a spin / in a flummox. Used in the context, 'Eeh, Arv'e had a mazzlin day, Ahr din't knar if A'm cumin or gannin', or 'A'm mazzled'." *BJ* re Cockfield, ca.1900. *EDD* distribution to 1900: esp. Nth

me

"uz, huz" Embleton, Newc 1897; 'us' for 'me' Coxhoe 1916; "us" *Dodd* MS Tanfield Lea C20/2. Used emphatically: "I love soup me" (Mr Soup on seaham.com website 2002); "Aa've just finisht work, me, like" S'm 2003 via BG. *Plus* "masell" Coxhoe 1916, "mesel – myself" Tanfield Lea 1960. See also **my**

meat food

"meat – food, e.g. rabbit meat [is] a lettuce, dandelions, etc." *JB* Shildon C20/mid. [OE mete '(solid) food']

meetin's at midway

"meetin's – midway down the pit; or where the full and empty corves or baskets pass each other" *Pitman's Pay* G'head 1820s; "Wen gannen up en doon th' shaft / Th' paitint caige did threetin / For te tuaik wor audin's life / If thae stopt it meeten" (at halfway) 'Th' Raw Between th'Caiges' *Armstrong* Tanfield 1880s, 1890s; "meetings – where the cages pass each other in the shaft, or where the full

meetin's cont.

and empty sets pass each other on a self-acting incline" *Nicholson* 1880; "meetins – wagons passing on gravity haulage" *Dodd* MS Tanfield Lea C20/2

meg a halfpenny

"a meg" (halfpenny) *Carlaw* Teesside 1870; "We'll never let a trashy meg / Between us myek discord" *NWC* 13 May 1893; "I haven't got a meg" *GP* S'm re C20/mid; "meg – small value coin (halfpenny?)" *Dodd* MS Tanfield Lea C20/2. *EDD* distribution to 1900: mag – general

meg to spit

"he's megging at us" *PG* H'pool 1998

meggy centipede, etc.

"meggy-monny-legs (a millipede) D'm. It is also called meg-monny-feet" *Brockett* Newc & Nth 1829; "meggy-mony-feet – a centipede" *Luckley* Alnwick 1870s. *EDD* distribution to 1900: esp. Sco. *Plus* "monifeet – centipede" *Dinsdale* mid-Tees 1849

mekanik colliery craftsman

ex. *Dodd* MS Tanfield Lea C20/2

mell hammer

"mell – a mallet" Finchale (1465); "a mell – a wooden sledge or beatle" *Kennet* 1690s as Nth; "mell – a wooden mallet or hammer, generally with a long handle" *Brockett* Newc & Nth 1829; "mell – the wooden mallet used by masons; also, any wooden mallet or beetle" *Atkinson* Cleve 1868; "Bring the mell, an' drive the post farther doon" *Luckley* Alnwick 1870s; 'caulking mallet' Green S'd 1885; "he's got a heed bit so's a mell" Ashington C20/mid; 'large wood or iron hammer' *Wade* South Moor 1966; "mell hammer – large hammer, e.g. 5lb, 10lb, 20lb" *JP* S'm C20/2. *EDD* distribution to 1900: Sco, Ire, Nth, Linx, Suff. NE 2001: in use. [AN mail pl. mals 'hammer, club']. *Plus* "mundie than mell" Gosforth C20/2 Q; "mundy – 56 lb hammer" Newc 2001 Q

mell to meddle

"The man that with this mater melys" (deals, is concerned) *Cuthbert* C15/mid; "melle no farther" *Raine* MS Rigton 1521; "to mell – to meddle 'Ise nouther mack nor mell'" *Kennet* 1690s as Yorks; "I will neither mack nor mar, for I'll no mell" *Bell* MS Newc 1830s; "mell –

mell cont.

to meddle" *Atkinson* Cleve 1868. *EDD* distribution to 1900: general. [OFr meller]

mell supper harvest supper

"ale in ye mell night" *Raine* MS Dishforth, 1672; "mel-supper – a supper and dance given at harvest home" *Bailey* Co.Durham 1810; "Mell Supper – the Kirn Supper, so called in Northumberland; [and?] in D'm" *Bell* MS Newc 1815; "Mell-supper – a supper and merry-making on the evening of the concluding reaping day – the feast of harvest home" *Brockett* Newc & Nth 1829; "Mell-supper – the harvest-supper" *Atkinson* Cleve 1868. *EDD* distribution to 1900: Nth. [ON mele 'corn'] See also **kirn supper**

mense 1. good manners, etc., 2. to grace, become/suit

1. "rule all wisely, & ye shal have much menske thereof " (credit) *Raine* MS Ussett, 1509; "Let iv'ry one his station mense / By acting like a man o' sense" *Allan's Tyneside Songs* p.208 1827; "mense – decency, propriety of conduct, good manners, kindness, hospitality. It also means an ornament or credit, as he is 'a mense to his family'" *Brockett* Newc & Nth 1829; "a mense to wor toon" *Allan's Tyneside Songs* p.240 1829; "Meat is good but Mence is better" *Bell* MS Newc 1830s; "mense – decency, civility, propriety of conduct: 'he has nowther mence nor sense'" *Atkinson* Cleve 1868; "thor's some hes been te skeul, an' still gets ne mair mense" *Haldane* Newc 1879; "mense – propriety" *Gibson* C'd 1880; "Mense – politeness, kindness... decency: 'I did it for meanse's sake'" *Palgrave* Hetton 1896; ex. *Nth Words* N'd 1938; "mense – 'newness' or best clothes" *JB* Shildon C20/mid; "essent mense ti say thanks – hasn't the manners to say thanks" *Dunn* B'p Auck 1950, sim. Consett C20/mid Q. *EDD* distribution to 1900: Sco, Ire, Nth, Linx. [ON mennska 'proper conduct']
2. "...friends beside, must all be there to mense the bride" *Chicken* Benwell 1720s; "mense – to grace, to ornament, to decorate: 'the pictures mense the room'" *Brockett* Newc & Nth 1829; "wor Peg shall hev a posey gown / to mense her when she comes to toon" *Allan's Tyneside Songs* p.304 1848; "Aw've dropp'd the gamblin' an' the beer / For nowt e'er seem'd te mense us" *Chater* Newc 1881 p.9; "Mense (vb) – to decorate,

mense cont.

e.g. 'mense the window'" *Palgrave* Hetton 1896

menseful/ly decently

"menseful – comely, graceful, becoming" *Ray* 1674; 'comely, graceful, manly' *Kennet* 1690s as Nth; "the good breeches that mencefully cover'd thy bum" *Bell* Newc 1812 p.43; "menseful – of good and becoming conduct; decent appropriate, neat... of things: 'a menseful chap, enow'" *Atkinson* Cleve 1868; "menseful – neat in appearance" S'd C20/2 Q; "menseful – neat, tidy" 2001 Q. *Plus* "Mally aw'm sure, just for mensefulness' syek / wad hev gien them thor teas an' a nice gordle-kyek" *Horsley* Jesmond 1891; "unmenseful – unbecoming, ill-mannered" *Atkinson* Cleve 1868

merle blackbird

exx. Geeson, N'd/ D'm 1969 re Nothumberland, *Crocker* Tees 1983. *EDD* distribution to 1900: Sco, Ire. [Fr merle]

messet, messan small dog

"messit or messan – a little dog, a sort of cur" *Brockett* Newc & Nth 1829; "messett or messett dog – for a little dog or lap dog" *Bell* MS Newc 1830s; "messet – small dog e.g. spaniel" *Dinsdale* mid-Tees 1849; "messan – any small dog" *Gibson* C'd 1880. *EDD* distribution to 1900: messan – Sco, Ire, N'd, C'd. [Gael. measan]

micey strange

"micey – strange" Newc 2001 Q; Oz in *Auf Wiedersehen Pet* series 2, 1992

mickle much, large

"mickle – much" *Kennet* 1690s as Nth; "and mickle mare" Rothbury C18/2; "put on the meikle pot" Newc C19/1 (Scots); "mickle wad ha' mair" *Atkinson* Cleve 1868; "candy see mickle a nounce" *Egglestone*, Weardale 1870s; "Little or mickle" (word noted as not common) *Palgrave* Hetton 1896. [OE micel, ON mikell]

midden muck heap

"knocked him in the head, & buried him in the muck-midding" *Raine* MS Batley 1689; "midding – a dung hill " *Ray* 1674; *Kennet* 1690s as W'd, D'm; "ah knaw when the Bishop cam te se us the houses were ah

midden cont.

wit'ned an the middens ah tyen to the quarry hole" *D'm Chron* 28 Apr 1865; "midden – a manure or muck-heap, a dunghill; any place or receptable for rubbish and dirt" *Atkinson* Cleve 1868; "muck midden" *Egglestone* Weardale 1870s; "midden – a dunghill, an ash heap" *Luckley* Alnwick 1870s; "midden – a mess" Stockton 2001 Q; "midden – rubbish dump" Ferryhill 2001 Q; "midden – dustbin" S'd 2001 Q; "midden – garden waste" B'd Castle. 2001 Q. *EDD* distribution to 1900: Sco, Ire, Nth, Mids, EA. [ME myddyng, likely from ON since Scand. cognates]. *Plus* "Middenstead – ash-heap" *Palgrave* Hetton 1896; "midnight mechanic – emptied the earth middens at the back of the house" *PHm* S'd C20/1; "I remember the midden men and the night soil men" *Northumbrian III* C20/2 re Crawcrook; "midden-cart" Palgrave Hetton 1896

midgy, midge's ee a small lamp

"midge's-ee – any thing diminutive" *Brockett* Newc & Nth 1829; "mistress or midgey – an oblong box without a front, carried upright, the use of which is to carry a lighted candle or small lamp in a current of air; a kind of lantern" *Nicholson* 1880; "Midgy – a kind of lamp used by putter lads. The height of the lamp was about 8 in., width 3 in., with open front. When first invented, they were simply little wooden boxes, with a hole at the bottom, through which the candle was thrust, and another hole at the top to let out the heat. Afterwards tin took the place of wood. The flame was sheltered by a piece of wood or tin about 2 in. high from the bottom of the lamp, and a similar piece from the top. The 'midgy' has now gone out of use" *Palgrave* Hetton 1896; "a midgy was an open fronted hand lamp used by miners when walking in by" *BW* West Auckland C20/mid; "mijee – small oil lamp (not safety)" *Dodd* MS Tanfield Lea C20/2. *EDD* distribution to 1900: N'd, D'm. See also **maggies**

mig liquid manure

ex. *Atkinson* Cleve 1868; "mig is the liquid flowing from a manure heap" *Wood* re rural Teesside C20/2. *EDD* distribution to 1900: esp. Yx. [OE miege, ON miga (vb)]

might [modal verb]

"whe knaws how far she meit gane" *Bell* Newc p.8 1812; "meet – might" *Pitman's Pay* G'head 1820s

mind to recall, remember, take note

"aw mind varry weel" *Allan's Tyneside Songs* p.238 1829; "aw mind it was warm wethor wen..." *Armstrong* Tanfield C19/2; "Aa mind yen day i' partiklar" *Haldane* Newc 1879; "Mind, noo! keep oot o' the clarts" *Embleton* Tyne 1897; "Aa dinnet mind what Aa sed" Coxhoe 1916; "it'll rain, mind!" (emphatic at end or start of sentence) *RM* Norton C20/mid; "I mind the time weel when..." *JS* Easington C20/mid; "mind, yor kiddin" *Dobson* Tyne 1970. *EDD* distribution to 1900: general. [OE gemynde 'mind' (noun)]. *Plus* "mind the trams" Tees 2002 Q

mingin' smelly, disgusting

"minging – smelly" Charver 2000–2002; "it was minging – disgusting, smelly; ex. abandoned Hawthorn shaft at Murton" 2003 E; "it was absoultely mingin'" (disgusting, of food) *GD* Seaham 2004; "mingin' – disgusting" *TR* Deneside 2004. [variant on taboo word]

minnie see **mother**

mint to intend

"I minted to strike at the other man" *Errington* p.91 Felling/Heworth re 1810s; "mint – to intend, to feign to do" *Atkinson* Cleve 1868. *EDD* distribution to 1900: Sco, Ire, Nth, EA. [OE myntan]. See also **excellent**

mirk dark, mirky

"candylles for Crystenmes to borne (burn) in the mirke mornynges" *Raine* MS York 1544; "mirk, murk – very dark" *Atkinson* Cleve 1868. *EDD* distribution to 1900: Sco, Ire, Nth, wMids

mistetched badly taught or trained

ex. Grose 1787 (of a horse, bad habits); "mis-tetch – bad habits" *Bailey* Co.Durham 1810; "mistetched – spoiled; said of a horse that has learnt vicious tricks" *Brockett* Newc & Nth 1829; "mistetched – ill-trained or mistrained" *Atkinson* Cleve 1868

the mister man, shopkeeper

"the mister in the shop" S'm 1960s via BG, sim *JP* S'm C20/2. [a courtesy title]

mixty-maxty a muddled mix

"mixty-maxty, mixy-maxy – any thing confusedly mixed" *Brockett* Newc & Nth 1829; title of book *Border notes and mixty-maxty* by *Crawhall* N'd 1880. *EDD* distribution to 1900: Sco, N'd. [from 'mixed']

mizzimazed confused, bewildered

ex. *ER* M'bro C20/2. *EDD* distribution to 1900: esp. Sth, SW

mizzle 1. slight rain (noun), 2. to rain lightly

"mizzle – slight rain" *Dinsdale* mid-Tees 1849; "mizul" *Dodd* MS Tanfield Lea C20/2; "mizzle – drizzle" *Dobson* Tyne 1973. *EDD* distribution to 1900: general. NE 2001: in use. [Du miezelen]
2. "If ye morning bee wette & misling, ye best way will bee to stay att hoame" *Raine* MS EYorks 1641; "15 Apr [1672] mizling, drizling, dagling, small rain" *Raine* MS Askham; "mizzling on" Middleton in Teesdale 2001 Q; "mizzle – spitting on to rain, light rain" Wheatley Hill 2002 Q. NE 2001: in use

mizzle to sneak away, go

"Eftor buying a bit mistletoe, aw determined to missle to the Butcher Market" *NM* vol.1 p.213 1888 re Newc; "the knight o' fairy tyel, that off wi' fair Miss Beauty mizzel'd" *Barrass* Stanley 1890s; 'mizzle – to disappear, go away" cenD'm 2001 Q; "mizzle – gone missing: 'my pen's mizzled again'" *Wood* Cleve 2002. *EDD* distribution to 1900: general. [compare Shelta (Irish gipsy) misli 'to go']

moggie see **maggies**

moider to perplex

"moidered – puzzled, bewildered, confused..." *Brockett* Newc & Nth 1829; 'to bewilder, to perplex' *Atkinson* Cleve 1868. *EDD* distribution to 1900: Sco, Ire, Nth, Mids

monged intoxicated, muddled

"monged – off one's head, usually due to drink or drugs" *Charver* 2000-2002. [OE has mangan 'to bewilder, mix' and gemongen 'mixed up']

monifeet see **meggy**

monkey 1. temper, 2. molten steel

1. "Mony a chep wad get his monkey up if his wife spok tiv 'im i' that way..." *Cuddy Cairt* Newc 1917; "at this Aa got me monkey up..."

monkey cont.

Wade West Stanley C20/1
2. "monkey – 'The man who fowt the monkey itha dust' – the monkey was the ladle of molten steel and the dust was the sand on the foundry floor" *IL* Tow Law C20/mid. *Plus* "monkey-hangers" – people of Hartlepool, according to song by Ned Corvan 1862; arguably more interestingly, the local football team's monkey 'mascot' was elected Mayor of Hartlepool, May 2002

montakitty playground game

ex. *Dobson* Tyne 1972. *EDD* distribution to 1900: N'd, Lakes

moor hen red grouse

"But the miners of Weardale are all valiant men, / They will fight till they die for their bonny moor hen" 1818 song

the morn the morrow, tomorrow

"the morn – tomorrow" *Brockett* Newc & Nth 1829; "all the pits are idle the morn" (cry of the caller) *Hitchin* re Seaham 1930s; "mawn neet – tomorrow night" *Dodd* MS Tanfield Lea C20/2; "he'll be there the morn" *Graham* Geordie 1979

mortal see **drunk**

moss uplands, moorlands, esp. boggy land

"o'er the moss... they came" *RR* Weardale 1569; "moss trooper – border freebooter" *EED*. [OE méos 'bog', ON mosa]

mother 1. **mam**, 2. **minnie**

1. "Mam" *FS* Wingate 1940s "...Aa sed ter me Mam in 1953" *MS* North Shields C20/2; "mams and dads" *Dobson* Tyne 1972, *Cate* p.119 B'p Auck area 1987; "me Mam" *VIZ* 72 (1995), S'd 2001 Q. *EDD* distribution to 1900: Sco, Yx, Lx, Mids, USA. *Plus* "mammy" *Pitman's Pay* G'head 1820s
2. "minny – mother" *Pitman's Pay* G'head 1820s; "minny – a fondling term for mother" *Brockett* Newc & Nth 1829; "fre the forst day ony on us ken'd wor minnie" *Allan's Tyneside Songs* p.535 1885. *EDD* distribution to 1900: Sco, Ire, N'd, C'd, W'd

motte 1. mound as mark, 2. *mons pubis*

1. 'a small button or any piece of bright substance to pitch at in the game of pitch and toss' *Bell* MS Newc 1815; "If more than one gambler wanted to be the chucker [in pitch n

motte cont.

toss]...then the choice was made by having the candidates throw a penny towards a marker on the ground. The mark might be a piece of paper, a little mound or a stone showing through the soil. The marker was known as 'the motte'." *LG* S'm C20/mid; "mot" (a piece of white boody used as target in a version of quoits) *Graham* Geordie 1979. *EDD* distribution to 1900: general. [Fr motte 'a butt to shoot at' or 'mound']
2. "mot – the pudenda of a female" *Bell* MS Newc 1815; sim. *LG* S'm C20/mid; *TP* S'd, 1960s, *Wood* M'bro 1960s

moudiewarp, moley rat, etc. the mole

"to Mary Beaton for a moldwarpe, 2d." *Raine* MS Wakefield 1683; "mold-warp" *Kennet* 1690s as Yorks; "moudy-warp" *Bailey* Co.Durham 1810; "moudy ratters – Northumberland for moles; also a trifling person" *Bell* MS Newc 1830s; "Moley rat – the only name known for the common mole" *Palgrave* Hetton 1896; "mowlee rat" *Dodd* MS Tanfield Lea C20/2; "moley-rat" Dawdon 2001 Q; "mowdy" B'p Auckland 2001 Q. *EDD* distribution to 1900: mouldywarp – general. [ME mold-warp 'earth-turner']. *Plus* "moudiheap – molehill" *Blenkinsopp* Teesdale 1931

mounge to grumble

"moungin' – grumbling, complaining" *Pitman's Pay* G'head 1820s; "and moungin' scratch'd his head" *Allan's Tyneside Songs* p.191 1824; "he's elwis gan moonging aboot" (moaning) *Graham* Geordie 1979. *EDD* distribution to 1900: Sco, Nth, sNotts

mow 1. a pile, 2. to pile up, to stack, 3. full up, 4. to have intercourse

1. "mow – a stack" *Brockett* Newc & Nth 1829. *EDD* distribution to 1900: general. [OE muga, ON muge 'a stack of hay']
2. "the wayne house dore which I had mowed up with turfes to keepe the wind from my horse" *Raine* MS Haslehead, 1647/48; "mow (pronounced 'moo') – to stack or pile up (corn in a barn)" *Dinsdale* mid-Tees 1849
3. "mowed off" (pronounced maoo-) eD'm 1990 per BG; "mowed up – no space left" *Dodd* MS Tanfield Lea C20/2; "mowed up" Tees 2002 Q. *EDD* distribution to 1900: esp. Yx, Mids. See also **stowed**

mow cont.

4. "to mow a woman... as he mow my Meggy" *Kennet* 1690s as Nth; "mow – to converse unlawfully" *Brockett* Newc & Nth 1829; 'to have intercourse (for a man)' *Dinsdale* mid-Tees 1849

mozzy mosquito

ex. *BL* Blaydon 1950s

muck (animal) excreta

"muck – dirt, dung for manure" *Brockett* Newc & Nth 1829; 'dirt, filth, especially excrement; foul weather' *Atkinson* Cleve 1868; "sum muck that sum e th' horses left lyen on th' rode" *Armstrong* Tanfield Lea 1880s, 1890s; "Here's a piece of coal as black as muck, / I hope it brings the best o' luck" (recited by first footer) *Hitchin* re Dalton-le-Dale p.25 1910s. *EDD* distribution to 1900: general. [ON myki]. *Plus* "muk-hak – fork or rake" Finchale 1465; "mukman – empties earth closets" *Dodd* MS Tanfield Lea C20/2

muds "muds – small nails used by cobblers" *Pitman's Pay* G'head 1820s; "muds – short thick nails driven into the heels of shoes or clogs" *Bell* MS Newc 1830s. *EDD* distribution to 1900: Sco, NE

mugger itinerant dealer

"mugger – a hawker of pots, an itinerant vender of earthenware. This trade is carried on to a great extent among the gipsy or Faa tribes in the Northern counties" *Brockett* Newc & Nth 1829; "The Vicar... was of manner meek / And gentle, though 'tis said he sometimes swore, / When wandering muggers day by day, came knocking at his door." *Stobbs* Woodhorn, C19/mid; "There resided principally in the West End of Tweedmouth a class of people who were known as muggers... their form of language was familiar to many who lived in that neighbourhood" *Nth Words* 1938; "Aa's sweetin like a mugger's cuddy" *Graham* Geordie 1979. *EDD* distribution to 1900: Sco, N'd, C'd, Yx. [from mug, i.e. pottery for sale; in example of the itinerant way of life: "For the last 10 years has travelled the country, and sold earthen pots and mugs in summer and coopered and mended lanthorns in winter" *Newc Courant* 12 Jan 1782]

mule large double ended coble

ex. *JH* Seaham C20/mid. *EDD* distribution
to 1900: N'd, Yx, with note much used in
herring fishing. *Plus* "fifie" – name *for* 'nearly
every double ended boat with a keel' *Hill*
Flamborough 1970s

mun must

ex. *Kennet* 1690s as Yorks; "aw mun away
tee"; "thou mun gang" *Bewick* Tyne 1790s;
"I munnet tell!" *Bells* re Carlisle 1802; "How,
smash! Skipper, what mun a' dee?" *Allan's
Tyneside Songs* p.27 1805; "aw mun gang"
Marshall G'head 1806; "canno', winno',
munno' for can not, will not, must not" *Bell*
MS Newc 1830s; "the beeldin seun mun gan"
Allan's Tyneside Songs p.234 1829; "if a keel
gets upset, maun we shut up the Tyne?"
Allan's Tyneside Songs p.367 1849; "mud
(long 'u') – pret. of must" *Gibson* C'd 1880;
"The end the mun defeat us" *Barrass* Stanley
1890s. *EDD* distribution to 1900: general.
[ON monu]. See also **have** (3)

mundy see **mell**

munter ugly

ex. *BL* Tyne pre-2000; "munter – to me it
always meant an ugly person, possibly more
so female than male" *SM* H/pool 2003

must able to, rather than has to

Of a walking stick left behind: "he mustn't
need it, for they couldn't walk without it" S'm
2002 per BG; "They mustn't have valued it"
Wheatley Hill 2003; "She mustn't like the look
of our Colin then" Crook 2004. See also **mun**

muthy humid

"muthy – close (weather)" *Blenkinsopp* Teesdale
1931. [ON moða]

my

"maa" *Haldane* Newc 1879; "me, ma, maw"
Armstrong Tanfield C19/2; "mee" *Allan's
Tyneside Songs* p.396 C19/mid; "maw", "me
bate" *Barrass* Stanley 1890s; "the tears rowled
doon ma cheeks like kidney-beans" Durham
1916; "ma" Tanfield Lea 1960; "me Aunt
Maggie" *Dobson* Tyne 1972

na no

"na" *Brockett* Newc & Nth 1829; *Graham* Geordie 1979; "nah" *Dobson* Tyne 1973; "noa" Seaham via BG 2003

nab promontory

"nab – head of a hill" *Ray* Nth 1737; 'the summit of a rock or mountain' *Grose* 1787; "nab, nabb – a protuberance, an elevated point, the rocky summit and outermost verge of a hill" *Brockett* Newc & Nth 1829; "nab – sharp fall at a hill range edge" *Wood* re Cleve. [ON nabbr; the Ordnance Survey online gazetteer gives examples in place-names only from Viking-settled areas, notably Nth Yx and Cumbria]

nack see **knack**

nadgy irritable

ex. *JR* Crook C20/mid

nae see **ne**

naggie, narkie, nasher see **turnip**

nantle to be casual

"nantle – to do something in an easy and careless manner" *Dinsdale* mid-Tees 1849. *EDD* distribution to 1900: Nth

nappy ale

"this good nappy ale" *Praise of Yorkshire Ale* C17 via *Raine* MS; "spirits strong and nappy beer" *Allan's Tyneside Songs* p.181 1824; "to be blithe ower a jug o' good nappy" *Allan's Tyneside Songs* p.245 1827; "seldom seen the warse o' nappy" *Pitman's Pay* G'head 1820s. *EDD* distribution to 1900: general

narvish nervous

"narvish – nervous" *Pitman's Pay* G'head 1820s; "it maks me narvish an' unlisty" *Embleton* Tyne 1897. *EDD* distribution to 1900: in this pronunciation N.I., N'd, C'd

nash to rush off

"nash – to move swiftly: 'He proper did a nash when me da turned up'" *Charver* 2000–2002; "nashing – leaving; gan nash – going to, often illicitly" S'd 2001 Q. [*OED* gives as slang 1812 on; compare Romany 'nash' to run]. See also **buroo**

naup to hit

"naup – to beat, to strike" *Brockett* Newc & Nth 1829; "to strike, inflict a blow (on the head) 'naup him'" *Atkinson* Cleve 1868; 'to strike as punishment' *Dinsdale* mid-Tees 1849. *EDD* distribution to 1900: Nth, Mids. [imitative]

ne no (adj.)

"ne occasion fort" (for it) *Bewick* Tyne 1790s; "it is ne fable" *Marshall* Newc p.23 1823; "nee leer [liar]" *Allan's Tyneside Songs* p.420 1862; "ta nee purpes" *Egglestone* Weardale 1870s; "this is a fust rate pie an' nee mistake" *Wearside Tales* 1879; "nee doot", "nee gud luck" *Armstrong* Tanfield C19/2; "I hev nee tatties" *Graham* Geordie 1979; "nee botha – no problem" Charver 2000-2002, S'm 2003 per BG. *Plus* "there's ne-where te park the car" *Dobson* Tyne 1972

neaf see **neif**

nearlies nearly, almost

"We neorlees hed words ower that" *Robson* Newc C20/1

neat cattle

"neat pl. nowt – an animal of the ox kind" *Atkinson* Cleve 1868. *EDD* distribution to 1900: Sco, Yx, Mids, etc. [OE néat] See also **nout**

neb see **nose**

nebody nobody

"nebody" *Armstrong* Tanfield C19/2, Coxhoe 1916. See also **nyen**

ned cake, knedde cake a cake or pastry

"knedde-cake – a cake kneaded with butter and baked on the girdle" *Brockett* Newc & Nth 1846; "knodden-cake – a kneaded i.e. yeast-based cake" *Dinsdale* mid-Tees 1849; "ned cake – a flat, current filled cake" AB re S'd C20/1; "ned kyek – baked on girdle" *Dodd* MS Tanfield Lea C20/2; "knedding cake – a cake kneaded with lard or butter and baked on a girdle" *Graham* Geordie 1979. [kneaded]

nedder adder

ex. Brockett as N'd 1846. *EDD* distribution to 1900: general; spelt nedder – Sco, Nth. [OE nædre]. See also **hagworm**

neep see **turnip**

neet night, tonight

'Good neet, hinny' *Brockett* Newc & Nth 1829; "Nut-crack Neet – All Hallows' Eve" *Dinsdale* mid-Tees 1849; "But what care they for that the neet?" *Barrass* Stanley 1890s; "Aw hell, lads! Not the neet" *Hay* Ushaw Moor C20/1; "are yer turning out the neet?" *IA* S'm 1950s, 60s; *EDD* distribution to 1900: in this pronunciation esp. Nth. [OE niht]. *Plus* "wuov his jasay neet cap on" *Bewick* Tyne 1790s

neether see **nowther**

neeze to sneeze

"neese, neeze – to sneeze" *Brockett* Newc & Nth 1829; "neeze" *Atkinson* Cleve 1868. *EDD* distribution to 1900: Sco, Ire, N'd, Yx, Lx. [ON hnjósa]

neif, neive fist

"with' thair nevys" *Cuthbert* C15/mid; "Much good do it you, Mrs Kate, with your scabbed neeves" *Raine* MS Newcastle, 1590; "neaf – the fist (Nth) "neif – hand or fist (D'm, W'd)" *Kennet* 1690s; "built up by Adam's aun neaves" (hands) *Allan's Tyneside Songs* p.52 ca.1800; "sticks and neeves they went pel-mel" *Bells* re Carlisle, 1802; "pummel... wi' yor neef" *Allan's Tyneside Songs* p.420 1862; "thor neeves wis fleein" *Armstrong* Tanfield C19/2. *EDD* distribution to 1900: Sco, Ire, Nth, eMids. [ON hnefi]. *Plus* "double-neif – the clenched fist" *Brockett* Newc & Nth 1829; "close-neived – niggardly, stingy, parsimonious" *Atkinson* Cleve 1868

neivel blow of the fist (noun and vb)

"neivel – to strike or beat with the fist" *Bailey* Co.Durham 1810; "he got on the lug such a nevel" *Bell* Newc 1812 p.42. *Plus* "neavil, nevel – to pummel, or beat with the fist" *Atkinson* Cleve 1868

nell-kneed knock-kneed

"nell-kneed – in-kneed" *Pitman's Pay* G'head 1820s. [knell 'to knock', OE cnyllan]

nesh soft

"thurgh harde and nesche" *Cuthbert* C15/mid; "the nesh bee can neither abide cold or wet" *Raine* MS EYorks 1648; "Flabby, as a nesh man, nesh grass" *Kennet* 1690s as D'm; "nash or naish – tender, weak, fragile, soft" *Brockett* Newc & Nth 1829. *EDD* distribution to 1900: general. [OE hnesce]

ness headland

"ness – a cape or projecting headland" *Atkinson* Cleve 1868. *EDD* distribution to 1900: Sco, Yx, Lx, I.Man, Linx, Shrop, Kt. [OE næs, ON nes; the Ordnance Survey online gazetteer gives examples around the UK but concentrated in Orkney and the Shetlands]

netty outside toilet

ex. *JG* Annfield Plain 1930s, "ootside netties" *Dobson* Tyne 1972; 'lavatory' *Graham* Geordie 1979. *EDD* distribution to 1900: N'd. NE 2001: in circulation. [?C18 nessy from necessary; ? Ital. cabinetti; *Raine* MS locates a possible early ex. "Robert Hovyngham sall make... at the other end of hys house a knyttyng" York 1419, in which case the root could be OE níd 'necessity']. *Plus* "to go to [the] Necessary" (public toilet) *Errington* p.67 Newcastle re 1800s; "lav" *Northumbrian III* C20/2 re Crawcrook; "oot back" G'head 2001 Q

neuk corner, nook, alcove

"his bedd noke" *Cuthbert* C15/mid; "laye in a newke nigh the fier" *Raine* MS Ebchester 1526; "neuk – a corner, nook... of field, room, box etc.: 't' neuk shop'" *Atkinson* Cleve 1868; "Aw sat i'the nuik, and my cutty aw smuik" *Street Piracy* Newc 1822. *EDD* distribution to 1900: in this pronunciation Sco, Nth. [cf. Norw nók 'hook, s.thing bent']. *Plus* "piss nyuk – urinal" *Dodd* MS Tanfield Lea C20/2

nevy nephew

"My fatha says 'is nevy hez t' hev 'is whippet put down" *CT* New Herrington 1930s; "nevvee – nephew" *Dodd* MS Tanfield Lea C20/2. *EDD* distribution to 1900: general

newcassel Newcastle upon Tyne

"the Newcassel cheps fancy they're clever" *Allan's Tyneside Songs* p.70 1805; "Neucassil" *Armstrong* Tanfield C19/2. See also **Gotham, toon**

nick a vertical cut (noun and vb)

"nicking – a working at the face of the coal... is the cutting of an upright cut into the face of the coal when it is kirved out below" *Bell* MS Newc 1815; "nick – the perpendicular groove made in the sides of a jud" *Brockett* Newc & Nth 1846; "nicking – a vertical cutting in the side or nook of a working-place" *Nicholson* 1880

nick-stick a form of tally

"nick-stick – a tally or notched stick by which accounts are kept after the ancient method" *Brockett* Newc & Nth 1829; *Nickstick* – title of magazine edited by Wm. Egglestone Weardale 1870s; "nick-sticks – a mode of reckoning which ladies well understand" (being in charge of household spending) *Pitman's Pay* G'head 1820s. *EDD* distribution to 1900: Sco, N'd, nYx

nicker to snigger

"the keel bullies nicker'd" *Allan's Tyneside Songs* p.306 1849; "nickering and hockering – sniggering and laughing" *Blenkinsopp* Teesdale 1931. *EDD* distribution to 1900: Sco, Nth, Mids. [imitative]

niest next

ex. *Pitman's Pay* G'head 1820s; "neest, niest, nest – next" *Brockett* Newc & Nth 1829. *EDD* distribution to 1900: general. [OE niehst]

nigh near (to)

"Aa wis nigh lossin me hat" *Graham* Geordie 1979. [OE neah] See also **varnigh**

nip to pinch

"nipping – pinching" *Brockett* Newc & Nth 1829; "an' nip wor lugs" *Allan's Tyneside Songs* p.353 1849. *EDD* distribution to 1900: general. *Plus* "a little nip or two" (small injury) *GC* Seaham C20/1

nithered feeling very cold

"netherd – starved with cold" *Grose* 1787; "nithered – extreme feeling of cold" *JB* Shildon C20/mid, *ER* M'bro C20/2, Trimdon 2002; "nithered, nithering" *JP* S'm C20/2. *EDD* distribution to 1900: Sco, N'd, C'd, Yx, wMids. NE 2001: in use. [OE niðerian 'to bring down']. See also **dazed**

nivvor never

"nivvor" Coxhoe 1916, "nivver heed!" *Atkinson* Cleve 1868; "nivor" *Armstrong* Tanfield C19/2, "nivvor – never" *Dobson* Tyne 1972. *EDD* distribution to 1900: general

nobbut only, just

"nobbit leave us alyen" *Allan's Tyneside Songs* p.308 1862; "nobbut – nothing but, only, simply: 'nobbut me'" *Atkinson* Cleve 1868; "beauty's nobbed skin deep" *Egglestone* Weardale 1870s; "when ah wiz nobbut

nobbut cont.

aboot sixteen ear ahd" *Embleton* Tyne 1897; "nobbut a good-lookin' nowt – handsome wastrel" *Dunn* B'p Auck 1950; "nobbut moderate – ill" *Dunn* B'p Auck 1950. *EDD* distribution to 1900: general

noo now

exx. *Parker* Tyne Valley p.69 1896, Coxhoe 1916; "he'll be here just noo" *Armstrong* Tanfield C19/2; "Is a sporrit noo prissint?" *Chater* Newc 1880; "every noos an thens" *Embleton* Tyne 1897; "noo – now" *Dobson* Tyne 1972. [OE nú]

nool, knowl to knock downwards

"nooled – checked, curbed, broken spirited" *Brockett* Newc & Nth 1829; "Noll [naul] – to strike" *Palgrave* Hetton 1896; "neuled down – weighed down" Spennymoor C20/mid; "knooled – dispirited" *Graham* Geordie 1979; "knowled – under the thumb – pronounced 'knooled'" *AM* South Shields C20/2; "noold – brow-beaten" *Dodd* MS Tanfield Lea C20/2. *EDD* distribution to 1900: Sco, Nth, Lincs, Corn

nor than

ex. *Ray* 1674; "mear diseases did her attend / nor I can name in half a year" Rothbury C18/2; "the yen better nor the tother" *Other Eye* Newc ca.1890; "siuner him nor me" *Dunn* B'p Auck 1950. *EDD* distribution to 1900: general

noration talk or noise

"Noration – a confused crowd, a noise" *Palgrave* Hetton 1896; "noration – a speech" S'm C20/mid per BG. *EDD* distribution to 1900: general, plus USA

nose 1. **neb**, 2. **sneck**, 3. **snook**, 4. **snib**, 5. **snitch**, 6. **beak**

1. "neb or nib – the nose. Also the beak on a bird" *Grose* 1787; "neb – bill of a bird" *Dinsdale* mid-Tees 1849; "the neb iv a duck" (beak) *Armstrong* Tanfield C19/2; "keep yer neb out" (don't be nosey) *IA* S'm 1950s,60s; sim. *JS* Easington C20/mid, B'd Castle 2001 Q, *AD* Hebburn 2003 Q; "neb – nose" *JB* Shildon C20/mid, *RM* Norton C20/mid, NShields C20/mid; "wet yor neb – have a drink" *Graham* Geordie 1979. *EDD* distribution to 1900: general. NE 2001: in use. [OE nebb]

nose cont.

Plus "nebby – nosey" D'ton C20/2, *JS* Easington C20/mid, Sedgefield 2001 Q.
2. "sneck" *JS* re Sacriston 1940s, *IA* S'm 1950s,60s, *RV* Winlaton C20/2, Wheatley Hill C20/2 Q; "snek – latch, nose" *Dodd* MS Tanfield Lea C20/2; "sneck or neb – nose" Barnard Castle 2001 Q; "sneck for nose; 'neb' not used" South Moor (Stanley) 2003 per BG. *EDD* distribution to 1900: N'd.
Plus "sneck lifter" (the price of a pint) via *Crocker* D'ton 1982
3. "snook" – The Ordnance Survey online gazetteer gives all five place-names with 'Snook' (headland) as in N'd. *Plus* "snoot – snout, nose" *Dodd* MS Tanfield Lea C20/2.
4. "snib – nose" Stockton 2001 Q. [?ON; compare Swed. snibb 'beak']
5. "snitch" *AT* Co.D'm C20/mid. [*OED* as slang]
6. "Blaa yor nesty dorty bubbly beak, hinny" *Windows* Newc 1917. See also **nab, ness**

not

"ye need-na be afraid" *Stobbs* Woodhorn C19/mid; "nut" *Egglestone* Weardale 1870s; "nut mee" *Wearside Tales* 1879. See also individual verbs

nout, nowt cattle

"nolt or nout – neat cattle" *Bailey* Co.Durham 1810; "nout or nolt – neat, or horned cattle of the ox species" *Brockett* Newc & Nth 1829; "Darlington Nowt Fair" *Dinsdale* mid-Tees 1849. *EDD* distribution to 1900: Sco, Nth, EA. [ON naut]. *Plus* "nowtman – herdsman, keeper of cattle" *Raine* MS Easington 1526; "nowtfoot – a cow heel" *Bell* MS Newc 1815; "some tripe and a nowt foot" *Allan's Tyneside Songs* p.227 1826. See also **neat**

nowt, nowse nothing

"I'll give him nowse at all" Bedlington 1761; "nowse" *Bewick* Tyne 1790s; "we think nowse on't" *Marshall* Newc 1823; "he de's nout nor wonnet de nout" *Bell* MS Newc 1815; "it was nowt but lees he teld him" *Marshall* Newc 1823 p.19; "aboot nowt – worthless" *Hull* MS wNewc 1880s; "half-nought (pronounced haff-nowght) – half-nothing, price too small to be worth mentioning" *Atkinson* Cleve 1868; "coal's nowt but cabbish staaks an' tatie peel-ins" *Haldane* Newc 1879; "ah's gud te nowt" (not up to anything) *Embleton* Tyne 1897;

nowt, nowse cont.

"Ye'll want for nowt ye've got" *EP* re ED'm 1940s; "it's neither nowt nor summat – neither one thing nor the other" *Dunn* B'p Auck 1950, sim. *Cate* B'p Auck area 1987 p.105; "thooz getten nowt!" *Dodd* MS Tanfield Lea C20/2; "nowtbutcanny" (of middling health) *Dobson* Tyne 1970; "the whole truth and nowt but the truth" *Irwin* Tyne 1970–71; "A got nowt" *VIZ* 72 (1995). *EDD* distribution to 1900: nowse – Sco, N'd, D'm. [OE nauht]
Plus "donot – an old and low word for a silly or good-for-nothing person of the female sex" *Bell* MS Newc 1815

nowther neither

"nouthir stande na gang" *Cuthbert* C15/mid; "nowther tipsy nor lame" *Street Piracy* Newc 1822; "nowther rhyme nor reason" *Haldane* Newc 1879; "nowther" Tanfield Lea, 1960, etc.

nutter someone who collects small coal

ex. Newc 2001 Q

nyen none, no one

"nane" *RR* Weardale 1569; "thous neahn deef" *Bewick* Tyne 1790s; "nyen the better" *Haldane* Newc 1879; "hevvin nyen on't" (wouldn't stand for it) *Hay* Ushaw Moor C20/1; "hes thee nyen? – don't you have any?" *Dunn* B'p Auck 1950. *EDD* distribution to 1900: in this pronunciation N'd, nYx. [OE nán]

a few oaths

"De'il rive their sark gangs hame to night"
Chicken Benwell 1720s; "crying, 'smash, man!
lower the sail!'" *Allan's Tyneside Songs* p.27
1805; "Begrike!" *Allan's Tyneside Songs* p.73
1806; "Ods heft!" *Allan's Tyneside Songs* p.75
1806; "Od smash my neavel!" *Marshall* G'head
1806; "Gad smash me sark" *Bell* p.37 Newc
1812; "Deel smash my heart!" *Bell* p.50 Newc
1812; "By my faicks!" *Allan's Tyneside Songs*
p.48 1812; "Dang Lunnun!" *Allan's Tyneside
Songs* p.50 1812; "Begox!" *Allan's Tyneside
Songs* p.51 1823; "'od bliss him!" *Allan's Tyneside
Songs* p.181 1824; "smash, marrow!" *Allan's
Tyneside Songs* p.217 1827; "By gock, thoo's
a quare 'un." *Palgrave* Hetton 1896; "Ohw
ballzit!" Newc C20/1 via RV; "yebuggarmar –
in approbation" *Dobson* Tyne 1970; "What the
frig are yuz aall taakin' aboot?" *VIZ* 34 1989

of

"i th' howl oh wounter" (winter) *Bewick* Tyne
1790s; "the lot on us" *Haldane* Newc 1879;
"oot i' bed" *Armstrong* Tanfield C19/2; "stalls
full ev apples" *Egglestone* Weardale 1870s

offens, oftens often

"offens, oftens – the plural of often" *Brockett*
Newc & Nth 1829; "oftens (pronounced
offens, off'ns) – often" *Atkinson* Cleve 1868;
"Oftens (of'ns)" *Palgrave* Hetton 1896.
EDD distribution to 1900: offens – D'm, Yx;
oftens – N'd, D'm, Yx, Lx, Lincs

ome fumes

"ome – the smoak, reek, stith or vapour of hot
liquids is call'd ome... as the ome of salt pans"
Kennet 1690s as D'm. *EDD* distribution to
1900: oam – Sco, D'm

oney only

"ye shud oney see thor little thatch hoose"
Allan's Tyneside Songs p.462 1862; "that's the
ootside on't ony" *Haldane* Newc 1879; "oney"
Tanfield Lea 1960

onsetter worker at foot of shaft

"onsetter – the person who attaches the corf
to the pit-rope at the bottom of the shaft"
Brockett Newc & Nth 1846; "onsetters – men
who put the full tubs in and take the empty
ones out of the cage at the shaft bottom"
Nicholson 1880; "the onsetter tyeuk the tubs
outa the cage and put Jonty in" *Hay* Ushaw
Moor C20/1; "onsetter – in charge of cage at

onsetter cont.

the bottom of shaft" *Northumbrian III* C20/2
re Durham collieries.

onstead establishment

"aaltegither we can brag ov a canny bit
'onsteed'" (shop and assets) *Cuddy Cairt* Newc
1917; 'the buildings on a farm' Viereck re
Gateshead, 1966. *EDD* distribution to 1900:
Sco, N'd, Lakes, Yx. Compare **heapstead**

ony 1. any, 2. at all (adv)

1. "ony amaunt e secrets" *Armstrong* Tanfield
C19/2; "ony" Coxhoe 1916; "onny – any"
Tanfield Lea 1960
2. "can ye caulk onney?" *Wearside Tales* 1879.
See also **oney**

onywhere anywhere

"he's onnywheer for a little apple" (is greedy)
Ashington C20/mid

oor hour

"aboot two oors" *Robson* Newc C20/1; "oor"
Armstrong Tanfield C19/2

oot out

exx. Coxhoe 1916, Tanfield Lea 1960; "arye
oot tonight?" S'm 1990 per BG

our see wor

outbye 1. outside, 2. towards the shaft or exit of
a pit

1. "out-by – a short way from home, not far
distant" *Brockett* Newc & Nth 1829; "outbye –
out of the way, remote" *Palgrave* Hetton 1896;
"It's varra caad oot bye" *Graham* Geordie
1979. *EDD* distribution to 1900: Sco, Nth
2. "I was alone... near 50 yeards out by"
Errington p.59 Felling/Heworth re 1800s;
"out-bye – the direction in any part of a mine
towards the shaft" *Nicholson* 1880; "out-bye –
at the shaft or bottom of the pit" *Pitman's Pay*
G'head 1820s; "technical, of a miner coming
towards the 'shaft' in order to get 'to bank'"
Palgrave Hetton 1896; "get out-bye as sharp
as you can" *JR* Seaham C20/1; 'places near the
shaft' *JM* Dawdon 1970s, sim *JP* S'm C20/2;
'[from] outwards to shaft' *Northumbrian III*
C20/2 re Durham collieries; "the gallowa's
wandered off outbye" *JM* Dawdon 1970s.
Plus 'bakby – away from coal face' *Dodd* MS
Tanfield Lea C20/2

ower over (prep. and adv.)

"owr... the hill" *Bewick* Tyne 1790s; "he gat ower wet" *Marshall* Newc 1823 p.15; "ower – over, too: 'ower little', 'ower large'; ower-tane – overtaken; out-ower – across, beyond or on the other side of a hill; ower-by – over the way" *Brockett* Newc & Nth 1829; "thoo's ower weel fed" *Armstrong* Tanfield C19/2; "ower an' ower" *Barrass* Stanley 1890s; "not ower far gone" Coxhoe 1916; "not owa grand – not too well" *Dodd* MS Tanfield Lea C20/2; "Far-ower clivvor" *Graham* Geordie 1979; "there's ower-many cars in th' street" S'm 2003 via BG; *EDD* distribution to 1900: in this pronunciation Sco, Ire, Nth, Notts, Lincs. See also **back ower, doon ower**

ower-bye across, over that way

"they had lived at her mother's – she leeved ower-bye" *Chater* Newc 1880. *EDD* distribution to 1900: Sco, N'd, C'd

owerman supervisor

"ower-man – an overseer" *Brockett* Newc & Nth 1846; "overman – the person who has the daily supervision and responsible charge of the mine, under the direction of the manager or under-manage" *Nicholson* 1880; "overman – man in charge, above the deputy and below the under manager" *JM* Dawdon 1970s. *EDD* distribution to 1900: Sco, NE

owse ox

"ousen or owsen – oxen" *Brockett* Newc & Nth 1829; "owse – ox – plural owsen" *Atkinson* Cleve 1868. *EDD* distribution to 1900: Sco, Nth

owse, owt anything

"they never gat owse better than..." *Bewick* Tyne 1790s; "Can they de owse..." *Marshall* G'head 1806; "as nice as owse" *Marshall* Newc 1823; "owse – any thing", "owt, ought – any thing" *Brockett* Newc & Nth 1829; "oswe, out – ought, anything" *Luckley* Alnwick 1870s; "owt" *Bell* Newc 1812 p.7; "ought (pronounced owght) – anything: 'ouwght or nowght'" *Atkinson* Cleve 1868; "Nor owt but me wiz shaken" *Barrass* Stanley 1890s; "Bob: 'Owt?' Tom: 'Nowt.'" *Windows* Newc 1917; "aw may drink, aw may fight, or dee owt" *Ross* Tyne C19/1 p.5; "has th' got owt f' nowt" (beggar's cry) *CT* New Herrington 1930s; "as funny as owt" S'm per BG, 2004. *EDD* distribution to 1900: owse – N'd. [OE áuht]

owther either

"owther – either" *Atkinson* Cleve 1868

ox

"Black Ox – misfortune: 'A! man, the Black Ox hesent stampt on your feet yet.'" *Bell* MS Newc 1815

oxo

"oxo – game of noughts and crosses" *JP* S'm 1990s, *Wood* Tees 2002

oxter armpit

"oxter, oxterns (Nth) an armpit, the armpits; Oxtar, Oxtars (D'm)" *Kennet* 1690s; "she has a babby under her oxter" *Bell* MS Newc 1839s; "Oxter – armpit: 'Oxter-bound,' stiff in arm and shoulder" *Palgrave* Hetton 1896; "i' the oxter pocket" (inside jacket pocket) *Eggleston* Upper Weardale 1877; "oxter – top pocket" *MG* Teesdale C20/2; "not his scalp but his right oxter" *Dobson* Tyne 1970; "he's got a boil in his oxter" Cockfield 2004 E; "hoxters" Wheatley Hill 2004 Q. *EDD* distribution to 1900: esp. Sco, Ire, Nth. NE 2001: in low use. [OE oxta]

paaky, parky, pawky choosy

"pauky – saucy, squeamish, scrupulously nice; also proud, insolent, cunning, artful" *Brockett* Newc & Nth 1829; "pauky – of a child hard to please" Dinsdale mid-Tees 1849; "pawky – impudent, semi-insolent: 'as pawky as a pyet'" *Atkinson* Cleve 1868; "pawky (paa:ki) – dainty" *Palgrave* Hetton 1896; "pawky – fussy, overly particular (esp. of a child)" *JB* Shildon C20/mid, Teesdale C20/2 Q; "parky – fussy about food" *Viereck* re Gateshead 1966, *Dodd* MS Tanfield Lea C20/2. *EDD* distribution to 1900: 'shrewd, precocious' Sco, Ire, Nth, Lincs. NE 2001: in use. *Plus* "we weren't all picky eaters" MS North Shields C20/2

paaky chilly

"Minditz paaky theneet" *Dobson* Tyne 1971

paas hands

ex. NShields C20/mid. [paws]

Pace Easter

"the fest of Pasche" *Cuthbert* C15/mid; "Pase Monday" *Raine* MS Ebchester, ca.1571; "Pasch – Easter" ('common' *Raine* MS re C19/2). *EDD* distribution to 1900: Sco, N'd, C'd, Yx, Lincs. [AN Pasche]

pace eggs, paste eggs decorated eggs at Eastertide

"Paste-eggs – eggs boiled hard and dyed or stained various colours, given to children about the time of Easter" *Brockett* Newc & Nth 1829; "ne place te bool wor peyste eggs noo..." *Allan's Tyneside Songs* p.396 C19/mid; "Pace-eggs – eggs boiled hard and stained of divers colours [used] on Easter Monday and Tuesday as playthings for children, and secondly as a viand" *Atkinson* Cleve 1868; "paste-egg – an egg boiled hard, and ornamented in various ways, used at Easter: 'Are ye gan t' the Pasture t' thraw yer paste-eggs?'" *Luckley* Alnwick 1870s; "An' to please the pit-laddies at Easter / A dishful o' giltey pyest-eggs" *Crawhall* Newc 1888; "Paste-eggs – eggs, dyed in a decoction of logwood chips and onion peel, and sold in shops or prepared at home during Easter" *Palgrave* Hetton 1896; "paste egg – a hard boiled Easter egg [for] boolin and jaapin..." *Graham* Geordie 1979; "'Pace', only in 'Pace-eggs' – eggs dyed and marbled brown for Easter with onion skins" *PG* H'pool C20/2, sim. *PE* Stockton 2003; "Paste eggs than Pace eggs" D'ton C20/mid,

pace eggs, paste eggs cont.

C20/2, sim. *JP* S'm C20/2; "paste-eggs – hard boiled eggs decorated at Easter. We used to break them open on Easter Monday usually by rolling them down a slope" *Wood* M'bro C20/2. *EDD* distribution to 1900: Pace eggs – Sco, Nth; Paste eggs – N'd, D'm, nYx, Lx. NE 2001: both forms in use

paddick frog

"paddock – a young frog" *Kennet* 1690s as D'm, 'Northumberland name for a frog' *Bell* MS Newc 1830s, 'frog' *Gibson* C'd 1880; "a padick" *Errington* p.34 Felling/Heworth re 1780s; "paddy – frog" *JB* Shildon C20/mid; "blawn up like a paddick" (full of food) *Lore and language* re N'd, C20/2. *EDD* distribution to 1900: general. [ON padda 'toad']. *Plus* "paddick's stuils" (toadstalls) *Allan's Tyneside Songs* p.376 C19/mid, "paddock-styul" *Luckley* Alnwick 1870s

pagged, etc. exhausted

"I'm proper pagged out"; "It was a real pag walking up Silksworth Row bank" *AB* re S'd C20/mid; "Aam paggered" (exhausted) *TR* Deneside 2004. *EDD* distribution to 1900: peg (vb) – general

palatic see **drunk**

pan crack unemployment benefit

'My mother explains that originally, on the means test, you got a 'chitty' which you gave to the grocer. It got you just enough food for a pan' *Wood* re M'bro/Stockton/Redcar C20/mid; "pancrack – living on benefits decided by means test" *ER* M'bro C20/2

panhaggerty, panacalty dish with meat and potatoes

"panacalty – a concoction of bacon, onions and sliced potatoes baked in a shallow dish in the huge oven." *Hitchin* p.22 re Dalton-le-Dale 1910s; "penaclty – bacon/potatoes/onions cooked in frying pan" *CT* New Herrington 1930s; "panhaggerty – a dish containing meat and potatoes" *Geeson* N'd/ D'm 1969; "pahnikitee – leftover edible food" *Dodd* MS Tanfield Lea C20/2; "panhaggerty, pan-hagglety – a dish containing potatoes, onions and grated cheese... sometimes left-over meat was used" *Graham* Geordie 1979; "panacalty – corn beef sliced and simmered with parboiled sliced potatoes, peas, gravy and anything else

panhaggerty, panacalty cont.

you can hoy into it" *Wood* re Teesside 2003, 'stuff fried up in pan' Roker C20/mid. *EDD* distribution to 1900: panhaggerty – N'd

pant drinking fountain, e.g. in Newcastle

"The buildinge of a sufficiente pannte in Sandgate" *Raine* MS Newcastle 1593; "pant – a public fountain. In Newcastle there are several..." *Brockett* Newc & Nth 1829; "she (the ghost) sports round the Pant" (Sandgate) *Allan's Tyneside Songs* p.300 1842; "pant – a fountain of water for public use" *Luckley* Alnwick 1870s; "pant – village water pump" *JB* Shildon C20/mid; "pant – a public fountain" *Geeson* N'd/D'm 1969. *EDD* distribution to 1900: Sco, Nth, Lincs. ['pant' is a known pre-Roman river name]

pap nipple

"pap – the breast: 'giving the child the pap'; [also] pappy – the breast" *Bell* MS Newc 1815; "paap – a pap, a teat" *Brockett* Newc & Nth 1846. *EDD* distribution to 1900: general. [?ON, compare Swed papp(e)]

pappa "the local word for faeces"

DN Seaton Burn, C20/2. [? Du pap 'soft matter', Du. pappekak]. *Plus* "Sid's pappered hesel" *VIZ* 37 ca.1990

parky see **paaky**

parlish dangerous, etc.

"parlish – perilous, dangerous, wonderful" *Brockett* Newc & Nth 1829; "parlish – dangerous" *Dinsdale* mid-Tees 1849; "parlish – remarkable " *Gibson* C'd 1880. *EDD* distribution to 1900: Nth. [parlous, perilous]

partrick partidge

ex. *Blenkinsopp* Teesdale 1931. *EDD* distribution to 1900: in this form, esp. Sco

pash 1. rotten, 2. rainfall

1."pash – anything rotten to softness: 'is rotten as pash'" *Bell* MS Newc 1815. *EDD* distribution to 1900: Nth, Lincs
2. "pash – a heavy fall of rain or snow" *Brockett* Newc & Nth 1829. *EDD* distribution to 1900: Nth, Mids. [compare Swed. paska 'to rain heavily"]. *Plus* "thunder-pash – thunder-storn" *Dinsdale* mid-Tees 1849. See also **plash**

paste eggs see **pace eggs**

pat-n-can an untidy mess

"Ee, this hoose looks just like a patt'n-can!" D'm 1950s; "padden can – somewhere very untidy" *PE* 2004E

patrens patterns (industrial context)

"patrens, patren-makers not patterns, etc." Tyneside 1930s Q. *EDD* distribution to 1900: in this form Sco, Ire, Lx, EA

pawky see **paaky**

pay 1. to beat, 2. tired out

"pay – to beat, to drub: 'the rascal pays his wife'" *Brockett* Newc & Nth 1829; "pay – to beat (a jacket etc.)" *Dinsdale* mid-Tees 1849; "Pay (pee:u) – 'I'll pay your bottom', a common threat to children" *Palgrave* Hetton 1896. *EDD* distribution to 1900: general. [pay in sense of 'pay back'?]
2. "we're aboot paid" (exhausted) *Todd* Tyne 1977; "paid – paid, exhausted" *Dodd* MS Tanfield Lea C20/2

paze to lever up

"paze – to raise, to force open" *Brockett* Newc & Nth 1846; "paze – to lever up (a weight)" *Dinsdale* mid-Tees 1849. *EDD* distribution to 1900: paise – general. [*OED* peise from OFr peser 'to weigh']

pea jacket sailor's jacket

"I'll have a new brown pea" *Bell-Harker* Newc C19/1; "pe-jacket – a jacket worn by the old Keelmen on the River Tyne" *Bell* MS Newc 1815; "pea jacket – the outer holiday dress of a keelman" *Pitman's Pay* G'head 1820s; "pea-jacket – a loose rough jacket or short covering with conical buttons of a small size, termed pea-buttons; much used in severe weather by mariners and by watermen on the Tyne" *Brockett* Newc & Nth 1829; "their old quid (tobacco) they'll pop in the pea-jacket cuff" *Bell* Newc 1812 p.44. Distribution: first noted in English 1721. [Du pij-jakker]

pee-dee, p.d. boy working on a keel

"P.D. ran to clear the anchor" *Allan's Tyneside Songs* p.27 1805; "pe-de – a boy employed on board the keel" *Bell* MS Newc 1815; "The keels were generally manned by the skipper, two keel bullies and a boy known as the 'Pee-Dee'" *Mitcalfe* re 1822 p.3; "pee-dee – a young

pee-dee, p.d. cont.

lad in a keel, who has charge of the rudder" *Brockett* Newc & Nth 1829; "pee-dee – a miniature marble; on the Tyne... a small boy" *Luckley* Alnwick 1870s. *EDD* distribution to 1900: N'd, D'm. [?Fr pédier for foot servant]

peesweep, peewit the lapwing

"pee-wit, peez-weep – the lapwing" *Brockett* Newc & Nth 1829; "peas weep – a plover so called from its crie" *Bell* MS Newc 1830s; "peewit – lapwing" *Dinsdale* mid-Tees 1849; "Peesweep – lapwing, or peewit" *Palgrave* Hetton 1896. *EDD* distribution to 1900: peesweep Sco, N'd – peewit – general. [imitative of call]. *Plus* "pee-wit-land – cold, wet, bad land which the pee-wit generally haunts" *Brockett* Newc & Nth 1829

peev alcoholic drink

"peevin, peevan" (a drink) *Yetholm Gypsies* 1882 p.46; "peeve – alcoholic drink: 'He was proper peeved-up last neet'" *Charver* 2000–2002 . [Romany 'peava', to drink]

peffy out of breath

ex. swD'm 2004 E

penker egg

"penker – small egg, the first egg(s) of a pullet" *JB* Shildon C20/mid. See also **marbles**

perishment a severe cold (infection)

"a perishment o' cou'd" *Atkinson* Cleve 1868; "Perishment – a violent chill is always described as a 'perishment of cold' (pa:rish:ment u kaa:d)" *Palgrave* Hetton 1896. *EDD* distribution to 1900: esp. D'm, Yx

pet term of endearment

"Ma comely pet" (to a girl) *Marshall* G'head 1806; "maa pet" (dear one, wife) *Haldane* Newc 1879; "pet – a term of endearment. Used between the sexes" *Wood* NE 2002; D'ton 1940s Q; Wheatley Hill 2003 Q. *EDD* distribution to 1900: general. *Plus* "petal", in common use, eD'm

peter waggy an articulated toy or puppet

"dancing and capering like a greet live Peter Wagg" *LPB* Newc 1820s; "peter-waggy – the Northern name for a Harlequin toy" *Brockett* Newc & Nth 1829; "When I go to Newcastle Fair / I'll buy my child a Peter Waggy" H Robson in *Fordyce* Newc 1826. *EDD* distribution to 1900: Tyne

peth path

"peth – a road up a steep hill (e.g. N'd, D'm)" *Brockett* Newc & Nth 1829; "peth – a road with a steep ascent, a path" *Luckley* Alnwick 1870s. *EDD* distribution to 1900: Sco, N'd. NE200: in street names. [OE pæð]

pew to snow

"pewing on – slight snow falling" Teesside 2001 Q. See also **pule**

phiz face

"phiz" Durham 1839; "a roond gud natur'd phiz" *Barrass* Stanley 1890s. [physiognomy]

pick mining tool

"colpickes – coal picks" Finchale 1354; "Pick is a Tool the Miners use to cut down the Cliffs and Rocks of stone to make passages in the Earth" Derbyshire, 1681; "pick – a tool used by a hewer. It consists of an iron about 18 inches long, steeled and sharpened at each end, and weighing from 3 to 6 lbs. in the centre of the head is a hole or eye into which is fixed a shaft of ash about 2½ feet long" *Nicholson* 1880

pick pitch

"it was pick night" *Bell* Newc 1812 p.10; "the neet was pick-dark" *Allan's Tyneside Songs* p.442 1862; "pick – pitch: 'as black as pick'" *Atkinson* Cleve 1868. [OE píc, Fr pic]

pickatree see **rainbird**

piggin a pot

"piggin – a wooden cylindrical porringer, made with staves, and bound with hoops like a pail; holds about a pint" *Bailey* Co.Durham 1810; "piggin – a iron pot with two ears, also a wooden pot with a handle" *Bell* MS Newc 1815. *EDD* distribution to 1900: general

pikelet crumpet

ex. N'd C20/mid via BG; "pikelet – a thin type of crumpet" *Wood* Cleve 2002. *EDD* distribution to 1900: esp. Yx, Lx, Mids. [Welsh bara pyglyd 'dark bread']

pillar remaining roof support of coal

"pillars – the rectangular masses of coal between the boards" *Brockett* Newc & Nth 1846; "broken-pillar working, the removal of the pillars left in the first working for the support of the roof" *Nicholson* 1880; 'A mining term for the square masses of coal left in a

pillar cont.

working to support the roof" *Graham* Geordie 1979; "pillars – 50 yard length of passage" *GC* Seaham C20/1. *EDD* distribution to 1900: N'd, D'm, Yx

pineapple weed herb *Matricuria matricurioides*

"half covered by pineapple weed and tufts of grass" *Cate*, B'p Auckland area 1987 p.128

piot magpie

"piots" Rothbury C18/2; "piet, pyet" *Atkinson* Cleve 1868; "pianet, pyanot, py'net" *Brockett* Newc & Nth 1829; "pye-annet – or young magpie, also the common term for the species in Northumberland" *Bell* MS Newc 1830s. *EDD* distribution to 1900: pyet – esp. Sco, Ire, Nth. [OFr pie]. *Plus* "nanpie – the magpie" *Atkinson* Cleve 1868. See also **maggies**

pirn cottonreel

"A cotton reel was a 'pirn'" *Nth Words* Northumberland, 1938. *EDD* distribution to 1900: Sco, Ire, N'd, C'd, Ches

pit coal mine

"pits not coal-mines, pitmen not miners" D'ton 1940s Q; "Pit – the only word in common talk for a mine. So, a miner is always 'pitman' or 'pittie,' and pit dress is 'pit-claes'" *Palgrave* Hetton 1896. *EDD* distribution to 1900: N'd, D'm, Yx. [OE pytt]

pitch n toss a game of chance

"Pitch an' Toss – two coins... spun in air till land: all heads (hoyer wins) or all tails (pays out even money). If lands heads and tails, is 'oneses', no result." Wade *South Moor* C20/mid; "Two old-fashioned cartwheel pennies were best for the game" *GP* S'm C20/mid; "'Pitch and toss' known as 'The hoy' was very popular with miners in the 50s, perhaps later, and had a little specialised vocabulary of its own. The 'hoyer' or 'chucker' of the two pennies sometimes had an assistant who collected the coins after each throw. He was known as a 'bevver' and for his 'bevving' might get a little tip if the chucker made a profit. The 3 possibilities were... 2 heads (chucker wins), 2 tails (chucker loses) and 1 head, 1 tail (no one wins). The last combination, I never knew why, was called '2 bikes'." *LG* S'm C20/mid

pit-heap surface at colliery

"when I got to the pit-heap / the banksman was closing the gate" West Stanley 20/1. *EDD* distribution to 1900: N'd, D'm. See also **heapstead**

pitman collier, mine worker

"the pitman's humble hyem" *MC* Tyne May 1881, etc. *EDD* distribution to 1900: N'd, eD'm. *Plus* "colliery lads" *Bell* Newc re Walker 1812 p.36; "pitties" *EDD* 1900; "wor Bob is a pit lad like the rest i the place" *D'm Chron* 28 Apr 1865

pitmatic, pitmatical 1. the craft of mining, 2. the lingo of North-East pitmen

1. "pitmatics – a jocose term for the technicalities of colliery working" *Heslop* 1890s. [on the model of mathematics] 2. "A great many of the lads, especially from the Durham district, had evidently never been in Newcastle previously, and the air of wonder with which they gazed at the crowds, at the buildings, and especially at the fine folks who occupied the windows, was very amusing. If the quality criticized and quizzed them, the lads returned the compliment, and it was entertaining enough to catch snatches of criticism on the manners and customs of the upper ten thousand of Newcastle, reduced to the purest 'pitmatical', shouted across the streets, as the men and lads belonging to collieries swept by where I stood in the crowd." *Newc Weekly Chron* 19 Apr 1873; "After a few minutes delay in the overman's cabin, thronged with men talking an unintelligible language, known, I was informed, as Pitmatic, we took our places in one of a long train of tubs, which, on a signal being given, started for the heart of the mine." *The Times* 21 Aug 1885 4/4; "I was also acquiring a new language. This was 'pitmatic'. It was a mixture of the broadest dialect of Durham and a number of words (often of foreign origin) used exclusively by pitmen when below ground." *Hitchin* re Seaham 1910s p.70; "The local miners [in Durham] have a curious lingo of their own, which they call 'pitmatik'... It is only used by the pitmen when they are talking among themselves... When the pitmen are exchanging stories of colliery life... they do it in 'pitmatik'...." Priestley *English Journey* ch.10 1934; "pitmatic – miners' dialect" *Dodd* MS Tanfield Lea

pitmatic, pitmatical cont.

C20/2; "Pitmatic Geordies or 'Yackers'" *Dobson* Tyne 1969; "it taalks deed pitmatick" *Irwin* Tyne 1970; "who needs pitman's shorthand when we've good north east pitmatic" *JM* Dawdon 1970s. *Plus* "I was taut the pit language and got on with my trade very well" *Errington* Felling/Heworth re 1790s p.42

pit-yacker pit worker, esp. hewer

"'Pit-yacker' is a self-descriptive term used by miners of the Durham coalfield. It has a half-derisive, half-humorous connotation, and stands in the same relation to pitmen as 'clodhopper' does to a farm labourer." *Hitchin* re Dalton-le-Dale 1910s (preface); "only pit-yackers spoke the pit-yackers' language" *Hitchin* re Seaham 1910s p.70; "a colliery workman who is rough in body and work and not very bright" *CT* New Herrington C20/mid; "pit-yakka – one who works under-ground" *McBurnie* Glebe Colliery, C20/mid; "pit-yakker" *Northumbrian III* Winlaton/Marley Hill C20/mid; 'a term of abuse applied to pitmen' *Graham* Geordie 1979. [source unknown] See also **yakker**

pittle to urinate

"pittle – to make water: 'pittle't all out'" *Bell* MS Newc 1830s; "Mary Anne she doesn't care a damn / She lifts up her petticoats and pittles like a man" *PHm* S'd C20/1; "pittle pot" *JS* Easington C20/mid, *CT* New Herrington 1930s ('kept under bed'). *Plus* "pittal – urine" *Dodd* MS Tanfield Lea C20/2. *EDD* distribution to 1900: in this form N'd, Yx, Lx, Der, Notts, EA. [piddle] See also **scoit**

pittly bed dandelion

ex. *GP* S'm C20/mid. *EDD* distribution to 1900: pittle-bed – N'd, Notts. *Plus* "pissy-bed – the dandelion plant" *Bell* MS Newc 1815; "there's a pink amang the pissy-beds" *Allan's Tyneside Songs* p.337 C19/1. *EDD* distribution to 1900: in this form Nth; piss-a-bed – general

pitterin' whinging

"Pittoring (pit:rún) – low-spirited, complain-ing: 'Ay, he's pitterin' on'" *Palgrave* Hetton 1896. *EDD* distribution to 1900: eD'm, EA [imitative]

plack a small coin

"no worth a plack" *Allan's Tyneside Songs* p.45

plack cont.

1812; "buzzems for a penny, rangers for a plack" *Scrapbook* Billy Purvis, C19/1; "plack – a small coin: 'We'll spend wor hinmost plack...'" *Pitman's Pay* G'head 1820s. *EDD* distribution to 1900: Sco, N'd, C'd, W'd, Lx. [Flem. placke 'small coin' C15]

plank insult re stupidity

"Yer plank!" (driver of another driver) S'm 2003 via BG

plantation any woodland, esp. managed

"Planting / Plantation" *Palgrave* Hetton 1896; "plantation" *TC* Parkside 1990s

plash/y 1. to splash, 2. wet, 3. rain

1. "plash – to splash; a heavy fall or even a shower of rain" *Brockett* Newc & Nth 1829; "plash – to splash" *Atkinson* Cleve 1868 2. "plashy – wet under foot: to plash in the dirt..." *Kennet* 1690s as Nth; "ploshy – miry, muddy" *Atkinson* Cleve 1868 3. "plash doon – downpour" *Dobson* Tyne 1973; 'a downpour of rain' *Graham* Geordie 1979. *EDD* distribution to 1900: Sco, Mids. NE 2001: not in use. [compare OE plæsc 'a pool', Swed plaska 'to splash']

plate slate clay

"plate – in mining, is slate clay... post (in mining) is sandstone" *Bell* MS Newc 1815

plate a rail (pit term)

"plait – plate, tub rail" *Dodd* MS Tanfield Lea C20/2

plate-pie a savoury or sweet pie baked and served in a deep plate

ex. *GJ* Spennymoor 1950s

ploat / plote 1. to pluck, 2. to rob, 3. to hit

1. "ploat – to pluck" *Grose* 1787; "plote – to pluck feathers; metaphorically, to chide vehemently..." *Brockett* Newc & Nth 1829; "plote – to pluck (a fowl)" Dinsdale, Teesdale 1849; "ploat – to strip off or pluck, e.g. feathers from a fowl; to plunder or rifle..." *Atkinson* Cleve 1868; "ti plot it like a guse" *Wearside Tales* 1879; "A blackberry bush or pitch that had been thoroughly picked was called 'ploted'" *JS* E'ton 1950s; "ploating a chicken or other bird meant pulling all the feathers off before cooking" *ER* M'bro C20/2, sim. *BF* Billingham C20/mid, NShields

ploat, plote cont.

C20/mid, Easington Colliery 2001 Q, Trimdon 2002 Q, Wheatley Hill 2004 Q; "plote – pluck or bring down" *Wade* South Moor 1966; "ploht – pluck chicken, remove dangerous loose stone [in a mine]" *Dodd* Tanfield C20/2; "ploat – to pluck and dress a bird" *JR* Sacriston C20/2. *Note* – not recognised by *EDD* which has 'plot – to scald'; *SED* (C20/mid) gives sense 'to pluck' from N'd, D'm, C'd, W'd, Yx. NE 2001: in low use. [Flem/Du ploten 'to pluck']
2. "to plunder or rifle: 'they'll ploat him'" *Atkinson* Cleve 1868; "ploat – to pilfer" Haswell 2001 Q; "ploat – to pluck or steal, not hit" South Moor (Stanley) 2003 per BG; "ploat – well and truly subject to crime: 'the area has been ploated by burglars'" *CC* Newc 2003. *EDD* distribution to 1900: nYx
3. to chide vehemently: 'how she plotes him'" *Brockett* Newc & Nth 1829"I ploated him" (I hit him) *ER* M'bro C20/2; 'to bash or hit' *JP* S'm C20/2; "Certainly in urban Teesside it means to 'inflict great violence upon'. It was always my cousin's favourite threat when I'd been teasing her (I'll ploat you)." *VW* M'bro 1980s; "ploat – not an ordinary punch but a hefty wallop, a great crushing knock-out blow." *JS* re Ch-le-St C20/2. *Plus* "plort – to punch or thump" *PG* H'pool 1998

plodge to wade

"plodge – to wade through water, to plunge" *Brockett* Newc & Nth 1829; 'to wade or walk through water' *Atkinson* Cleve 1868; "to paddle; we went plodging or had a plodge at the seaside" *HP* South Gosforth C20/mid; 'to paddle in the sea' *IL* Tow Law C20/mid, *Wood* Tees 2002; "ploj – wade" *Dodd* MS Tanfield Lea C20/2; 'to wade in water with bare feet' *Graham* Geordie 1979 "gannin plodge" East Boldon 1985. *EDD* distribution to 1900: N'd, D'm, C'd, Yx. NE 2001: in common use

plook, pluke pimple

"plook – a pimple, scab" *Atkinson* Cleve 1868; "ez rank ez flesh-flees on a sheep pluk" *Egglestone* Weardale 1870s; 'pimples' *Embleton* Newc 1897. *EDD* distribution to 1900: Sco, N'd, C'd, Yx. [Gael. pluc]. *Plus* "plooky, plooky-faced – pimpled" *Brockett* Newc & Nth 1829

plote see **ploat**

plother wet and muddy

"plother – very wet mud especially if including animal manure" *Wood* re rural Teesside C20/2

plout to struggle to walk

"to plout through snow" *MG* Teesdale C20/2. *EDD* distribution to 1900: Sco, Ire, C'd

pluffer pea-shooter

"get a piece of elderberry, about nine inches long and ¾ inch in diameter. Hollow out the pith with a screwdriver or six inch nail and this makes an ideal peashooter or 'pluffer'." *Northumbrian III* C20/2 re Co.Durham; "wi' thor bit bows an' arrers and pea-pluffers" (pea-shooters) *Dobson* Tyne 1970–71; 'a tube used as a pea-shooter' *Graham* Geordie 1979. *EDD* distribution to 1900: Sco, N'd. *Plus* "pluff – to blow in the face; to explode gunpowder" *Brockett* Newc & Nth 1829. [compare Du ploffen 'to puff, explode']

poke sack, bag

"ii seckes, iii pooks" Cockerton 1612 via *Atkinson* no.30; "a poke – a sack, a bag" *Kennet* 1690s as Nth; "Poverty writes her name on radle, pat or meal-pock" Durham 1839; 'a narrow bag of the sack description' *Atkinson* Cleve 1868; "a poke o' cwols" *Luckley* Alnwick 1870s; "Poke – a sack, or bag (common). 'Flour-poke." *Palgrave* Hetton 1896. *EDD* distribution to 1900: general. [AN poque] See also **bait poke**

pollis police(man)

"the pollis cam" (emphasis on first syllable) *Allan's Tyneside Songs* p.382 1851; "a good heart beats within him for he knocks the pollis doon" *Allan's Tyneside Songs* p.423 1862; "Ah telt a pollis aboot it" *Egglestone* Weardale 1870s; "a pollis pulled us oot at last" *Robson* Newc C20/1; "the pollisses – Jackson en Jones" *Armstrong* Tanfield C19/2; "Pollis – police" *Palgrave* Hetton 1896, Tanfield Lea, 1960. etc.; "poliss – tribal constabulary" *Dobson* Tyne 1970; "a sergeant and a poliss" *Irwin* Tyne 1970–71; "Morpeth polisses versus Ashington polisses" *Irwin* Tyne 1970; "phoned the polisses" S'd 2003 via BG. *Plus* "bobby" *Allan's Tyneside Songs* p.501 1881; "gissie" S'd 1890; "poliss point" (traffic light) Newc, 1966 per BG

pooda gunpowder

"pooda – mine explosive" *Dodd* MS Tanfield Lea C20/2

popple the common corn cockle

ex. *Atkinson* Cleve 1868. *EDD* distribution to 1900: Sco, Ire, N'd, C'd, Yx, Linx, EA

poppy-pill opium

ex. *Pitman's Pay* G'head 1820s. *EDD* distribution to 1900: obsol

porrage porridge

"porrage – hasty-pudding or porridge – oatmeal mixed in boiling water and stirred on the fire till it be considerably thickened. In Durham it is poddish. 'Put on the poddish-pot'" *Brockett* Newc & Nth 1829

porriwiggle the tadpole

ex. *Atkinson* Cleve 1868. *EDD* distribution to 1900: Yx, Leics, EA, Sur. [polliwog 'wagging head']

poss to agitate, to wash

"poss – to dash violently in the water, to beat; 'to poss clothes' in what is called a poss-tub" *Brockett* Newc & Nth 1829; "Poss – to wash clothes by putting them in a 'poss-tub' of soap and water, and thumping them with a 'poss-stick,' or short-legged staff, in some places called a 'dolly'" *Palgrave* Hetton 1896; "to poss the clothes" *RM* Norton C20/mid; "only if you're possing them in a poss-tub" *PG* H'pool C20/2; "a picture of some Seaham women indulging in the long forgotten art of double possing" *S'd Echo* 7 Jan 1965; "poss – wash in hot water" *LL* Tyneside, 1974. *EDD* distribution to 1900: Sco, Nth, wMids. [Fr pousser]. *Plus* "possing tub and staff" *MWN* 19 May 1860; "possing-stick, poss-stick – the staff [used to poss]" *Atkinson* Cleve 1868; "...the paraphernalia of the laundry: a poss-tub, scrubbing brush, bars of yellow soap and the mighty mangle" *Hitchin* re Dalton-le-Dale p.21 1910s; "poss-stick – a heavy piece of wood with a stalk and heavy foot" *Graham* Geordie 1979, Roker C20/mid; *HP* South Gosforth C20/mid; "poss tub – kept in yard half full of water" *Dodd* MS Tanfield Lea C20/2, Dinnington 1950s Q; "the pounding of primeval poss-tubs" *Dobson* Tyne 1970; "posh – to agitate, e.g. a fire [cf. poss]" *Dinsdale* mid-Tees 1849; "dolly, dolly-tub – a washing-tub in the form of a barrel" *Atkinson* Cleve 1868

post sandstone

exx. *Brockett* Newc & Nth 1846 (in pit), *Nicholson* 1880. *EDD* distribution to 1900: Sco, N'd, C'd, Yx, Northants

pot 1. earthenware mug, 2. plaster cast on broken limb, 3. lobster pot, etc.

1. "in private they were o'er a pot" *Chicken* Benwell 1720s; "pots o'erturn'd, and glasses broken!" *Pitman's Pay* G'head 1820s; "the boody pots (of beer) went roon an' roond" *Barrass* Stanley 1890s; "pot – an earthenware mug: 'a pot o' coffee'" S'm 1990s per BG. *EDD* distribution to 1900: Nth, Mids. *Plus* "pot py – meat and dough boiled" *Dodd* MS Tanfield Lea C20/2
2. "pot – the cast on a broken leg" *GP* S'm 1990s. *Plus* "chalk – a plaster cast" S'd 2001 Q
3. 'trap... for crabs and lobsters... invariably called a pot in cobles' *Hill* Flamborough 1970s

pote poet

exx. *Haldane* Newc 1879, *Armstrong* Tanfield C19/2

pout, paut to kick

"pout – to kick or strike with the feet" *Brockett* Newc & Nth 1829; "paut, poat – to kick gently or move with the feet" *Atkinson* Cleve 1868; "paut – to finger or paw" *Blenkinsopp* Teesdale 1931. *EDD* distribution to 1900: general. [OE potian]

pow top of head

"carrot-pow'd Jenny's Jacky" *Marshall* G'head 1806; "Time laid his cauld hand on his pow" *Allan's Tyneside Songs* p.354 1849; "pow – the poll or head (human)" *Atkinson* Cleve 1868. *EDD* distribution to 1900: Sco, Ire, Nth, Mids [poll]. *Plus* "crut – top of head" N.Shields C20/mid Q; "pow-head – a tadpole before it has legs" *Brockett* Newc & Nth 1829

powl, powlen pole

"the powl tuen down" *Marshall* Newc 1823 p.23; "aw dream'd aw was at the North Powl" *Ross* Tyne p.23 C19/1; "powlens" (wooden poles, levers) *Egglestone* Weardale 1870s

priest

"Priest (praest) – a clergyman is always so called" *Palgrave* Hetton 1896

prod a goad

"prod – a prick" *Bailey* Co.Durham 1810; 'a prick or skewer' *Brockett* Newc & Nth 1846. *EDD* distribution to 1900: general

prog to poke or prick

"prog, proggle – to prick, to pierce; a prog; progly – prickly" *Brockett* Newc & Nth 1829; "they wez buzy proggin' me aall ower" *Robson* Newc C20/1; "Aa progged it wi' one o' Polly's hat pins" *Robson* Newc C20/1; "to poke with s.thing pointed or sharp, hence proggie mat" South Shields C20/2 Q (see next entry); "...any feul knaas that sheep canna prog" *Dobson* Tyne 1972 *EDD* distribution to 1900: general

proggie mat home-made rug

"proggy mat – made from hessian base with woven lengths of fabric" *CT* New Herrington 1930s; "a proggie mat made with clippings of cloth about 2 inches long and a progger" *JS* Easington C20/mid; "progee mat – home-made rug" *Dodd* MS Tanfield Lea C20/2; "it takes ten sheep to make one proggy mat..." *Dobson* Tyne 1972. See also **clooty, hookie mat**

proggles prickles, etc.

"prog, proggle – to prick, to pierce; a prog; progly – prickly" *Brockett* Newc & Nth 1829; "progils" (prickles of a hedgehog) *Armstrong* Tanfield C19/2; "proggle – a thorn" *Palgrave* Hetton 1896. *EDD* distribution to 1900: N'd, D'm, wMids

proggly prickly

"proggly – prickly" *Luckley* Alnwick 1870s, Wade *South Moor*, 1966; "Progily" (hedgehog nickname) *Armstrong* Tanfield C19/2

pross to gossip

att. *Brockett* Newc & Nth 1846, Blenkinsopp Tees 1931. *EDD* distribution to 1900: D'm, Yx, Lincs. [prose]

puar pure, very

"Ise pure weel" *EDD* wYx 1900; "'Puar' and 'puarly' are used to emphasise something: 'It's puarly mint, man'" *Charver* 2000–2002. *Plus* "clean gyen", "clean daft" *Hull* MS wNewc 1880s

pubble plump

"pubble – plump, full: usually said of corn or grain when well perfected" *Bailey* Co.Durham

pubble cont.

1810; "as pubble as a partridge" *Atkinson* Cleve 1868. *EDD* distribution to 1900: Nth. [?Fris. pumpel]

puddick undersize fish

'any fish too small to sell in a market' *GP* S'm C20/mid. [?paddick]

puddings intestines

"A'll pull thy puddin's oot!" *Palgrave* Hetton 1896. *EDD* distribution to 1900: Sco, Nth, Ches, Lincs

puffler pit representative

'spokesman/negotiator for a team on a shift of men down the pit' New Herrington C20/mid; "puffler – man in charge of long wall in mine" Sacriston C20/2 per BG

pug, puggie to rob a bird's nest

"pug a nest – to destroy or spoil a (bird's) nest" Spennymoor C20/mid; "a nest that was robbed and destroyed was puggied as in 'some rotten bugger has puggied it'" *JS* Easington, 1950s; "if we destroyed a nest we 'puggied it'" *JR* Sacriston C20/2

pule to sleet

"pule – to sleet, or to fall as a mixture of snow and sleet: ''t pules an' snaws sae' *Atkinson* Cleve 1868. *EDD* distribution to 1900: Sco, N'd, nYx. See also **pew**

pump to break wind

exx. *CT* New Herrington 1930s *CP* S'm 1996, *Dodd* MS Tanfield Lea C20/2, etc.; "pump off" Teesside 2001 Q. *EDD* distribution to 1900: Sco, neLx. NE 2001: in use. *Plus* "another word we used at school was to boff" *PG* H'pool C20/2; "trump – the politer term" *CT* New Herrington 1930s

punch to kick

"punch – to strike with the feet, to thrust as with a point" *Brockett* Newc & Nth 1829; "punch – noun/vb – kick" *Dinsdale* mid-Tees 1849; "punch – to kick about with the feet in bed in a restless manner: 'Lie still an' dinna punch us that way'" *Luckley* Alnwick 1870s. *EDD* distribution to 1900: Sco, Nth. See also **bunch**

puoy punt pole

"puoy – a long pole with an iron fork at the end, used by keelmen on the Tyne to puoy or push their keels on" *Bell* MS Newc 1815; "puoy, puy or pouie – a long pole, with an iron spike or spikes, at the end; used in propelling keels in shallow water, or when it is inconvenient to use sails or oars" *Brockett* Newc & Nth 1829; "Bobby Gowlan' comes puoying his keel up" *Green* Wearside 1879 re C19/1. *EDD* distribution to 1900: puy – N'd, D'm, Notts, Lincs, EA

puss brown hare

ex. B'd Castle 2001 Q. *EDD* distribution to 1900: Sco, N'd, C'd, Yx

put to push, propel

'to but, to push with the horns' *Meriton* nYx 1683; "to putte – to push with head or horns as a cow" *Kennet* 1690s as Yx; "putting the tram" *Collier's Rant* Newc C18/2; "putting a keel" *Brockett* Newc & Nth 1829; "efter putting the men three fives" (tubs) Shield Row C20/1; "to propel a keel with a powey is called to put or to set" *Graham* Geordie 1979. *Note:* a considerable range of contexts is given for the word 'put' in *Heslop*. *Plus* "puttin in kaad – becoming cold" *Dodd* MS Tanfield Lea C20/2

putter a youth employed in moving coal tubs

"putter – a boy who works the tram" *Pitman's Pay* G'head 1820s; "putter – a boy in the workings of a coal pit who pushes or propels the corf or corves on a tram or rolley along the rolley way from where the hewer is working to the foot of the shaft" *Bell* MS Newc 1830s; "Putters are commonly young men from 16 to 20 years old" *Brockett* Newc & Nth 1846; "hand-putter or barrowman – one who puts without the assistance of a pony" *Nicholson* 1880; "pony-putter – a lad who brings the tubs from the working places to the flat with a pony" *Nicholson* 1880; "The 'putter' is a lad who 'puts,' or shoves the full tubs from the hewer's 'cavil' to the 'flat', and takes the empty ones in to him" *Palgrave* Hetton 1896; "person who transports tubs to the coal-face from a flat or passer-by. Sometimes by hand or pony." *McBurnie* Glebe Colliery, C20/mid; "putter – works with the tubs" *JM* Dawdon 1970s. *EDD* distribution to 1900: Sco, N'd, D'm, Lx, Yx, Ches. See also **foal**

putting the job of propelling tubs of coal in a pit

"my putting's a' done" *Collier's Rant* Newc C18/2; "putting-hewer – a young hewer who is liable to be called upon to put if necessary" *Nicholson* 1880. *EDD* distribution to 1900: N'd, D'm

qu— see also **tw—, wh—**

quarles quarries

"quarles – a large flat brick made of fire clay and used for flews in hot walls, etc." *Bell* MS Newc 1815; "Engine house was completed in November 1935. We are told that it will be in use for about 60 years. We are putting this note on the quarrels hoping it will be found." Dawdon Colliery Dec 1935

quean, wheen 1. woman, 2. disreputable woman

1. "this is a gloomy quean, says Tommy Linn" *NChorister* D'm, C18/2; "quean – a term of abuse to a female; [but] not always used in a reproachful sense: 'a sturdy quean', 'a good-like quean'" *Brockett* Newc & Nth 1829; "weean – a female, a woman, a wife [quean]" *Atkinson* Cleve 1868; "wander aboot like the rest o' young queens" *Barrass* Stanley 1890s. *EDD* distribution to 1900: Sco, Nth, S.W. [OE cwéne '(any) woman'
2. "Thou art a base, beggerlie, scurvie queane" *Raine* MS Newcastle 1607. *EDD* distribution to 1900: Sco, Nth

queen-cat, wheen-cat she-cat

"wheen-cat – a queen-cat... " *Ray* 1674 *Grose* 1787; "queen-cat" *Dinsdale* mid-Tees 1849; "queenie and carl-cat" *GP* S'm 1950s; "queenie" eD'm. 2001 Q; "tom-cat and queen-cat" Seaburn C20/2 Q. *EDD* distribution to 1900: C'D, D'm, Yx. *Plus* "bess-cat" Teesdale. C20/2 Q. See also **carle**

queens heads postage stamps

"put on twee Queens' heads" *Egglestone* Weardale 1870s. *EDD* distribution to 1900: Sco, Nth

quex goose

"a broad quex – a brood goose" *Bell* MS Newc 1830s

quey, whye young heifer

'A heifer of any age up to 3 years, or until she has a calf' (*EDD*); "excellent queys from 2 to 3 years old" *Newc Courant* 7 Oct 1826; "whye or quey – a heifer" *Bailey* Co.Durham 1810; "quey – generally pronounced whye" *Brockett* Newc & Nth 1829; "your whey's doon i' the born" *Parker* Tyne Valley 1896 p.69; "Quey stirk (waay stau:k) – 2-year-old heifer" *Palgrave* Hetton 1896; "quey – a heifer"

quey, whye cont.

Upper Teesdale 2001 Q. *EDD* distribution to 1900: Sco, Nth, eMids. [ON kvíga]

quick (of trees and bushes)

1. "quicken-tree – the mountain ash" *Brockett* Newc & Nth 1846. [OE cwic – 'living']
2. hedging plants: "qwhykwode – thorns, quick-wood hedge" Finchale (1487–8) "quicks – young hawthorn trees or bushes" *Bell* MS Newc 1815; "wicks – plants [for a hedge]" *Atkinson* Cleve 1868. See also **whick**

r the Northumberland burr

"a difficulty in pronouncing the letter r, which they cannot deliver from the tongue without a horrid jarring in the throat" Defoe *A tour of the whole island* 1720s; "the rough sound of 'r', as it is pronounced by the natives of Durham, who sound it in their throats with a disagreeable rattling." 1798 per Beal p.167 1999; "maek gam of wor bur" *Allan's Tyneside Songs* p.50 1812; "an' say wor burr becomes us weel" *Oliver* Newc 1824 p.8 (re Newcastle); "The Northumbrian growls it out from the bottom of his throat" *Haldane* Newc 1879 p.9; "the Geordie 'R'" *Dobson* Tyne 1970..." this is both rolling and gutteral" *Dobson* Tyne 1969

raa see **raw**

rackless thoughtless, careless

ex. *Viereck* re Gateshead, 1966. *EDD* distribution to 1900: Sco, Nth. [ON rǽkja, OE récan]. *Plus* "rack – to care: 'never rack you'" *Grose* 1787

rack, rax out change, improve

'said of weather going to improve' *MG* Teesdale C20/2; Middleton in Teesdale 2001 Q; "to rax out – to clear up [of weather]" *Brockett* Newc & Nth 1829. [?ON rek; compare Eng. rack 'flying clouds']

racken, recken-crook pot-hanger

"one paire of rackes, a paire of tonges and a reckon crooke with a paire of pott kilps" Darlington via Atkinson no.24 1610; "racen, a racken or racen – pot-hangers in Yorkshire; in the bishoprick of Durham a racen-crouk" *Kennet* 1690s; recken-cruck – a crook hung on a bar in the chimney of most country houses, on which they hung the kale pot on" *Bell* MS Newc 1830s; "Recking-crook (krook) not (kruok) – a crook hanging over the fire for pans to hang from" *Palgrave* Hetton 1896. *EDD* distribution to 1900: Nth, Lincs. [OE racente, ON rekendr 'chain']. See also **brandreth**

rackle violent

'violent, headstrong' *Pitman's Pay* G'head 1820s; 'rackle – disorderly (of a person)' *Dinsdale* mid-Tees 1849

radge rage, wildness

"when that childre play and rage" (romp), "Cuthbert, it acords noht the to rage" (of

radge cont.

Cuthbert as a child playing) *Cuthbert* C15/mid; "radged – furious mad" nYx 1890s per *EDD*; "he flew into a raj (rage, but pronounced radge)" *IA* S'm 1950s, 60s; "radge" (noun, adj or verb) *Charver* 2000-2002

radgy an angry or wild person

"He's a proper radgee" *Charver* 2000–2002; "radgie – charva, specifically of the aggressive persuasion" www.urbanDictionary.com; "radgie-gadgie – angry old man" Newc 2001 Q

raff heap, refuse, lumber, etc.

"raff – abundance, a great quantity, a great number: 'a raff of fellows'" *Brockett* Newc & Nth 1846; *EDD* distribution to 1900: general. [compare Swed. raffs 'rubbish']. *Plus* "raff-yard – timberyard" *Dinsdale* mid-Tees 1849 [compare Gm Raf 'beam of wood']; "raff-yard – scrapyard" *Dobson* Tyne 1973

raffled snarled up

"P.D. ran te clear the anchor / 'It's raffled.' right loudly he roar'd" *Allan's Tyneside Songs* p.27 1805; "raffle – to become confused in one's intellect: 'he is beginning to raffle'" *Atkinson* Cleve 1868. *EDD* distribution to 1900: N'd, W'd, Yx, Lx. [?ravel from Du. rafelen 'to tangle']

rageous furious, violent

"rageous – in a rage, in excessive pain, violent" *Brockett* Newc & Nth 1829; "that dog o' yours is rageous" wYx C20/mid per *EDD*; "rageous – outrageous (violent and delirious)" *Palgrave* Hetton 1896. *EDD* distribution to 1900: Nth, Lincs. [OFr rageux]

raggies ragworms

'used as fishing bait' *DP* S'm 2000

raim see **rame**

raggy 'stony, of shale'

ex. *Barrass* Consett 1893

rain-bird woodpecker

"rain-birds, rain-fowl – popular names for woodpeckers" *Brockett* Newc & Nth 1829. *EDD* distribution to 1900: general. ['said to be vociferous when rain is impending' *OED*]. *Plus* "pickatree – woodpecker" *Brockett* Newc & Nth 1829. *EDD* distribution to 1900: N'd, W'd, Yx

rake course, direction, stretch

"Whyt Barne Rake" *Durham* C16/2; "ratch – the straight course of a navgiable river. The word is used on the Tyne in the same sense as Reach on the Thames. The Newcastle keelmen generally call it Rack." *Brockett* Newc & Nth 1829; "a rake to Hartley Burn" (journey) C'd 1880 per *EDD*. [ON rák, OE raécan]. *Plus* "she's raking up the dyke" *Allan's Tyneside Songs* p.29 1812; "rack – reach" *Pitman's Pay* G'head 1820s; "rax – to reach" *Brockett* Newc & Nth 1829

ram rancid

"ram – foetid, rank...: 'a ram smell', 'a ram taste'" *Brockett* Newc & Nth 1829; "ram – acrid or pungent (of a smell)" *Dinsdale* mid-Tees 1849; "ma pipe's varry ram an ah mun hed rimed oot" *Embleton* Tyne 1897; 'rancid' *CT* New Herrington 1930s; "ram – rancid (re butter, bacon)" *JB* Shildon C20/mid. *EDD* distribution to 1900: Nth, Ches, Lincs, Dor. [cf. Ice. ramr]

ramage rough

"ramage – violent, rude, as the man was very ramage with the lass" *Bell* MS Newc 1830s. [OFr ramage]

rame, raim to complain, moan, etc.

"to rame – to weep or cry" *Kennet* 1690s as D'm; "rame, ream – to cry aloud, to ask over and over again in a teasing manner; raming, reaming – crying" *Brockett* Newc & Nth 1829; "rame. To ply one with questions, as children love to do: 'What's tha ramin' o' me for?' 'He just raimed my life out for sixpence'" *Palgrave* Hetton 1896; "raim – grumble excessively" *Dodd* MS Tanfield Lea C20/2; "to talk or call fretfully: 'he just raimed away...'" *Graham* Geordie 1979; "raim – to moan" Ferryhill 2001 Q; "stop riming on about that" *JS* Easington C20/mid. *EDD* distribution to 1900: Sco, Nth, part of Mids. [ON hreim-r 'a scream or cry']

rammel 1. brushwood. 2. types of stone, 3. to ramble

1. "for carreage of rammell 5s." *Raine* MS York 1584; "rammel meaning rubbish: 'the boot sale was full of rammel'" *TH* Wheatley Hill 2002. *EDD* distribution to 1900: esp. Sco, Nth, Mids. [AN ramaille 'branches, loppings']

rammel cont.

2. rammel – a thin piece of coarse cannel coal which lies at the top of the marketable coal" *Bell* MS Newc 1830s; "ramble – a thin stratum of shale, often found lying immediately above the seam of coal" *Nicholson* 1880; "rammul – small stone from mine roof" *Dodd* MS Tanfield Lea C20/2; 'rammel – stone that gets mixed with the coal' Wade South Moor 1966. *EDD* distribution to 1900: N'd, C'd, D'm, Ches, Shrop
3. "deeth rammels on throo lane an' square" *Allan's Tyneside Songs* p.241 1829

rampageous boisterous, disorderly

ex. *JS* Easington C20/mid; 'over the top' *MB* Coxhoe C20/mid; "rampageous – rough" Sedgefield 2001 Q. *EDD* distribution to 1900: general

ramstam impetuous

"ramstam – thoughtless: 'a rackle ram-stam wife'" *Pitman's Pay* G'head 1820s. *EDD* distribution to 1900: Sco, Ire, N'd, Northants, Beds

randy a noisy, vulgar woman (without immoral connotations)

"D'ye want me to make a randy of meself?" *AK* re N'd 1940s. *EDD* distribution to 1900: general

range see **rench**

rant be voluble, etc.

"rant – evangelise, angry uncontrolled speech" *Dodd* MS Tanfield Lea C20/2; 'a lively song with chorus' *Graham* Geordie 1979. *EDD* distribution to 1900: general. [Du ranten 'to rave']. *Plus* "ranty – excited; wild with passion, drink or excitement" *Atkinson* Cleve 1868; "Ranters – Primitive Methodists" *Palgrave* Hetton 1896

rap to signal from shaft to engine room

"he rapped 'Men On' to the brakesman / and away Aa went in the cage" West Stanley C20/1; "the' rapped the cage ter bank" *Hay* Ushaw Moor C20/1; "then the banksman will rap them (the men) down" *GP* S'm C20/mid. *EDD* distribution to 1900: N'd, D'm, nStaffs [imitative, noted C14 on]

rapper 1. signal mechanism at pit shaft, 2. flexible metal strip used in N'd/D'm version of sword dancing

1."rapper – a lever placed at the top of a shaft or inclined plane, to one end of which a hammer is attached, and to the other a line, communicating with the bottom of the shaft or incline. Its use is to give signals when everything is ready at the bottom for drawing away" *Nicholson* 1880. *EDD* distribution to 1900: N'd, D'm, wYx
2. "the rapper... was [probably] discovered by accident when mining tools were adapted to be used as improvised swords" www.rapper.org.uk. [the metal strip with handles each end probably started off as an implement to scrape down horses (and pit ponies?)]. *Plus* "wafter – play sword" *Graham* Tyne 1980

raspberry 1. **rasp**, 2. **hindberry**

1. ex. *Grose* 1787; "rasp – raspberry, both the bush and its fruit" *Brockett* Newc & Nth 1829; *Dinsdale* mid-Tees 1849; *Palgrave* Hetton 1896; eD'm 2001 Q. *EDD* distribution to 1900: Sco, Ire, Nth, Mids. NE 2001: in use
2. "hind-berries – raspberries" *Ray* Nth 1674; 'raspberries (*Rubus Idæus*)' *Bailey* Co.Durham 1810; *Brockett* Newc & Nth 1829

ratch see **rake**

ratchet hound

"[people suppose] the noise of the wild swans flying high upon the heights, to be spirits, or (as they call them here in the North) Gabriel-Ratchets" *Raine* MS 1647; "Gabriel-ratchet (pronounced Gaabrl-ratchet) – a name for a yelping sound heard at night, more or less resembling the cry of hounds or yelping of dogs" *Atkinson* Cleve 1868. *EDD* distribution to 1900: ratch – Sco, N'd, Lakes. [OE ræce]

ratherlings mostly

'for the most part' *Brockett* Newc & Nth 1846

ratten rat

"ratten – the... rat" *Brockett* Newc & Nth 1829; *Dinsdale* mid-Tees 1849. *EDD* distribution to 1900: Sco, Nth, Ches, Der, Shrop. [ME raton]

rattle-scawp mischievous fellow

Palgrave Hetton 1896. *EDD* distribution to 1900: NE

rattly-bags see **thunnor**

raw, raa row of terrace houses

"of the towne on the este rawe" (east row or street) *Cuthbert* C15/mid; "We leve i' yen raw" *Marshall* G'head 1806; "raw – a row of buildings, the side of a street" *Brockett* Newc & Nth 1829; "the folks o' wor raw" *Allan's Tyneside Songs* p.359 1849; "a colliery raw" Jesmond 1891; "roond the raws ... the youngsters hugg'd the teup" *Barrass* Stanley 1890s; "the pit raa" *Graham* Geordie 1979; "raa – terrace row" Thornley 2001 Q. *EDD* distribution to 1900: Sco, Nth

rax to stretch

"and raxed him where he stood" (stretched himself to full height) Reed *Border Ballads* C16; "rax – to stretch or strain: riving and raxing" *Atkinson* Cleve 1868; "rax – to stretch; to strain" *Nicholson* 1880; "He raxed his-sel' oot" *Palgrave* Hetton 1896; "to rax yourself to the point of injury, e.g. strain or sprain" Darlington 1940s (Q); "rax that blether an' we'll myek a foot ball" *Luckley* Alnwick 1870s; "rax – [to] stretch, strain (an object)" *JB* Shildon C20/mid; "he's raxed hissell – strained a muscle" *Dunn* B'p Auck 1950s, sim. D'ton 1940s Q; "rax me new shoes for us" *IA* S'm 1950s, 60s, *GP* S'm 1950s; "I've raxed me bike" (bent frame) cenD'm 2001 Q; "to rax out – to make item fit easier" Wheatley Hill 2002 Q; "divvent swing on the chair or you'll rax it" *AD* Hebburn 2003 Q. *EDD* distribution to 1900: Sco, Ire, Nth, Lincs. [OE raxan]

reckling runt of litter

"reckling – an unhealthy child, pig or lamb; the nestling, or smaller bird in a nest" *Grose* 1787; "wreckling... the youngest or weakest of the breed among animals" *Brockett* Newc & Nth 1829; "My sister was 18 and my brother 14 when I was born, so I was the 'recklin'" *JB* Shildon, 1930s, 1940s, sim. *GP* S'm C20/mid; "A recklin is the runt of a pig litter" *Wood* re rural Teesside C20/2. *EDD* distribution to 1900: Sco, Nth, Mids. NE 2001: in use. [ON recklingr 'an exile']

red to tidy, clean, etc.

"red – to untangle or separate" *Grose* 1787; "red – to put in order, to clear, to disentangle: 'to red up the house'" *Brockett* Newc & Nth 1829, "pronounced in D'm, reet" 1846; "red (up) – to tidy up (one's hair)" *Dinsdale* mid-Tees 1849; "ye shud red up yer place", "red yor hair" *Luckley* Alnwick 1870s; "redding –

red cont.

clearing away the stones produced by blasting, falls, &c." *Nicholson* 1880, sim. *Dodd* MS Tanfield Lea C20/2; "daily housework was always 'redding up'" *Nth Words* Northumberland, 1938. *EDD* distribution to 1900: Sco, N'd. [redden 'to make ready']. *Plus* "redding-comb – a comb for the hair" *Brockett* Newc & Nth 1829

reed red

"reed" *Anderson* Newcastle 1593; "a read why calf" Darlington, 1610 per Atkinson no.25; "leyke twe little reed tatees" *Bewick* Tyne 1790s; "reed an' blue fire" *Allan's Tyneside Songs* p.415 1853; "as reed as a fox" *Lakeland* re C'd 1856; "his fingers was reed raw" *Dunn* B'p Auck 1950, "reed raa" *Dodd* MS Tanfield Lea C20/2. *EDD* distribution to 1900: in this pronunciaton Sco, NI, N'd, C'd. [OE réad]

reek smoke (noun and vb)

"reek – smoke... in the North they pronoune it reek and use it indifferently for all sorts of smoak" *Kennet* 1690s; "whei cowers biv the chimlay reek?" *Allan's Tyneside Songs* p.51 1823; "Reek (rae:k) – smoke, e.g. Baccy-reek, Powder-reek" *Palgrave* Hetton 1896; "powder-reek" *Wade* South Moor 1966; "reek – pipe smoke" *Dunn* B'p Auck 1950; "the chimleys reekin badly" *Graham* Geordie 1979. *EDD* distribution to 1900: general. [OE réc, ON reykr]. *Plus* "reeky – smoky *Atkinson* Cleve 1868

reesty rancid esp. of bacon

"reasty – rancid, particularly applied to bacon" *Brockett* Newc & Nth 1829, "...spoilt by long keeping" 1846; "reesty – rancid, discoloured and having a bad taste" *Atkinson* Cleve 1868; 'rotten (of bacon)' *JB* Shildon C20/mid. *EDD* distribution to 1900: reasty – general. [OFr resté 'left over, stale']

reet right (noun and adj.)

"reet" *Bewick* Tyne 1790s; "reet frae wrang discerning" *Allan's Tyneside Songs* p.45 1812; "reet as a tripet" *Haldane* Newc 1879; "thoo's aboot reet there, Tommy" *Embleton* Tyne 1897; "reet forrard" (straight ahead) ?N'd, *NCM* 1900–1901; "not reet iv his head" *Graham* Geordie 1979. *EDD* distribution to 1900: in this pronunciation Nth

rench, etc. to rinse

ex. *Brockett* Newc & Nth 1829; "range the pot out" *Palgrave* Hetton 1896; "wrench out a cup" ER M'bro C20/2; "rainch" Thornley 2001 Q. *EDD* distribution to 1900: general. [ON hræinsa 'to cleanse']

renky well-shaped

"rencky – great and boisterous" *Kennet* 1690s as Yx; "renky – tall and well-made, athletic" *Atkinson* Cleve 1868. *EDD* distribution to 1900: nYx. *Plus* "renty – well-shaped... of horses or cows" *Grose* 1787

rezzy reservoir

ex. Trimdon C20/2 Q

rice, rise brushwood

"None shall cut rise... on Allenton Common" *Raine* MS Hexham, 1664; "rice – hedging wood" *Bailey* Co.Durham 1810; "rice – dead thorns fixed to form a fence" *Luckley* Alnwick 1870s extra; 'brushwood' *Smith* Weardale 1883. *EDD* distribution to 1900: general. [OE hrís]

ride to ride on a plundering expeditions

"ride – to go out on horseback to rob; rider – a moss-trooper, or robber on the Borders" *Brockett* Newc & Nth 1829. *EDD* distribution to 1900: Sco, N'd, C'd, W'd – now obsol. [OE gerídan]. *Plus* 'a raid' e.g. poem *RR* D'm C16/mid

rieve, reave to plunder

"thai slew, thai brent, thai robbed, thai reved" *Cuthbert* C15/mid. *EDD* distribution to 1900: Sco, Ire, N'd, C'd, Yx. [OE réafian]. *Plus* "riever, reaver – a border thief" per *EDD*

rift to belch

"rift – to belch; also to plow out grass land" *Bailey* Co.Durham 1810; "riften – belching" *Dunn* B'p Auck 1950. *EDD* distribution to 1900: Sco, Ire, Nth, Mids. [ON ripta 'to break']

rig ridge

"rygg" *Cuthbert* C15/mid; "coming over the Dry-rig" *RR* Weardale 1569; "rig – a ridge, an eminence; rig-and-fur, rig-and-rein – ridge and furrow" *Brockett* Newc & Nth 1829; "rigg – the ridge of any object: 'Ah'll lig thee on tha' rigg' (back)" *Atkinson* Cleve 1868; "Furrows are called 'rigs'" *Palgrave* Hetton 1896. *EDD*

rig cont.

distribution to 1900: in this pronunciation Sco, Ire, Nth, Mids, EA. [OE hrycge, ON hrycg]

riddy ready

"awl riddy" *Armstrong* Tanfield C19/2

rime to clean out with a driling motion

"rimed out – cleaned out" (of a pipe) Embleton Newc 1897. *EDD* distribution to 1900: N'd, W'd, Yx, Lx, Lincs, Dor. [OE rýman 'to make room']

rind hoar frost

ex. *Dinsdale* mid-Tees 1849; "Rind – rime, hoar-frost: 'There's a heavy (or, thick) rind on'" *Palgrave* Hetton 1896. *EDD* distribution to 1900: Sco, NE. [dubious OE hrinde]

ripe to rifle

"ripe – to search, to steal privately, to plunder: 'to ripe for stones in the foundation of an old wall', 'he riped the nest'" *Brockett* Newc & Nth 1829; 'to quarry stones' *Dinsdale* mid-Tees 1849; "ripe – to rifle or search: 'Aw catch'd him ripin' maw breeches pocket'" *Luckley* Alnwick 1870s. *EDD* distribution to 1900: Sco, Nth. [OE rýpan]

rive 1. to tear, rip, 2. a rent

1. "the yong man sarke, of some ryvyng had a marke" *Cuthbert* C15/mid; "I shall rive him out of the earth that ever giveth him one grote of my geare" *Raine* MS Newcastle, 1586; "paid for fellying of wood and ryving of spilys" (Bishop of Durham's accounts, ca. 1515) via *Brockett* Newc 1846; "De'il rive their sark gangs hame tonight" *Chicken* Benwell 1720s; "rove my breeks" *Marshall* G'head 1806; "rive – to separate into parts by applying force to each side" *Brockett* Newc & Nth 1829; "he was fit to rive swarth" (to tear up the ground with vexation) *Atkinson* Cleve 1868; "rave – did rive, tore" *Dinsdale* mid-Tees 1849; "rovven – p.p. of rive: 'rovven fra tegither' (torn asunder)" *Atkinson* Cleve 1868; "Please sir, he's ruvven a leaf out" *Palgrave* Hetton 1896; "hes rovven his claes te bits" *Dunn* B'p Auck 1950. *EDD* distribution to 1900: esp. Sco, Ire, Nth, EA. NE 2001: in common use. [ON rífa]
2. "rive – a rent or tear" *Brockett* Newc & Nth 1829; 'a rent in a garment' *Graham* Geordie 1979; 'large tear or rip' *JP* S'm C20/2

rock hard, tough

"they'll think we're rock" *VIZ* 37 ca.1990

rolley four-wheel vehicle

"rolley – a small waggon (with four little wheels) for conveying the corf" *Bell* MS Newc 1830s; 'similar in construction to a tram but larger; a long carriage for conveying the corfs or tubs of coals from the crane or flat to the bottom of the shaft, drawn by horses; *Brockett* Newc & Nth 1846; 'a carriage used to carry corves along the horse-roads underground. The rolley was contrived as an improvement upon the tram, upon which a single corf was placed; a horse drawing one, two, or three corves at a time' *Nicholson* 1880; "rolley – what is called a 'trolly' in some parts, i.e. an open waggon for carrying heavy goods, such as beer-barrels or packing-cases" *Palgrave* Hetton 1896; "rolly – four-wheeled, flat, farm cart, with front wheels plus small driver's platform swivelling" *JB* Shildon C20/mid; "rolley – Pitmatic for trolley" *Leslie* Newc 1992. *EDD* distribution to 1900: N'd, D'm, Yx, Lincs, Norf, i.e. East coast

rolly way road in pit

"rolley-way – the under-ground waggon-way along which the rolleys travel" *Brockett* Newc & Nth 1829; 'way laid with iron on which the rolley travels' *Bell* MS Newc 1830s; 'the horse road underground' *Nicholson* 1880; 'haulage road' *Northumbrian III* C20/2 re Durham collieries; "rolleewai – underground railway" *Dodd* MS Tanfield Lea C20/2, Dinnington 1950s Q

roof upper surface of pit tunnel

"roof closing (large fall in coal mine)" *JM* Thornaby C20/2

rook, roke mist

"rook, rouk – a mist or fog" *Brockett* Newc & Nth 1829; "rook – mist, rooky – misty – the mist or sea fret" *Bell* MS Newc 1830s; "roaky – misty" *Dinsdale* mid-Tees 1849; "roke – a thick fog" *Atkinson* Cleve 1868; "It's a thick rook the neet" *Palgrave* Hetton 1896. *EDD* distribution to 1900: roak – general. [?ON, compare reek]. *Plus* "roky – foggy" *Atkinson* Cleve 1868; "rooky" *Palgrave* Hetton 1896

roondabout traffic roundabout

"roondaboot" *Dobson* Tyne 1972 (preferred to circle)

roondy coal marketable for domestic use

"lumps o' roondy coal" *Allan's Tyneside Songs* p.516 1872; "Then, smack! the roondie an' the small / Aw skelps off the back-end" *Barrass* Stanley 1892; 'large lump of coal' *JM* Thornaby C20/2, *Dodd* MS Tanfield Lea C20/2; "artefacts... constructed from bits of roondy coal" *Dobson* Tyne 1970; "roundies – round coal" Ferryhill Seaham 2001 Q. [i.e. a useful size when coal to be placed on the fire with tongs]

roop/y hoarse

"a roop – of the North a hoarsness, and hoars voic[e]s occasioned by a cold" *Kennet* 1690s; "roup – hoarsnees of voice – to be roupy, to be hoarse" *Bell* MS Newc 1830s; "roopy – husky (of the voice). (Always used)" *Palgrave* Hetton 1896. *EDD* distribution to 1900: roupy – general. *Plus* "rooped – hoarse: 'He's roop'd wuv a sair throat'" *Luckley* Alnwick 1870s

rout, rowt 1. to bellow, 2. a loud noise

1. "the rowtinge and blaringe" *Raine* MS EYorks 1641; "rowting – bellowing of an ox" *Bailey* Co.Durham 1810; "roughting – the lowing or bellowing of cattle" *Bell* MS Newc 1815. *EDD* distribution to 1900: Sco, Ire, Nth, Lincs. NE 2001: not in use. [ON rauta]. *Plus* "blorting – to bellow" Middleton in Teesdale 2001 Q
2. "div'nt ye mak' sic a rout" *Allan's Tyneside Songs* p.47 1812

rowk to search

"to search or look: 'I rowked in a drawer'" *MG* Teesdale C20/2. *EDD* distribution to 1900: roak – N'd, C'd; roke – wYx, etc.

rowst arousing

"rowst – get the men to work after their blaa (breather) was finished" *JS* Easington C20/mid

rozzel, rozin – to warm

"rossel – to heat, to roast" *Brockett* Newc & Nth 1829; "rozzle – resin. Also, to warm oneself: 'He rozzled his hide'" (by the fire) *Palgrave* Hetton 1896; "rozzel yor shins" *Graham* Geordie 1979. *EDD* distribution to 1900: Nth, Lincs, Shrop. *Plus* "rozzla – very hot day" *Dodd* MS Tanfield Lea C20/2; "rozin'd – comfortably tipsy" *Pitman's Pay* G'head 1820s; "he rosin'd wor gobs wiv a glass o' French brandy" *Allan's Tyneside Songs* p.295 1842

runch wild mustard

"runches. runch balls – charlock when it is dry and withered" *Kennet* 1690s as Nth; "runch – a general name for wild mustard, white mustard, and wild radish" *Bailey* Co.Durham 1810. *EDD* distribution to 1900: Sco, N'd, C'd, Yx. [?AN runche 'bramble']

S

sackless innocent, ineffective

"sackless – innocent, faultless" *Ray* 1674; "a sackless man goeing to jaole" *Raine* MS Croukley 1681; "a sackless dog" *Oiling* G'head 1826; 'simple, weak, helpless, innocent' *Brockett* Newc & Nth 1829; 'simple, easy to be imposed upon, and born down' *Bell* MS Newc 1830s; 'foolish, senseless' *Palgrave* Hetton 1896; "he's a greet sackless cuddy" *Graham* Geordie 1979; "I was working with a Stokesley joiner who described another joiner, whom he considered incompetent, as sackless", "a sackless nowt" *Wood* C20/2; 'idiotic' *Dodd* MS Tanfield Lea C20/2; 'drunk' Weardale, Teesdale 2001 Q; 'silly' Wheatley Hill 2002 Q; "ye sackless bugger!" cen D'm Q 2001. *EDD* distribution to 1900: Sco, Nth. NE 2001: in use. [ON saklauss]

sair, sare sore(ly), bad(ly)

"sare – much, greatly: as sare hurt, sare pained" *Bailey* Co.Durham 1810; "sare – sore, painful; very much, greatly, intensely: 'sare hadden' very much distressed by pain or sickness" *Brockett* Newc & Nth 1829; "he oft had sair wark for ti myek a bit fend" *Allan's Tyneside Songs* p.489 1862; "sair upset" *Barrass* Stanley 1890s; "bonny an' sair – very upset" *Dunn* B'p Auck 1950. *EDD* distribution to 1900: in this pronunciation Sco, Nth [OE sár]

Sand-dancers folk of South Shields

2002 per BG. [possibly from Arab seamen settled there in the 1920s]

Sandies Scotsmen

"the Sandies, frae Scotland" *Allan's Tyneside Songs* p.441 C19/mid. [likely from 'Alexander' as a forename]

sand-shoes plimsolls

ex. GJ Spennymoor 1950s; *Dodd* MS Tanfield Lea C20/2

sand-strake

"sand-strake is the first range of strakes or planks laid next the keel" *Wm Scoresby* (Whity) 1820 qu. *OED*; "sandstrake" *C/GR* Amble C20/2. *EDD* distribution to 1900: N'd. [ME strake]. *Plus* 'strake or single range of plank from bow to stern in a coble' *Hill* Flamborough 1970s

Santy Santa Claus

"Santee Klaas" *Dodd* MS Tanfield Lea C20/2; S'm 1990s per BG. *Plus* "Afore w' gan t' bed an' th' fires damped down ar's ganna send a note t' Santa. If mi motha an' fatha 'll help us spell an' a can hev a small piece o' paper arl tell'm wat best gift a want then fowld it tight an hoy it up th' chimla. If it dissent come down e'll hev gorrit. If it diz come down arl try again till it dissent." *CT* New Herrington 1930s

sandwich

"a ham sangwidge and a pint o' Borton" *Cuddy Cairt* Newc 1917; "bacon samidges" *VIZ* 72 (1995)

sark shirt, shift

"the yong man sarke " *Cuthbert* C15/mid; "brave ruffled sark" *Bells* re Carlisle 1802; "my pit sark" *Marshall* G'head 1806; "when I cam to Walker wark / I had ne coat nor ne pit sark" *Bell* Newc 1812 p.36; "Dolly Coxon's pawned her sark" (shift) *Allan's Tyneside Songs* p.29 1812; "sark – shirt... smock, a shift" *Bell* MS Newc 1830s; "sark – a shirt; also a shift or chemise: 'stripped tiv his sark-sleeves'" *Atkinson* Cleve 1868; "she gat oot i' bed wi nowt but hor sark" (slip) *Armstrong* Tanfield C19/2. *EDD* distribution to 1900: Sco, Ire, Nth. [ON serkr, OE serc; notably forms part of the word 'berserker' (a raging Viking warrior, either because of his 'bear-shirt' or 'bare-shirt']. *Plus* "top-sark – rough woollen over-shirt" *Gibson* C'd 1880; "body-sark – vest" *Utpon* 1950 N'd, D'm. See also **shart**

sartin certain

"aw's sartin" *Allan's Tyneside Songs* p.410 C19/mid; "sartin – certain" Tanfield Lea, 1960. *EDD* distribution to 1900: in this pronunciation Ire, Eng

sarve to serve

"he's chatcht it, and sarve him reet" *Parker* Tyne Valley 1896 p.87

satisfised satisfied

"Satisfised. The invariable mispronunciation of 'satisfied.' (saat:is:faa:yzd.)" *Palgrave* Hetton 1896

saugh the willow

"saugh – the great round-leaved willow" *Brockett* Newc & Nth 1846. *EDD* distribution to 1900: Sco, Nth, EA. [OE Ang salh]. *Plus* "sauve" Dinsdale mid-Tees 1849

sca— see also **ska—**

scad to scald

"scadding of peas – a custom in the North of boiling the common grey-peas in their shell" *Grose* 1787; "skadded his gob – with hot tea" *PHm* S'd C20/1; "a big pint pot full o' scaddin' het sweet tea" *Grieves* Tyne 1975

scallion young onion

"Scallion – a young onion, before the bulb has formed. A favourite dish is scallion and lettuce" *Palgrave* Hetton 1896; 'spring onions' *JB* Shildon C20/mid

scar cliff, bare place on hillside

"Salt Skare / Salt Skars, Long-Skares" rocks off the Tees per John Seller *The English Pilot* 1671 vol.1 p.11; "scarre – a cliff or lone rock on the dry land" *Grose* 1787; "scar (sometimes pronounced scaur) – the face of a precipitous rock, or stony bank; a rocky surface, at the foot of the sea-cliffs, or below the barrow beach, nearly awash" *Atkinson* Cleve 1868. *EDD* distribution to 1900: Sco, Ire, Nth, Mids. [ON sker 'sea-reef']

scarecrow 1. **flaycraw**, 2. other

1. "flaa craw – a stick stuck in the middle of a field or garden and dressed with old cloaths to frighten birds" *Bell* MS Newc 1815; "a flae craw" *Wearside Tales* 1879; "flaycrow and scallywag came from the dales, and the Scottish influence appears with tattybogle used twice" *Crocker* 1983
2. "flay-boggle – a hobgoblin, an apparition; also a scarecrow" *Atkinson* Cleve 1868; "tatee-bogle – a scarecrow in a potato field" *Brockett* Newc & Nth 1829; "tattie boggle" Newc 2001 Q

scart scratch (noun and vb)

"sic a dream as gar'd me scart me lug" *Allan's Tyneside Songs* p.312 1827; "Threat, 'may the Deil scart you frae top to tae'" *Bell* MS Newc 1830s; "I divvent care the scart iv a nail for his politics" *Parker* Tyne Valley 1896 p.79. *EDD* distribution to 1900: Sco, Ire, N'd, C'd, Yx. See also **scrat**

Scenty Eddie effeminate man

"Scenty Eddie – said of anyone effeminate; believed to be a comment on Edward VIII when he visited the North East as Prince of Wales" *BL* Winlaton 1950s

scobbie chaffinch

"Scobbie – chaffinch. Not so common as 'sheelie'" *Palgrave* Hetton 1896. *EDD* distribution to 1900: D'm, C'd, W'd, Yx, Warks

scoit to urinate

ex. *GP* S'm C20/2. [ON skjóta, OE scéotan 'to shoot']. See also **pittle**

scon to punish

"scon – to strike or inflict punishment; a common word amongst the coal miners" *Brockett* Newc & Nth 1846

sconce pretence, trick (noun and vb)

"Man, it's as plain as A B C, for all 'twad seem a sconce" *Barrass* Stanley 1890s. *EDD* distribution to 1900: N'd, Yx. "sconce – to bear tales which are untrue or magnified" *Atkinson* Cleve 1868

sconce a seat

"sconce – a fixed seat at one side of the fire-place in the old large open chimney" *Brockett* Newc & Nth 1829; "skonss – seat near fire" *Dodd* MS Tanfield Lea C20/2; 'a seat at the side of an old chimney' *Graham* Geordie 1979. *EDD* distribution to 1900: Sco, Nth. *Plus* "sconce – a screen" *Atkinson* Cleve 1868

scoot to squirt, etc.

'to squirt' *Graham* Geordie 1979. *EDD* distribution to 1900: general. *Plus* "skooted – go quickly" *Dodd* MS Tanfield Lea C20/2. [ON skjóta, OE scéotan]

scooter syringe

exx. *Bell* MS Newc 1815; *Brockett* Newc & Nth 1829; *Luckley* Alnwick 1870s; 'a squirt or syringe' *Embleton* Tyne 1897

scoury stone whitener

"scoury stone – a product used to whiten the doorstep" Spennymoor C20/mid Q

scrab crabapple

"nuttes, scrabbes & egges" *Durham* C16/2; "scrab – a wild apple, the crab" *Brockett* Newc & Nth 1829. *EDD* distribution to 1900: N'd.

scrab cont.

[variant of crab; or cf. Swed skrabba]. *Plus* "scrab apples – fir cones" *Luckley* Alnwick 1870s

scraffle 1. to scramble, 2. to search for, with hands

1. "a shot tower se hee / that biv it ye might scraffle to heaven"*Allan's Tyneside Songs* p.48 1812; "scraffle – to scramble, to climb up by the help of the hands; scraffling – working hard to obatin a livelihood" *Brockett* Newc & Nth 1829; "I came scraffling my way through the market" *Atkinson* Cleve 1868; "what ivvor set me to scraffle inte that waggon?" *Haldane* Newc 1879. *EDD* distribution to 1900: Sco, Nth, Northants, Warks. [?Du schrabbelen] 2. "skraflin – searching with hand" *Dodd* MS Tanfield Lea C20/2. *Plus* "grafun – search, using hand" *Dodd* MS Tanfield Lea C20/2; "grafflin – searching for something with one's hand" *Graham* Geordie 1979

scrammel to **scramble**

exx. *Bell* MS Newc 1815, *Pitman's Pay* G'head 1820s, *CT* New Herrington 1930s; "nip intiv the sail locker there, scrammel ower the spare sails..." *Green* Wearside 1879 re C19/1

scran food

"rob them o' scran" *Pitman's Pay* G'head 1820s; "scran – food, victuals: 'scran-time' (meal-time)" *Atkinson* Cleve 1868; 'food' *Graham* Geordie 1979. Charver 2000-2002; "went to pick some scran up" (fast food?) N'd per BG 2004. *EDD* distribution to 1900: general, plus USA. [?Romany scran 'food']

scranch to crunch

"scranch – to grind any hard or crackling substance between the teeth" *Brockett* Newc & Nth 1829, Geeson, N'd/ D'm 1969. *EDD* distribution to 1900: general. [compare Flem. schranzen]. *Plus* "scranchings... the bits and pieces of hard fried batter which used to be found in a pennorth of chips" *AK* Newc 1950s; "scranchum – a sort of thin hard baked spice or ginger bread" *Bell* MS Newc 1815; "skranshum – overcooked pork skin" *Dodd* MS Tanfield Lea C20/2

scrat to scratch

exx. *Atkinson* Cleve 1868, *Geeson* N'd/ D'm 1969; "scratting around for odd jobs" *Wood* Tees 2002. *EDD* distribution to 1900: general. [?AN escrat – thus *Geeson*]. See also **scart**

screeners pit surface workers

"screeners" (surface workers who sorted coal by sizes) *Armstrong* Tanfield C19/2

scribbly jack etc. yellow-hammer

ex. Crook C20/2 Q; "scribble-chat – yellow-hammer" Newton Aycliffe 2001 Q. [from pattern on eggs?]

scringe to grate, to squeeze

"skreenge or skringe – to squeeze violently" *Brockett* Newc & Nth 1829; "scringed his teeth" *Armstrong* Tanfield C19/2; "when a boy sharpens his slate-pencil with a knife, he says it makes his teeth 'scringe'" *Palgrave* Hetton 1896; "skrinjed teeth – grated teeth" *Dodd* MS Tanfield Lea C20/2. *EDD* distribution to 1900: Sco, Ire, Yx, Mids, EA, Kt. [variant of cringe?]

scrog/gy bush(y)

"scrog – a stunted bush or shrub; scroggy – full of old stunted trees or bushes" *Brockett* Newc & Nth 1829; "scroggy – rugged, rough, rude, as scroggy briers" *Bell* MS Newc 1830s. *EDD* distribution to 1900: Sco, Ire, Nth, EA

scrow a mess

ex. *TP* Alston, 2003 [pron. 'au']. *EDD* as disorder, uproar

scrub to rub

"Where Aw horse the scrubbin full uns (tubs) / Up for eighteen pence a score" *Barrass* Stanley 1890s; "there wiz a fahl o' styen... an he gat scubb'd and scrush'd varry bad" *Embleton* Tyne 1897; "you scrub past broken timbers" *Moreland*, Dawdon 1980. [compare MDu schrubben]

scrudge to crowd

"Ye niver see'd the church sae scrudg'd as we wur there thegither" *Marshall* Newc 1823; "skrudge – to crowd or squeeze close" *Atkinson* Cleve 1868; "scrudge – nearly the same as 'scrounge'" *Luckley* Alnwick 1870s. *EDD* distribution to 1900: scrouge – general [Fr escrager, escracer (Atkinson)]

scrunch to crush or crowd together

"scrounge or scrunge – to crowd, to squeeze" *Brockett* Newc & Nth 1829; "'What are ye scroungin' us for?" *Luckley* Alnwick 1870s; *KH* Stockton C20/2. *EDD* distribution to 1900: general

scrush crush (noun and vb)

"scrubb'd and scrush'd varry bad" *Embleton* Tyne 1897; "skrush – crush" *Dodd* MS Tanfield Lea C20/2; 'a crush' *IA* S'm 1950s, 60s. *EDD* distribution to 1900: N.I., Notts, Essex, Dev. NE 2001: in use

scud 1. to speed, 2. to hit, 3. to skim

"to skud or skud away – to make haste" *Kennet* 1690s as Yorks; "scud – small clouds... or to run scudding along" *Bell* MS Newc 1815
2. "scudded 'em aal ower" (balls in a game) *GP* S'm 1950s; "scudded 'em – beat them up" S'm 1990s per BG. [compare Sco skudge, 'to buffet', Du schudden 'to shake']
3. "scud – to remove a superficial covering, (to skim with a spade)" *Atkinson* Cleve 1868

scudder a beating

ex. EP Southwick C20/mid

scufter to do fussily

ex. *Dinsdale* mid-Tees 1849.
EDD distribution to 1900: Nth

scug to hide

"skugg" *Bailey* Co.Durham 1810; "scug yourselves away" *Atkinson* Cleve 1868.
EDD distribution to 1900: Sco, Nth.
[ON skugge 'shadow']

scumfish to smother

"she thout she wad ha' been skumfeesht wi the steyth" *Bewick* Tyne 1790s; "scumfish – to smother, to suffocate with smoke" *Brockett* Newc & Nth 1829; "Aw was half scumfish'd wi' the stoor" *Luckley* Alnwick 1870s; "amaist scumfish'd" *Embleton* Tyne 1897; "skumfish – lack of air causing illness or death" *Dodd* MS Tanfield Lea C20/2; "to choke with smoke: 'The chimley's been smokin' till aa's fair scumfished'" *Graham* Geordie 1979; "fair scumfished – exhausted" Gateshead 2001 Q. *EDD* distribution to 1900: Sco, Nth, Lancs]
[AN descomforter 'to destroy, make grieve'].
See also **mafted, smoor**

scunner 1. a dislike, an aversion, etc., 2. to dislike

1. "dinna spier (ask) how things is gan for fear ye git a scunner (sharp answer)" *Northumbrian Words III* C20/mid re Kielder; "he's tyen a scunner at her" *Graham* Geordie 1979; "skunna – strong aversion to" *Dodd* MS Tanfield Lea

scunner cont.

C20/2. *EDD* distribution to 1900: Sco, N.I., N'd, Yx, Lx
2. "scunner – to nauseate, to feel disgust, to loathe; to shy, as a horse...; a man... who shrinks through fear" *Brockett* Newc & Nth 1829; "scunner – to be afraid, to turn from or avoid...' she never scunnered it'" *Bell* MS Newc 1830s; "Scunner – to flinch, or give signs of pain. 'He never scunnered that blow on the heed'" *Palgrave* Hetton 1896; 'to dislike, reject' *Dobson* Tyne 1973; "scunner – to shudder with dislike" Ashington 2001 Q. *EDD* distribution to 1900: Sco, Ire, N'd

scutboard stern of coble

'stout transverse board secured over the top of the stern... also scudboard' *Hill* Flamborough 1970s. *Plus* "scut-top not board" *FT* Cullercoats 2003; "scut" C/GR Amble C20/2. [ON scutr stem or stern of vessel; or from scut 'tail']

se see **so**

sea-coal 1. coal as opposed to charcoal, 2. coal shipped by sea, 3. coal found on the shore, 4. coal mined from under the sea

1. "sæ-col" (the mineral jet) ca. 1050; "carbo maris" (sea-coal) – coal as opposed to other fuels, Medival Latin; "carbones maritimi" Finchale (1358-9). [OE cól – any hot burning substance, wood, charcoal, etc.]
2. "The City of London, and Parts adjacent, as also all the South of England, are supplied with Coals, called therefore Sea-coal, from Newcastle upon Tyne, and from the coast of Durham and Northumberland." Defoe *Tour through the Whole Island of Great Britain* 1720s
3. "The vaynes of the se-coles be sometyme upon clives of the se, as round about Coket Island." Leland, C16; "Along the coast road between Sunderland and Seaham Harbour, we came upon quite a number of men riding or wheeling bicycles loaded with two or three small sacks of coal. I heard afterwards that these men descend very steep and dangerous cliffs near Seaham Harbour and pick up coal from the shore. They were now going to Sunderland to sell the coal."*JB* Priestley 1934; "recycled coal from sea-shore' *GP* S'm 1950s.
4. "sea coal – coal worked from under the bed of the sea" *Nicholson* 1880; 'coal from under the sea' Dawdon C20/2

sea-fret coastal fog

"Quite often in June sea-frets or fogs hide the sun from us when the days are longest" *Coulthard*, 1934, p.57; "sea-fret – a west mist or haze proceeding from the sea inland" *Brockett* Newc & Nth 1846; "sea-fret / fret – fine rain, heavy mist" *JB* Shildon C20/mid, *Graham* Geordie 1979, S'm 2000 per BG; "fret – a mist, or sea-fog" *Palgrave* Hetton 1896. *EDD* distribution to 1900: NE coast. NE 2001: in use

seaves rushes

"he began the seiues graythe" *Cuthbert* C15/mid; "seaves – rushes" *Kennet* 1690s as Nth; "seave – a rush; seavy – overgrown with rushes: 'seavy ground' (Hexhamshire)" *Brockett* Newc & Nth 1829; "seve-light – a rush light" *Atkinson* Cleve 1868. *EDD* distribution to 1900: Nth, Ches, Lincs. [ON sef]

sec such

"T' was seck a bang an' sec a flash" *Lakeland* re C'd C20; "en seck like" *Egglestone* Weardale 1870s; "sek – such" *JB* Shildon C20/mid. *EDD* distribution to 1900: seck – N'd, C'd. W'd. [OE swelc]. See also **so**

see

"aw so" (I saw) *Bewick* Tyne 1790s; "And Ralphey fra St Nich'las spire / Seed aw the world around him" *Marshall* Newc 1823 p.18; "Aw seed it" *Brockett* Newc & Nth 1829, *NWC* 16 Jan 1886, Sup., p.5, *Dunn* B'p Auck 1950, *Dodd* MS Tanfield Lea C20/2, etc.

seem'ly seemingly

'common for apparently' *Palgrave* Hetton 1896

seggy second

"seggy – second (in children's games)" *Wood* Cleve 2002

segs blakeys, half-moon of metal to fit front and back of soles of shoes

"there was nothing quite like sliding to school on your segs making nice sparks for all of 2 days before they became quite blunt" (seaham.com website 2002). [segment]

sel' self

ex. *Ray* 1674; "by the sel on't" (under its own power, by itself) *Allan's Tyneside Songs* p.203 1827; "sell – pronoun, self: mysell, hissell,

sel' cont.

hersell, yoursell. Plural, sells" *Brockett* Newc & Nth 1829

selled, selt sold

"sell'd" *Meriton* nYx 1683; "Sen t' horses was selt" *Lakeland* re C'd 1856. NE 2001: in use. [OE selde (pret.)]

sen since

"sen, sin, sune – since" *Brockett* Newc & Nth 1829; "sen-sine, sin-sine – since such and such a time" *Atkinson* Cleve 1868" *Atkinson* Cleve 1868

set 1. to accompany someone, or start them on their way, 2. to employ (set on), 3. to propel, 4. to put in place, 5. to free (set away)

1. "The did me entreat / to set them up street" *Street Piracy* (Newcastle, 1822); 'to accompany one a part of the distance he is going' *Dinsdale* mid-Tees 1849; "I will set you home", "I was setten part of the way" *Atkinson* Cleve 1868; "She knew that he wad wait ootside, te ... set hor hyem" *Barrass* Stanley 1890s; "set yi yem? – take you home?" *Dodd* MS Tanfield Lea C20/2
2. "Gan down to Scotty Owen / He's sure to set yer on" *Lore and language* re Houghton Pit, 1920s
3. "set – to propel, to push forward: 'setting a keel' *Brockett* Newc & Nth 1829
4. "aw wish thou wad set some buttons o' my trousers" *Green* Wearside 1879 re C19/1; "Set is the ordinary expression for 'put' e.g. 'set on the dishes', 'set out the fowls' (drive them out of doors), etc." *Palgrave* Hetton 1896
5. "th' ducks must be awl set away" (freed) *Armstrong* Tanfield C19/2

set a sequence of tubs

"the full set... of 65 tubs" *Hitchin* re Seaham 1930s p.109; 'a number of tubs the manager decides shall be hauled by any electric or compressed driven hauler' *McBurnie* Glebe Colliery, C20/mid; "bump the set – get into trouble" *Dodd* MS Tanfield Lea C20/2

set pot washing vessel

'iron pot set in brickwork with fire grate under to boil washing' *CT* New Herrington 1930s; 'a large iron bowl incased in brick, with a fire underneath, used for boiling' Spennymoor C20/mid; "large cast iron bowl with wooden lid; filled with water, fire set

set pot cont.

underneath for washing clothes" *GP* S'm C20/mid

seugh a channel

"seugh or saugh – a wet ditch; also a sub-terranean vault or channel, cut through a hill to drain a mine" *Grose* 1787. *EDD* distribution to 1900: Sco, N'd, C'd, Lx, Ches. [compare Du zoeg]

seun soon

"seughn, seun" *Bewick* Tyne 1790s; "seun empty" *Allan's Tyneside Songs* p.191 1824; "syun" Durham 1916; "syun" Tanfield Lea 1960, etc.

shackle wrist

"shackle – the wrist; Scots, shackle-bone – the wrist bone" *Brockett* Newc & Nth 1829; "shackle b'yan – wrist bone" *Dinsdale* mid-Tees 1849; "shekel – wrist" *MG* Teesdale C20/2. [abbrev. of shackle-bone]

shades curtains

"shaids" *Dodd* MS Tanfield Lea C20/2. *EDD* distribution to 1900: eD'm, nYx, wYx

shale 1. to drag feet, 2. to peel

1. "shale – to drag or scrape feet on ground esp. shaling" *Dinsdale* mid-Tees 1849. *EDD* distribution to 1900: general.
2. "shale – to peel, to shell" *Brockett* Newc & Nth 1829

shall 1. positive forms, 2. negative forms

1. "this sall be thine" *Cuthbert* C15/mid; "I's gie ye..." *Bell* Newc 1812 p.38; "wese – we will or shall" *Brockett* Newc & Nth 1829; "Ise – I shall, and sometimes I am" *Brockett* Newc & Nth 1846; "ye shud only seen us gannin'" *Allan's Tyneside Songs* p.451 1862. *EDD* distribution to 1900: sall – Sco, Nth
2. "ye shanna gan aside us" *Marshall* G'head 1806; "sannot – shall not" *Dinsdale* mid-Tees 1849

shangy 1. a disturbance, 2. scrap iron

1. "shangy – a hubbub or row or crowdy main where one fights over another" *Bell* MS Newc 1815. *EDD* distribution to 1900: N'd
2. "shangy – scrap iron" Newc 2001 Q

sharen, share cow dung

"sharen... cow sharen – cow dung" *Bell* MS Newc 1815; "Share – cow-dung" *Palgrave* Hetton 1896. *EDD* distribution to 1900: general. [OE scearn, ON skarn]. *Plus* "scarn-bcc – a beetle" *Brockett* Newc & Nth 1846

sharp sudden, quick

"mak' sharp! – make haste!" *Atkinson* Cleve 1868; "[Aal sharp did] – /Aa:l shaap dae:d/ – I'll do it quickly" *Palgrave* Hetton 1896; "mak sharp – get a move on" *Dunn* B'p Auck 1950; "ye're reet, it's sharper that way" S'm 2003 per BG

shart shirt

"sharte" *Anderson* Newcastle 1568; "my shart lap" (shirt tail) *Errington* p.67 Felling/Heworth re 1800s; "sharts and shifts were wet wi' sweet" (at dancing) *Allan's Tyneside Songs* p.155 1827 "wiv the varry sharts on that they were born in" (stripped to the waist) *Wearside Tales* 1879; "shairt" *JR* Crook C20/mid; "shart" *JS* re Sacriston C20/2, Dinnington 1950s Q, etc. *Plus* "body shart – vest" *JO* re High Thornley/Rowland's Gill 1930s–1940s in *Nth Words*; "at the face they generally wore a body shart (sleeved vest) and pit hoggers (cotton pants fastened below the knee with tape)" *Northumbrian III* C20/mid re Winlaton/Marley Hill

shearers, shears automatic face cutting machines in the mines

"it's AFC's and shearers that cut and load the coal" Moreland, Dawdon 1980; "Oh! me lads ye shud see 'em gannin / The shears fra the 'retreaters' leave the advancin faces stannin" *Taylor* Dawdon C20/2

sheelie see **chaffinch**

shem shame

ex. *Brockett* 1829 re Newc; "for shem", "shem o' them" *Barrass* Stanley 1890s; "I was shem – embarrassed, ashamed" S'd 2001 Q. *EDD* distribution to 1900: in this pronunciation Sco, Ire, N'd

shibbin'-leather shoe-lace

ex. *Dinsdale* mid-Tees 1849; "shibb'n" *Atkinson* Cleve 1868. *EDD* distribution to 1900: D'm, Yx. [shoe-band]. See also **whang**

shiel seasonal shelter

"About the beginynge of Aprill they take the moste parte of there cattell & go with them upe onto highe landes – towarde the Borders of Scotlands, & there buylde them lodges or sheales." *Raine* MS 1542; "as it were Nomades... who frome the moneth of Aprill unto August, lye out scattering and summering (as they tearme it) with their cattell in little cottages here and there which they call Sheales and Shealings" Camden 1600 qu. Reed *Border Ballads* p.27; "shiel, shieling – originally a temporary hut or cabin for those who had the care of sheep on the moors" *Brockett* Newc & Nth 1829; "shield – such turf houses as shepherds build to watch their flocks on the moors, also fishermen's houses" *Bell* MS Newc 1830s; "The word 'shiel', from which Shields is derived, means a shelter, in this case for fishermen" *Coulthard* p.125–6 1934. [ME schéle – ?southernisation of ON skále, or skiól 'a shelter']

Shields South and North Shields

"Up wi' smoky Shields" *Allan's Tyneside Songs* p.31 1812; "sum keelmen wer' gaun doon te Sheels" *Allan's Tyneside Songs* p.219 1827; "tegether like the folks iv Sheels" *Allan's Tyneside Songs* p.237 1829

shifter 1. part-time pit worker; surface worker, 2. superintendant

1. "shifters – underground workmen employed at miscellaneous work, such as timbering rolleyways, taking up bottom stone or taking down top to make height where necessary, setting doors, building stoppings, redding falls, &c." *Nicholson* 1880; "Aw'm a poor aud shifter noo" *Barrass* Stanley 1890s
2. "mahsta shifta – in charge of night shift" *Dodd* MS Tanfield Lea C20/2; "master-shifter – a person who has responsible charge of the mine during the night" *Nicholson* 1880. *EDD* distribution to 1900: N'd, D'm

shiggy to wriggle

"shiggy down ropes" Newc 1940s via AK; "shiggy sweets out of a bag" *BL* Spennymoor C20/mid

shigs shares

"shigs and arters" (share of left-over apple-core, etc.) South Shields C20/2 Q

shill to shell

"shill – to shell (peas)" *Dinsdale* mid-Tees 1849; 'to separate, to shell' *Atkinson* Cleve 1868; "shillin' them beans" *Wearside Tales* 1879. *EDD* distribution to 1900: general

shippen cow-house

exx. Ray 1674, *Brockett* Newc & Nth 1829. *EDD* distribution to 1900: general. [OE scypen]

shire to decant

"Shire – to pour off water or any liquid in such a way as to leave the sediment" *Palgrave* Hetton 1896. *EDD* distribution to 1900: Sco, Ire, Nth. [OE scíran 'to clarify']

shirley way of working a coal-pile

"shirley – [to] repeatedly shovel mixture of coal and coal dust to top of pile, to reveal larger pieces of coal" *JB* Shildon C20/mid

shive a slice

"a shive oh butter an breed" *Bewick* Tyne 1790s, sim. *Graham* Geordie 1979; "shive – a slice, as [of] a loaf, an apple, a turnip (ON skífa)" *Atkinson* Cleve 1858; "It is easy from a cut loaf to steal a shive" *Palgrave* Hetton 1896; exx. *AT* Co.D'm C20/mid, Ferryhill 2001 Q. *EDD* distribution to 1900: general. [ON skíva, OFris skíve]

shog, shoggle to jog

"shoggle – to shake, to joggle" *Brockett* Newc & Nth 1829; "shog, shoggle" *Atkinson* Cleve 1868; "shog" *Wearside Tales* 1879. *EDD* distribution to 1900: general

shoon shoes

"my half shoon" *Collier's Rant* Newc C18/2; "to cobble their canny pit shoon" *Bell* Newc 1812 p.39; "Her high-heel'd shoon wi' buckles breet", "half-shoon – old shoes with the toes cut off" *Pitman's Pay* G'head 1820s; "shun" *MG* Teesdale C20/2. *EDD* distribution to 1900: in this form, Sco, Ire, Nth, Mids. [OE plural scón (pronounced 'shoon')]

shoor sure

"Awze sure of thee impidence!" *Bewick* Tyne 1790s; "Aw shoor aw dinnot knaw what the lads are gettin' to now" *JS* South Shields C19/mid; "aw shoor aw will" *Armstrong* Tanfield C19/2; "Aa's shooer!" S'm 2003 via BG

shoother shoulder

"braid shouthers" *Bewick* Tyne 1790s; "strite frae the shoother" *Barrass* Stanley 1890s. *EDD* distribution to 1900: in this pronunciation esp. Sco, N'd, Lx, Ches. *Plus* "shull-bane – the shoulder bone" *Brockett* Newc & Nth 1829

shot to throw

"shot it over here will you?" *PG* H'pool 1998, as commoner than 'hoy'

shotstick rod to ram charge etc., home

"Shotstick – a round stick on which a paper cartridge is rolled (mining term)" *Palgrave* Hetton 1896; "he chased me wi' the shot-stick/ But Aw lick'd him te the flat!" *Barrass* Stanley 1892

shuggy swing 1. **shuggy**, 2. **shuggy shew**, 3. **shuggy-boat**

1. "Give me a shuggy... a 'shuggy' is also a see-saw" *Palgrave* Hetton 1896; "a swing is a 'shuggy' [in mining villages]... on Tyneside it is a 'hiky'." *Nth Words* 1938
2. "shuggy-shew – a swing" *Grose* 1787; 'a swing for children' *Bell* MS Newc 1815; 'a swing, a long rope fastened at each end and thrown over a beam' *Brockett* Newc & Nth 1829; "gannin' up in a shuggy shoo" *Robson* Newc C20/1. *EDD* distribution to 1900: Sco, Ire, M'd, nYx, Northants
3. "shuggy-boat – small fairground swing for two children, with upholstered ropes like bell-ropes" *JB* Shildon C20/mid; 'those big boat-like swings that a number of people can get in that you get at old-fashioned fairgrounds' *PG* H'pool C20/2; "lorchin like a shuggyboat" *Dobson* Tyne 1969; "shuggyboat – a swing... with seats across like a boat" *Graham* Geordie 1979. *EDD* distribution to 1900: N'd, Tyne. NE 2001: in use

shull, shool shovel

"on[e] dozen shoolis" *Raine* MS Durham City 1543-54; "spades, shewlys & gades" *Durham* C16/2; "shull or shuil – a spade or shovel" *Brockett* Newc & Nth 1829; "showell" *CT* New Herrington 1930s; "shool" Tanfield Lea, 1960; "a shyeul o' coal" *Dobson* Tyne 1969. *EDD* distribution to 1900: general. [OE scufl]

si— see also under **sy—**

sic, sicken such

"for euery sik defaute" *Anderson* Newcastle 1480; "to play them sicken a part" *RR* Weardale 1569; "in sike a fear" Rothbury C18/2; "sic, sik, sike – such" *Brockett* Newc & Nth 1829; "sik (with long 'i'), sike – such; sikan before vowels" *Atkinson* Cleve 1868; "Av nivvor knaan sike like – never known anything like it" *Dunn* B'p Auck 1950. *EDD* distribution to 1900: sic – Sco, Ire, Nth; sike – Yx, Lx. [OE swilc]. *Plus* "sic-leyke fwoak" (similar) *Bewick* Tyne 1790s. See also **sec**

siddle to pick out

"Siddle – to pick out or choose the best of anything" *Palgrave* Hetton 1896

sill base statum

"sill – (in mining) the bed" *Bell* MS Newc 1815. *EDD* distribution to 1900: N'd, D'm, C'd, Staffs. [OE, ON syll]

sile see **syle**

siller silver

"siller buckles on his knee" 'Bobby Shaftoe' C18; "silla, silva – silver" *Dodd* MS Tanfield Lea C20/2. *EDD* distribution to 1900: in this pronunciation Sco, N'd, C'd

sin syne ago, since then

"sixty years sin seyne" *Bewick* Tyne 1790s; "sine – afterwards" *Brockett* Newc & Nth 1829; "Sin – since, ago" *Palgrave* Hetton 1896. *EDD* distribution to 1900: since – Sco, Ire, Nth, EA

sind to rinse

"sind – to wash out, to rinse" *Brockett* Newc & Nth 1829, *Dinsdale* mid-Tees 1849. *EDD* distribution to 1900: Sco, Nth. [ME sind]

singin' hinny cake with currants

"singing hinny – a cake made of flour, butter and currants and baked on a girdle – and gets their name from the quantity of butter causing them to fizz on the girdle – sometimes called 'spice fizzers'" *Bell* MS Newc 1815; "strang lyac'd tea and singin' hinnies" *Pitman's Pay* G'head 1820s; "singin-hinnie or stinging-hinny – a rich kneaded cake; indispensable in a pitman's family" *Brockett* Newc & Nth 1829; "Maw granny likes spice singin' hinnies" *Crawhall* Newc 1888; "Singing hinny – a kind of girdle-cake, common among old folk. (Name imported from the North.) Now generally called Spice Cake" *Palgrave* Hetton 1896

sipe to leak or ooze out

"to sipe – to soak or drain. 'to sipe thro'"
Kennet 1690s as Nth; "sipe – to drain a pot
or other vessel: "he's siping the pots" i.e. he's
draining the pots after other people's drinking" *Bell* MS Newc 1815; "sipe – to leak, to
ooze or drain out slowly through a small
crevice" *Brockett* Newc & Nth 1829; "The
watter's sipin' oot" *Palgrave* Hetton 1896.
EDD distribution to 1900: Sco, Nth, EA.
[OE sypian]. *Plus* "sipings – the drainings of
a vessel after any fluid has been poured out
of it" *Bailey* Co.Durham 1810; "siping – a very
small feeder of water" *Nicholson* 1880

sivin etc. seven

"seevent" (seventh) *Bewick* Tyne 1790s;
"seeben" *Egglestone*, Weardale 1870s; "sivin"
Dobson Tyne 1972; "sivinty" *Armstrong* Tanfield
C19/2. *EDD* distribution to 1900: in this
pronunciation esp. Ire

sk— see also under **sc—**

skabbee underhand tactics

ex. *Dodd* MS Tanfield Lea C20/2.
EDD distribution to 1900: N'd, Lx, Mids

skale to spread

"to skale – skaling – to dress on clean grass
land in the Spring intended to be laid away
for meadows" *Bell* MS Newc 1815

skane, skeen to shell

'to cut shell fish out the the shell' (*EDD*);
"we're skaning mussels" nYx 1873 per *EDD*;
"skeen or scaled mussels" *JH* S'm C20/mid;
"skaning – cleaning limpets for use as bait"
Amble per BG 2003. [perhaps from Gaelic
sgain 'a knife']

skankin' disgusting

"skankin – foul-smelling, bad, stinking"
Charver 2000–2002

skate a kite

"scate – a paper kite" *Bell* MS Newc 1815;
"Paper-skyetts" (kites) *Crawhall* Newc 1888.
[?variant of kite]

skeel wooden pail

"skeel – a cylindrical milking pail, with a
handle made by one of the staves being a little
longer than the rest" *Bailey* Co.Durham 1810;
"Skeel – a peculiarly-shaped bucket (broader

skeel cont.

at bottom than top, with upright stave projecting from rim, to serve as a handle), formerly
used in colliery villages to carry water for
household use. They were carried on women's
heads on a 'wase', and a piece of wood was
made to float on the top, to prevent the water
from splashing over" *Palgrave* Hetton 1896.
EDD distribution to 1900: Sco, Nth, wMids.
[ON skjóla 'pail']

skeet a guide runner

'wooden lining for pit shaft' *GP* S'm C20/mid;
"skeets – cage guides in pit shaft" *Dodd* MS
Tanfield Lea C20/2. *EDD* distribution to 1900:
N'd, D'm. *Plus* 'skid, transverse log or sleeper
used for launching [a coble]' *Hill* Flamborough
1970s. [?ON skjótt 'swift']

skeets boots

"skeets – boots esp. football boots" Newc
2001 Q

skeffin' nasty

"skeffin' – disgusting, generally" *TR* Deneside
2004

skeg a glance

"skeg – a quick glance: 'have a skeg'" *Wood*
Cleve 2002. *EDD* distribution to 1900: Yx

skelly to squint

"she skelly's wiv her eyes" *Allan's Tyneside Songs*
p.149 1827. *EDD* distribution to 1900: Sco,
Ire, Nth. [?from ON; compare Norw skjelga]

skelp to slap or hit

"skelp 'im and batter 'im" *Allan's Tyneside
Songs* p.70 1805; "the drums they're skelpin"
Marshall G'head 1806; "skelp – to slap, to
strike with the open hand" *Bailey* Co.Durham
1810; "skelp – to beat – as that child deserves
to be skelped" *Bell* MS Newc 1830s; "the
roondie an' the small Aw skelps off the back-
end" *Barrass* Stanley 1890s; "aa had mare
than me share o' skelpins" *Robson* Newc
C20/1; "Aal skelp thee lug'ole" *Dunn* B'p
Auck 1950; 'to strike with the open hand
particularly on the behind or the cheek'
Graham Geordie 1979. *EDD* distribution to
1900: Sco, Ire, Nth, Mids. NE 2001: in use.
[compare Ice. sklefa]

skemmy pigeon

"see the skemmies tiv his duckit flee" Tyne *MC* May 1881; "Skemmy – the common blue or farmer's pigeon, often kept by boys as a pet" *Palgrave* Hetton 1896; "he (the miner) gambles with his pigeons or 'skemmies'" *Coulthard* p.71 1934; "skemmie would be a poor bird, a bird below standard" South Moor (Stanley) 2003 per BG. *EDD* distribution to 1900: N'd, D'm. *Plus* "skemmie... thin/small/weak" *CT* New Herrington 1930s. See also **cushat**

skep 1. basket, 2. frame for winding long baited line on prior to fishing

1. "skepe – a basket...made of whicker work or rushes" Finchale 1397; "she bair thre skepful of sand to the said alter" *Raine* MS Sedgefield 1570; "skep – a basket of rushes or wicker work" *Brockett* Newc & Nth 1829; 'a basket of willow or flag-fabric' *Atkinson* Cleve 1868; "skep – cattle-feeder" Teesdale 2001 Q. *EDD* distribution to 1900: general. NE 2001: low use. [OE sceppe, ON skeppa]. See also **bee-hive**
2. 'willow pallet on which a baited long line was coiled' *Hill* Flamborough 1970s; Yorx 2003 per BG. *Plus* "swill not skep" *FT* Cullercoats 2003; "swole – box or frame for lines" *C/GR* Amble C20/2

skeul 1. school, 2. to gamble

1. "skeul" *Bewick* Tyne 1790s; "trainin skeals fur thievs an pickpockets" *MWN* 3 Mar 1860; "has thee been skyul?", "skiul-boss – teacher" *Dunn* B'p Auck 1950. *EDD* distribution to 1900: in this pronunciation Yx, C'd
2. "skyull'd away the pay" Tyne *MC* May 1881

skilly gruel, thin porridge

"skilly – oatmeal and water" *Robson 1849* Tyne; "Wat is breed en skilly for / But just te muaik ye smaul?" (re prison) *Armstrong* Tanfield C19/2; "Skilly is very weak compared [to crowdie]" *Nth Words* Blyth, 1938; "skillee – soup (jail)" *Dodd* MS Tanfield Lea C20/2. *EDD* distribution to 1900: general / slang. NE 2001: in low use. [from skilligalee]

skinch 'pax' (a truce) in children's games

"Skinch – meaning he is not liable to be caught and made prisoner" *Palgrave* Hetton 1896; "skinch on high, skinch on wood" att. *GP* S'm C20/mid; "skinch was common in our

skinch cont.

street in Easington, you crossed your fingers as you claimed it" *JS* Easington C20/mid; "skincheez" (pax) *Dobson* Tyne 1970–71. *Plus* "kingy – truce" *Wood* Eaglescliffe 2002

skipper captain of a boat

"The keels were generally manned by the skipper, two keel bullies and a boy known as the 'Pee-Dee'" *Mitcalfe* p.3 re 1822; "if owt in the keel was deun rang, the skipper wad curse" *Allan's Tyneside Songs* p.153 1827. *EDD* distribution to 1900: esp. Sco, N'd. [MDu schipper]

skit sarcasm, practical joking, etc.

"took some skit – meant took some scoff or leg pulling" *JS* Easington 1950s. *EDD* distribution to 1900: general

skite exit (noun and vb)

"I cam aboard the Admiral and bade them stryke in the Kyngys name of England, and they bade me skyte..." 1449 *English Trade* pp.274–5; "The putter lad had teun his skite" *Barrass* Stanley 1890s; "skite off – run away" *ER* M'bro C20/2, Teesside 2001 Q. *EDD* distribution to 1900: N'd, C'd, Yx. [ON skýt— with sense 'shoot'; or compare Norw. skit 'dirt, filth']

skitter/s diarrhoea

"skitter – (verb)... vulgar name for the diarrhoea" *Brockett* Newc & Nth 1829; "the screaming skitters" *Dobson* Tyne 1970; "inter-intestinal skitters" *Dobson* Tyne 1972; "the gallowa... skitters there an' awl" Moreland, Dawdon 1980. *EDD* distribution to 1900: Sco, C'd, Yx, S.W.

skrike yell

"at what tyme the said Herrison wyfe gave a skrike" *Raine* MS Lanchester ca.1573; "[he] gave a skrike, & turned round, & fell downe dead" *Raine* MS EYorks, 1668; "Aw gav a skrike" *Allan's Tyneside Songs* p.182 1824; 'to shriek or crie out' *Bell* MS Newc 1830s; 'to scream, shriek' *Atkinson* Cleve 1868; "he gav a greet skrike" *Embleton* Tyne 1897. *EDD* distribution to 1900: Sco, Ire, Nth, Mids. [ON skrikja 'to scream', compare Norw. skrika (vb)]

slabs, slabstones sink and draining board

ex. *GP* S'm 1950s

sladder to spill

ex. *Blenkinsopp* Teesdale 1931.
EDD distribution to 1900: Nth

sladdery muddy

"sladdery walking" *Brockett* Newc & Nth
1829; "sladdery – dirty, muddy, e.g. of road"
Dinsdale mid-Tees 1849; 'muddy' *Blenkinsopp*
Teesdale 1931

slaister to do s.thing poorly

"slaistering – doing any thing in a awkward,
untidy manner" *Brockett* Newc & Nth 1829;
"slayster – leaves work in unfinished state"
(?noun) *Nth Words* N'd, 1938; "a lax/languid/
sluggish way of going about one's work –
'slaisterin about with that bucket and mop'"
BJ re Cockfield C20/mid; "howay man gie
ower slaisterin' on – dragging the feet" *Dunn*
B'p Auck 1950; "slaistering – to trail feet"
Weardale, Teesdale 2001 Q. *EDD* distribution
to 1900: Sco, Nth

slake tidal mud

"slake – accumulation of mud or slime,
especially in a river" *Brockett* Newc & Nth
1829; 'soft muddy ground left bare by the tide
EDD 1900; "Jarra Slax" *Irwin* Tyne 1970–71.
EDD distribution to 1900: Sco, N'd, Tyne,
D'm, C'd

slape slippery

'slippery, smooth' *Brockett* Newc & Nth
1829; "as slape as glass" *Atkinson* Cleve 1868.
EDD distribution to 1900: Nth and parts of
Mids. NE 2001: not in use. [ON sleipur]
See also **slippy**

slaita slater

"slaita – roof repairer" *Dodd* MS Tanfield Lea
C20/2

slavver 1. to drool, dribble, 2. to talk nonsense,
3. nonsense

1. "remarks on slavering" Bedlington, 1761;
"blutherin and sl[a]verin" (of a baby) *Bewick*
Tyne 1790s; "Slavering Nell" *Marshall* G'head
1806; "slaver – to eject saliva from the mouth"
Atkinson Cleve 1868. *EDD* distribution to 1900:
general. [?ON; compare Ice. slafra]
2. "ye slaverin cull" (talking nonsense)
Allan's Tyneside Songs p.221 1827; "slavverin'
on" (talking nonsense) *GP* S'm C20/mid.
EDD distribution to 1900: Yx, Lincs

slavver cont.

3. "slavva – drivel" *Dodd* MS Tanfield Lea
C20/2; "slavver – saliva; cheek, impudence;
or just talk" *Wood* Tees 2002

sleck small coal

"sleck – small pit-coal" *Ray* 1674, *Grose*
1787, *Dodd* MS Tanfield Lea C20/2.
EDD distribution to 1900: esp. Nth, Mids.
[?Flem. sleck]

sleck to quench

"sleck – to cool in water; to quench: 'to sleck
your thirst'" *Brockett* Newc & Nth 1829;
Atkinson Cleve 1868. See also **slocken**

sled pit transport

"sled or sledge – a wooden frame upon
which the corves were drawn previous to
the introduction of wheels and rails, and still
used occasionally in leading to a stow-board"
Nicholson 1880

slee sly

"If they be never so slee" *Noah's Ark* Newc
C15/16; "he was sorry that he had dronke
to anie such slee carle as he was" *Raine* MS
Langhorsley 1606; "slee" Durham 1916, *Dodd*
MS Tanfield Lea C20/2. *EDD* distribution to
1900: in this pronunciation Sco, N'd, D'm,
C'd

slem poorly done

"slem – to work shoddily" *Blenkinsopp* Teesdale
1931; "slem – bad, ill-done (of work); untrust-
worthy (of a worker)" *Atkinson* Cleve 1868.
EDD distribution to 1900: Lakes, Yx

slip pinafore

"slip – a child's pinafore" *Brockett* Newc & Nth
1829; "slip – a sort of child's apron" *Luckley*
Alnwick 1870s; "a pinafore was a 'slip'" *Nth
Words* Northumberland, 1938; *Graham*
Geordie 1979

slippy slippery

exx. *Brockett* Newc & Nth 1829, *Luckley* Alnwick
1870s; "Slippy – slippery (always used)"
Palgrave Hetton 1896. *EDD* distribution to
1900: general. NE 2001: in common use

slocken to quench

"a fyre to slokyn" *Cuthbert* C15/mid; "the lime
was slockened" *Raine* MS Newcastle 1654; 'to
put out or extinguish' *Kennet* 1690s as Nth;

slocken cont.

"Get slocken'd lads! fadder pays aw'." *Bells* (nC'd) 1815; "to slocken your thirst" *Brockett* Newc & Nth 1829; "monny watters cannut slocken luv" *Moore* Weardale 1859; "wad he' slockened ony bit drouth 'at he might a had" *Haldane* Newc 1879. *EDD* distribution to 1900: Sco, Ire, Nth, eMids. [ON slokna]. See also **sleck**

slogger to walk untidily

"Slogger – to walk with the stockings hanging loosely" *Palgrave* Hetton 1896. *EDD* distribution to 1900: Sco, N'd, D'm, Northants

slush 1. hardworking / hardworker, 2. to work hard, 3. a greedy drinker

1. "slush hewer – a hard working coal miner" Wade *South Moor* C20/mid; "The slush, ay!" cried aud Bill McGee / He works ower hard, ne doot..." *Barrass* Stanley 1890s. *EDD* distribution to 1900: Yx
2. "Aw slush an' fill like fire and fun" *Barrass* Stanley 1890s. *EDD* distribution to 1900: Yx
3. "slush – a person greedy of drink" *Pitman's Pay* G'head 1820s; 'a reproachful term for a dirty person, a greedy eater' *Brockett* Newc & Nth 1829; 'a greedy eater or drinker' *Luckley* Alnwick 1870s. *EDD* distribution to 1900: Nth

smack to taste

"an' smack'd the yell" (ale) *Allan's Tyneside Songs* p.299 1831. *EDD* distribution to 1900: Sco, Lakes. [OE smæc (noun)] See also **smatch**

smally small

"a smally bairn" *Brockett* Newc & Nth 1829; "smally – little, puny, undergrown" *Atkinson* Cleve 1868; "Aw'm just a smaaly laddy" *Barrass* Stanley 1890s; "Smally (smaa:li): 'That's a smally bit bairn'" *Palgrave* Hetton 1896. *EDD* distribution to 1900: Sco, NE

smash to crush

ex. Bailey D'm 1810. [compare Norw. smaska 'to crush']. See also **oaths**

smasher fruit pie about 4 inches diameter

"smasher – a small standing pie of goose-berries" *Bell MS* Newc 1815. *EDD* distribution to 1900: N'd, nYx

smatch 1. to overcook, 2. flavour (noun)

1. "smatched – bit burned, off-taste" *Blenkinsopp* Teesdale 1931

smatch cont.

2. "smatch – a savour, flavour or taste: 'a smatch o' London'" *Atkinson* Cleve 1868. *EDD* distribution to 1900: esp. Nth, Mids. [OE smæc]. See also **smack**

smit 1. any infection, 2. to infect

1. "smit, smittle – infection" *Brockett* Newc & Nth 1829; "Smit – an infectious disease: 'He'll get the smit'" (i. e. catch the disease) *Palgrave* Hetton 1896; "got the smit" (a cold) *CT* New Herrington 1930s; "more precisely 'the smit,' e.g. the flu – but, yes, it's any infection: 'he's got the smit'" *PG* H'pool C20/2. *EDD* distribution to 1900: Sco, D'm, Yx. [OE smitte 'polution']. *Plus* "smit was also used in taking a fancy to a young man or woman to the extent that they eventually clicked and went out steady" *JS* Easington C20/mid; "got the smit – pregnant" S'd 2001 Q
2. "smit, smittle – to infect" *Brockett* Newc & Nth 1829; "smit – to infect" *Dinsdale* mid-Tees 1849; *Todd* Tyne 1977

smittle, smittlish 1. contagious, 2. to infect, 3. infection (noun)

1. "smittleish – infectious" *Grose* 1787; "smittle, smittlish – infectious, contagious" *Brockett* Newc & Nth 1829; "its smittal when owt new o' that kind's started" *Haldane* Newc 1879; "Is't smittle?" (Is it catching?) *Palgrave* Hetton 1896; "smittle – infectious Upper Teesdale Q 2001. *EDD* distribution to 1900: Sco, Nth
2. "smittle – to infect" *Ray* 1674; *Atkinson* Cleve 1868. *EDD* distribution to 1900: Sco, Nth, eMids
3. "smittle – infection" *Dinsdale* mid-Tees 1849; *Atkinson* Cleve 1868. *EDD* distribution to 1900: D'm, Yx

smock shift

"smock – the under linen of a female" *Brockett* Newc & Nth 1829. *EDD* distribution to 1900: general. See also **sark**

smoggies the people of Teesside

ex. *Wood* 2003

smoor to smother

exx. *Bell MS* Newc 1815, *Dinsdale* mid-Tees 1849; "smoor, smorr, smurr – to smother" *Atkinson* Cleve 1868. *EDD* distribution to 1900: Sco, Ire, Nth, eMids, EA. [?MDu smören]. See also **scumfish**

snake stones ammonites

"snake-stones – petrified shell fish or ammonites" *Brockett* Newc & Nth 1829, *Atkinson* Cleve 1868. *EDD* distribution to 1900: nYx and parts of Mids

snagger a knife for harvesting turnips with a an extra point on the back of the blade

"when the ground was frosty, the point was stuck in the turnip to get a grip to pull it out by, then the blade side was used to top and tail it" *SM* Ho'ton/Penshaw C20/mid. *EDD* distribution to 1900: Sco, C'd, Yx. [?ON; compare Norw. snag 'spike']. See also **turnip**

snanny, snammy, snarter see **turnip**

sneck door latch: 1. noun, 2. verb

1. "gat hyem... and when lifting the sneck..." *Allan's Tyneside Songs* p.142 1816; "sneck – the latch or fastening of a door or gate" *Brockett* Newc & Nth 1829; "sneck – the latch (small bar of metal) of a door or wicket" *Atkinson* Cleve 1868" *Atkinson* Cleve 1868; "lift t' snek en cum in" *Egglestone* Weardale 1870s; "Aa lifted the sneck an' waaked reet in" *Other Eye* Newc ca.1890; "sneck – horizontal bar at an outdoor gate *plus* the pivoted thumb-lever which lifts the sneck... 'rattle the sneck' – vibrate the thumb-lever without "lifting the 'latch' to draw attention to caller" *JB* Shildon C20/mid; "netty sneck" *IA* S'm 1950s,60s; "my dad always used to tell me not to leave the sneck up when I went to his allotment i.e. keep the gate securely closed" *RM* Norton C20/mid; "sneck-lifter – the price of a pint" *Crocker* Tees 1983; "cage sneck – a movable part of the cage by which the tubs are kept in the cage during their passage in the shaft" *Nicholson* 1888; "he clambered up it (i.e. backyard gate), using the sneck for a toe-hold" *Cate* p.70 B'p Auckland area 1987; "sneck – catch on a yale lock" *GD* S'm 2002. *EDD* distribution to 1900: Sco, Ire, Nth, Mids, EA; as vb – Sco, Nth, Mids. NE 2001: in use. [ME sneck 'latch', compare OE twí-snæcce 'two-pronged']. *Plus* "sneck in snout – expression meaning a spanner in the works" Spennymoor C20/mid; compare "a sneck before one's snout" *EDD* C'd, Yx, Derbys, 1900. See also **nose, snib**
2. "sneck – latch [the door]" *Ray* 1674; "to sneck a door – to shut it, or latch it" *Kennet* 1690s as Nth; "...it is also used as a verb: 'to sneck the door'" *Brockett* Newc & Nth 1829

sned 1. to cut, 2. handle

1. "sned – to lop, to cut: 'to sned sticks'" *Brockett* Newc & Nth 1829; "sneddin' – fine line, offcuts of fishing line" *GP* S'm 1950s. *EDD* distribution to 1900: Sco, Ire, Nth. [OE snædan]
2. "sned – the long shank or handel of a scythe" *Brockett* Newc & Nth 1829. *EDD* distribution to 1900: snead – general

snedder slim

"snedder – slim, slender: 'a snether woman'" *Kennet* 1690s as D'm. *EDD* distribution to 1900: D'm; snether – Yx

snell sharp, keen

"snell – sharp, cold, as a 'snell wind', a sharp piercing wind, 'a snell morning', a bitter cold morning" *Kennet* 1690s as D'm; "snell – sharp, keen: as snell air" *Bailey* Co.Durham 1810. *EDD* distribution to 1900: Sco, Ire, Nth, Lincs [OE snel, ON snjallr]

snew snowed

"it snew all day" *Brockett* Newc & Nth 1829; "snew – did snow" *Dinsdale* mid-Tees 1849. *EDD* distribution to 1900: general

snib latch

"snib than sneck" (door latch) *KH* Stockton C20/2; "snib – the swivelling bit of wood that serves to shut a cupboard door or gate" (E). *EDD* distribution to 1900: Sco, Ire. See also **nose**

snicket see **cut**

snig an eel

ex. *Brockett* Newc & Nth 1829. *EDD* distribution to 1900: general (not Sco)

sniggle snare (noun and vb)

"to sniggle, to fish for eels" *Brockett* Newc & Nth 1829; "snickle, sniggle – a snare or wire for the capture of hares or rabbits" *Atkinson* Cleve 1868; "snigglies – wire noose for catching rabbits" *GP* S'm 1950s. *EDD* distribution to 1900: general

snirls, snurls nostrils

"snurls – nostrils" *Kennet* 1690s as Nth; "snirls, snirrels (pronounced snolls) – the nostrils" *Atkinson* Cleve 1868. *EDD* distribution to 1900: N'd, C'd, Yx

snitch see **nose**

snite to wipe

"snite your nose" *Ray* 1674; "snite – to wipe the nose [by hand]" *Atkinson* Cleve 1868. *EDD* distribution to 1900: Yx, Lincs, EA. [OE snýtan, ON snýta]

snod smooth (noun and vb)

"snod, snog – smoothe, sleek... as He is snodly gear'd or snogly gear'd... wheat ears are said to be 'snod' when they have no beards or awms" *Kennet* 1690s as D'm; "snod, snodden – to smooth down" *Dinsdale* mid-Tees 1849; "snod – a careful, close person" *Robson* Tyne 1849; "gay and snod – cunning" *Tyneside Grammar* 1880s. *EDD* distribution to 1900: Sco, N'd, Yx, Lx. [compare ON snoðinn 'bald']

snood the short piece of line that linked hook to main fishing line

ex. Amble per BG 2003; "snood with hook attached" *JH* S'm C20/mid. *EDD* distribution to 1900: Sco, N.I., N'd, nYx, Derbys, Suff, Kt. [OE snód]

snook, etc. to sniff

"a little black bitch...snoaking at a juniper bush" *Raine* MS Ushaw, 1674/75; "to snawk – to smell" *Kennet* 1690s as Nth; "snoke – to smell, to pry about curiously..." *Brockett* Newc & Nth 1829' "snoke, snook – to smell at; also pronounced snoork", "tak' a lang snoork" *Atkinson* Cleve 1868; "snorkin' 'n' snoor'n'" (snorting) *Egglestone* Weardale 1870s; "snowkin' like pigs at a sew" *Gibson* C'd 1880. *EDD* distribution to 1900: Sco, Ire, Nth. [?ON; compare Norw. snöka, Swed. snoka 'to sniff']

snook headland

e.g. west end of Holy Island. *EDD* distribution to 1900: N'd, etc. [the 5 uses of 'snook' as a place-name in England available via the Ordnance Survey online gazetteer are in N'd]. See also **nose**

snotter to have a runny nose

"snotters – bubbles: 'he snotters and sleeps' [of] a man who falls a sleep when he is drunk" *Bell* MS Newc 1830s; "snotter – to snivel, to sob or cry" *Brockett* Newc & Nth 1829. *EDD* distribution to 1900: Sco, Ire, Nth, parts of Mids. *Plus* "snotterclout – handkerchief" *Graham* Geordie 1979. *EDD* distribution to 1900: N'd, nYx

so

"see doon sat Andra" *Bewick* Tyne 1790s; "sae, se" *Marshall* G'head 1806; "se fast" *Armstrong* Tanfield C19/2; "se" Durham 1916, Tanfield Lea, 1960. *EDD* distribution to 1900: sae – Sco; see – N'd; soa – Yx. See also **sec**

soft mild and wet

"Soft – wet (of the weather)" *Palgrave* Hetton 1896. *EDD* distribution to 1900: general

sonsy lucky, pleasant

"sonsy – lucky" *Bell* MS Newc 1815; "soncy or sonsy – pleasant, agreeable, engaging; as applied to a person's looks" *Brockett* Newc & Nth 1829; "Sonsy – nice, jolly-looking, stout (of persons). Imported from the North, and not commonly heard" *Palgrave* Hetton 1896; "sonsee – pleasant" *Dodd* MS Tanfield Lea C20/2. *EDD* distribution to 1900: Sco, Ire, Nth. NE 2001: not in use. [?Gaelic]. *Plus* "[a witness] did heare the said Jane Patterson... call the said Elizabeth Scott, 'unsoncy read-headed fox', and that she was ill to meet withall first in a morninge" *Raine* MS Swalwell 1618

soom to swim

"to soom through Tyne" *Allan's Tyneside Songs* p.70 1805; "we'll a' soom or sink" *Allan's Tyneside Songs* p.71 1805; "soom – the Northumbrian pronunciation of swim; soomer – a swimmer: 'a top soomer'" *Brockett* Newc & Nth 1829; "ah's gan to hev a soom doon at Cullercoats" *Embleton* Tyne 1897; "soom – to swim" Tanfield Lea 1960. *EDD* distribution to 1900: Sco, N'd, C'd

soss 1. to fall, 2. a fall

"soss – to fall with force; to cause anything to fall so into water" *Atkinson* Cleve 1868; "a clumsy, heavy fall: 'he tumbled soss into the gutter'" *Luckley* Alnwick 1870s. *EDD* distribution to 1900: Sco, Nth, eMids. [imitative]
2. 'a heavy, clumsy fall; the sound caused by the act of falling *Brockett* Newc & Nth 1829; "a heavy fall: 'He went down with such a soss'" *Palgrave* Hetton 1896. *Plus* "soss, marra!" (sorry, when bumping into someone) *TC* re Dawdon Pit, C20/2

soss to lap up

'to lap like a dog' *Bailey* Co.Durham 1810; "soss – to lap up (e.g. milk, of a dog)" *Dinsdale* mid-Tees 1849; "to lap water etc., as a dog does" *Atkinson* Cleve 1868. *EDD* distribution to 1900: Nth, EA

sossenger sausage

"Ah'll fry the' a sossenger te the supper" *Egglestone* Weardale 1870s. *EDD* distribution to 1900: sausinger – D'm, Yx, Lx, wMids

spales, spiles 1. splinters, 2. 'stakes used in making an embankment' *EDD*

1. "spale, spail, spyel, spell – a chipping of wood, or splinter" *Brockett* Newc & Nth 1829; "spales or spyalls – refuse chips for firing" *Bell* MS Newc 1830s. *EDD* distribution to 1900: general. See also **spell, spelk**
2. "paid for fellying of wood and ryving of spilys' (Bishop of Durham's accounts, ca. 1515) via Brockett Newc 1846; "The Spiles" (made ground near Seaham North Dock) *GP* 1998. *EDD* distribution to 1900: N'd, C'd, W'd, Lx, EA. [variant of piles]

spane to wean

"Her lambs were not then spained" *Raine* MS Whalton 1605/06; "sp[y]aned – weaned" *Bailey* Co.Durham 1810; "he's a face that would spyen a calf" *Bell* MS Newc 1815; "spean, spaen or spane – to wean a child; to deprive a creature of its mother's milk" *Brockett* Newc & Nth 1829. *EDD* distribution to 1900: Sco, Ire, Nth. [OFr espanir]

spang to spring in the air

"spangin' – jumping, leaping: 'a flea... amang war blankets spangen'" *Pitman's Pay* G'head 1820s; "spang – to leap with elastic force, to spring" Brockett Newc & Nth 1829. *EDD* distribution to 1900: Sco, Ire, Nth

spanghew to fling hard

"spanghew – to throw with violence. The word is sometimes used to express a barbarous operation on the toad, a reptile to which rustics have a great antipathy" *Brockett* Newc & Nth 1829; 'to cause to move with force or velocity' *Atkinson* Cleve 1868; 'to fling, project, e.g. a frog' *Gibson* C'd 1880; "spanghew'd – spread out, flattened" *Egglestone* Weardale 1877. *EDD* distribution to 1900: Sco, Nth, parts of Mids. *Plus* "spangued out – forced out by pressure" (of a pit prop) *Wade* South Moor 1966

spar to close

"spar, spare – to shut, to close. A very common word in the North" *Brockett* Newc & Nth 1829. *EDD* distribution to 1900: Sco, N'd, C'd, W'd, Derbys, Norf. [MDu sparre, OFr esparre]

spark 1. to splash, 2. to hit

1. "to splash, to make foul with mud: 'I've spark'd my boots'" *Brockett* Newc & Nth 1829. *EDD* distribution to 1900: Sco, N.I. N'd
2. "spark – to hit someone" Charver 2000–2002

sparty marshy

"sparty-ground – ground wet, and with rushes here and there" *Brockett* Newc & Nth 1846. *EDD* distribution to 1900: Sco, N'd, D'm. [spart 'dwarf rush']

speel to climb

"speel, speil – to climb, to clamber" *Brockett* Newc & Nth 1829. *EDD* distribution to 1900: Sco, Ire, N'd, C'd. *Plus* "then doon te Sheels a' hands did speel" *Allan's Tyneside Songs* p.416 1862

speir to ask, enquire

"of me to spir" *Cuthbert* C15/mid; "he would speere them there lease againe" *Raine* MS Ryton 1662; "I'm laith to spier questions on moon shiney nights" N'd C19 per BG Texts p.93; "Speer – inquire. This word is rare, being an importation from the North" *Palgrave* Hetton 1896; "dinna spier how things is gan" *Northumbrian Words III* C20/mid re Kielder. *EDD* distribution to 1900: speer – Sco, Ire, Nth, parts of Mids. [OE spyrian, ON spyrja]

spelk splinter, splint, etc.

"Four spelkes athwart, and one top spelk are sufficient" (in constructing a hive) *Raine* MS 1648; "the splints or splinters of wood used in binding up of broken bones are called spelks" *Kennet* 1690s; "spelk – a small plinter from wood... also... a tall raw boned lad: 'hes [sic] a spelk of a fellow'" *Bell* MS Newc 1815; "spelk – a small splinter, a thatching stick; a little, slender creature" *Brockett* Newc & Nth 1829; "spelks – hazel pins used in thatching" *Dinsdale* mid-Tees 1849; "A slim-built, smaal spelk ov a lad" *Barrass* Stanley 1890s; "spelk – a thorn or splinter in the flesh. Also of anything insignificant: 'A spelk of a thing', 'He's just a spelk of a lad'" *Palgrave* Hetton 1896;

spelk cont.

"spelk – wood splinter, small weak person" *Dodd* MS Tanfield Lea C20/2; "Aw've getten a spelk i' my hand" *Graham* Geordie 1979. *EDD* distribution to 1900: Sco, Nth. NE 2001: in use. [OE spelc] See next entry

spell splinter, etc.

"spelles" *Raine* MS EYorks 1641; "spale, spail, spyel, spell – a chipping of wood, or splinter" *Brockett* Newc & Nth 1829; "spell – splinter" *Dinsdale* mid-Tees 1849; *Atkinson* Cleve 1868; "spell, not spelk" D'ton C20/mid, C20/2, B'd Catle, Teesdale 2001 Q; "Why did the magician give up magic? Because he one of his spells got stuck in his finger" *Wood* Cleve 2002. *EDD* distribution to 1900: Sco, Ire, Nth, Mids. [ON spela] See also **spelk, spales**

spennish licorice

"Spanish – licorice, or Spanish juice. (Pron. 'Spennish.')" *Palgrave* Hetton 1896; "spennish" NShields C20/mid Q

spice 1. gingerbread, 2. (imported) dried fruit esp. currants

1. "spice – gingerbread" *Brockett* Newc & Nth 1829. *EDD* distribution to 1900: N'd, D'm, C'd, nYx
2. "spice – dried fruit. Hence, spice-cake, a cake full of currants" *Brockett* Newc & Nth 1829; "Spice – the only name known for currant-cake. 'Cake' always means tea-cake" *Palgrave* Hetton 1896. *EDD* distribution to 1900: N'd, Yx, D'm, Derbys

spice-kyek tea-cake

"a good speyce suet keayk" *Bewick* Tyne 1790s; "then Sunday comes – wi' friends te tea, / when spice-kyeks florish..." *Wilson* Newc C19/mid; "spice-cakes – teacakes enriched with currants" *Atkinson* Cleve 1868; "a spice loaf is made of dough and mixed with raisins, currants, allspice, ginger and different other aromatics" *Embleton* Tyne 1897. *EDD* distribution to 1900: D'm, Yx. *Plus* "fizzer – a singing hinnie without spice" *Brockett* Newc & Nth 1846

spiles see **spales**

spink a spark

"a spink of fire – a spark" *Kennet* 1690s as D'm; "spink – a spark of fire or light" *Brockett* Newc & Nth 1829; "not a spink of leet" *Bell*

spink cont.

MS Newc 1830s. *EDD* distribution to 1900: D'm. See also **chaffinch**

spletter pit worker

"the spletter, his daddy" *Marshall* G'head 1806. [from split? compare: "ma heed's fit to splet" *Cuddy Cairt* Newc 1917]

spout narrow entry ot crab pot

'way into a Flamborough pot for a crab' *Hill* 1970s; "'monk' not 'spout'" *FT* Cullercoats 2003

sprent sprinkled

ex. *Dinsdale* mid-Tees 1849. *EDD* distribution to 1900: sprent as inf. of vb – esp. Sco, Nth

spuggy sparrow

"Looks tha, thar's a spuggy, man!" *Palgrave* Hetton 1896; "spuggy – any common-or-garden little bird, not just a sparrow. I remember the kids I taught in Hull in the 70s divided birds into two kinds – spuggies and seagulls; i.e. land birds and sea birds." *JS* from Chester-le-Street C20/mid; "there gans a spuggi" East Boldon 1985; 'a sparrow, also a spiritualist' *ER* M'bro C20/2; "spuggy or spacka" *IA* S'm 1950s,60s; "spuggie or spug" Roker C20/mid; "ah want gyeuses not spuggies" *Dobson* Tyne 1970–71; "spuggy – any small bird" *JR* Sacriston C20/2; spuggy – sparrow S'd 2002 Q. *EDD* distribution to 1900: eD'm; spug – Sco, N'd, Warks, Worcs. NE 2001: in use. *Plus* "to take a spuggy's ticket – to climb over a fence to get free view of football/cricket match" *LG* re Seaham C20th/mid; "spuggy's ticket – a free look obtained at a paying spectacle, usually from up a height" *AK* Tyneside, 1950s; "Dickyhedgie – the hedge-sparrow" *Palgrave* Hetton 1896; "cuddy – the hedge-sparrow" *Atkinson* Cleve 1868

squally-mashed obliterated

ex. *GP* S'm C20/mid. *Plus* "molly-squash – to inflict great violence upon" *Wood* M'bro C20/2; "mangle-shredded" *CT* New Herrington 1930s [variant on smash?]

squeaker young pigeon

ex. Gosforth C20/2 Q. *EDD* distribution to 1900: Sth (of swift, partidge)

squench to quench

ex. *Dinsdale* mid-Tees 1849. *EDD* distribution to 1900: general. [variant of quench]

squitts quits

"skwitts – all square after gambling" *Dodd* MS Tanfield Lea C20/2; "squits – equal, even" (ending a contest) *Wood* Tees 2002

staithe jetty, landing stage

"staith – often pronounced steeth or steith, a place to lay up and to load coals at... The word occurs in a demise from the Prior of Tynemouth, *AD* 1338" *Brockett* Newc & Nth 1829; "staith – a quay, a permanent stage or platform by the water-side to facilitate shipping or landing goods; an embankment or sea-wall" *Atkinson* Cleve 1868; "Staithes (stae:uths) – the shipping stage belonging to a colliery" *Palgrave* Hetton 1896. *EDD* distribution to 1900: Sco, Nth, Lincs, EA. [ON stǫð, OE stæð 'shore']

stanchels uprights, bars

"iron for stanshalls of wyndowes" *Raine* MS Embleton N'd 1586; "door stanchels" *Oliver* Newc 1824 p.16; *Allan's Tyneside Songs* p.237 1829; "Doorstaingels ('g' soft, as in 'angel') – door-frames" *Palgrave* Hetton 1896. *EDD* distribution to 1900: Sco, Tyne – obsol. [OFr estanchele]

stane, styen stone

"leanin on the hud steahyn" (mantlepiece?) *Bewick* Tyne 1790s; "styen-caad" *Dunn* B'p Auck 1950. *EDD* distribution to 1900: stane – Sco, N'd; steean – Nth; styen – D'm, C'd. [OE stán]

stang a pole

"the said Jane did so abuse her husband [that she] was carried upon a stang about the towne" *Raine* MS Heighington, 1609; "stang – wooden bar or pole" *Ray* 1674; "stang – a piece of wood used by butchers to keep the feet of sheep, etc. extended till cold" *Bell* MS Newc 1830s. *EDD* distribution to 1900: Sco, Nth, Mids. [OE stæng, ON stǫng]

stang sting

"stang – the sting of a bee etc." *Bell* MS Newc 1815; "stang – to shoot with pain, as in the tooth-ache" *Brockett* Newc & Nth 1829. *EDD* distribution to 1900: esp. Sco, Nth, Lincs. [ON stanga (vb)]. See also **dragonfly**

stangie ?hen-pecked husband

"the snobs and stangies i' the Garth" *Allan's Tyneside Songs* p.310 1827; "an' at a stangie's shop a bowt / a cover for me heed, man" *Allan's Tyneside Songs* p.298 1831

staple pit access

"the staple... its purpose was to lower full tubs to another level" *Hitchin* re Seaham p.69 1910s

starling 1. **stiggie**, 2. **stashie**, 3. **stinker**

1. "stiggie" Gosforth C20/2 Q
2. "stashies" *CT* Co.D'm, C20
3. "stinker" cenD'm 2001, *PE* Seaton Carew C20/1; *Wood* re Teesside 2004

starn stars

"starn – stars; starneys – little stars" *Bell* MS Newc 1815. *EDD* distribution to 1900: Sco, Nth. [ON stjarna (star)]

starp to walk with long strides

ex. *AT* Co.D'm C20/mid

starrish strong (of drug)

"starrish – powerful; as medicine that is too much for the strength of the patient" *Brockett* Newc & Nth 1829. *EDD* distribution to 1900: N'd. [from steer adj. 'strong', OE stiere]

starving cold

"starve[d] – to suffer from extreme cold" *Atkinson* Cleve 1868; "When my parents were v. cold they said they were starving." *DH* Consett, mid C20th; "starved or starving meaning cold" D'ton 1940s Q. *EDD* distribution to 1900: general. [OE steorfan 'to perish']

stee ladder

exx. *Ray* 1674, *Bailey* Co.Durham 1810; "stee or stey" *Brockett* Newc & Nth 1829; "stee" *Dinsdale* mid-Tees 1849; "stee, stegh" *Atkinson* Cleve 1868; "tak hehd o' this stee – ladder" *Dunn* B'p Auck 1950; *JB* Shildon C20/mid; Upper Teesdale 2001 Q. *EDD* distribution to 1900: sty – Nth, eMids. [ON stige]. *Plus* "lether – Northumberland for ladder" *Bell* MS Newc 1830s

steek to shut, fasten

"[she] steekit dor and window" *Reed Border Ballads* C16; "steek the heck – shut the door" *Bailey* Co.Durham 1810; "steek – to put a stick or steek over the sneck of a door to prevent it being opened – so to steek the windows or door is to make them fast" *Bell* MS Newc 1830s; "steck – to shut, close or fasten, often pronounced steek: 'steck t' heck', 'steck thy een'" *Atkinson* Cleve 1868. *EDD* distribution to 1900: Sco, Ire, Nth. [ME steken (vb), OE staca 'stake']

steg a gander

"I am neyther goos-steler nor steg steiler"
Raine MS Sedgefield ca.1570; "steg – a gander"
Bailey Co.Durham 1810; "steg – a gander"
Upper Teesdale 2001 Q; *EDD* distribution
to 1900: Sco, Ire, Nth, EA. [ON steggi 'a
male bird']

stell a large open drain

ex. *Bailey* Co.Durham 1810. *EDD* distribution
to 1900: Nth

stemples staples in a wall serving as a vertical
ladder

"stemples... a rude and apparently dangerous
staircase" (in lead mine) *Alston* 1833. *EDD*
distribution to 1900: Sco, Yx, Derbys, Card,
Corn

stick strike (noun and vb)

"stick – a stand or combination among workmen, generally in regard to wages; what is
elsewhere called a strike" *Brockett* Newc &
Nth 1829; 'among colliers means when they
confederate not to work without advanced
wages' *Bell* MS Newc 1830s. *EDD* distribution
to 1900: N'd, D'm

stick an' clout umbrella

"Stick and Clout – cant name for an umbrella"
Palgrave Hetton 1896

sticks furniture

"And when we flit, the landlord stops / Ma
sticks till a' the rent be paid" *Pitman's Pay*
G'head 1820s

stife poor air

"stife – close, oppressive, occasioning difficulty
of breathing: 'as stife as a dungeon'" *Atkinson*
Cleve 1868; "it teuk us aall wor time te see yen
anuther in the kitchin, an' the stife wez aaful"
Robson Newc C20/1; "a fug in the air I always
associate with frying chips – 'stife' would be
coming from the pan" *PG* H'pool C20/2; "lead
miners used to call the smoke and fumes from
explosives 'the stife' – you would walk back
through it to the face, cap lamp just lighting
the rails, unable to breathe" *SV* E; "I have
heard that 'stife' or 'stithe' was the cloud of
gas or whatever that was given off after shot-
blasting down the mines" *DE* Shildon C20/2;
"open the door and let the stife out" Markse
C20/2 via *Wood*; "thors an aaful stife inheor"
(smell) *Dobson* Tyne 1970; "styfe – choking

stife cont.

smoke" *Graham* Geordie 1979; "stife – used
down the mines and also used to describe the
blue fog from an overheated and greasy oven"
2000 E (unsourced); "stife – thick smoke"
Upper Teesdale 2001 Q; Tyneside, B'd Castle
2001 Q. *EDD* distribution to 1900: Sco, N'd,
D'm, C'd, Pem, Suff. NE 2001: in use. [ON
stifla – to choke]. See also **stithe**

stifey fuggy, stifling

"stifey – close, suffocating" *Atkinson* Cleve
1868; "frying chips... the room would be
'stifey': 'By, it's stifie in here!'" *PG* H'pool
C20/2. "stifie – stifling" Teesside 2001 Q

stime dim light

"stime – a dim ray of light" *Dinsdale* mid-Tees
1849; "'A canno' see a stime' – often said by
one whose eye-sight is bad" *Palgrave* Hetton
1896. *EDD* distribution to 1900: Sco, Ire, Nth

stirk young cow or ox

"stirkis – young male cattle in their first year"
Finchale 1447-8; "sturk – young bullock or
heifer" *Ray* 1674; "stirk – a yearling ox or
heifer" *Bailey* Co.Durham 1810; "stirk – heifer,
1-2 years old" *Dinsdale* mid-Tees 1849. *EDD*
distribution to 1900: Sco, Ire, Nth, Mids.
[OE stirc 'calf']

stite as soon as, sooner, rather

"Stite – equally, as soon: 'Stite him as me' (the
sense is often 'much rather')" *Palgrave* Hetton
1896; "A might stite gan hyem" (might as
well...) *Nth Words*, Seaton Sluice, 1938. "myt
as styt – may as well" *Dodd* MS Tanfield Lea
C20/2. *EDD* distribution to 1900: NE. [as tite]
See also **astite, tite**

stithe bad atmosphere

"stithe – hard, sever, pungent" *Ray* 1674;
"she thout she wad ha' been skumfeesht
wi the steyth" *Bewick* Tyne 1790s; "stithe –
strong, stiff, e.g. stithe cheese" *Grose* 1787;
"styth – foul air: 'Through smoke and styth'"
Pitman's Pay G'head 1820s; 'a black suffocating
damp in a colliery' *Brockett* Newc & Nth 1829;
"stithe – pungent smell" *Dinsdale* mid-Tees
1849; "stithe – carbonic acid gas, often found
in old workings, and evolved in most shallow
mines" *Nicholson* 1880; "stithe – unpleasant,
smokey atmosphere" *JB* Shildon C20/mid;
"stythe – the products of the combustion of
fire-damp" *Nicholson* 1880; "my mother said

stithe cont.

stithe" (Horden): "the kitchen was full of stithe' (steam, etc.)" *JR* Sacriston C20/2; "styth – mine gas, CO^2" *Dodd* MS Tanfield Lea C20/2; "stythe (with hard th) – gas, methane" South Moor (Stanley) 2003 per BG. *EDD* distribution to 1900: esp. N'd, D'm, C'd, nYx. [OE stið 'strong, harsh']. See also **stife**

stob post

"stob – a stump, a post" *Pitman's Pay* G'head 1820s; "stob – pointed stick" *Dinsdale* mid-Tees 1849; "stob – the stump of a tree; a short post" *Atkinson* Cleve 1868; "stack stob – pointed stick used in thatching stacks" *JB* Shildon C20/mid; 'also a gibbet' *Graham* Geordie 1979. *EDD* distribution to 1900: Sco, Ire, Nth, Leics, Northants, USA. [?C14 variant of stub]. *Plus* "stoop – a gatepost. Upper Teesdale 2001 Q

stobbie unfledged bird

ex. *Palgrave* Hetton 1896. *EDD* distribution to 1900: eD'm

stone-men pit workers

"stone-men – men employed in driving stone drifts, taking up bottom, or taking down top stone to make height for horses, &c." *Nicholson* 1880; 'The Stoneman's Song' Johnny Handle 1958

stooks supporting pillar of coal

"stook – the remains of the pillar of coal after it has been jenkined" *Pitman's Pay* G'head 1820s; [in reducing the pillars of coal...] "this last bit is the stook" *Hitchin* re Seaham 1920s p.106; "stooks – coal pillars left to support roof" *Dodd* MS Tanfield Lea C20/2. *EDD* distribution to 1900: Sco, NE, Northants

stoppings barrier put up in pit

"stoppings – a barrier of plank, brick or stone... in a coal mine" *Brockett* Newc & Nth 1846; "stopping – a wall built in any excavation for the purpose of conducting air further into the mine" *Nicholson* 1880; 'brick wall in pit' *JR* Seaham C20/1. *EDD* distribution to 1900: N'd, D'm, nYx, nStaffs

stopple pipe-stem

"a pipe stopple – a piece of a tobacco pipe" *Bell* MS Newc 1815; "if he haddent bad teeth he wad eaten the stopple" *Allan's Tyneside Songs* p.219 1817; "Pipe-stopple – stem of tobacco-pipe" *Palgrave* Hetton 1896. *EDD* distribution to 1900: general. [MDu stapel 'stem']

storken to congeal

"storkin or storken – to grow stiff: as melted fat cooled again" *Bailey* Co.Durham 1810; "stirken – to cool and stiffen, as gravy does /stau:kn/" *Palgrave* Hetton 1896. *EDD* distribution to 1900: Ork, Nth. [ON storkna]

stot an ox

"stottes – male cattle from one to four years old" *Finchale* (1363-4); "iiii stotys pris xl (pound)" Reed *Border ballads* re 1582 p.26; "a gowden stote" *Raine* MS ?Durham 1581; 'young bullock or steer' *Ray* 1674; 'a two years old ox' *Bailey* Co.Durham 1810; 'a young ox from one to four years old' *Brockett* Newc & Nth 1829; 'bull stirk' Upper Teesdale 2001 Q. *EDD* distribution to 1900: Sco, Nth, Derbys, Lincs, Sx. [OE stot, ON stútr]

stot 1. to bounce, move quickly (intrans.), 2. to (make) bounce (trans.)

1. "stot – to rebound from the ground, to strike any elastic body so as to cause it to rebound" *Brockett* Newc & Nth 1829; "aw'd see him stot bi me... on his aud wooden peg" *Allan's Tyneside Songs* p.490 1862; "By, he wes stottin" (jumping up and down with anger) *Hay* Ushaw Moor C20/1; "stotting down with rain" *JS* Easington 1950s; "the hailstones wis stotin [sic] off the hoose-tops" *Graham* Geordie 1979; "stot out!" – stop that!, keep away! *TR* S'm, 2002; "a stotting headache" Blyth 2003 per BG; "stot along – hurry" Wheatley Hill 2002 Q.
2. "stot the ball" *IA* S'm 1950s,60s; *HP* South Gosforth C20/mid; "Aa'll stot ye" S'm 2000 per BG. *EDD* distribution to 1900: Sco, N'd, C'd. NE 2001: in common use. ["The Dutch verb 'stoten' is closer [than stuiten]... the [Dutch] word for 'tappets' by the way is 'kleppstotters'." Peter Cain. The vb is first noted in Scotland 1513, in the NE C19]

stotty (cake) flat round loaf

"Oven bottom cake is known as 'stotty cake' in mining villages" *Nth Words* Northumberland 1938; "stotty kyek" *PHm* S'd C20/1; "stotty cuak – usually made from surplus dough after bread making, also the oven has sufficiently cooled" *CT* New Herrington 1930s; "stottee kyek – large flat loaf" *Dodd* MS Tanfield Lea C20/2; "the State Stotty-Cake factories" *Dobson* Tyne 1970; "stotty-cake – flat loaves,

stotty (cake) cont.

oven-bottom bread" *LL* Tyneside 1974, *Graham* Geordie 1979, Wheatley Hill 2004 Q, etc. NE 2001: in use. [from 'stot' (to bounce) in sense of resilience of a yeast-based bread. Term made popular by commercial bakers?]. *Plus* "stotty-bun" S'm 2002 per BG. See also **fadge**

stound hurt (noun/vb)

"stound – to ache, to smart, to be in pain" *Brockett* Newc & Nth 1829; 'numbing pain caused by a blow' *Dinsdale* mid-Tees 1849; 'an ache, pang' *Gibson* C'd 1880. *EDD* distribution to 1900: general. [?OFr estoner]

stour 1. dust in motion, 2. disturbance, commotion, riot

1. "stour – dust" *Bailey* Co.Durham 1810; "ye'll get yor een a' full o' stour" *Allan's Tyneside Songs* p.245 1827; "dust floating in the air: 'midst dust and stour'" *Pitman's Pay* G'head 1820s; "stoor – dust in motion; stoory – dusty" *Brockett* Newc & Nth 1829; "Stoury Sunday" (re snow storm) *Alston* 1833; "such a stour – dust from sweeping up" *Nth Words*, N'd 1938. *EDD* distribution to 1900: Sco, Ire, Nth, Derbys
2. "he wex sa hate (hot) in slike a stour" (commotion, struggle) *Cuthbert* C15/mid; "was sore wounded in that stour" *RR* Weardale 1569; "arms and armour... that sav'd wor lads in mony a stour" *Allan's Tyneside Songs* p.303 1848; "dinnet clash the door / or myek ony idle stor" *Allan's Tyneside Songs* p.478 1863; "what a stor mun he' been at his disappearance" *Haldane* Newc 1879; "When Aa cum hyem sic a stoor wis on" *Other Eye* Newc ca.1890. [AN estur 'tumult']

stoury gruel

"stoury – oatmeal and beer warmed together with a little sugar added to it" *Bell* MS Newc 1815; "water gruell with ginger and sugar" *Bell* MS Newc 1830s

stowed (off) packed out, crowded

"stowed off with homework" *JS* Easington 1950s; 'shaft bottom road full of coal-tubs' *Northumbrian III* C20/2 re Durham collieries; "stowd off – no more room" *Dodd* MS Tanfield Lea C20/2; eDm C20/2, Tyne, nwD'm 2001 Q; "stowed off – fed up" Ch-le-St 2002, South Moor (Stanley) 2003 Q; "stowed out" *PG* H'pool 1998, S'd 2003 Q. *EDD* distribution to 1900: Sco, NE

stramash to devastate, devastation

"stramash – to beat, to bang, to break irreparably, to destroy; [noun] a complete otherthrow, with great breakage and confusion: 'he made a sad stramash amang the pots and pans'" *Brockett* Newc & Nth 1829; "stramash – to dash or smash in pieces" *Atkinson* Cleve 1868. *EDD* distribution to 1900: Sco, Yx. [variant on smash?]

stramp to trample (upon)

'to tread on' *Bell* MS Newc 1815; 'trample' *Palgrave* Hetton 1896, *Dodd* MS Tanfield Lea C20/2; "dinna stramp ower the clean floor" *Graham* Geordie 1979. *EDD* distribution to 1900: esp. Sco, NE. [variant of tramp]

stravaigin' wandering about

"Wiv a' the stravagin aw wanted a munch" *Marshall* Newc 1823; "stravaigin' – strolling about" *Pitman's Pay* G'head 1820s; "cum stravagin' this way" *Allan's Tyneside Songs* p.244 1842. *EDD* distribution to 1900: Sco, Ire, N'd, Australia. [Med.Latin extravagare]. *Plus* "vaig – to wander, to roam (Fr vaguer)" *Brockett* Newc & Nth 1829

strenkle to sprinkle

"and strenkill it (holy water) opon hir" *Cuthbert* C15/mid; "strenkle a leapyt (little bit?) ov sugar ont" *Bewick* Tyne 1790s; "strinkle – to scatter grain down to fowls: "strinkle a handful of corn to them" *Bell* MS Newc 1815. *EDD* distribution to 1900: N'd; strinkle – Sco, Nth, eMids, EA

strike

"struck up, re rabbit mating" *JR* Crook C20/mid

strike to kick

"strike – to kick, as a horse does" *Atkinson* Cleve 1868; "streaik – struck, tossed" *Eggleston* Weardale 1877. *EDD* distribution to 1900: Sco, Yx, nLincs

strite straight

ex. Durham 1916; "strite off yem" *Armstrong* Tanfield C19/2. *EDD* distribution to 1900: in this pronunciation Yx

strunt/y the tail

"strunt – the tail or rump; strunty – any thing short or contracted" *Brockett* Newc & Nth 1849. *EDD* distribution to 1900: Sco, Yx, eMids, EA

stumor something or someone striking

"a stumor of a goal" *JS* re Ryhope 1950s; "stiumor – an incompetent person" *GP* S'm C20/mid; 'sort of person – usually female – whose behaviour makes one gasp, either because it is so stupid, or so shrewd' *Viereck* re Gateshead 1966; "styooma – difficult person or situation" *Dodd* MS Tanfield Lea C20/2; "stumer – an unusual person, also means stupid" *Dobson* Tyne 1973

suit

"'you'd suit it' rather than 'it'd suit you'" *AK* re Newc C20/mid

summat, summick something

"summic" *Allan's Tyneside Songs* p.420 1862; "summic, summat... 'tell you summic'" *Haldane* Newc 1879; "nowt or summat" *Cate* p.105 B'p Auckland area 1987; "summuk" *Dodd* MS Tanfield Lea C20/2; "summik like that" *VIZ* 51 1990s. [summat equals somewhat]

sump place where water collects (in pit)

"Sumps are holes sunk in Drifts to the depth of two or three yards, more or less" Derbyshire, 1681; "sump – a dirty settling of water *Bell* MS Newc 1815; "Sump wet – wet to the skin" *Palgrave* Hetton 1896; "sump-wet – very wet" *Dodd* MS Tanfield Lea C20/2; 'at the bottom of the shaft, a standage for water' Wade *South Moor* C20/mid. *EDD* distribution to 1900: general

sunshower raining whilst the sun is shining

ex. *JS* Easington C20/mid, ER M'bro C20/2

sup drink (noun/vb)

"sup – a small quantity of any liquid" *Atkinson* Cleve 1868; "Ah try'd a sup tea" *Egglestone* Weardale 1870s; "Sup (suop) – a drop: 'A sup rain', 'ha'e a sup milk, will tha?'" *Palgrave* Hetton 1896; "sup up, the dog's won – everything is fine today" Spennymoor C20/mid

swads (pea) pods

ex. *Bell* MS Newc 1815, "beans... swads an' all" *Green* Wearside 1879 re C19/1; "swad – a peascod" *Brockett* Newc & Nth 1829; "swads an' all" *Wearside Tales* 1879. *EDD* distribution to 1900: Nth, EA

swaimish bashful

"swameish – shy, bashful" *Bailey* Co.Durham 1810; "swamish, sweamish" *Brockett* Newc &

swaimish cont.

Nth 1829; "swaimish, swaimous – hesitating, diffident, bashful or shy: 'I felt swaimish at asking'" *Atkinson* Cleve 1868. *EDD* distribution to 1900: esp. C'd, Yx. [AN escoymous 'squeamish']

swally a dip

"swelly or swally – a small basin or dish in the strata produced by undulation" *Nicholson* 1880; "Thor's a hitch an' then a swally" *Barrass* Stanley 1890s; "Swalley (swaul:i) – a hollow place: 'The village lies right in a swalley'" *Palgrave* Hetton 1896; *JR* Seaham C20/1; "swallee – dip in ground" *Dodd* MS Tanfield Lea C20/2; "a depression in the roadway underground" *JM* Thoraby C20/2. *EDD* distribution to 1900: N'd, D'm, wYx, Warks, Glos

swang swamp

ex. *Pitman's Pay* G'head 1820s. *EDD* distribution to 1900: Nth. [?swamp; but note OE wang 'flat plain']

swape steering oar

"swape – a long oar used on board of the keels in the Tyne to steer by" *Bell* MS Newc 1815. *EDD* distribution to 1900: Tyne, Yx, Lincs. [ON sveip – of circular motion]. *Plus* "there's a nasty turn with a double swape" (?bend in passage in pit) *Moreland* Dawdon 1980

swarth a fetch

"swarth – the ghost of a dying man" *Ray* 1674 re C'd; 'the spirit or ghost of a dying man called in Yorkshire a waft' *Kennet* 1690s. *EDD* distribution to 1900: C'd, Yx. [OE swart 'black'; compare also Sco warth/wraith]. See also **waff**

swattle swallow noisily

"to swattle some yell" *Allan's Tyneside Songs* p.187 1824. *EDD* distribution to 1900: Sco, Nth, EA

sweal to flare

"swale, sweal – to singe or burn, to waste or blaze away" *Ray* 1674; "swealing of a candle: meeting or guttering of a candle, as proverbial saying in the north, see how the candle sweals" *Kennet* 1690s; "swale, sweal – to singe or burn, as to sweal a hog. Also to waste or blaze away, as, the candle sweals" *Grose* 1787; "sweal – to

sweal cont.

melt, to waste or blaze, to burn away rapidly, as a candle when exposed to the wind" *Brockett* Newc & Nth 1829; "sweal – to gutter, as a candle does in a current of air" *Nicholson* 1880; "sweelin doon the wind" *Barrass* Stanley 1890s; "sweal / sweadle – to waste away as candle in wind" *Blenkinsopp* Teesdale 1931; "swale – [to] burn heather on moors" *JB* Shildon C20/mid. *EDD* distribution to 1900: general. [OE swǽlan 'to burn']

sweir stubborn

"Hawkie is a sweir beast and Hawkie winna wade the watter" C19/1 via *Graham* Geordie 1979. [OE swǽr 'grievous, difficult', ON svárr]

swill large shallow basket

"swil – a sort of flat wide basket used by flesh carriers and fish wives in Newcastle *Bell* MS Newc 1815; 'a round basket of unpeeled willows' *Brockett* Newc & Nth 1846. *EDD* distribution to 1900: Nth, EA

swipes drink, ?ale

"as stale as swipes kept ower lang i' the huddock" *Allan's Tyneside Songs* p.188 1824. *EDD* distribution to 1900: Sco, Yx, Lx, IoMan

sy— see also **si—**

syke, sike runlet

"unto the full letch or sike of the said more" *Raine* MS Winston 1606; "sike – little rivulet" *Ray* 1674; "syke – a small brook" *Bailey* Co.Durham 1810; "sike – ditch, water-channel" *Dinsdale* mid-Tees 1849; "syke – a streamlet, a rill of water; a small run draining out of a bog" *Atkinson* Cleve 1868. *EDD* distribution to 1900: Sco, Nth, EA. [ON sík, ON síc]

syle rafter

"syles – principal rafters of a house" *Bailey* Co.Durham 1810. *EDD* distribution to 1900: Sco, Nth. [OE sýl 'pillar']

syle strainer

"a mylke syle" *Raine* MS ?York, 1553/54; 'a strainer' *Atkinson* Cleve 1868; 'a sieve' Upper Teesdale 2001 Q. *EDD* distribution to 1900: general. {?ON; compare Swed. sil]

t', th' the

"t' byuk" Durham 1916; sim. *Moore* Weardale 1859, *JB* Shildon C20/mid; "all th' meat" (the) *Armstrong* Tanfield C19/2. *EDD* distribution to 1900: C'd, Yx, Lx

taa toe

"tae – the toe, according to the Scottish form" *Brockett* Newc & Nth 1829; "taas – toes" *Dodd* MS Tanfield Lea C20/2. *EDD* distribution to 1900: tae – Sco; teea – Yx

taak talk

"meynde what their o taokin about" *Bewick* Tyne 1790s; "taak" Durham 1916, *Haldane* Newc 1879; "whee's A taakin te – who am I talking to" *Dunn* B'p Auck 1950. *Plus* "a taaky chep" *Haldane* Newc 1879

tab cigarette

"gizza draw of your tab" *JS* Easington 1950s; "giz a tab" *Dobson* Tyne 1970; "heyegorrenny-tabswespatzon" (filter tips) East Boldon 1985; "tab ends" *VIZ* 96 (1999). NE 2001: in use. [brand-name 'Ogden's Tabs']. *Plus* "a butt was called a dump" *JS* Easington 1950s, sim. *Graham* Geordie 1979; "giz a swaller" (a turn on a cigarette) IA S'm 1950s,60s; "binger – cigarette end...' save me your binger'" *ER* M'bro C20/2; "pitchy kissy, knocky downy, blowy ower – cigarette card games" *ER* M'bro C20/2

tack horse gear

ex. *GP* S'm C20/2. *EDD* distribution to 1900: Ire, wMids. [tackle] *Plus* "tack – smokeable narcotic of dubious strength" Charver 2000–2002

tadger 1. a child, 2. a tadpole, 3. penis

1, 2. exx. *JP* S'm 1960s
3. "Doctor Tadger" *Dobson* Tyne 1972; "tadger" *PG* H'pool C20/2; "me todger" *VIZ* 45, 1990s. *Plus* "dog pyntle" Reed *Border ballads* p.24 re C16; "chucky" eD'm 1990; "kellee" *Dodd* MS Tanfield Lea C20/2

taggerman scrap dealer

ex. *GP* S'm 1950s. [tagger 'tinned sheet iron']

taistrel a rogue

"tastrill – a cunning rogue" *Grose* 1787; "taistrel, testril – a rude or prankish kid" Brockett Newc & Nth 1846; 'a wastrel' *Gibson* C'd 1880; 'an ill-mannered boy; one given to

taistrel cont.

playing pranks' *Palgrave* Hetton 1896. *EDD* distribution to 1900: Sco, Nth. [a sixpence]

tak take: 1. **tak** forms, 2. **tyek** forms

1. "tack – to take" *Brockett* Newc & Nth 1829; "tak' ho'd – to undertake an office or special performance or duty" *Atkinson* Cleve 1868; "t' traction engines... cud tak't up te Kil'ope Cross" *Egglestone* Weardale 1870s; "aw'se gawn ti tak it tiv the maister's house" *Wearside Tales* 1879; "tak the wite" (take the weight) *JS* Easington C20/mid; "Aam ganni tak off – run away" *Dunn* B'p Auck 1950; "teuk the lead" *Bewick* Tyne 1790s; "Aw champt the bit an' teuk the bridle" *Barrass* Stanley 1890s; "thai had the childe tane" *Cuthbert* C15/mid; "a journey ta'en" *RR* Weardale 1569; "she's teun a fit" *Armstrong* Tanfield C19/2; "they've tuen'd up [the pavement]" *Allan's Tyneside Songs* p.245 1827; "teun hyem on a barrow" *Allan's Tyneside Songs* p.252 1829; "aw've teun the yaller fever wi' snuffin goold dust" *Allan's Tyneside Songs* p.400 C19/mid; "'well tune with,' i.e. is very popular" *Palgrave* Hetton 1896, 'admired' Durham 1916; "yu'v tack'n a hamma t' crack a nut" *CT* New Herrington 1930s; "tyun ahad – fire well lit" *Dodd* MS Tanfield Lea C20/2; "I went to the football but all the seats were chun" *JP* S'm C20/2. *EDD* distribution to 1900: tak – Sco, Nth, Mids
2. "tyek – take" *Pitman's Pay* G'head 1820s; "t'yak" *Brockett* Newc & Nth 1829; "tuaik" *Armstrong* Tanfield C19/2; "tyek" *Barrass* Stanley 1890s, Tanfield Lea, 1960; "tyekkin in watta – nerves spoiling contestant's game" *Dodd* MS Tanfield Lea C20/2; "tekkin' a broon" *Irwin* Tyne 1970; "ye wouldn't hev tu tek it yem afta" *VIZ* 34 (1989)

tally tallow

"he'd skin a louse for its tally" Ashington C20/mid

tallyman any due collector

"on pay-day a stream of tallymen, club agents, money-lenders and insurance men passed through the house" *Hitchin* re Dalton-le-Dale p.18 1910s; "tallyman or tick man" *IA* S'm 1950s, 60s; 'due collector, HP instalment collector' *EP* Southwick C20/mid; "talleeman – credit collector" *Dodd* MS Tanfield Lea C20/2; 'due collector' D'm 2001 Q, Trimdon 2002 Q. [AN tallie]. *Plus* "provvy man" – Tyneside C20/mid Q

tang, teng 1. to sting, 2. the tongue of a buckle

1. "tang, teng – to sting" *Brockett* Newc & Nth 1829; "tenged – stung" *Kennet* 1690s as Yorks, sim. *Atkinson* Cleve 1868. *EDD* distribution to 1900: Nth, eMids. [ON tunge 'sharp point'] See also **dragonfly**

2. "tang – the tongue of a buckle; the prong of a knife or other article which runs into and is fixed in the handle" *Atkinson* Cleve 1868

tappy-lappy in a rush, headlong

"commin tappy lappy owr the Stob-Cross Hill" *Bewick* Tyne 1790s; 'as hard as you can, applied to running' *Brockett* Newc & Nth 1829; "away we went, tappy-lappy down the lonnin" *Allan's Tyneside Songs* p.505 1891; 'pell-mell, helter-skelter' *Palgrave* Hetton 1896; "tappee-lapee – happy-go-lucky" *Dodd* MS Tanfield Lea C20/2; "gannin' tappy-lappy oot the toon in a cloud o' dust" *Dobson* Tyne 1971; "the twee boxers went ti'd tappy-lappy...", 'to rush aimlessly and blindly' *Graham* Geordie 1979; "ter gan up ter toon, tappy lappy" MS North Shields C20/2. *EDD* distribution to 1900: Nth. *Plus* "gannin tap-happy doon the lonnin" (happily, cheerfully) *BL* Winlaton 1950s

tara, tata see **goodbye**

tarry-tout tarred string

"Tarry towt – a single strand of rope steeped in tar. *Palgrave* Hetton 1896; "hemp rope tarred for use in wet conditions" *McBurnie* Glebe Colliery C20/mid; 'thick treated string used to tie hewer's token to tub' *GP* S'm 1950s. *EDD* distribution to 1900: eD'm]. *Plus* "tooty tar – a piece of rope impregnated with tar handy for lighting fires" *JG* Annfield Plain 1930s

tatie potato 1. **tatie**, 2. **tettie, tattie**, 3. **chetty**

1. "tatees an soat" (salt) *Bewick* Tyne 1790s; "She peels the taties wi' her teeth" *Pitman's Pay* G'head 1820s; "the Tatie Market" *Allan's Tyneside Songs* p.237 1829; "taties, tripe, and greens" *Allan's Tyneside Songs* p.197 1838; "ther was ony amount o' tatees en turnips" *Egglestone* Weardale 1870s; "tormuts and carrots and taties" *Allan's Tyneside Songs* p.554 1891 re S'd; "tatie – potato, or a stupid person" Charver 2000–2002

2. "aw've tetties te boil" *Allan's Tyneside Songs* p.399 C19/mid; "Ye're just the scrubbiest bits o' tetties I ivver saw" *Parker* Tyne Valley 1896 p.79; "Tetties Aa-laa Fish Shop" (chips)

tatie cont.

Windows Newc 1917; "tetty-flavoured crisps" *Dobson* Tyne 1972; "I hev nee tatties" *Graham* Geordie 1979; "tattie watta" *VIZ* 48, 1990s; "tattie boggle" Newc 2001 Q; "tatties" Barnard Castle 2001 Q; "it hit me like a sack a tatties" Newc 2004 per BG

3. "chetties" *JP* S'm C20/2; "chyetties" Tyneside 2001 Q; "chetties" Thornley 2001 Q; "the chetties set on [to boil]" *JR* Sacriston C20/2; "the tchetties set on [to boil]" Sacriston 2004 E; "chats – small potatoes not worth peeling, ususally fried in skins" *Wood* Tees 2002. *EDD* distribution to 1900: general; 'tattie' typical of Sco? NE 2001: in common use. *Plus* "tatie pit" (small-scale coal mine) S'm C20/2 via BG; "Tettyhowkaz – agricultural or peasant Geordies" *Dobson* Tyne 1970; "tatie-pie – potato clamp (heap of potatoes covered in straw then earth, for storage)" *JB* Shildon C20/mid. See also **scarecrow**

tatty tattoo

ex. Tyne 2003 Q

tave 1. senseless action, 2. heavy walking

1. "taving – random or delirious motion" Brockett Newc & Nth 1846; "tave (pronounced teeav) – to sprawl or fidget about" *Atkinson* Cleve 1868

2. "t'yav, tave – to walk laboriously e.g. over a ploughed field" *Dinsdale* mid-Tees 1849; "taav – to wade in mud" *Blenkinsopp* Teesdale 1931. *EDD* distribution to 1900: general [?ON; compare Norw. tava 'to toil']

taw see **marbles**

tawm, tome fishing line (e.g. of horsehair)

"tome – a hair line for fishing" *Grose* 1787 as C'd; "tawm" *Bailey* Co.Durham 1810; "tawm, tome, tam – a fishing line: ' a long twine tam'" *Brockett* Newc & Nth 1829; 'pull'n horse hairs oot ed tail te mak fish'n taums' *Egglestone* Weardale 1870s. *EDD* distribution to 1900: esp. Sco, Nth. [ON taumr 'cord, line']

taws 1. leather strap, 2. punishment with same

1. 'a leather strap used by schoolmasters for chastising children' *Brockett* Newc & Nth 1829; 'a leather strap partly cut into long strips, tails or tags' *Luckley* Alnwick 1870s; "Taws (taa:z, taaz) – a leathern strap for punishing naughty children, to be seen hanging up in many cottages. It is like a carriage-window strap,

taws cont.

cut into a fringe at one end" *Palgrave* Hetton 1896. *EDD* distribution to 1900: Sco, Ire, N'd, D'm, C'd

2. "you could hear them screamin' as they got thor taws" Tynemouth C20/1 re training ship; "taws – punishment" *Dodd* MS Tanfield Lea C20/2; "a good towsin'" – a good thrashing Tynemouth C20/2 Q

te see **to**

tee too

"aw mun away tee" *Bewick* Tyne 1790s; "Prince Albert tee" *Allan's Tyneside Songs* p.303 1848; "tee – too" Tanfield Lea 1960

teem to pour out (transitive)

"[penalty] for temynge fylthee tubbs in the water of Ouse" *Raine* MS York, 1540s; "team – to empty a cart, by turning it up, to pour out" *Bailey* Co.Durham 1810; "it was just like teamin' cau'd watter down mi back" *Egglestone* Weardale 1870s; "teem – to pour out: 'teem oot the milk'" *Luckley* Alnwick 1870s; "A teapot with a well-turned spout is called a 'good teemer.'" *Palgrave* Hetton 1896; 'referred to tipping a load of coals, bricks or sand off a lorry or cart in the street as well as pouring down with rain' *JS* Easington C20/mid; "teemoot the scaddin' het oil" *Dobson* Tyne 1970–71; "team oot the tea" *Graham* Geordie 1979; "teem that out down the sink" *Wood* Tyne 2002. *EDD* distribution to 1900: general. [ON tæma 'to empty']. *Plus* "On the staiths, 'teemers' put the brakes on to the wagons, open the bottom and let the coal into the hoppers" *Coulthard* p.108 1934 re Ashington

tell

"wyse monkes...teld him thus" *Cuthbert* C15/mid; "it was nowt but lees he teld him" *Marshall* p.19 Newc 1823; "yen o' the beuks thet tellt ye hoo it's aall dyun" *Robson* Newc C20/1; "Ah telt a pollis aboot it" *Egglestone* Weardale 1870s; "a telt th'" (I told you so) *CT* New Herrington 1930s; "Aah towld ye he cudna be telt" *Leslie* Newc 1992. *EDD* distribution to 1900: telled – general; telt – Sco, Nth. [OE pret. tealde]

temse a fine sieve

"temes – a temse, a sieve of hair cloth" (for flour preparation) Finchale 1449-50; "tempse – a fine cloth or silk sieve" *Bell* MS Newc

temse cont.

1815; "temse – a sieve made of hair, used in the dressing of flour" *Atkinson* Cleve 1868. *EDD* distribution to 1900: general. [OE temesian (vb)]

teng see **tang**

teufit lapwing

"tewfet" *Grose* 1787; "tuiffit – the lapwing or plover; tuiffit-land – cold, wet, bad land only fit for the tuiffit" *Brockett* Newc & Nth 1829; "tuffit – a lapwing" *Dinsdale* mid-Tees 1849. *EDD* distribution to 1900: Nth

teum see **toom**

tew, chew 1. to work hard, 2. to mess about, aggravate, trouble, 3. (noun) hard work, trouble

1. "thou is a tuing sow" (energetic lass) *Chicken* Benwell 1720s; "tew – to struggle, toil: 'we had to tue on wi' a nasty scabby roof'" *Pitman's Pay* G'head 1820s; "tue – to labour long, to work hard, to be fatigued by repeated or continued exertion: 'tuing on', 'a tuing life', 'sare tues'" *Brockett* Newc & Nth 1829; "to tue – to labour till tired, or diligently: 'here have I been tuing all day for you and your bairns' – a usual salutation by the wife on her husband's return from an ale house" *Bell* MS Newc 1830s; "tew – to toil, to take trouble, to fidget or move uneasily: 'a tewing bairn' (a restless child), 'a tewing hay-time' (a wet and unfavourable season)" *Atkinson* Cleve 1868; "choo-in – exhausting... physically rough" *Dodd* MS Tanfield Lea C20/2; "Aa've tew'd at the job till Aa's paid (exhausted)" *Graham* Geordie 1979; "tew on – to bother or struggle on" Sacriston 2004 E. *EDD* distribution to 1900: esp. Sco, Nth, eMids, Lincs. [OE tawian, to work at, also to harass]

2. "tewing – teazing, disordering, harassing" *Bailey* Co.Durham 1810; "tew – to tire; to ruffle, mess up" *Dinsdale* mid-Tees 1849; "She fairly tewed his life out" *Palgrave* Hetton 1896; "'tewing,' of work, means tedious" *Palgrave* Hetton 1896; "tewed – fatigued: 'it's been a tewing job'" *Wade* South Moor C20/mid; "chewed to death – harassed" Spennymoor C20/mid Q, *Dunn* B'p Auck 1950; "stop chewing me about" (stop messing me about) *PG* H'pool C20/2; "tew – to tumble about, to ruffle, to rumple" *Dobson* Tyne 1973 (as archaic); "a right tew on" (an awkward job) B'p Auckland 2001 Q; "tewed meaning

tew, chew cont.

overworked" Upper Teesdale 2001 Q; "chewed" eD'm 2001 Q; "cannot be tewed" (bothered with) *KH* Stockton C20/2, eD'm, B.Auck Q 2001. *EDD* distribution to 1900: Sco, Nth, Lincs. NE 2001: in use
3. "we reach'd the Moor wi' sairish tews" *Allan's Tyneside Songs* p.139 1816; "We'd sair tues amang us to manage wor keel" *Allan's Tyneside Songs* p.442 1862; "'too much chew' – too much of a carry-on to do something... or simply 'chewy', an adjective for a task difficult to perform" *PG* H'pool C20/2; "getting a lot of chew" (hassle) *KH* Stockton C20/2; "tyoo – chew, laboured effort" *Dodd* MS Tanfield Lea C20/2. *Plus* "chewy – an adjective for a task difficult to perform" *PG* H'pool C20/2. *Plus* "tew – bless you!" (anon., hopefully with a sense of shame, 2000 Q)

thack thatch (noun and vb)

"ryvyng of thak" *Cuthbert* C15/mid; "thack, theak, theaking – thatch [noun]", "thach, theak – to thatch" *Atkinson* Cleve 1868. *EDD* distribution to 1900: general. [OE þacian]. See also **theek**

tharf kyek a bread or biscuit

"they never gat owse better than thaaf keahyk" *Bewick* Tyne 1790s; "tharf cake, a girdle cake made of flour and water" *Bell* MS Newc 1815; "thauf-cake or tharf-cake – a cake made of unfermented dough – chiefly of rye and barley – rolled very thin and baked hard [for keeping]" *Brockett* Newc & Nth 1829; "tharf cyek – made of dough left over... also called fadge cake, and is commonly eaten at tea time" *Embleton* Tyne 1897. *EDD* distribution to 1900: Nth, Derbys. [OE þeorf 'unleavened'; perf-bred in *Cursor Mundi* C14/1]. *Plus* "tharfish – somewhat reluctant or backward; shy, timorous: 'a tharfish kind of a bairn'" *Atkinson* Cleve 1868

that

"at – that, which" *Atkinson* Cleve 1868; "let somebody talk et hez seen t'world" *Egglestone* Weardale 1870s. *EDD* distribution to 1900: at – Nth, Sco, Ire. ['at is either a reduced form or genuinely reflects ON at]. *Plus* "Aw'll sing ye the best thit Aw knaw" *Barrass* Stanley 1890s. *Note:* 'that' is commoner as relative pronoun than 'which'

thee see **thoo**

theek to thatch

"wi' ae lock o' his gowden hair / we'll theek our nest when it grows bare" Reed *Border Ballads* C16; "Wor canny houses duffit theek'd— Wor canny wives within 'em—" (?thatched like a dovecot) *Oiling* G'head 1826. *EDD* distribution to 1900: Nth, Lincs, Northants. [?OE þeccan]. *Plus* "Jemmy Grame the theaker lad" *Bewick* Tyne 1790s

them those (demon. adj.)

"gie us some o them new'uns" S'm 2000 per BG, etc. *EDD* distribution to 1900: general. [OE þæm, oblique case]

there see **thor**

thereckly directly

ex. *Wearside Tales* 1879; "she'll be dry thereckely" *Haldane* Newc 1879; "(the) rekklee – directly" *Dodd* MS Tanfield Lea C20/2

they, them (pronoun)

"a place th' call Stanley" (they) *Armstrong* Tanfield C19/2; "thae, tha" (they) *Armstrong* Tanfield C19/2; "them thit wis prisint" *Armstrong* Tanfield C19/2; "thame" (them) *Embleton* Newc 1897; "they think it's great, them" N'd 2004 pr BG

thill the floor of a coal seam, etc.

"thill – in mining, clay" *Bell* MS Newc 1815; "thill – the surface upon which a tram runs" *Pitman's Pay* G'head 1820s; "thill – the bottom stone of a coal seam" *Brockett* Newc & Nth 1846, *Nicholson* 1880. *EDD* distribution to 1900: N'd, D'm, Yx

thir, thur – these

"thir folk in earth I made of nought" *Noah's Ark* Newc C15/16; "thir Weardale-men" *RR* Weardale 1569; "thur – these" *Kennet* 1690s as Yorks; "thur, thor – these, those" *Brockett* Newc & Nth 1829; "thur" – these *Eggleston* Weardale 1870s. *EDD* distribution to 1900: Sco, N.I., Nth; thor more typical of NE, thir of Sco. [*Cursor Mundi* C14/1 first uses thir as plural of this; compare ON þeir].
See also **thor**

thirl drill, twist?

"the cauld blasts o' the winter wind / that thirl'd thro' my heart" Newc C19/1 (Scots); 'to pierce or stab, to perforate, to bore *Brockett* Newc & Nth 1829. *EDD* distribution to 1900: Sco, Ire, Nth, Mids

thivel stick

"thivel – a stick for stirring hasty pudding" *Luckley* Alnwick 1870s; "nee bigger then a thyvel" *Egglestone* Weardale 1870s. *EDD* distribution to 1900: Sco, Nth. [?ON; compare OIce þefja 'to make thick']

thocking panting, gasping?

"thockin and blowin" *Bewick* Tyne 1790s. *EDD* distribution to 1900: Tyne

thoft, toft – thwart or cross-seat in a coble (small boat)

"thoft" *FT* re Northumberland 2003, Whitby 2003 per BG; "carlin toft" foremost toft *Hill* Flamborough 1970s, "carling thoft" *FT* re Northumberland 2003. *EDD* distribution to 1900: Sco, N'd, nYx, nLincs. [OE þofte, ON popta]

thon that

"thon – that (over there)" *JB* Shildon C20/mid; "thon's" (that is) *Todd* Tyne 1977. *EDD* distribution to 1900: Sco, Ire, N'd, D'm. [only recorded 1800 plus – formation from yon]

thonder yonder

exx. *Bell* MS Newc 1815, *Luckley* Alnwick 1870s, *Dodd* MS Tanfield Lea C20/2; "torn [turn] off thonder" *Haldane* Newc 1879. *EDD* distribution to 1900: Sco, Ire, N'd, wMids, EA. [from yonder]

thoo, tha, thee you (sg): 1. nom.sg. (subject), 2. acc.sg. (object), 3. gen. (possessive)

1. nom.sg.: "thous neahn deef" *Bewick* Tyne 1790s; "How's tou?" *Bells* re Carlisle, 1802; "Thou naws" *Marshall* G'head 1806; "cannot thoo...?" *NWC* 16 Jan 1886, Sup. p.5; "thoo gans", "again thoo come back" *Egglestone* Weardale 1870s; "how is ta?" *Haldane* Newc 1879; "thoo best o' wives" *Barrass* Stanley 1890s; "where is the gannin the day, Bill?" *Embleton* Tyne 1897; "thoo sees" Durham 1916, *Dodd* MS Tanfield Lea C20/2. *EDD* distribution to 1900: thoo – Sco, Nth. [OE þú]

thoo, tha, thee cont.

2. acc.sg.: "thee" *Collier's Wedding* Newc 1720s; "aw'll sing thee a tune" *Allan's Tyneside Songs* p.88 1807; "it waz kind o' thee" (oblique) *Egglestone* Weardale 1870s; "Aw wad knock th' doon" *Armstrong* Tanfield C19/2; "te thoo" *Barrass* Stanley 1890s; "tha" – you (nom/acc.sg.) Durham 1916' "Aa'll tell thee" Durham 1916 [OE þé]
3. gen. "thee Fayther" *Bewick* Tyne 1790s; "thee twee breests" *Moore* Weardale 1859; "tha ni'em" *Egglestone* Weardale 1870s; "thaa" *Haldane*, Newc 1879; "thee beuk en thee slate" *Armstrong* Tanfield C19/2; "thee care – your car" *Dunn* B'p Auck 1950. [OE þín] See also **ye** (pl.)

thor 1. those, 2. their, 3. there

1. "thur, thor – these, those" *Brockett* Newc & Nth 1829; "thor drinks" *Barrass* Stanley 1890s. [generally reckoned a variant of thir, but possibly distinct]
2. "thor prairs" *Armstrong* Tanfield C19/2; "thor evil star" *Barrass* Stanley 1890s; "thor – their, they're" *Dobson* Tyne 1972
3. "thor issent a doot" *Allan's Tyneside Songs* p.243 1842; "thor's" (there is) *Barrass* Stanley 1890s, Tanfield Lea 1960

thowle oak tholepin

ex. *Hill* Flamborough 1970s; "thowle" *C/GR* Amble C20/2

thowt thought (pret.vb)

"aw thowt" *Wearside Tales* 1879, *Armstrong* Tanfield C19/2, Durham 1916, Tanfield Lea, 1960

thrang, throng 1. crowd, 2. crowded, 3. busy

1, "off, helter-skelter wi' the thrang" *Allan's Tyneside Songs* p.298 1831; "it middle at thrang in iverybody's shop" *MWN* 16 Nov 1861; "thrang, throng – a confused crowd; a state of bustle, confusion: 'i' t' varry thrang on 't'" *Atkinson* Cleve 1868; "Ah follow'd t'thrang" *Egglestone* Weardale 1870s; "mixt up e th' thrang" (crowd, throng) *Armstrong* Tanfield C19/2. [OE geþrang, ON þrǫng]
2. "as thrang as three in a bed", "as thrang as hens on a muck midden" *Egglestone* Weardale 1870s; "throng – busy; inconveniently crowded (always used)" *Palgrave* Hetton 1896; "thrung – crowded" *Dobson* Tyne 1973

thrang, throng cont.

3. "throng in getting in [i.e. carting away] the Roman monuments lately dug up neare Adle Mill" *Raine* MS 1702; "nit ower thrang wi' wark" *Bells* re Carlisle, 1802; "As throng as Thropp's wife when she hanged herself with the dishclout" *Raine* MS as current saying C19/2; "the condition of being very busy: 'T' missis's in a vast o' thrang wiv her cheeses'" *Atkinson* Cleve 1868; "ye better come back the morn, hinny, wor very thrang the day, ye see" *Luckley* Alnwick 1870s; "he wis varry thrang wi' summic" *Haldane* Newc 1879; "thrang – throng, busy" Tanfield Lea 1960. *EDD* distribution to 1900: Sco, Ire, Nth, Mids. *Plus* "heaving – really crowded" *GP* S'm C20/2, etc.

thraw, thraa to throw

"thrawn owrboard" *Bell* Newc 1812 p.8; "as fast as I could thraw a coal" *Bell* Newc 1812 p.37; "thae started to thraw" (vomit) *Armstrong* Tanfield C19/2. *EDD* distribution to 1900: in this pronunciation Sco, Ire, Nth. [OE þraéwan]

threap 1. to rebuke, 2. to insist

1. ex. *Ray* 1674; "threap, threapen – to blame, rebuke, reprove or chide" *Grose* 1787. [OE þréapian 'to rebuke']
2. "Yet still aw cannot help but wonder / When aw's threept out o' what's se clear" (argued) *Pitman's Pay* G'head 1820s; 'to persist vehemently in assertion or argument' *Brockett* Newc & Nth 1829; "she threeps doon it is" *Embleton* Tyne 1897. *EDD* distribution to 1900: general

thrimmel to trickle (money)

"thrimmel – to draw money reluctantly from the pocket... 'The parish now, wi' miser's care, / Mun thrirnmel out some sma' relief'", "the reckoning they / Get thrimmel'd out, and toddle hyem" *Pitman's Pay* G'head 1820s; "Wor geordies [guineas] now we thrimmel'd oot" *Marshall* Newc 1823. *EDD* distribution to 1900: thrimble – Sco, Nth

thropple, thrapple windpipe, throat

"ma thropple was ready to gizen (crack with thirst)" *Allan's Tyneside Songs* p.49 1812; "thropple – throat, windpipe" *Palgrave* Hetton 1896; "thrapple – throat" Ashington C20/2. *EDD* distribution to 1900: thrapple – Sco, N'd

throstle the thrush

exx. *Grose* 1787, *Atkinson* Cleve 1868; "whissel'd like a throssel" *Egglestone* Weardale 1870s; "the song-thrush is sometimes called 'thros'le,' but more often 'greybird'" *Palgrave* Hetton 1896. *EDD* distribution to 1900: general. [OE þrostl]

thrum to purr

exx. *Dobson* Tyne 1973; "the cat's... thrummin" *Graham* Geordie 1979. *EDD* distribution to 1900: Sco, Nth, EA. [imitative]. *Plus* "three-thrums – the purr of a cat" *Tyneside Grammar* 1880s; "thrums – wool for rug making" *Dodd* MS Tanfield Lea C20/2

thunnor thunder

ex. *Brockett* Newc & Nth 1829. *EDD* distribution to 1900: in this pronunciation Sco, Nth, Derbys, Lincs. [OE þunor]. *Plus* "thunner-pash – thunder-shower" Dinsdale mid-Tees 1849, *Egglestone* Weardale 1877; "thunner-stane – quartz pebble" *Dinsdale* mid-Tees 1849; "rattly-bags – thunder" *LG* S'm C20/2

tidy-betty a fender (for kitchen range)

"Tidy betty – a short fender across the grate, without a bottom" *Palgrave* Hetton 1896; *MR* S'm 1930s. *EDD* distribution to 1900: D'm, Yx, Lincs, Derbys

tiggy game of tag

"tiggy – the child's game of 'touch'" *Palgrave* Hetton 1896; "tig or tiggy for a children's chasing game" *RM* Norton C20/mid; "tuggie than tiggy" Gosforth C20/2 Q. *Plus* "thou... was ower bissy tiggen on woh Jemmy Grame" *Bewick* Tyne 1790s; "tig" *Brockett* Newc & Nth 1829, *KH* Stockton C20/2, M'bro, Stockton. D'ton 2001 Q; "tacky – a game in which one is appointed to pursue and catch the others" *Viereck* re Gateshead 1966. *EDD* distribution to 1900: tig – Nth, Corn. NE 2001: in use. See also **kicky-can**

tied obliged

"obliged, compelled, sure, certain: 'I'm tied to go'" *Brockett* Newc & Nth 1829; "A's tied to gan" (forced to go) *Palgrave* Hetton 1896. *EDD* distribution to 1900: in this sense Sco, Nth, Notts, Lincs

till to

"they thought tul a' had their prey", "for tul have been at home again" *RR* Weardale 1569; "till – to or unto. It is still quite common in many parts of N'd" *Brockett* Newc & Nth 1846; "til um – to him" *Dinsdale* mid-Tees 1849; "he did nowt till her" *Luckley* Alnwick 1870s – extra. *EDD* distribution to 1900: esp. Sco, Ire, Nth, Mids. [ON, OE (Northumbrian) til]

timmer timber

ex. *Brockett* Newc & Nth 1829; "keep ya timmer in" – 'look after youself' *Northumbrian III* 1990 re Backforth; "just the right timmer – just the right size" *McBurnie* Glebe Colliery, C20/mid. *EDD* distribution to 1900: in this pronunciation Sco, Nth. *Plus* "This [i.e.beer] was the kind o' belly timmir / For myekin pitmen strang and tuiff" *Pitman's Pay* pt.3, Gateshead 1829; "belly-timber – food" *Atkinson* Cleve 1868

tite soon

"sho als tite was hale" (immediately) *Cuthbert* C15/mid; "I may as tite be a ladye as thou a lord" *Raine* MS Durham, 1587; "titter – rather, sooner" *Bailey* Co.Durham 1810; "tite – soon, easily, well" *Brockett* Newc & Nth 1829; "Ah wad as tite gan as stay" *Atkinson* Cleve 1868, "I was there titter than you" *Atkinson* Cleve 1868; "Aa might as tight deun wivoot" *Other Eye* Newc, ca.1890. *EDD* distribution to 1900: Sco, Nth. [ON títt 'often']. See also **stite**

titty sister

"Care... wi' his blear-e'ed titty, Grief" *Pitman's Pay* G'head 1820s. *EDD* distribution to 1900: Sco, Nth

tium see **toom**

to, tiv, tin etc.

"rudely they fell tea their meat" Rothbury C18/2; "tid" (to it) *Marshall* G'head 1806; "frev a needle tiv an anchor" *Marshall* G'head 1806; "tiv-a-tee – to a T" *Brockett* Newc & Nth 1829; "tin (before vowel) – to" *Dinsdale* mid-Tees 1849; "up tut knees ie dyke watter" M'bro *MWN* 28 Jan 1860; "tud" (to it, to the) *Egglestone* Weardale 1877; "te", "ti", "tiv him" *Barrass* Stanley 1890s; "arl good things cum tivva n'end" *CT* New Herrington 1930s. *EDD* distribution to 1900: tiv – N'd, C'd, wD'm, Yx.

tod fox

"tod – a name for the fox" *Brockett* Newc & Nth 1829; "if you sarra (serve) the tod / you maun bear up his tale'" *Bell* MS Newc 1830s. *EDD* distribution to 1900: Sco, Ire, Nth, Lincs

toit to totter

"toyte – to totter like old age" *Pitman's Pay* G'head 1820s, *Gibson* C'd 1880. *EDD* distribution to 1900: Sco, NE, Corn. *Plus* "toitle – to upset" (?to tip up) *Blenkinsopp* Teesdale 1931

tomahawk pit tool (combined pick and hammer)

"tomahawk – a type of hammer used by man laying railway in the pit. Head 1 ft long with chisel and hammer ends; shaft 2 feet long" *McBurnie* Glebe Colliery C20/mid. *EDD* distribution to 1900: wYx

tommy-shop a system using vouchers issued as part of pay (common early C19)

"Tommee shop – where miners compelled to shop (now obsolete)" *Dodd* MS Tanfield Lea C20/2; "the pay ticket, otherwise the ticket directing the deduction for 'tommy'; 'tommy' being one of the names for 'truck'" *MWN* 21 Apr 1860. *Plus* "tommy boxes – food tins of local steelworkers" *ER* M'bro C20/2; "tommy box" Teesside steelworks 2001 Q

too see **tee**

toom, teum, chum empty

"some tounes wex nere tome" *Cuthbert* C15/mid; "toom, tume – empty" *Ray* 1674; "toom, teum, tume – empty, void" *Kennet* 1690s as Nth; "ju-um – empty" *Grose* 1787; "'a tyum cellar" *Bell* MS Newc 1815; "toom or teum – empty: 'a teum cart'" *Brockett* Newc & Nth 1846; "Aw've fill'd an' sent away the tubs thit com in teum"; "Aw rattled the full uns an' teum uns alang" *Barrass* Stanley 1890s; "ah brak a tyum teapot" *Embleton* Tyne 1897; "tyum meant empty" *Hitchin* re Seaham p.70 1910s; "an empty tub was called a 'tuman'... we referred to anything empty as 'tume'" *BW* West Auckland C20/mid; "chum – empty" *Dodd* MS Tanfield Lea C20/2; "chum uns" (empty tubs) *JP* S'm C20/2, *Wade South Moor* C20/mid, *JM* Dawdon 1980; "chummins, chummings – often wrote as plural for chum, when referring to a load of empty tubs" *McBurnie* Glebe Colliery

toom, teum, chum cont.

C20/mid. *EDD* distribution to 1900: Sco, Ire, Nth. [OE tóm, ON tómr]

toon town

"low parts of the toon" Durham 1916; "Newcassel is at yence byeth a toon and a county" *Allan's Tyneside Songs* p.158 1840; "gan to th' toon" *Armstrong* Tanfield C19/2; "Canny Toon – Newcastle" *Dobson* Tyne 1973; "Toon army" (Newcastle United supporters) 1970s? [OE tún]

toot look-out

"keep toot – act as a look-out" Charver 2000–2002. *EDD* distribution to 1900: Yx, Lx, Mids. [also source of place-names like Toot Hill]

top prepared section of coal face

"top – the portion of a coal seam after the nicking and kirving processes are performed, left to be detached by the 'shot'" *Brockett* Newc & Nth 1846

topping crest

"toppin – crest e.g. of a bird, or a person's hair" *Dinsdale* mid-Tees 1849; "'cyem 'er topping!' (comb...) – take some of the conceit out of her" *Hull* MS wNewc 1880s. *EDD* distribution to 1900: esp. Sco, Nth

toppy choppy

"toppy – choppy sea" Hutton Henry 2001 Q

torfle to fall down and die (of animals)

ex. Brockett Newc & Nth 1846; "towp, towple – to totter or fall over" *Atkinson* Cleve 1868. *EDD* distribution to 1900: Sco, Nth

tormit see **turnip**

torn to turn

"she torned the lock", "aw torned roond" *Armstrong* Tanfield C19/2; "torned" Durham 1916

tosser coin

"Aa hevvent got a tosser" att. *GP* S'm C20/2. See also **pitch n toss**

tram vehicle for coal

"tram – a small sledge, used in collieries, for conveying the corf" *Bell* MS Newc 1815; "tram – a small carriage upon which a corf or basket is placed; or it sometimes means two

tram cont.

boys who have charge of this carriage, the one drawing and the other pushing it" *Pitman's Pay* G'head 1820s; "tram – a small carriage on four wheels... used in coal mines to bring the coals from the hewers to the crane" *Brockett* Newc & Nth 1846; "tram – a wooden carriage upon which the corves used to be conveyed along a tramway. The term still applies to the part of a tub to which the box is bolted" *Nicholson* 1880; "Strictly speaking, a bogey has the flange on the wheel, while in the case of the tram, the flange is on the rail" *Palgrave* Hetton 1896; "Down the pit, a bogey with an iron pin about two feet long, at each of the four corners, to prevent the timber and rails from falling off, would be called a 'horney tram'" *Palgrave* Hetton 1896; "A tram... had a bogey like a coal-tub, but in place of a superstructure of wood it had four metal bars, one at each corner. Usually these were used for transporting props." *Hitchin* re Seaham 1920s p.79. *EDD* distribution to 1900: N'd, D'm. [first recorded ca. 1800]. *Plus* "off the way – off the boards on which the tram ought to run" *Pitman's Pay* G'head 1820s

trapper boy worker in pit

"trapper – a lad who the charge of a door in the mine, for preserving the circulation of the air" *Pitman's Pay* G'head 1820s; "trapper – a boy whose business it is to attend to the trap-doors in a coal-mine [for ventilation]" *Brockett* Newc & Nth 1829; "trapper – a little boy, whose employment consists in opening and shutting a trap-door when required for the passage of tubs" *Nicholson* 1880. *EDD* distribution to 1900: N'd, D'm. [from trap 'a ventilating door in a pit' (*EDD*)]

trashing tiring

"I had a lovely holiday but the journey was very trashing" *AK* Newc 1950s; "trashed – worn out, e.g 'aam trashed'" G'head 2003 (E). *EDD* distribution to 1900: Sco, Nth. *Plus* "trash – exhausting work" *Dodd* MS Tanfield Lea C20/2

tret treated, pret. of 'to treat'

"he tret them so kind", "hoo thae ad been tret" *Armstrong* Tanfield C19/2; "the bairns had been badly tretten" *Graham* Geordie 1979; "the miners tret them (the ponies) kindly for they earned a man his pay"

tret cont.

Moreland, Dawdon 1980; "the neighbours tret your house just like their own" *JM* Dawdon 1980. *EDD* distribution to 1900: tret – Sco. [OFr tretier]

trig true

"trig – true, faithful: 'my loyalty's trig' (from song *Canny Newcastle*)" *Brockett* Newc & Nth 1829; "Jim Jemieson kens that your courage is trig" *Allan's Tyneside Songs* p.299 1842. *EDD* distribution to 1900: general. [ON tryggr 'trusty']

trig to stuff

"to trig – to overeat" *Dinsdale* mid-Tees 1849; "trigg'd with a good dinner" *Atkinson* Cleve 1868. *EDD* distribution to 1900: Nth, Lincs

trigged out dessed smartly

ex. *Dinsdale* mid-Tees 1849. *EDD* distribution to 1900: ?Yx. [for rigged? cf. troll for roll, trolley/rolley

trinnels dowels

"wooden pegs... to fasten the planks" on a keelboat – *Mitcalfe* re 1822

trod footpath

"trod – a beaten path" *Bailey* Co.Durham 1810; 'a beaten foot path through a field' *Brockett* Newc & Nth 1829; "a green trod" *Blenkinsopp* Teesdale 1931; "Ther's good trods garn till t' top" *Lakeland* re C'd C20. *EDD* distribution to 1900: Nth, Lincs. [OE trod 'treading']. *Plus* "foot-gang – the path from a cottage etc across a field to the road" *Bell* MS Newc 1815

troll roll

"troll – to roll or be rolled" *Atkinson* Cleve 1868. *EDD* distribution to 1900: general

trollibags intestines

"black puddings [from] Tib Trollibag's stand" *Bell* Newc 1812 p.41; "Gallowgate for trolley bags" *Allan's Tyneside Songs* p.29 1812; "trollibobs, trollibogs – entrails: 'tripes and trollibobs'" *Atkinson* Cleve 1868. *EDD* distribution to 1900: trollibags – Sco, Nth, EA; trollibobs – Yx, Lx, Worcs, Suf, Hants

trousers

"pulled up mee troosers" *Parker* Tyne Valley 1896 p.69. *Plus* "foston trousers – tied with string at knees" *PH* S'd, 1950s; "fustins" (pit

trousers cont.

trousers) *Northumbrian III* 1990 re Backworth. See also **breeks, keks**

trots a bar or stick of wood with snood (short line) and hook attached

"to put the trots in – a method of fishing from the beach. A trot was placed on the sand at low tide; the suction of the sand buried and held the trot secure; at the next low tide, the trot could be checked to see if a fish was hooked." *JH* S'm C20/mid

tub mine vehicle

"tub – an open-topped box of wood or iron, bolted to a tram; used in conveying coals from the working places to the surface" *Nicholson* 1880; "Tub. (too:b, toob, tuob) – a coal-waggon used down the pit, holding from 6 to 8 cwt." *Palgrave* Hetton 1896. *EDD* distribution to 1900: in this sense NE. [ME tubbe]

tufty buns small bread rolls

'small bread buns' *TM* Parkside 1950s; "tuffies – small bread rolls" *IA* S'm 1950s, 60s, GD (Co.D'm) C20/2, Thornley 2001 Q. [compare "tough cake" (plain bun), eD'm, sDev, *EDD* 1900]

tug to rob a bird nest

"tug – to rob, to destroy: 'to tug a nest'" *Brockett* Newc & Nth 1829; *Palgrave* Hetton 1896. *EDD* distribution to 1900: in this sense N'd, D'm. *Plus* "huggee – rob bird's nest" *Dodd* MS Tanfield Lea C20/2

tunger – see **turnip**

tup 1. ram, 2. tub of coal marking holiday break

1. "Mr Donkin's tups will be shown at Sandoe, on the 21st instant" *Newc Courant* 2 Aug 1823; exx. *Dinsdale* mid-Tees 1849, *Atkinson* Cleve 1868; "Tup (tyoop) – a 'tupe' or 'teup' is a ram" *Palgrave* Hetton 1896; "tup – male (entire) sheep, ram" *JB* Shildon C20/mid. *EDD* distribution to 1900: general
2. "tyup – the last basket or corf sent up out of the pit at the end of the year. The name is got from a tup's horn accompanying it. 'Bussin' the tyup' is covering the coals with lighted candles, which the lads beg, borrow, or steal, for the occasion. It is an expression of their joy at the gaudy days or holidays which take place generally after this event" *Pitman's*

tup cont.

Pay G'head 1820s; "roond the raws one heul doo day, the youngsters hugg'd the teup" *Barrass* Stanley 1890s

turnip – 1. **tornip**, etc., 2. **bagie**, 3. **naggie**, 4. **narkie**, 5. **nasher**, 6. **neep**, 7. **snadger**, **snadgie**, 8. **snagger**, 9. **snanny**. 10. **snarter**, 11. **snasha**, 12. **tunger**, **tungie**, 13. **yammy**

1. "I had to lead turnups upon a sledge" *Errington* Felling/Heworth re 1790s p.42; "tormit – turnip" *Pitman's Pay* G'head 1820s, Tanfield Lea 1960, *Graham* Geordie 1979; "iz big iz a turmit" *Allan's Tyneside Songs* p.418 1862; "on'y three turmots iv a five yacker field" *Wearside Tales* 1879 ; "turnip snagging, when turnip pinching" *JR* Crook C20/mid; "turnap lanterns" *Lakeland* re C'd C20; "tonnup or snashie" *BW* Middle Herrington C20/mid; "turnep – turnip *or* swede" *JB* Shildon C20/mid. *EDD* distribution to 1900: tonnup eYx. [first element implies 'round' (cf. 'tower') either from French tour or cf. Swed. tur; second element is næp, a root vegetable, from OE / Latin.]
2. "...in the North [Nothumberland] they [turnips] were 'bagies'" *Nth Words*, 1938; "howing the baigies – hoeing the turnips" *Nth Words*, N'd, 1938; "bagie or baggie – one variety of the Swedish turnip, the purple top" Geeson, N'd/ D'm 1969; "bagie" *Dobson* Tyne 1969, Blyth, Newbiggin 2002 Q. [Swed. rutabaga; Geeson's 1969 claim that 'rutabaga' is Latin does not seem justified]. *Note:* also used in USA
3. "naggies – turnip lanterns" Jarrow 1970s per Graham Lewis; "nagger" Wheatley Hill 2004 Q; "naggie" S'm 2002 Q
4. "narkie" *JP* re Sunderland C20/2, S'd 2001 Q; "narkie kickin'" (game) Southwick 1980s; "narky" Hoton, S.Hylton 2002 Q
5. "nasher" *CT* New Herrington, C20/mid; 'because the animals used to gnash it' *SM* Ho'ton/Penshaw C20/2; "nashy" S'd 2001 Q
6. "neep" Tyneside C20/mid, S'd, B Auck, Blyth, Newbiggin 2002 Q. [OE næp – also source of second element in **turnip**]
7. "snadger" *FS* Shotton Colliery 1930s, *TP* S'd 1960s, Birtley 2003 per BG, Ch-le-St 2002, Stanley, Hoton, Ch-le-ST 2002 Q; "Turnips are 'snadgers' on Tyneside" *Nth Words* 1938; "snadgers or snannies" *RV* Winlaton 1950s; "snadgie" Cleadon Park, South Shields, Tyneside C20/2 Q, "snajie" South Shields C20/2 Q. [?variant of 'snagger'

turnip cont.

– see next entry]
8. "snagger or tunger" *JM* Thornaby C20/2; "snaggers – definitely at Easington Colliery for turnip." *JS* Easington C20/mid; "been hoein' snaggers – turnips" *Dunn* B'p Auck 1950; "My friend fron Horden knew the orange one as a Snagger" (E); "snagger – when too frosty to pull [turnip] out by top, you stick the point of the snagger in to get a grip, then the main blade for topping and tailing. Hand harvesting continued until about 1990; every farm would have turnips as a crop" *SM* Ho'ton/Penshaw C20/2; "snagger" South Moor (Stanley) 2003 per BG, Wear Valley, B'p Auck, H'pool, Lanchester, Fencehouses 1930s, Stanley C20/2, Ch-le-St, Thornley, Wheatley Hill, Wingate 2002 2001 Q. [derived from the tool for harvesting the crop, thus "tunnip snaggin'" (harvesting) Saltburn, Cleveland C20/2 per *Wood*]
9. "In Seaton Burn it was 'snanny' and we had to run fast to avoid getting 'arses skelped' when we nicked them from the farmer's fields" *DN* Seaton Burn, C20/2; "snanny" *KE* Winlaton mid 20C/mid, *MB* Coxhoe C20/mid, Dinnington 1950s, *RV* Winlaton 1950s, Gosforth C20/2, Gateshead 2001 Q; "snammy" NShields C20/mid
10. "snarter" *JP* S'm C20/2. [?ON snarr, neut.snart 'severe, sharp']
11. "snasha" *Dodd* MS Tanfield Lea C20/2; "tonnup or snashie" *BW* Middle Herrington C20/mid
12. "I seem to remember people also saying 'tunjer'" *FS* Shotton Colliery 1930s; "snagger or tunger" *JM* Thornaby C20/2; "tungie-snackin'" (harvesting) M'bro per *Wood* C20/2; "tungy" M'bro 2001 Q
13. "yammy" S'd 2001 Q
Note: The variety of terms attest the importance of this crop as both animal and human feed ("Turnips... form the chief winter feed for sheep" *Coulthard* p.62 1934); it would be a standard crop on every farm, and its familiarity might have led to the diversity of names

tuther (the) other

"the tother" *Tyneside grammar* 1880s; "the yen better nor the tother" *Other Eye* Newc ca.1890; "the tuther month" *Barrass* Stanley 1890s; *JB* Shildon C20/mid; *Dodd* MS Tanfield Lea C20/2. *EDD* distribution to 1900: general

twang 1. boast, affectation, vanity,
2. talking posh, 3. local intonation, dialect

1. "Yet some may think't a twang" *Shields Song Book* (South Shields, 1826); *EDD* distribution to 1900: in sense 'a lie' – N'd, Lincs, Glos
2. "twang as in some one talking affectedly ower posh" *JS* Easington C20/mid. *Plus* "twangy – with odd or affected intonation" *Atkinson* Cleve 1868
3. "wor aad Newcassel Twang" *Allan's Tyneside Songs* p.576 ca.1890; 'intonation' Benny Graham 1980s per BG; "twang – dialect" Ferryhill 2001 Q. *EDD* distribution to 1900: Sco, Nth, Mids. [imitative]

twank to smack, etc.

ex. *GP* S'm C20/mid; 'to punish with a strap or cane' *Graham* Geordie 1979. *EDD* distribution to 1900: Nth, Lincs, EA. [imitative]. *Plus* "twankin' – playing truant" *GP* S'm 1960s

twat 1. the female genitalia, 2. term of insult

1. ex. S'm 1950s, etc.
2. "y' bad-moothed little twat" *VIZ* 42 ca.1990; "whether you think im a twat or not" (seaham.com website 2002)

twattle to fondle

"twattle – to treat caressingly, to fondle, to coax" *Atkinson* Cleve 1868. *EDD* distribution to 1900: Yx. [from twat]. *Plus* "be-twattled – confounded, overpowered, stupified, infatuated" *Brockett* Newc & Nth 1829; "betottled, betwattled – bewildered, confused or confounded, stupefied" *Atkinson* Cleve 1868

twee two

"either ane or twa" *RR* Weardale 1569; "twee horns full of grease" *Collier's Rant* Newc, C18/2; "leyke twe little reed tatees" *Bewick* Tyne 1790s; "twea – two" *Bailey* Co.Durham 1810; "its eyes like twee little pyerl buttons did shine" *Allan's Tyneside Songs* p.142 1816; "twea – two; tweasome – two in company" *Brockett* Newc & Nth 1829; "an' cut him in twee halves" 'Lambton Worm' 1867; "a twee-shillin'-bit" *Egglestone* Weardale 1870s; "atween the twee leets" (at twilight) *Embleton* Tyne 1897; "twee twinnies" *Embleton* Tyne 1897; *EP* Southwick C20/mid; "twe – two" Tanfield Lea, 1960. *EDD* distribution to 1900: twa – Sco, Yx; twe – N'd; twee – Tyne; tweeah – eYx. NE 2001: no longer in use, perhaps

twee cont.

because of similarity to and risk of confusion with 'three'. [OE twá]. See also **atwee**

twilt quilt

"Her twilted petticoat" *Pitman's Pay* G'head 1820s; "twilt – a bed cover" *Brockett* Newc & Nth 1829, *Atkinson* Cleve 1868; "twult – a quilt" *Luckley* Alnwick 1870s. *EDD* distribution to 1900: Sco, Nth, EA

twinnie a twin

"Mary Jane an Dorothy Ann, them's twee twinnies" Embleton *Embleton* Tyne 1897; 'either of a pair of twins' *EP* Southwick C20/mid

twiny fretful

"twiny – fretful, uneasy" *Dinsdale* mid-Tees 1849; 'peevish, fretful' *Atkinson* Cleve 1868. *EDD* distribution to 1900: Nth. *Plus* "twine – to cry" *Brockett* Newc & Nth 1829

twist(y) 1. to moan, complain,
2. whingeing (adj), 3. a quarrel

1. "twisting – discontented" *Palgrave* Hetton 1896; 'subdued complaining, crying (by child)' *JB* Shildon C20/mid; 'to whinge' *JP* S'm C20/2; "to twist / twine – to complain" B'd Castle 2001 Q; "twistin on" cenDm 2001 Q. NE 2001: in use
2. "twisty – cross, out of humour" *Atkinson* Cleve 1868; "Where aal the twisty, twiney, bad-tempered aad beggars come frev 'at gets puttin inti cabins beats me!" *Haldane* Newc 1879; "a twisty bairn" *IA* S'm 1950s,60s, sim. Gateshead 2001 Q. *EDD* distribution to 1900: N'd, C'd, Yx; "twisting" eD'm. NE 2001: in use
3. "Twist – quarrel, disagreement: 'They're all atwist', 'Hes thoo hadden a twist?'" *Palgrave* Hetton 1896

twitchbell see **earwig**

twok to steal (esp. a car), to joyride

"D/side Twocker Squad" (grafitti, S'm, 2000); "If Elton John is so ****ing rich, how come his wig looks like it's been twocked of a ****-soden tramp?" (Letter to *VIZ*, 2001). [taking without owner's consent]

tyke, tike dog

ex. *Kennet* 1690s as Yx; "mony a tike did him attend" Rothbury C18/2; "landlords were

tyke, tike cont.

styen-hearted tykes" *Allan's Tyneside Songs*
p.177 1824 Newc; "tike or tyke – a blunt or
vulgar fellow... also a name for a dog" *Brockett*
Newc & Nth 1829; "tike tyke – a dog, a cur;
a churlish or mean and low person; (playfully)
a hungry child: ' a nest of hungry tykes'
(a family)" *Atkinson* Cleve 1868; "Tyke –
Yorkshire person" *JB* Shildon C20/mid.
EDD distribution to 1900: Sco, Ire, Nth,
Mids, EA, USA. [ON tík 'female dog']

tyooth tooth

ex. Durham 1916. See also **axletooth,
(tooth)wark**

tyun see **tak**

understrapper underling

"undastrappa" *Dodd* MS Tanfield Lea C20/2; *Graham* Geordie 1979. [*OED* exx. 1700 on]

unket ?unusual

"uncots – treasure, queer things or out-of-the-way things, stored by as valuables" *Bell* MS Newc 1815; "unket, unkenned – strange or relating [to] strangers: 'an unkett folk'" *Bell* MS Newc 1830s. *EDD* distribution to 1900: general. [ME unkidd 'uncouth']

upaheight high up

"up-aheet" *Egglestone* Weardale 1877; "up a hyt" *Dodd* MS Tanfield Lea C20/2; "up-aheyte" *Todd* Tyne 1977; *GP* S'm 1998. *EDD* distribution to 1900: N'd, W'd, Yx

upcast mine shaft

"an upcast (pronounced upkest) shaft in a coal-mine is one used to promote a circulation or upward draft of air" *Brockett* Newc & Nth 1846; 'the shaft by which the return air is discharged from the mine' *Nicholson* 1880. *EDD* distribution to 1900: Sco, N'd, D'm

upcast to reproach

"upcast – to upbraid; [noun] a taunt, reproach" *Brockett* Newc & Nth 1829; "Upcast – throw in one's teeth, taunt with" *Palgrave* Hetton 1896; "gie ower up-kesting that – stop reminding me" *Dunn* B'p Auck 1950. *EDD* distribution to 1900: Sco, Ire, Nth. *Plus* "upkast – reminder of past grievance" *Dodd* MS Tanfield Lea C20/2. See also **cast**

upgrown adult

"Upgrown – grown up, adult (always used)" *Palgrave* Hetton 1896. *EDD* distribution to 1900: general

urchin hedgehog

"p[ai]d for 4 urcheons' heads, 6 d." *Raine* MS Whitekirk 1673/74; "Tommy Linn had no saddle to put on, but two urchin skins" *NChorister* D'm C18/2; 'a hedgehog, also a dwarfish... or deformed person' *Bell* MS Newc 1830s; "hurchin, or urchin – a hedgehog" *Brockett* Newc & Nth 1846. *EDD* distribution to 1900: general. [AN herison, hereson 'hedgehog']

urled pinched

'stinted in growth' *Brockett* Newc & Nth 1829; 'pinched with cold' *Dinsdale* mid-Tees 1849. *EDD* distribution to 1900: Nth

us see **me, we**

vage a struggle to do something

"it's a vage to reach" *MG* Teesdale C20/2; 'something that's an effort or a struggle to do' Middleton in Teesdale (E). [?related to voyage]

varnigh very nearly

"thor eggs wad jawp an' var-ny crack a styen" *MC* Tyne May 1881; "thouse varney ten minits late" West Stanley C20/1; "vannear" *Lakeland* re C'd C20; "its vennigh kennor – near knocking off time" *Dunn* B'p Auck 1950; *Dodd* MS Tanfield Lea C20/2. ['varry' (very) plus 'nigh']

varry very

"its varra true, sed Jenny the Gardner" *Bewick* Tyne 1790s; "a varra deeal" (a large quantity) *Atkinson* Cleve 1868; *Wearside Tales* 1879; "varry painful" *Dobson* Tyne 1972. *EDD* distribution to 1900: in this pronunciation Yx

vast vast amount, a lot (of)

"sheed seen a vast o' the warld" *Bewick* Tyne 1790s; "I've seen a vast of obstinate awd men like you" *JS* South Shields C19/mid; "kindness dis a vast" *Allan's Tyneside Songs* p.477 1863; "he's a vast aader nor he leuks" *Haldane* Newc 1879; "thor wis a vast o' folk i' the chapel" *Graham* Geordie 1979. *EDD* distribution to 1900: general

vend combination of North East pit-owners to regulate the price of coal (C19/1)

"vends – a limited sale of coal, as arranged by the 'trade': 'They were not hamper'd. then wi' vends'" *Pitman's Pay* G'head 1820s. *EDD* distribution to 1900: esp. N'd, D'm

viewer pit manager

"Viewer – the manager of a coal-mine. So, 'under-viewer' (under-manager)" *Palgrave* Hetton 1896; 'the manager of a colliery' *Graham* Geordie 1979. *EDD* distribution to 1900: N'd, D'm, Staffs

vine pencil

"vine-pencil – a black lead pencil" *Brockett* Newc & Nth 1829; "Vine – a lead-pencil (always used). 'Pencil' always means slate-pencil" *Palgrave* Hetton 1896; 'pencil' Spennymoor C20/mid, *Viereck* re Gateshead 1966, Dobson 9 Newc 1974. *EDD* distribution to 1900: N'd, D'm, C'd. [vine charcoal, used

vine cont.

for writing]. *Plus* "keely-vine – a black-lead pencil" *Brockett* Newc & Nth 1829

vision television

ex. *IL* Tow Law C20/2

waak to walk

"in Aa waaks as large as life" *Tyneside grammar* 1880s; "Aw...wawk'd gotherly in" *Barrass* Stanley 1890s; "waakin'" Durham 1916. *Allan's Tyneside Songs* p.217 1837. See also **wark** (work/pain)

waal coal face

"waal – wall, hard coal face" *Dodd* MS Tanfield Lea C20/2

waff 1. air, 2. a spirit

1. "waff o' cawd – a slight cold" (infection) *Pitman's Pay* G'head 1820s; "waff – a slight motion of the hand; a slight puff of wind" *Brockett* Newc & Nth 1846; 'rush of air' *Dobson* Newc 1974. *EDD* distribution to 1900: Sco, Nth. [waft?; compare Norw. veift 'puff of wind']
2. "the spirit or ghost of a dying man called in Yorkshire a waft" *Kennet* 1690s; "waff – an apparition in the exact resemblance of a person, supposed to be seen just before or soon after death" *Brockett* Newc & Nth 1829; "waff – fetch, doppelganger" *Dinsdale* mid-Tees 1849. *EDD* distribution to 1900: Sco, N'd, Yx

play the wag play truant

"thor's ne playce te play the wag noo" *Allan's Tyneside Songs* p.396 C19/mid; "aa cud hev tyeken a prize for wez (who's) playin' the wag" *Robson* Newc C20/1; "ye played the wag from Sunday Skeul as weel" *Irwin* Tyne 1970–71. *EDD* distribution to 1900: N'd, D'm, Lx, Oxf, London, Australia. *Plus* "play the nick – truancy" *Dodd* MS Tanfield Lea C20/2

wag at the wa' pendulum clock

ex. *Allan's Tyneside Songs* p.485 1862. *EDD* distribution to 1900: Sco, N'd

waggonway track for coal vehicles

"waggon way – a rail way on which the coals are conveyed from the Pits in waggons to the staiths on the Tyne, Wear, and Blyth" *Bell* MS Newc 1815; "these days there was ne iron rails, the waggon-ways were wood" (re Stephenson's time) *Allan's Tyneside Songs* p.463 1862; "wagon-way – the railway upon which the coals are taken away from the screens. the rolley-way is also called the wagon-way" *Nicholson* 1880. *EDD* distribution to 1900: N'd, D'm. *Plus* "a wagonway-man... was a general handyman, an experienced miner, who had a

waggonway cont.

vague authority over the boys in his district" *Hitchin* re Seaham p.65 1910s

waggy see **peter waggy**

wailer pit worker

"wailer – a person employed on the pit heap at the mouth of the pit to wail or pick out the stones and brasses from out of amongst the coals" *Bell* MS Newc 1815; "waila – cleaning coal in picking belts" *Dodd* MS Tanfield Lea C20/2

wairsh insipid

"Life wad be varra wairch without 'em" (lasses) *Pitman's Pay* G'head 1820s; "wairsh, wearch, werch – thin, watery, weak, insipid" *Brockett* Newc & Nth 1829; "she hezzent put ony salt i' the breid, an' its as wairsh as waiter", "also weak, wishy-washy: 'wairsh port'" *Luckley* Alnwick 1870s; "wairsh – tasteless" Tanfield Lea 1960. *EDD* distribution to 1900: esp. Sco, Ire, Nth, Mids [ME werische]. *Plus* "Warsh (waa:sh) – faint, from loss of food" *Palgrave* Hetton 1896

wake see **lyke wake**

waked woke

"next mornin he waked up" *Haldane* Newc 1879; "waked up" Durham 1916

walls-end quality coal

"Walls-End – a name extensively used for Newcastle coals... The coals from this place being at one time of the most valuable description, other coalowners began to append to the name of their coals the favourite term of Walls-end, no matter from whence they came" *Brockett* Newc & Nth 1846; "best Dawdon wallsend" *GP* S'm re 1946

wallyment, wullemot guillemot

"wullemot / wullyment – the guillemot" *Heslop* Tyne 1890s. *Plus* "Bairn, thou's as white as a wallyment" (?) *Parker* Tyne Valley 1896 p.65

wame belly

"weary byens and empty wyem" *Pitman's Pay* G'head 1820s; "had fu' been the wame o' Bob Cranky" *Allan's Tyneside Songs* p.96 1814; "wame – the womb or belly" *Bell* MS Newc 1815. *EDD* distribution to 1900: Sco, Nth, Derbys. *Plus* "give us yell and aw'll drink ma wameful" *Bell* Newc 1812 p.89

wang-tooth molar

"wang-tooth – the jaw-tooth" *Grose* 1787; "wang-tooth – a molar tooth or grinder" *Atkinson* Cleve 1868. *EDD* distribution to 1900: Nth, Derbys, Lincs. [OE wang 'cheek']

wankle wobbly, uncertain

"wankle – wobbly, wavery" *Ray* 1674; "wankle weather – uncertain, changeable" *Kennet* 1690s as Nth; "wankle – uncertain" *Bailey* Co.Durham 1810; "as wankle as a wet seck" *Gibson* C'd 1880; 'weak, tottering' *Smith* Weardale 1883. *EDD* distribution to 1900: general. [OE wancol]

wappies wasps

ex. *JO* re High Thornley/Rowlands Gill, 1930s–1940s in *Nth Words*. *EDD* distribution to 1900: N'd. *Plus* "waps – a wasp" *Grose* 1787.

play war be very angry, etc.

"Me mam'll play war with me" *AK* Tyne mid 20C

wark 1. work (noun), 2. to work

1. "when I cam to Walker wark / I had ne coat nor ne pit sark" *Bell* Newc 1812 p.36; "awl kines e wark" *Armstrong* Tanfield C19/2; "when things gan wrang wi' wark or pay" *Barrass* Stanley 1890s; "ye'll nivvor need te gan te wark" *Dobson* Tyne 1972. *EDD* distribution to 1900: in this pronunciation Sco, Nth. *Plus* "wark-folks – labourers, workpeople" *Brockett* Newc & Nth 1829; "waukrife" (work experienced) *Wearside Tales* 1879
2. "he can neither wark nor want" *Brockett* Newc & Nth 1829; "he's warked as debbity" Tyne *MC* May 1881

wark 1. to ache, 2. ache, pain

1. "wark – to ake" *Ray* 1674; "my head werkes, my teeth werke" *Kennet* 1690s as D'm; Embleton, Newc 1897. *EDD* distribution to 1900: Sco, Nth, eMids, EA Shrop
2. "wark – an ache, sharp pain: 'teeath-wark', 'heead-wark'" *Atkinson* Cleve 1868; "tiuthwark – toothache" *Dunn* B'p Auck 1950; "bellywark" Weardale, Teesdale 2001 Q. [OE wærc 'pain']. *Plus* "aixes – bodily pains or the ague" *Bell* MS Newc 1815. See also **waak** (walk)

warrant, warnd to be sure, be certain

"I'll warr'nt ye've had a merry day" *Chicken* Benwell 1720s; "aw warn't ye aw thought they luck'd pretty" *Allan's Tyneside Songs* p.48 1812;

warrant, warnd cont.

"Aa's warned – I warrant" *Haldane* Newc 1879; "Aa warnstha" (I daresay) *Tyneside grammar* 1880s; "ah warnd thoo hezn't been abed ahl neet, noo?" *Embleton* Tyne 1897; "A wairn'd a will" (I bet I will) *CT* New Herrington 1930s; "Aa-warnd ye think yorsel' clivvor?" *Graham* Geordie 1979. *EDD* distribution to 1900: general. [OFr warantir]

warse, warst worse, worst

"warse – worse" *Kennet* 1690s as Nth; "mickle the better and no' the war" *Bell* MS Newc 1830s; "gettin warse and warse" *Haldane* Newc 1879; "warst" Durham 1916; "warse" Tanfield Lea, 1960. *EDD* distribution to 1900: in this pronunciation Sco, Nth

warsle to wrestle

"warsel – struggle" *Pitman's Pay* G'head 1820s; "warsle – to strive, to wrestle" *Brockett* Newc & Nth 1829. *EDD* distribution to 1900: Sco, Ire, N'd, W'd, C'd, Yx

was 1. was (preterite singular), 2. were (pret. pl.)

1. "wis leukin at" *Bewick* Tyne 1790s; "he wis comin yem" *Armstrong* Tanfield C19/2; "wes" Durham 1916, Tanfield Lea, 1960; "I war flayed to tell ye a plain tale" ?N'd, *NCM* 1900–1901
2. "Wor cares war few" *Barrass* Stanley 1890s; "we wannit iv a partickler hurry" *Wearside Tales* 1879; "what we war tawkin' about" *Allan's Tyneside Songs* p.444 1862

wath a ford

ex. *Dinsdale* mid-Tees 1849. *EDD* distribution to 1900: Sco, Nth, Lincs. [ON vað]

watter water

"waiter or waeter – the Newcastle pronunciation of water" *Brockett* Newc & Nth 1829; "rum weak as watter" *Allan's Tyneside Songs* p.246 1827; "he had smelt the salt wetter" *Allan's Tyneside Songs* p.221 1842; "waiter" *Luckley* Alnwick 1870s; "neebody sud drink watter" *Haldane* Newc 1879; "it wes cummin doon hyel wettor" *Cuddy Cairt* Newc 1917, sim. *Brockett* Newc & Nth 1846; "gone ower watter – emigrated" *Dunn* B'p Auck 1950; "wettor" *Todd* Tyne 1977. *EDD* distribution to 1900: in this pronunciation esp. Sco, Nth

wattie see **hare**

waup curlew

"when the waups are on the heights" *Northumbrian Words III* C20/mid re Kielder

wavy tin corrugated iron

att. *GP* S'm 1980s of Houghton Pit workers in Seaham

wawk see **waak**

waxa see **excellent**

waysgoose day out

"Waysgoose – day trip of the workpeople belonging to a firm or company" *Palgrave* Hetton 1896 [term first noted 1683]

we, us

"as wuh say" (we) *Dobson* Tyne 1972; "worra wuz ganna dee?" *VIZ* 48; "worsells" (ourselves) *Barrass* Stanley 1890s; "huz" *Marshall* G'head 1806, *Barrass* Stanley 1890s; "huz colliers" *Allan's Tyneside Songs* p.177 1824. See also **me**

weans children

'children, little ones' *Pitman's Pay* G'head 1820s; *Bell* MS Newc 1830s; "weeans, weeans – wee-ones, children (Sco. weans)" *Brockett* Newc & Nth 1829. *EDD* distribution to 1900: Sco, Ire, Nth, Lincs. ['wee one']. See also **bairn**

wedge money

ex. G'head 2001 Q. See also **brass, lowie**

weel well

"weel eneugh" *Bewick* Tyne 1790s; "Walker pit's deun weel for me" *Bell* Newc 1812 p.36; "Ye may weel ax" *Parker* Tyne Valley 1896 p.87 "weel" Tanfield Lea, 1960. *EDD* distribution to 1900: in this pronunciation Sco, Nth

weeny tiny

"weeny – very little" *Brockett* Newc & Nth 1846; "tiny... Only heard once, from a native of S. Shields" *Palgrave* Hetton 1896; *Dodd* MS Tanfield Lea C20/2. *EDD* distribution to 1900: general

wend 1. to go, 2. a turning

1. ex. *Ray* 1674
2. "wend or wiend – a narrow street or small court (D'ton, Stockton)" *Brockett* Newc & Nth 1829. *EDD* distribution to 1900: Sco, D'm, W'd. [OE windan 'to turn, go']

weshin', wishin' washing

"wishinge" *Anderson* Newcastle 1624; "a rainy weshin' day" T. Wilson *Allan's Tyneside Songs* p.264 1831. *EDD* distribution to 1900: wesh – C'd, Yx, Lx, Mids

whang shoelace, thong

"whangs – leather thongs" *Grose* 1787, *Bailey* Co.Durham 1810; 'a small leather thong such as is used for tying shoes', 'a belt round the waist' *Brockett* Newc & Nth 1846; "whaing (hwaeng) – boot-lace" *Palgrave* Hetton 1896. *EDD* distribution to 1900: Sco, Ire, Nth, Mids. NE 2001: not in use. [thwang 'thong'] See also **shibbin'-leather**

what

"whatten – what kind of, what: 'whatten o'clock is it?'" *Brockett* Newc & Nth 1829; "a divvent naw warrit means" *CT* New Herrington 1930s; "what'n humour he's in" *Dunn* B'p Auck 1950. *EDD* distribution to 1900: general

what for why

"what for nut?" (why not) *Green* Wearside 1879 re C19/1; "What for de they put oranges intiv the pigs' mooths?"* *NWC* 16 Jan 1886 Sup. p.5; "what for? says the Pee-dee" *Allan's Tyneside Songs* p.153 1927; "what are ye off school for?" D, S'm 2003. [after model of Old English 'for hwi...?' (for what, why)]. *Plus* "'Cos for! – reply to 'What for?'" *FS* Shotton Colliery 1930s. *Wey thoo maun be a fuyl not te knaa that – It's becaas they cannot put them intiv the pigs onywhor else."

whe who

"whe's that with ye?" *Chicken* Benwell 1720s; "whe dos thou tig on wee?" *Bewick* Tyne 1790s; "whe's thou, man?" *Allan's Tyneside Songs* p.293 1825; "and show'd plain whee was rook and whee was pigeon" *Allan's Tyneside Songs* p.238 1829; "'It's time for ye ti tak a wife,' said Smoggins to his son. 'Whee's sall Aa tak?' axes the young hopeful." Newc C19/2; "wheese thee think thou's taaking te?" Shield Row C20/1; "think weel, maw man, wi' whe ye play" *Allan's Tyneside Songs* p.417 1862; "Ah divvent care whese ghost ye are" *Irwin* Tyne 1970; "weezon the bar?" East Boldon 1985. *EDD* distribution to 1900: in this pronunciation Nth. [OE hwa 'who', hwæs 'whose' – in direct questions]

wheezles wheeze (noun and vb)

1. wheezles (respiratory disease): "cats wi' the wheezles" *Barrass* Stanley 1890s
2. "wheezle – to wheeze" *Dinsdale* mid-Tees 1849. *EDD* distribution to 1900: esp. Sco, N.I., D'm, C'd

whemmel to overturn

"whemmel, whommel or whummel – to turn upside down, to tumble over" *Brockett* Newc & Nth 1829; 'to upset or turn over' *Atkinson* Cleve 1868; 'to up-turn a barrow to empty it' *Smith* Weardale 1883. *EDD* distribution to 1900: Sco, Ire, Nth, Mids. [whelm]

wherry boat esp. on the Tyne

"the vessel came in contact with a small Highland wherry from Mull and Icolmkill, which immediately sunk" *Newc Courant* 17 Aug 1822 p.4; "Aw thowt aw'd myek a voyage to Shiels / Iv Jemmy Joneson's whurry" *Allan's Tyneside Songs* p.51 1823; "whurry – wherry, large boat; a sort of barge or lighter" *Brockett* Newc & Nth 1829; "Aw've the wherry o' poor Jimmy Johnson / An' aw hev both the oars, mast and sail" *Ross* Tyne p.1 C19/1. *EDD* distribution to 1900: Sco, EA. *Note* example in store at Beamish Open Air Museum gives dimension 42ft x 19 ft, with 4ft 6 in draft when loaded

whey see **quey**

whick alive, lively

"whick – quick – used in the cry of fresh fish at Newcastle: 'whick-an-alive'" *Bell* MS Newc 1815; "whick – alive e.g. which-hedge" *Dinsdale* mid-Tees 1849; "as whick as onny lop (flea)" Tyne *MC* May 1881. [quick, OE cwic] See also **quick**

whickens couchgrass

"quickens or quicken grass – a general name for all creeping or stoloniferous grasses or plants, which give the farmer so much trouble to eradicate" *Bailey* Co.Durham 1810; "wicken-grass, wickens – twitch, couch or couch-grass" *Atkinson* Cleve 1868. See also **quicks**

whiet quiet

"can't you be whiet, whiles?" *Smith* Weardale 1883; "ther tongues nivver lay whyte" *Lakeland* re C'd 1901

while until

"while that thou come again" *Noah's Ark* Newc C15/16; "a yonge black calfe, to be brong up about house whel saint tillinmas" Darlington 1610 via Atkinson no.25; "Nor to presu[m]e for sell, whylles they have [r]ong the corne bell" *Durham* C16/2; "while – until, before: "wait while I come", "not while night" *Atkinson* Cleve 1868; "Ah'll be stayin while Friday" *Wood* re Cleveland C20/2. *EDD* distribution to 1900: Sco, Nth, Mids. [OE hwíle]

whiles sometimes

"whiles gannin', whiles baith fairly down", "...march away, whiles in, whiles out o' step" *Marshall* G'head 1806; "it rains whiles" *Brockett* Newc & Nth 1829; "she's kind o' kittle i' the temper, whiles" *Embleton* Tyne 1897; "A whiles think hes aal right" *Dunn* B'p Auck 1950; "whiles" Alston 2001 Q. *EDD* distribution to 1900: general

whilk which (rel.pron.)

"whilk – who, which what.... whilk – somebody, a certain person" *Kennet* 1690s as D'm; "aw whilk while" Rothbury C18/2; "whilks Trunks? i.e. which is trumps?" *Bell* MS Newc 1815; "whilk – which" *Pitman's Pay* G'head 1820s, *Moore* Weardale 1859, *Atkinson* Cleve 1868; "any yan o' whilk" *Egglestone* Weardale 1870s. *EDD* distribution to 1900: in this pronunciation Sco, Yx [OE hwilc]

whin hard stone

"whynn – hard stone – in mining" *Bell* MS Newc 1815; "whin or whinstone.—greenstone; an igneous rock; but the term is usually applied by borers and sinkers to any exceptionally hard rock that emits a sharp sound under the hammer or chisel; usually a greenstone or siliceous sandstone" *Nicholson* 1880. *EDD* distribution to 1900: Sco, Nth

whinge to whine, complain

"dinna whinge and whipe" *Marshall* G'head 1806; "haud you whinjin gob" *Allan's Tyneside Songs* p.361 1849; D'ton 1940s Q. *EDD* distribution to 1900: Sco, Ire, Nth [?OE hwinsian]

whins gorse bushes

"xiii loods of furres or whynnes" *Raine* MS Castle Eden 1576/77; "whinns, for baking" expenses, Sherburn Hospital, 1686 via *Brockett*

whins cont.

Newc & Nth 1846; "lay drunk amang the whins" *Allan's Tyneside Songs* p.207 1827; "the whins and bents and strang sea air" *Allan's Tyneside Songs* p.468 1862. *EDD* distribution to 1900: general. NE 2001: in use. [ON? compare Norw. hvine]. *Plus* "whinney-bush" *Wood* re rural Teesside C20/2, Trimdon 2002 Q

whisht peace, quiet

"had thy wisht" *Marshall* G'head 1806; "as whisht as a mouse" *Bells* re Carlisle 1802; "whisht! – be silent, hush!" *Brockett* Newc & Nth 1829; "whisht lads, haad yor gobs..." 'Lambton Worm' 1867; "Whisht (hwisht). hush!" *Palgrave* Hetton 1896. *EDD* distribution to 1900: general

whussel to whistle

"the fifes are whuslin' lood an' clear" *Marshall* G'head 1806; "whussel – a corruption of whistle" *Brockett* Newc & Nth 1829; "whusseld" (pret.) *Barrass* Stanley 1890s. *EDD* distribution to 1900: Sco, N.I., C'd, N'd

why well!, why!

"Wi aw thowt there was ne harm in that, man" *Street Piracy* Newc 1822; "Y man!" *Egglestone* Weardale 1870s; "Wey!" (well, why...) *Tyneside grammar* 1880s; "wey! – why!" Tanfield Lea 1960; "why like?" *VIZ* 78 1996

why-aye! certainly, of course

"Ae-hy" (why-aye) *Bewick* Tyne 1790s; "eigh-wye – a careless mode of expressing assent – yes, yes" *Brockett* Newc & Nth 1829; "wia – well, yes, why!" *Dinsdale* mid-Tees 1849; "Wey ay (wai:aa:y) (why, ay!) – to be sure! (v. common)" *Palgrave* Hetton 1896; "why aye hinny – certainly darling" *Dobson* Tyne 1969; "why-aye – definitely yes" *JB* Shildon C20/mid, 'undoubtedly' *Dodd* MS Tanfield Lea C20/2, 'of course' *Graham* Geordie 1979. *EDD* distribution to 1900: why-aye – eD'm, nYx, eYx

wicken-grass, wicks see **whickens, quick**

wife, wifie woman

"to man or wyfe" *Cuthbert* C15/mid; "a fitt seete for brydgrumes, bryds, and sike wyves to sit in" *Raine* MS Chester-le-Street 1612; "awd wife" *Allan's Tyneside Songs* p.237 1829; "wife – any woman, whether married or not" *Brockett* Newc & Nth 1829; "astonished the wifie did

wife, wifie cont.

seem" *Allan's Tyneside Songs* p.308 1862; 'any staid woman' *Graham* Geordie 1979. *EDD* distribution to 1900: wifie – Sco. [OE wif-mon]

will 1. present tense, 2. past tense

1. "will for shall, and would for should... passim in the North Countreye" *Brockett* Newc & Nth 1829; "winnot – will not" *Dinsdale* mid-Tees 1849; "aw winnot believe't" *Green* Wearside 1879; "aw wunna hev barley breed" *Luckley* Alnwick 1870s; "twinnit wesh" (will not work) *Chater* Newc 1880; "winnet" *Barrass* Stanley 1890s; "winnut – won't" *Dunn* B'p Auck 1950; "wee-ant" (won't) *Wood* re Cleveland C20/2; *EDD* distribution to 1900: winna – Sco, Nth, Mids; winnut etc. Nth, Derbys
2. "it wad set aw his wits astear" Rothbury C18/2; "if he haddent bad teeth he wad eaten the stopple" *Allan's Tyneside Songs* p.219 1817; "you wad thought his feet was myed o' styen" *Allan's Tyneside Songs* p.155 1827; "whe iver wad thowt..." *Allan's Tyneside Songs* p.243 1842; "eff aw hadn't been a good scholar, aw wad lost me set" *Wearside Tales* 1879; "wadn't, wadint" *Armstrong* Tanfield C19/2; "neebody wad knawn nowt" *Other Eye* Newc ca.1890; "wadint – wouldn't" *Dodd* MS Tanfield Lea C20/2

willock whelk

"willicks – the shell fish periwinkle" *Bell* MS Newc 1815; "willock – standard black whelk on rocks below high tide; buck willock – same but yellow shell; bull willock – same as buck, yellow, but 'massive', only found out at sea, attached selves to crab pots etc., seeking the bait." *JH* S'm C20/mid; "the willick or periwinkle is a small univalve mollusc found on the rocks of the Geordieland coast" *Dobson* Tyne 1972. *EDD* distribution to 1900: general. [OE wioloc]. *Plus* "bull-willik" S'd, S'm 2001 Q; "pennywilks" *Allan's Tyneside Songs* p.406 1862

win to access coal underground

"for wynenge stones to the said worke, viii d." *Raine* MS Embleton, N'd, 1584; "win – to get: as winning stones, to get stones in a quarry" *Bailey* Co.Durham 1810; "during this month a seam of coal, four feet 2 inches thick, was won at Greencroft Colliery" *Latimer, Records* re Aug 1840; "win – to get (something) by

win cont.

effort" *Dinsdale* mid-Tees 1849; "win – to reach, attain to: "wan yamm" (home) *Atkinson* Cleve 1868; "win – coal is won when it is proved and a position attained so that it can be worked and brought to bank" *Nicholson* 1880. *EDD* distribution to 1900: Sco, N'd, D'm, Yx. [OE gewinnan]

wind-berry bilberry

"wind-berry – billberry or whortleberry" *Ray* 1674; "win- or wind-berry – a bilbury or wortleberry" *Grose* 1787. *EDD* distribution to 1900: wimberry – esp. Lx, wMids. See also **bleaberry**

windy pick pneumatic pick

"small pneumatic drill used in hewing" *JM* Dawdon 1980. *Plus* "pompom – pneumatic drill in pit" *JR* Seaham C20/1; "jigger" *BL* Winlaton 1960s,70s

witch-wood the mountain ash

ex. *Brockett* Newc & Nth 1829. *EDD* distribution to 1900: Nth, Suff

wite 1. punishment, blame, 2. to blame, punish, 3. weight

1. "Od [God's] wheyte leet on him!" *Bells* re Carlisle 1802; "Wite – blame: 'He got the wyte on't'" *Palgrave* Hetton 1896
2. "G—d wheyte her... for beheavin se to maw bayrne" *Bewick* Tyne, 1790s; "wite – to reproach, to blame" *Atkinson* Cleve 1868. *EDD* distribution to 1900: esp. Sco, Ire, Nth. [OE wítan 'to blame']
3. "wite" (weight) *Armstrong* Tanfield C19/2

with

"what he did weed" (with it), "puft wea pride" Rothbury C18/2; "wiv, woh" *Bewick* Tyne 1790s; "wiv – with, esp. before vowel: "wiv 'imself'" *Atkinson* Cleve 1868; "wiv us / win us" *Tyneside grammar* 1880s; "wid" (with it) *Armstrong* Tanfield C19/2; "wi' – with, wiv before a vowel" Tanfield Lea 1960. *Plus* "wivoot – without" *Atkinson* Cleve 1868, Tanfield Lea 1960

wizzen'd dried, shrivelled

"wizened – dried, shrivelled, shrunk" *Bailey* Co.Durham 1810; "as a wizzen'd aud wife" *Bell* MS Newc 1815; "wizened, wizzened, wizzent" *Brockett* Newc & Nth 1829. *EDD* distribution to 1900: Esp. Sco, Nth. [OE wisnian, ON visna] See also **guizzen, kizzen**

wobbit no...

"Wobbit – an introductory word: 'Wobbit thou'll not'" *Palgrave* Hetton 1896. *EDD* distribution to 1900: D'm, Lincs. [why plus but]

wokey damp

"wooky – moist, sappy" *Kennet* 1690s as D'm; "voky – damp, moist, juicy [plus weaky]" *Brockett* Newc & Nth 1829; "weaky, weeky – moist, watery, juicy, full of sap" *Atkinson* Cleve 1868. *EDD* distribution to 1900: weaky – Nth, Worcs; woky, oakey – D'm; voky – N'd

wor our

"this is wor pay week" *Collier's Rant* Newc C18/2; "wor – our; worsells – ourselves" *Brockett* Newc & Nth 1829; "wor Nan" (wife of speaker) *Armstrong* Tanfield C19/2; "Our – used in calling members of a family: 'Coom hayer, oor Jumzie!'" *Palgrave* Hetton 1896; "worsells" Durham 1916; "Wor lads at th' church social an' a want t' see we 'es dancing wi" *CT* New Herrington 1930s; "wor pit village" *Irwin* Tyne 1970. [OE úre]

worm dragon, serpent

"the Long Worm of Lambton is celebrated at Lambton near Chester le Street, Durham, and its well, hill etc. shown..." *Bell* MS Newc 1830s. *EDD* distribution to 1900: Sco, N'd. [OE wyrm 'worm, reptile, dragon' i.e. animal of serpentine form]. See also **hagworm**

worrit, werrit to worry, torment

"werrit – to tease. Not so violent a metaphor as tue" *Brockett* Newc & Nth 1829; "he set his dog on to worrit wor cat" *Graham* Geordie 1979. *EDD* distribution to 1900: general

wow treacle?

"wowy an' bread – bread and treacle" *Dunn* B'p Auck 1950; "treacle-wow – treacle beer" *Pitman's Pay* G'head 1820s

wowl to howl

"wowl – to cry or howl" *Pitman's Pay* G'head 1820s; *Palgrave* Hetton 1896. *EDD* distribution to 1900: in this form, esp. NE, EA. *Plus* "wowly – irritable" *MB* Coxhoe C20/mid. See also **yowl**

wrang wrong

"eff he thinks aw'se a fule, he's a lang way wrang" *Wearside Tales* 1879, etc.

(get) wrang get into trouble, be told off

"you'll get wrong off your Mam, etc." *FS* Wingate 1940s; "yihll get rang" *JP* S'm C20/2; "I got him wrong – got him into trouble" 2001 Q. *EDD* distribution to 1900: phrase – Sco, N'd, Yx, Lx. NE 2001: in use

wrought worked

"wrought out – worn out" *Pitman's Pay* G'head 1820s; "Geordy wrout hard" *Haldane* Newc 1879

wuddy noose

"jilted, dreamt of knife and wuddy" *Newcastle Magazine* p.177 14 Aug 1872. *EDD* distribution to 1900: Sco, N'd, nYx. [withy]

wunter winter

"i th' howl oh wounter" *Bewick* Tyne 1790s

x

the mark a pitman was expected to make (rather than a signature) on the Yearly Bonds, setting out terms of pit pay and employment in the first half of the 19th century. "My maternal grandfather used an X when signing a document – an operation that scared him stiff." *Hitchin* re Dalton-le-Dale 1910s p.15

yacker acre

ex. *Dinsdale* mid-Tees 1849; "a five yacker field" *Wearside Tales* 1879. See also **yakker**

yaits oats

"yets" *Grose* 1787 re N'd; "yaits" *Bailey* Co.Durham 1810; "yeats, hay and grass" Rothbury C18/2. [OE átan]. See also **haver**

yak etc. the oak

"trees of ake" *Raine* MS Durham 1439; "akes" *Bell* MS Newc 1830s; "a twig o' yeck" *Pitman's Pay* G'head 1820s; "he's as hard as yek and iron" *Brockett* Newc & Nth 1829. [OE ác]

yakker ?worker

"yacker – a labourer" *RM* Norton C20/mid; "Yackas and Keekers – the excavating Geordies or pit-men" *Dobson* Tyne 1970; "yakka – ignorant deviation of pitman" *Dodd* MS Tanfield Lea C20/2; "yacker – pit lad" NShields C20/mid Q; "yacker – pit worker (hewer)" Wheatley Hill 2002 Q; "coal yacker" (miner) *JM* Thornaby C20/2; "pit yakker – a pitman" *Graham* Geordie 1979 (where source as 'yark', a heavy blow); "farm-yakkers" *Wood* Cleve 2002; "aad yakker" meaning old pit worker, *GD* Co.D'm 2004 E. [possibly yacker derived from yark or hack; less likely 'yacker' meaning chatterbox, an Australian word first noted in print in the UK in 1959 or 'yakka', strenuous labour, from Aborigine into Australian English 1847]. See also **pit-yacker**

yal, yell ale, beer

"some drank yell" *Bells* re Carlisle 1802; "yal – ale" *Bailey* Co.Durham 1810; "tyest the yell and stop a bit" *Pitman's Pay* G'head 1820s; "nowther yal ner porter" *Egglestone* Weardale 1870s; "a quiet pint o' yell" *Barrass* Stanley 1890s; "ower-much yall – too much to drink" *Dunn* B'p Auck 1950. [OE ealu]

yallow yellow

"yallow – yellow" *Dinsdale* mid-Tees 1849; "as yallow as a marigowld" *Egglestone* Weardale 1870s

yammer 1. to talk incessantly, complain

1. "yammering and shouting" *Bewick* Tyne 1790s; "yammer – to cry like a dog in pain" *Bailey* Co.Durham 1810; "yammering on frae morn till neet" *Pitman's Pay* G'head 1820s; "yammer – to fret, to whine, to complain" *Brockett* Newc & Nth 1829; "yammerin'

yammer cont.

hoonds" *Allan's Tyneside Songs* p.236 1829; "yammer – to rattle on" *Gibson* C'd 1880; "yammering – continually grumbling" *Nth Words* Whickham, N'd 1938; "yammerin' – always nagging" *Nth Words* N'd 1938; "stop yammering on about it" *IA* S'm 1950s,60s; "giv ower yammerin" *Graham* Geordie 1979. *EDD* distribution to 1900: Sco, Ire, Nth, Mids, USA. [OE geomrian, MDu jammeren]. *Plus* "a ranterfied priest / that gets paid for his lees an' his yammer" *Allan's Tyneside Songs* p.366 1849

yammy see **turnip**

yan, ane one

"ilk ane fra othir" *Cuthbert* C15/mid; "either ane or twa" *RR* Weardale 1569; "yan – one; yance – once" *Kennet* 1690s as Nth; "Ane neet gannin hame" *Street Piracy* Newc 1822; "yan neat" (one night) *Marshall* G'head 1806; "every yen" (everyone) *Oiling* G'head 1826; "that yan day" *Egglestone* Weardale 1870s; "yen o' wor hewers" *Haldane* Newc 1879; "yen an' twenty weeks" *MC* Tyne May 1881; "A cannot gie ye yan" *Dunn* B'p Auck 1950. [OE án (with long vowel) remained 'an' in the North, with the 'a' breaking to 'ia', 'ie', etc.] NE 2001: "yan, twee, tree" reported in use Upper Weardale ca.1940 Q

yance once

"yance (ance) – once" *Bailey* Co.Durham 1810; "yance mare aw's free" *Armstrong* Tanfield C19/2; "yence – once" Tanfield Lea 1960; yans bitt'n, twicet shy" cenD'm C20/2 Q. [ME ánes]. *Plus* "wonce" *Allan's Tyneside Songs* p.238 1829

yare ready, active

"yare – sharp, ready" *Kennet* 1690s as D'm; 'nimble, ready' Ray 1737. *EDD* distribution to 1900: general. [OE gearu pronounced yaru]. *Note:* At the opening of Shakespeare's *Tempest*, does the boatswain's use of 'what cheer', 'yare', 'ahold' suggest the scene is set on a collier?

yark to thrash

"yark or yerk – to wrench or twist forcibly; to jerk" plus "yark – to beat soundly, to correct severely" *Brockett* Newc & Nth 1829; "yarking – violent, as yarking pains – also to beat as 'I'll yark you weil'" *Bell* MS Newc 1830s; "aw'll

yark cont.

yark his byens" *Allan's Tyneside Songs* p.420 1862; "yark – to strike, to flog" *Atkinson* Cleve 1868; "aw'll yark yor hide" *Luckley* Alnwick 1870s, *Other Eye* Newc ca.1890; "givvum agud yarkin" *Dobson* Tyne 1970-71. *EDD* distribution to 1900: in this sense Sco, Nth. [ME yerk]. *Plus* "yark – a sharp blow" *Todd* Tyne 1977

yarp to talk on and on

"yarp – to yammer on" *PG* H'pool C20/2; "yarp on" (talking nonsense) *ER* M'bro C20/2. [?harp on]

yaud, yade a horse

"yade – a horse (Nth); yaud – a horse in Yorkshire" *Kennet* 1690s; "it's a running yade, says Tommy Linn" *NChorister* D'm C18/2; "he was a yawde steiller" *Raine* MS ?Durham 1564; "yaude – a horse" *Bailey* Co.Durham 1810; "yad – a worn-out horse" *Pitman's Pay* G'head 1820s; "yaud or yawd – a horse, a jade" *Brockett* Newc & Nth 1829; "yaud, yode – a nag, a mare" *Atkinson* Cleve 1868. *EDD* distribution to 1900: Sco, Nth. [ON jälda 'mare']

yaup to yelp

"yaup – to cry loudly and incessantly, to lament; to yelp as a dog" *Brockett* Newc & Nth 1829. *EDD* distribution to 1900: Sco, Nth, Mids. [imitative; compare yap, yelp]

ye you (pl.)

"ye" *Cuthbert* C15/mid; "ye pay no les" *Durham* C16/2; "with ye" (sg) *Collier's Wedding* Newc 1720s; "yil" (you will) *Armstrong* Tanfield C19/2; "to a stranger...'ye' (yae)" *Palgrave* Hetton 1896; "just like yee and me" *Irwin* Tyne 1970; "ye've not even started, ye!" S'm per BG 2003. *EDD* distribution to 1900: general. [OE gé pronounced yay]. See also **thoo, you**

year, eer

"year – used for the plural as well as the singular: 'I henna seen him this twenty year'" *Brockett* Newc & Nth 1846; "these mony eers" *Haldane* Newc 1879; "when ah wiz nobbut aboot sixteen ear ahd" *Embleton* Tyne 1897; "six year" S'm 1990 per BG. [OE gear, neut. plural, pronounced year]. *Plus* "In Durham, yule-tide was a double holiday, for we... shared hogmanay with the Scots. We

year, eer cont.

called this Newrus." *Hitchin* re Dalton-le-Dale p.22 1910s

yearth, orth earth

"yearth" *Pitman's Pay* G'head 1820s; "the goold frae the yerth" *Allan's Tyneside Songs* p.367 1849; "yerth" Dinsdale, mid Tees 1849; "this mighty orth" *Allan's Tyneside Songs* p.421 1862; "orth" *Barrass* nD'm 1893. *Plus* "yerd – a fox earth" *Bailey* Co.Durham 1810

yeble able

"as lang as wour yebble" *Marshall* G'head 1806; "bein yeble te buy" *Barrass* Stanley 1890s. *Plus* "yeblins – maybe – or perhaps" *Bell* MS Newc 1815; "yables, yeblins, yeablesae, yebblesee – perhaps; cf. ablins" *Brockett* Newc & Nth 1829.

yeckey echo

"wor vera hills yeckey the peels" *Oiling* G'head 1826

yell whole

"then a yel heap o' stuff" *Allan's Tyneside Songs* p.313 1827; "the yell o' the lot" *Allan's Tyneside Songs* p.408 1862; "a yell hedgehog" *Armstrong* Tanfield C19/2; "yell watta – excessive rain, water from top and bottom of miners' working place" *Dodd* MS Tanfield Lea C20/2. *EDD* distribution to 1900: in this pronunciation N'd, C'd. See also **yal**

yellow-yowley yellow-hammer

"yellow-yowley – a Northern name for the yellow bunting or yellow hammer" *Brockett* Newc & Nth 1829; "they've a bunch ov hair upon their jaws / just like a yowley's nest" *Allan's Tyneside Songs* p.468 1862; "Yowley or yellow yowley (yuw-li) – the yellow-hammer" *Palgrave* Hetton 1896; "yella-yowlee" *Dodd* MS Tanfield Lea C20/2. *EDD* distribution to 1900: Sco, Ire, Nth

yem see **hame**

yep, aup ape

"yap – ape" *Bailey* Co.Durham 1810; "aup – a wayward child; an ape" *Brockett* Newc & Nth 1829; "yap, yep – an opprobrious epithet to a youngster; ape" *Brockett* Newc & Nth 1829; "aup – mischievous child" *Dinsdale* mid-Tees 1849

yest yeast

ex. *ER* M'bro C20/2. [OE (Ang) ?gest, LWS gist pronounced yist]. *Plus* "yesty kyek" (stotty cake) *BL* Blaydon 1940s–1960s. See also **barm**

yet, yate 1. gate, 2. roadway, 3. right of way

1. "the toune yate" *Cuthbert* C15/mid; "yat – gate" *Bailey* Co.Durham 1810; "fit to loup a yett or stile" *Pitman's Pay* G'head 1820s; "as old as Pandon-yate" *Brockett* Newc & Nth 1829; "he saa him clim ower a yett" (stile?) *Haldane* Newc 1879; "the Moor Yate" *Bell* re Long Benton Newc 1812 p.106; "iron yets" *Egglestone* Weardale 1870s. [OE geat pronounced yat]
2. "at the bryge ende apon the yatt" *Anderson* Newcastle 1503; "yet or yate also is used for a village street" *Bell* MS Tyne 1830s
3. "O yet! O yet! O yet! O yet!" 'make way' *Durham* C16/2; sim. in Denham tracts C19. See also **gate**

yetlin' pan, cauldron

"yetlings pro fixis – pans for cooking fish" Finchale 1411; "yecklin, yetlin – a cast metal pot with three legs used for making broth in" *Bell* MS Newc 1815; "yetling – a small metal pan or boiler wtih a bow handle" *Brockett* Newc & Nth 1829; "yettlin – a hemispherical metal pot with three legs and a bow handle, much used for boiling porridge and pota-toes'" *Luckley* Alnwick 1870s; "away he gans te the fire an' lifts off the yetlin' boilin' an' steamin'" "(kettle) *Haldane* Newc 1879; "kail pot or yettlin" *Nth Words* Alnwick re 1880 approx. *EDD* distribution to 1900: Sco, Nth. [ME yet, OE geótan 'to pour']

yewd went

"yewd, yod – went; yewing – going" *Ray* 1674; "yed" (went) *Gill* re Lincs C17/1. [OE éode]. See also **go**

yon that (at a distance)

"What's yon?" *Atkinson* Cleve 1868; "Yon (adj.), Yonder (adv.). That, there; generally, of objects pointed out. Sometimes, of distant things" *Palgrave* Hetton 1896; "yon – that (over there)" *JB* Shildon C20/mid. *EDD* distribution to 1900: general. [OE geon pronounced yon]. See also **thon**

you

"yuz" (plural) *VIZ* 34 (1989); "Wheer's you's ganning?" Fellgate 2003 per BG; "where-as yous been?" S'm per BG 2004; "how sad R use" S'm grafitti, 2004. [after Irish/Liverpool there is a tendency to create a new plural (yous, ye's)]. See also **thoo, ye**

yor 1. you're, 2. your

1. "aw think yor reet" *Allan's Tyneside Songs* p.494 1871
2. "yor" *Armstrong* Tanfield C19/2, Tanfield Lea 1960; "yer severence pay" *Dobson* Tyne 1972. *Plus* "yorsel – yourself" Tanfield Lea 1960, "yersel – youself" *Dobson* Tyne 1972

young 'un lad, youngster

"an' sweers 'twas the deevil or else 'twas a yungin" *Allan's Tyneside Songs* p.467 1862; "our young 'un" (a younger brother) *IA* S'm 1950s, 60s. NE 2001: in use

yowl to howl

ex. *Kennet* 1690s as Nth; "youl – to howl like a dog" *Bailey* Co.Durham 1810; "aw yool'd oot" *Allan's Tyneside Songs* p.53 1823; "startid yowlan" *Lakeland* re C'd C20. *EDD* distribution to 1900: general. See also **wowl**

yuck to chuck

"yuck uz that hammer ower" / "we got yucked owt o the pub last neet" *JR* Sacriston C20/2 – alternative to hoy. *EDD* distribution to 1900: ?Yx

yuke itch (noun and vb)

"yewk – the [itc]h (D'm)... to yuck – to itch, to have an itching in the skin (Nth)" *Kennet* 1690s; "yuke – to itch" *Bailey* Co.Durham 1810; "uke – to itch" *Atkinson* Cleve 1868. *EDD* distribution to 1900: yewk – esp. Sco, Ire, Nth. [ME yeke, MDu jeuken]

Yule the Christmas season

"Yule – the time of Christmas" *Brockett* Newc & Nth 1829; "merry were the days o' yule" *Allan's Tyneside Songs* p.354 1849; "Yule – Christmas. Hence 'Yule-dough', 'Yule-clog'. Yuletide 'is becoming commoner than it was a short time ago, but most people say 'Christmas'" *Palgrave* Hetton 1896. *EDD* distribution to 1900: Sco, Nth, eMids. [OE geól, pronounced yole, ON jól]. *Plus* "Yu-gams – Christmas games" *Ray* 1674. See also **Kersmas**

yule-clog yule log

ex. *Dinsdale* mid-Tees 1849; "Yule-clog –
the large log specially provided for burning,
and burnt, on Christmas Eve" *Atkinson* Cleve
1868; "Yule-clog" *Palgrave* Hetton 1896. *EDD*
distribution to 1900: N'd, D'm, W'd, Yx

yule-doo Christmas biscuit, etc.

"a kind of baby or little image of paste" Brand
Popular Antiquities 1795 via *EDD;* "Yule-dough
– a figure of a woman made of paste and
spices meant as a remembrance of the Virgin
Mary, given to young persons on Christmas
Day" *Bell* MS Newc 1815; "Yule-dough – a
Christmas cake, or rather a little image of
paste studded with currants" *Brockett* Newc
& Nth 1829; "Yule doo – a small image made
of dough, with a couple of currants for eyes"
Luckley Alnwick 1870s; "roond the raws one
heul doo day, the youngsters hugg'd the teup"
Barrass Stanley 1890s; "hule-doo/yule-doo – a
figure made in gingerbread or dough... hands
touched in front and two eyes of currants"
Heslop Tyne 1880s; "'Yule-doo' is a kind of
currant cake made in shape of a baby and
given to children at Christmas. Not so many
years ago the 'putter lad' expected his 'hewer'
to bring him the 'yule-doo'. If the hewer
failed to bring one, the putter would take the
hewer's clothes, put them into a 'tub', fill it up
with rubbish, and send it 'to bank'; or if the
'doo' was not well made, the putter nailed it
to a tub and wrote the hewer's name underneath" *Palgrave* Hetton 1896; "Yule-do:
These small cakes made with ginger or
currants were often formed into small figures,
with dried fruit for eyes, and were given to
children, we now know them better as gingerbread men." Farne website [re C20/1?];
"Yull-doo – gingerbread man with hands
joined" *Dobson* Newc 1974. *EDD* distribution
to 1900: NE. *Plus* "Yoodle-doo – Xmas box
to putter" *JP* S'm re C20/mid

yuuk huge

ex. *Dodd* MS Tanfield Lea C20/2

yuven etc. oven

"yown, yune – an oven" *Atkinson* Cleve 1868;
"yuven" *Armstrong* Tanfield C19/2. Embleton
Newc 1897; "the inside o' the uven wez reed
het" *Robson* Newc C20/1; "A hev a bakin' o'
bread i' th' yuven" *Dunn* B'p Auck 1950

izzard z

"izzard, izzet – the letter z" *Brockett* Newc
& Nth 1829, *Dinsdale* mid-Tees 1849.
EDD distribution to 1900: general

zookers

"Zookers – a sort of exclamation" *Bell* MS
Newc 1815

Bibliography

This bibliography contains references to critical works and studies of dialect. For main texts and dictionaries, used as sources, please refer to the abbreviations of printed sources on pp.186–190.

Alford, H. (1864) *The Queen's English* London.

'The Bombardment of Berry Edge', written in Newcastle, 1856. [Newcastle Central Library, Local Tracts, vol.12]

Beal, J.C. (1999) *English Pronunciation in the Eighteenth Century: Thomas Spence's 'Grand Repository of the English Language'* Oxford.

Brunner, K. (1963) *An Outline of Middle English Grammar* Oxford.

Clarke, J.F. (1977) 'Workers in the Tyneside Shipyards in the Nineteenth Century', pp.109–131 in *Essay in Tyneside Labour History* ed. Norman McCord, Newcastle.

Edwards, V.K. *et al.* (1984) *The Grammar of English Dialects: A Survey of Research* London.

Ellis, S. (1985) 'Scandinavian Influences on Cumbrian Dialect', pp.161–7 in *The Scandinavians in Cumbria* ed Baldwin, John R. & Whyte, Ian D., Edinburgh.

Flom, George T. (1900) *Scandinavian Influence on Southern Lowland Scotch: A Contribution to the Study of the Linguistic Relations of English and Scandinavian* Columbia University Germanic Studies vol.1 no.1, New York.

Fox, A. (2000) *Oral and Literate Culture in England 1500–1700* Oxford.

Herman, A. (2003) *The Scottish Enlightenment* London.

Houghton, T. (2003) *Rara Avis in Terris: or the Compleat Miner* London.

Kastovsky, D. (1992) 'Scandinvian Influence' pp.320–336 in *The Cambridge History of the English Language* vol.1 ed. Hogg, R.M. Cambridge.

Kemble, J.M. (1845) 'On the North Anglian Dialect' *Philological Society Proceedings 2*, pp.119–130

Kerswill P.E. (1984) 'Social and Linguistic Aspects of Durham (e:)' *Journal of the International Phonetic Association* 14, pp.13–30.

Kerswill, P.E. (1987) 'Levels of Linguistic Variation in Durham' *Journal of Linguistics* 23, pp.25–49

Kolb, E. (1966) *Phonological Atlas of the Northern Region* Bern.

Lawson, J. (1932, 1944) *A Man's Life* London.

Lee, J. (1950) *Weardale Memories and Traditions* Consett.

Llewellyn, E.C. (1936) *The Influence of Low Dutch on the English Vocabulary* Publications of the Philological Society, no.12.

Lynne, P. (1997) 'The Influence of Class and Gender: Female Political Organisations in Co. Durham during the Inter-war Years' *North East History* vol.31, pp.43–64.

Haswell, G.H. (1895) *The Maister: A Century of Tyneside Life* London.

McIntosh, A. *et al.* (1986) (eds) *A Linguistic Atlas of Late Medieval England* 4 vols, Aberdeen.

Mitcalfe, W.S. (1937) 'The History of the Keelmen and their Strike in 1822' *Archaeologia Aeliana* 4th series, vol.14, pp.1–16.

Meriton, G.A. (1683) *Yorkshire Dialogue* (repr. Yorks. Dialect Soc. as Reprint 2, 1959, ed Cawley, A.C.)

Moorman, F.M. (ed.) (1916) *Yorkshire Dialect Poems 1673–1915* London.

Musgrove, F. (1990) *The North of England: A History from Roman Times to the Present* Oxford.

Orton, H. (1933) *The Phonology of a South Durham Dialect: Descriptive, Historical, and Comparative* London.

Orton, H. *et al.* (1978) (eds) *The Linguistic Atlas of England* London.

Petyt, K.M. (1980) *The Study of Dialect* London.

Rothwell, W.M. *et al.* (1992) *Anglo-Norman Dictionary.*

Shields, M. (1974) 'Dialects of North Eastern England' *Lore & Language* 10, pp.3–9.

Strang, B. (1970) *A History of English* London.

Trudgill P. (1990) *The Dialects of England* Oxford.

Upton, C. *et al.* (1987) (eds) *Word Maps: A Dialect Atlas of England* Beckenham.

Upton, C. *et al.* (1994) (eds) *Survey of English Dialects: Dictionary and Grammar* London.

Viereck, W. (1966) *Phonematische Analyse des Dialekts von Gateshead-upon-Tyne, Co. Durham* Hamburg.

Vikar, A. (1922) *Contributions to the History of Durham Dialects* Malmö.

Wade, E. (1978) 'The Patter of the Northumberland and Durham Coalfield' *Bulletin of the NE Group for the Study of Labour History* vol.12, pp.21–29.

Wade, F. (1966) *The Story of South Moor* (typescript).

Wakelin, M.F. (1972) *English Dialects* London.

Wall, A. (1898) 'Scandinavian Elements in the English Dialects' *Anglia* vol.20, pp.45–135.

Sources and abbreviations

Initials alone usually represent individual communications, as part of the Durham & Tyneside Dialect Group's questionnaire survey of 2001 – marked Q – or subsequent discussion and correspondence. Bear in mind such entries may relate to an earlier state of dialect. E marks an e-mail response to the website www.pitmatic.co.uk with the same provisos.

Abbreviations of place names

B'd Castle – Barnard Castle
B'p Auck – Bishop Auckland
C'd – Cumberland
Ch-le-St – Chester-le-Street
Cleve – Cleveland
D'm – Durham (county)
D'ton – Darlington
e – east
G'head – Gateshead
Hetton – Hetton-le-Hole
Ho'ton – Houghton-le-Spring
H'pool – Hartlepool
Ire – Ireland
Lx – Lancashrre
n, N – north
N'd – Northumberland
Newc – Newcastle

N.I. – Northern Ireland
Nth – North of England
Sco – Scotland
s, S – south
S.Shields – South Shields
S'd – Sunderland
S'm - Seaham
Tyne – Tyneside
w – west
W'd – Westmorland
Yx – Yorkshire
Plus standard county name abbreviations

Note: in the context of distribution to 1900, reckoned via the *EDD* (*English Dialect Dictionary*), Nth imples counties of England from the Humber north; NE implies a combination of Northumberland, Co. Durham and Cleveland.

Abbreviations relating to language

adj – adjective
adv – adverb
AN – Anglo-Norman (also known as OFr, Old Fench)
C – century
Dan Danish
Du – Dutch
ex. – example (from)
Flem – Flemish

Fr – French
Fris – Frisian
Gm – German
Ice – Icelandic
intrans. – intransitive verb
M – middle period
ME – Middle English (ca.1100–1450)
ModE – Modern English (ca.1450 on)
O – old period

Abbreviations relating to language cont.

obsol. – obsolete, out of use

OE – Old English, the language of the Anglo-
Saxons to ca.1100

ON – Old Norse, the language of the Vikings

p.pt. – past or passive participle

prep. – preposition

pret. – preterite or past tense

Swed – Swedish

trans. – transitive verb

vb. – verb

Abbreviations of printed sources

3M – Third Marquis of Londonderry *Letter to
Lord Ashley* 1842

Aberdeens. 1993 – William Morris Wilson *Speak
of the North East* (1993)

Allan's Tyneside Songs – C19/mid, *Allan's Illustrated
Edition of Tyneside Songs,* ed. David Harker
(Newcastle upon Tyne, 1972) (specific page
or date supplied where necessary)

Alston 1833 – Thomas Sopwith *An Account of
the Mining Districts of Alston Moor, Weardale, and
Teesdale* (W.Davison, Alnwick, 1833) [BL]

Anderson – JJ Anderson *Records of Early English
Drama* vol.7, Newcastle-upon-Tyne (Toronto,
1982) (Gives company records relating to
mystery play performances)

Armstrong Tanfield C19/2 – poems of Tommy
Armstrong via Ross Forbes (ed.) *Polisses and
candymen: the complete works of Tommy Armstrong,
the pitman poet* (The Tommy Armstrong Trust,
Consett, 1987)

Ashington C20/mid – Joe Holland in *Northern,
Geordie, Posh and other languages* compiled by
Jean Crocker, 1986 (Joe started school in 1924)

Atkinson Cleve 1868 – *A glossary of the Cleveland
dialect* by JC Atkinson (London, 1868)
[particularly useful for analysis of words
and careful definitions]

Atkinson D'ton (plus date) – JA Atkinson *et al.
Darlington Wills 1600-1625* (Surtees Society
vol.201, 1993) than

Bailey Co.D'm 1810 – John Bailey's *General view
of the agriculture of the County of Durham* (1810)
(apparently an independent effort)

Barrass Consett 1897 – Alexander Barrass
The Pitman's Social Neet (Consett, 1897)

Bedlington 1761 – anon. *The will of a certain
northern vicar* (London, 1765) [NCL L042
vol.10] (deliver'd in sixty one / by me, the
vicar of B - d - - - g - - n)

Bell Newc 1812 – *Rhymes of Northern Bards* ed.
John Bell (Newcastle, 1812) *Bell* MS Newc 1815
or *Bell* MS Newc 1830s – Newcastle University
Bell-White MS 12

Bells – *A Garland of Bells*, printed for John Bell,
Newcastle, 1815

Bell-Harker – Newc C19/1 – Dave Harker (ed.)
Songs from the Manuscript Collection of John Bell
(Surtees Society, vol.196, 1985)

Bewick Tyne 1790s – Thomas Bewick *The howdy
and the upgetting – two tales of sixty years sin seyne,
as related by the late Thomas Bewick of Newcastle,
in the Tyne Side dialect* (London: printed for the
admirers of native merit, 1850)

Blenkinsopp Teesdale 1931 – RW Blenkinsopp
The Teesdale dialect (Barnard Castle, 1931)

'Bobby Shaftoe' C18 – with variants from RR
Terry *Salt Sea Ballads* (London, 1931)

Boldon Book c.1185 ed. David Austin (Chichester,
1982)

Brockett Newc & Nth 1846 – John Trotter
Brockett *A glossary of North Country words in use...*
(Newcastle: T. & J. Hodgson, 1825), second edn
1829, third edn 1846 [Brockett died 1842, aged
54; his main collecting seems to have been work
of the 1810s, 1820s]

Brockie D'm 1886 – Wm Brockie *Legends and
Superstitions of County Durham* (Sunderland, 1886)

Carlaw Teesside 1870 – Thomas Carlaw *A
choice collection of original Teesside songs, comic
and sentimental* (Stockton, 1870)

Cate B'p Auck 1987 – Dick Cate *Ghost dog* (1987)

Charver 2000–2002 – from contributions to
Newcastle Stuff, 2000–2002, the magazine edited
by Marshal Hall

Chater, Newc (plus date) – *Chater's Illustrated
Annual* 1880s [NCL]

Abbreviations of printed sources cont.

Chicken Benwell 1720s – Edward Chicken, *The collier's wedding* (second edn, Newcastle, 1764) Written 1720s re miners at Benwell

Coulthard 1934 – EM Coulthard *From Tweed to Tees: a short geography of North Eastern England* Edinburgh, London: Johnston, 1934

Coxhoe 1916 – John Salisbury *Me and Jake* (London, 1916) via Beamish

Crawhall Newc 1888 – *Newcassel Songs, 1888* – Joseph Crawhall ed. *A Beuk o' Newcassel Sangs* (Newcastle, 1888)

Crawhall N'd 1880 – Joseph Crawhall *Border notes and mixty-maxty* (1880)

Cresswell Newc 1883 – James Creswell *Local and other songs* (Newcastle, 1883)

Crocker (place) 1983 – Jean Crocker *Accent on the North East* (Darlington, 1983)

Cuddy Cairt – 'The Cuddy-Cairt' (a Jacky Robison story) in *Tyneside Stories and Recitations, collected, edited and retold by CE Catcheside-Warrington* (Windows, Newcastle, 1917)

Cuthbert C15/mid – *The Life or St Cuthbert in English Verse c. AD 1450* (Durham: Surtees Society vol.87, 1891)

Denham Tracts – MA Denham *The Denham Tracts* (London, 1892)

Derbyshire, 1681 – Thomas Houghton *Rara Avis in Terris: or the Compleat Miner* (London, William Soper, 1681) Book 2 includes a glossary, relevant to lead mining in Derbyshire, with very few words coinciding with North East usage

Dinsdale mid-Tees 1849 – Frederick T Dinsdale's *A Glossary of Provincial Words used in Teesdale in the County of Durham* (London, 1849) The area covered is from Middleton in Teesdale to Darlington and north of the Tees for 9 or 10 miles along this route.

Dobson Tyne 1969 – *Larn yersel Geordie* (1969)

Dobson Tyne 1970 – *Hist'ry o' the Geordies, Advanced Geordie palaver*

Dobson Tyne 1970/71 – *Hadrian and the Geordie Wall, Stotty Cake Row*

Dobson Tyne 1971 – *Supergeordie*

Dobson Tyne 1972 – *Aald Geordie's Almanack*

Dobson Tyne 1973 – *A light-hearted guide to Geordieland*

Dobson Tyne 1974 – *A Geordie dictionary*

Dodd MS Tanfield Lea C20/2 – handwritten card index at Beamish Open Air Museum. 1950s on

Douglas – Dave Douglas *Pit talk in Co. Durham* (1973)

D'm Chron – *Durham Chronicle*

Dunn B'p Auck C20/mid – Nelson Dunn 'Dinna Tark si Fond' tape casette 2002. (specifically Evenwood/Ranwshaws ca.1950)

Durham 1590s – ed. B Colgrave and CE Wright, 'An Elizabethan poem about Durham' in *Durham University Journal* vol.32 (n.s.1) 1940, 161–8

Durham 1839 – *The British Minstrel* Newcastle Central Library, Local Tracts vol.11

East Boldon ca. 1985 – via Gerry Ash, pub quiz, ca. 1985

EDD – *English Dialect Dictionary* ed. Joseph Wright (6 vols, Oxford 1898–1905) This presents accumulated information from ca. 1700 to the 1890s – thus 'to 1900', not 'at 1900'

Egglestone Weardale 1870s – William Egglestone, *Betty Podkin's visit to Auckland Flower Show* (Stanhope, 1876) and *Betty Podkin's letter ted Queen on Cleopatra's Needle* (London, 1877)

Egglestone Weardale 1886 – WM Egglestone, *Weardale names of field and fell* (Stanhope, 1886)

Elliot Tyne 1971 – *The Geordie Bible* (ca. 1971)

Embleton Tyne 1897 – D Embleton *Local dialect dialogues* ca.1897

English trade – *English trade in the Middle Ages* by L Salzman (Oxford, 1931)

Errington Felling/Heworth (plus date) – *Coals on rail or the reason of my wrighting: the autobiography of Anthony Errington from 1778 to around 1825* ed. PEH Hair (Liverpool University Press, 1988)

Finchale (date) – *Deeds of Finchale Priory* ed. *J Raine* MS (Surtees Society, vol.6, 1837) [based on the glossary – comments date from 1837]

Fordyce Newc 1826 – W ?T Fordyce *The Newcastle Song Book 1826*

Fox – Adam Fox *Oral and literature culture in England 1500–1700* (OUP 2000)

Geeson N'd/D'm 1969 – Cecil Geeson *A Northumberland and Durham word book* (Newcastle: Hill 1969) [contains a fair amount of retropective material; some useful etymological notes]

Abbreviations of printed sources cont.

Gibson C'd 1880 – Alexander C Gibson's *The Folk-Speech of Cumberland* (London 1880) [Entries relevant to North East dialect are selected from the glossary on pp.163–208]

Gill – Alexander Gil's *Logonomia Anglica* (2nd edn, London 1621) [re Lincolnshire]

Graham Geordie 1979 – Frank Graham *The New Geordie Dictionary* (Newcastle) [includes a fair proportion of historic material]

Green Wearside 1879 – John Green *Tales and ballads of Wearside* (Sunderland 1879) re C19/1

Grieves Tyne 1975 – *Original stories and poems by Harry Grieves of Holywell* (1975-7)

Grose 1787 – Francis Grose's *Provincial Glossary*

Haldane Newc 1879 – Harry Haldane's pamphlet *Geordie's Last* (second edition, Newcastle: *The Daily Journal*, 1879)

Hay Ushaw Moor C20/1 – James Hay *Spider and other tales of pit village life* (Amra Imprint, Seaham, 2003)

Heslop N'd 1890s – R Oliver Heslop *Northumberland Words: A glossary of words used in the County of Northumberland and on the Tyneside* (2 vols, English Dialect Society, 1893–4), first appeared as a series of articles in the *Newcastle Evening Chronicle*, in the 1880s [often retrospective]

Hill Flamborough 1970s – R Oliver Hill and JEG McKee *The English Coble* (National Maritime Museum, 1978)

Hitchin re Dalton-le-Dale 1910s, Seaham 1920s – George Hitchin *Pit-Yacker* (Cape, London, 1962)

Horsley Jesmond 1891 – James Horsley 'Lays of Jesmond & Tyneside songs and poems' (Newcastle, 1891)

Hull MS wNewc 1880s – Rev. JE Hull 'A popular introduction to the Tyneside dialect', typescript in the Archives of the Natural History Society of Northumbria, Hancock Museum [partly published and overlapping with his *Tyneside Grammar*]

Irwin 1970 – *The Geordie Joke Book* by Dick Irwin and Scott Dobson (1970)

Irwin 1970/1971 – *Geordie at the club* (1971 or earlier), *Geordie on the beer* (1971 or earlier)

Jamieson Scots Dictionary 1808 – John Jamieson *An etymological dictionary of the Scottish language* (2 vols, Edinburgh, 1808)

Johnson – Margot Johnson 'The Geordie: coins, lamps ships or people?' *Northern Notes* vol.2 (1969-1970) pt 4, pp.47-50

Kennet (place) 1690s – Bishop *Kennet's* 'Etymological Collections of English Words and Provincial Expressions', a manuscript dictionary surviving as British Library MS Lansdowne 1033 (vol. 99 of Bishop *Kennet's* Collection), compiled in the 1690s. [Words anticipated in Ray are not included]

Lakeland 2003 – *Lakeland Dialect* vol.64 (2003)

Latimer Records – John Latimer *Local Records* (Newcastle, 1857)

Leslie Newc 1992 – Stephen Leslie ed. *Offishal Geordie Dictionary including Euro-Geordie* (Berwick 1992)

LL – Mike Shields: 'Dialects of North-East England', *Lore & Language* 10, 1974, pp.3–9) – covering an up to 5 miles north and south of the Lower Tyne

Lloyd – *Come all ye bold miners* ed. AL Lloyd (1978)

Lore and language – *Northumbrian lore and language* compiled by Jean Crocker (1980s)

Luckley Alnwick 1870s – John Lamb Luckley's *The Alnwick Language* in Newcastle Central Library.

McBurnie Glebe Colliery, C20/mid – Geordie McBurney, 'Pitman's glossary' as taken down by Ada Radford ca.1970 re period 1924–1968

The Maister Shields C19/1 – George H Haswell *The Maister: a century of Tyneside life* (London: Walter Scott, 1895) [esp. re period 1800–1840 in Shields and Tynemouth]

Marshall G'head 1806 – *The Northern Minstrel or Gateshead Songster* ed. J Marshall (Gateshead, 1806)

Marshall Newc 1823 – *A collection of original Newcastle songs* (Newcastle: J Marshall, 4th edn, 1823)

MC – *The Monthly Chronicle* Newcastle, 1880s

Meriton nYx 1683 – George Meriton *A Yorkshire dialogue* 1683 repr. Yorks Dialect Soc 1959

Mitcalfe – W.Stanley Mitcalfe 'The history of the keelmen and their strike in 1822' *Archaeologia Aeliana* 4th series, vol.14 , 1937 1–16

Mitford Newc C19/2 – 'Pitman's Courtship' by William Mitford in *A Beuk o' Newcassel Sangs* ed. Joseph Cawhall, 1888

Abbreviations of printed sources cont.

Moore Weardale 1859 – Thomas Moore *The Song of Solomon in the Durham Dialect as spoken at St John's Chapel, Weardale,* 1859

MWN – Middlesbrough Weekly News

NChorister D'm 1809 – *North-County Chorister* ed. J Ritson (Durham, 1802; London, 1809)

NCM N'd 1900 – *Northern Counties Magazine* (Newcastle, vol.1, 1900-1901) 'A tale of Dead Lad's Rigg' by Halliwell Sutcliffe

NDN – Northern Daily News

N'd 1995 (rural/children) – Andrea Simmelbauer 'The dialect of Northumberland: a lexical investigation' *Anglistische Forschungen* 275 (2000) 145–147 [involving 58 schoolchildren from rural backgrounds]

Newc Courant – Newcastle Courant

Newc Jnl – Newcastle Journal

Nicholson 1880 – WE Nicholson *A glossary of terms used in the coal trade of Northumberland and Durham* (Newcastle, 1888) [Nicholson recognises and draws on a previous list of mining words, GC Greenwell's 1849 glossary with the same title]

NM – Northern Magpie vols.1–2, 1888–1889 (Newcastle based)

Noah's Ark Newc C15/16 – as printed in Henry Bourne's *History of Newcastle* (1736)

Northumbrian III – Northumbrian Words and Ways vol.3, compiled by Jean Crocker, 1990

NT – Northern Tribune vol.1 1854

Nth Words 1938 – *Old North Country Words* 1938, Newcastle Central Library L427.8

NWC – Newcastle Weekly Chronicle

Oiling G'd 1826 – Thomas Wilson 'The oiling of Dicky's wig' from the *Tyne Mercury* 18 Jul 1826

Oliver Newc 1824 – Wm Oliver *Collection of original local songs and other pieces* (Newcastle, 1824)

Other Eye – His Other Eye anon. pamphlet, ca.1890, Newcastle. [NCL Central Library, Local Tracts vol.42]

Owen Macdonald – "Dying words of... Owen Macdonald" broadsheet, 1752 [Newcastle Central Library]

Palgrave Hetton 1896 – FMT Palgrave: *A list of words and phrases in everyday use by the natives of Hetton-le-Hole in the County of Durham* (English Dialect Society, vol.74, 1896)

Parker Tyne Valley 1896 – Joseph Parker *Tyne folk: masks, faces and shadows* (London, 1896) [Includes dialect speech from area around Haltwhistle, Wylam, Corbridge, Acomb, Matfen, Ovington, etc.]

Pitman's Pay G'head 1820s – written by Thomas Wilson, published in three parts in the journal *The Newcastle Magazine* in 1826, 1828, 1830. [A 'collected' edition, with glossary, was issued with an introduction by the author, in 1843, also used here]

Purvis C19/mid – Life of Billy Purvis (Newcastle & Sunderland, 1875)

Raine MS – James Raine, BL MS Egerton 2868 [uses wills of the Diocese of Durham, wills of the Diocese of York, and records of trials held in York Castle, plus some early printed books and diaries]

Raistrick Yx – *Old Yorkshire Dales* (Arthur Raistrick, 1967)

Ray 1674 – John Ray *Collection of English words, not generally used* (London, 1674). Also 1737 edition

Reed Border ballads (date) – James Reed *The Border Ballads* (Stocksfield, 1991)

Ritson N'd 1793 – *The Northumberland Garland* (Newcastle, 1793, London 1809)

RLS – Robert Louis Stevenson *The Merry Men* 1891 [Scottish dialect]

Robson Newc C20/1 – WJ Robson *The Adventures of Jackie Robison* Newcastle, 1890s

Robson Tyne 1849 – JP Robson *Songs of the Bards of the Tyne* (Newcastle ca.1849) [includes glossary]

RR Weardale 1569 – 'The Rookhope Ride' in *The Bishopric Garland* ed. J Ritson (Stockton, 1784, Newcastle 1908)

Ross Tyne C19/1 – John Ross (printer) *Songs of the Tyne, being a collection of popular local songs*

Rothbury, C18/2 – 'Ecky's Mare' in J Ritson (ed.) *Newcastle Garland*

Scrapbook Tyne – *Scrapbook of Tyneside songs* [Newcastle Central Library L427.82]

S'd Echo – Sunderland Echo

Shields Song Book (South Shields, 1826)

Smith Weardale 1883 – W. Herbert Smith *Walks in Weardale* (Claypath, Durham, 1883)

Abbreviations of printed sources cont.

Spennymoor C20/mid – taken down by Jean Crocker "in conversation with a lady from Spennymoor concerning words which related to household objects... used normally in her young days" and published in *Accent on the North East: dialect jottings* (Darlington, 1983)

Stobbs Woodhorn C19/mid – John Stobbs *Snelly the Tyelyor: a Northumbrian Legend anent the Shadowless Man* (und.) [Newcastle Central Library, Local Tracts, vol.104/9]

Street Piracy (Newcastle, 1822) – *A new song entitled Street Piracy, or, Lantern Justice, to which is added, The dying reflections of Poor Snap* (Newcastle Central Library, Local Tracts, vol.104/12)

Stukeley – William Stukeley *Itinerarium curiosum* (London, 1776) vol.2 *Iter Boreale*

RS Surtees *Handley Cross* (London, 1854)

Tanfield Lea 1960 – from a list compiled by the local Women's Institute and forwarded by Gerry Ash

Taylor Dawdon C20/2 – Ernie Taylor, dialect songs at Dawdon Pit

Todd Tyne 1974 – George Todd *Todd's Geordie words and phrases* (Newc, 1977)

Tweddell Cleve 1875 – GM Tweddell *Rhymes and Sketches to illustrate the Cleveland Dialect* (Stokesley, 1875) [includes glossary]

Tyneside grammar 1880s – JE Hull 'A grammar of Tyneside' *The Vasculum* (Newcastle) vol.8 no.4 (1922) 55–60, 105–107, 117–121 [re Belsay, Stocksfield, Whittonstall on west, Blyth, Cleadon on east; period 1870-1890]

Upton 1950 – Clive Upton *Survey of English Dialects – dictionary and grammar* (London, 1994)

Viereck – Wolfgang Viereck *Phonetische Analyse des Dialekts von Gateshead-upon-Tyne / Co. Durham* (Hamburg, 1966)

Wade *South Moor* C20/mid – Fred Wade *The story of South Moor: a mining village situated in the north western part of Co.Durham* typescript, 1966 plus Fred Wade *Annfield Plain*, typescript 1966, and *The Story of West Stanley* (typescript 1956)

Weardale Nickstick – magazine edited by Wm Egglestone in 1870s [BL]

West Stanley C20/1 – 'Johnny Fry the Putter' via Fred Wade *Story of West Stanley* pp.372–3

Wilson Newc C19/mid – Joe Wilson 'Cum te maw shop'

Windows – Tyneside Stories and Recitations, collected, edited and retold by CE Catcheside-Warrington (Windows, Newcastle, 1917)

Wood M'bro 2002, etc. – Vic Wood, inc. website www.communigate.co.uk/ne/teesspeak/

Yetholm Gypsies – Joseph Lucas *The Yetholm history of the Gypsies* (Kelso, 1882)

Contact note

Bill Griffiths is Co-ordinator of the Durham & Tyneside Dialect Group, set up in 1998 "to promote the awareness of dialect English as spoken now and formerly in the North East". In 2001, with funding from Tomorrow's History, a dialect questionnaire was distributed; over 500 responses received, and many 'new' words reported, giving an indication of how little attention had been paid to the region's dialect over the past 50 years or more.

The DTDG provide talks for local community groups, issue a newsletter three times a year, and maintain a website at www.pitmatic.co.uk – all useful ways of disseminating and collecting dialect information, and keeping in touch with dialect enthusiasts in the region (and beyond). Continuing collaboration with the Centre for Northern Studies at Northumbria University in Newcastle has produced a number of publications; while to the south, a friendly association with Vic Wood and the Lower Tees Dialect Survey has helped assess dialect developments in both areas. The DTDG have a stall at the Durham Miners Gala (second Saturday in June) and hold a dialect day each year in Newcastle as part of the Heritage Open Days scheme.

If you would like further information or want to participate, you are welcome to get in touch with Bill Griffiths either through the Centre for Northern Studies, Northumbria University, Newcastle upon Tyne NE1 8ST, or direct at 21 Alfred Street, Seaham, Co.Durham SR7 7LH.

Notes

Notes

Notes